ALEISTER CROWLEY
AND THE AEON OF HORUS

History · Magick · Psychedelia · UFOlogy

PAUL WESTON

AVALONIAN ÆON
PUBLICATIONS

Aleister Crowley and the Aeon of Horus
Copyright © 2009, 2014 Paul Weston
First edition published 2009
This second edition published 2014 by
Avalonian Aeon Publications, Glastonbury, England.

All rights reserved.
No part of this publication may be reproduced or used in any form or by any means without written permission from the Publisher and the author except for review purposes.

The right of Paul Weston to be identified as the author and of the Work has been asserted by him in accordance with the Copyright, Designs and Patents Act 1988.

ISBN: 978-0-9557696-4-1

A CIP catalogue record for this book is available from the British Library.

Design and text styling by
Bernard Chandler, Glastonbury. www.graffik.co.uk
Cover illustration by Yuri Leitch
Text set in Monotype Plantin 10/12pt

Printed and Bound in Great Britain by
CPI Antony Rowe, Chippenham and Eastbourne

DEDICATION

To
Aleister Crowley,
Jack Parsons,
Robert Anton Wilson.

And also in memory of
John Keel
who died during the writing of this work.

ABOUT THE AUTHOR

Paul is a Psychic Questing, Reiki,
Crowley, Fellowship of Isis, Scientology, Adi Da,
Kriya Yoga, Mother Meera, Druid, Osho, Gurdjieff,
Anthony Robbins firewalking, UFOlogical,
Avalon of the Heart, 2012 kind of guy.
He lives in Glastonbury.

www.aleistercrowley666.co.uk
www.mysteriumartorius.co.uk
www.avalonianaeon.com
www.avalonianaeon.blogspot.com

Also published by the same Author:
Mysterium Artorius
Arthurian Grail Glastonbury Studies
Avalonian Aeon -
From Glastonbury Festival to 2012
A Personal Occult Odyssey

ACKNOWLEDGEMENTS

Mother Meera. Cosmic Trigger darshans July 23rd 2007/2008 framed the unexpected development of this book. February 2009 sent me to Egypt. Om Namo Bhagavate Mata Meera.

Rachel, Michael and Leo. The main encouragement to write it.

Yuri Leitch. For a magnificent rendering of my vision of the cover for this work. www.yurileitch.co.uk

Andrew Collins. For demonstrating with *The Cygnus Mystery* the efficacy of the Cult of Lam, for powerful times in Cairo; and permission to use his Stele of Revealing photograph. www.andrewcollins.com

Chandira Hensey. For major involvement in the nineties phase of this material and continuing support.

Caroline Wise. For support, inspiration, and the timely living flame leela.

Oliver Gillespie. For providing me with Jimmy Page's *Lucifer Rising* music in time for my Cairo adventure.

Phil Stretch. For feeding my head with an outstanding sequence of DVDs, thus preventing brain explosion during crucial phases of the writing.

Richard Sprigg. For helping me to realise that an important detail needed to be better expressed.

Aleister Crowley quotations used with permission, copyright OTO.

CONTENTS

PREFACE ... 9
The Mystery of History ... 11
Crowley and the Aeon ... 13

INTRODUCTION -
THE ENIGMA: BEYOND THE LEGEND OF INFAMY ... 19

FIN DE SIECLE ZEITGEIST ... 24

THE BOOK OF THE LAW ... 29

GNOSTIC REVIVAL ... 36

GURDJIEFF, TIBET, AND THE KALI YUGA ... 44

ABSOLUTE ELSEWHERE:
THE MORNING OF THE MAGICIANS ... 50
Prologue ... 50
Hippy Reich ... 51
Banality of Evil? ... 54
Hitler the Occult Messiah ... 55
Fantastic Realism ... 58
The Demons of Houston Stewart Chamberlain ... 60
Guido von List and Theosophy ... 61
Theozoology and the New Templars ... 62
Thule: Polar Gnosis and Politics ... 64
Himmler: the Grail and Ancestral Heritage ... 67
Illumination ... 72
In Defence of Blavatsky and Steiner ... 73
Beelzebub and the Beast ... 76

CROWLEY AND THE NAZIS ... 79

THE MAGICAL BATTLE OF BRITAIN ... 82
The 1588 Hermetic Espionage Matrix ... 82
Spookiness ... 86
Finest Hour ... 89
Golden Eye of Horus: The Spy who Fed me Mexican Brain Poison ... 92

CONTENTS

THE BABALON WORKING 101
  Apocalyptic Alchemy 101
  Living Flame 103
  Enter LRH 105
  The Holy Whore 106
  Nag Hammadi Plasmate 112
  Perfect Mind 114
  Tangential Ripples 116
  Black Pilgrimage 117

THE REBIRTH OF WITCHCRAFT 122
  The Sabbath of the Goat 123
  The Golden Bough 125
  Aradia 127
  The Margaret Murray Controversy 129
  The White Goddess 133
  Priestess 136
  Gerald Gardner and the Wiccan Mythos 138
  Jack Parsons and "The Witchcraft" 145
  King of the Witches 148

OPENING THE DOORS: THE PSYCHEDELIC EXPERIENCE 151
  Return of the Sacramental Mysteries 152
  Goodbye to Berlin. Hello to Sgt Pepper 153
  Jailbreak from the Consensus Prison 157
  The Most Dangerous Man in America 162

SYMPATHY FOR THE DEVIL 167
  Strange Days 167
  Helter Skelter 170
  Lucifer Rising 173

A MAN SURROUNDED BY A WHIRLWIND OF SAND 177

EXTRA-TERRESTRIAL GNOSIS 189
  Thelemic UFOlogy and the Cult of Lam 189
  Things Seen in the Sky and Rumours of Wars 196
  Advent of the Ether Ships 199
  The Nazi Contactee at the Portal of the UFO Era 201
  Multidimensional Mojave 205
  The Flying Saucer Vision 212
  Our Lady of Space 215
  Ultraterrestrials 216
  Enlightenment 218

CONTENTS

CHAPEL PERILOUS: ADVENTURES IN THE GOBLIN UNIVERSE 220
Loch Ness Leviathan and the Boleskine Kiblah 221
Call of Cthulhu: Wail of Sumer? 229
Mothman 241
Men in Black 244
Wilhelm Reich's Contact with Space 250
Orgone Bioforms 254
Ahrimanic Dark Gods 258
Secret Chiefs 261

COSMIC TRIGGER 263
Illuminati 263
Sirius Mystery 264
Sufism 267
Dog Days 269
Models and Metaphors 271
Ordeal of the Abyss 272

THE MONTAUK LEGEND:
CONSPIRICISM AS A MAGICAL PROCESS OF INITIATION 275
Paranoiac Preliminaries 275
Space-Time Project 279
Babalon Ripples 287
The Men-an-Tol Crowley Myth 291
Pyramids and Sacred Grids 293
Inspired Forth-Speaker of Montauk 295
Montauk-Thule 299
The Black Sun, Swastika, and Shin 306

SECRET CIPHER: THE KEY OF IT ALL? 310

THE PSYCHOLOGY OF THELEMA 323
Maps of the Territory 324
The Magickal Diary 331
The Leary Eight Circuit Model 332
Circuit One: Bio-Survival 332
Circuit Two: Emotional-Territorial 334
Circuit Three: Semantic Symbol Dexterity 336
Circuit Four: Socio-Sexual 337
Magnetic Centre and the Kundalini Alchemy of Shin:
  Stirrings of the Secret Lover 339
Peak Experiences and New Existentialism:
  A Fifth Circuit Aside 344
To Infinity and Beyond: A Meta-programming,
  Neurogenetic, Non-local, Magical Revival 346

CONTENTS

APPENDIX A: NOTES TOWARDS A MODERN HISTORY
OF THE STELE OF REVEALING 356

APPENDIX B: L. RON HUBBARD
AND THE BABALON WORKING 361

ILLUSTRATIONS 376
The Stele of Revealing 376
The Grid Page from The Book of the Law 377
The Qabalistic Tree of Life 378

BIBLIOGRAPHY 379

INTRODUCTORY INDEX 384

PREFACE

'Write & find ecstasy in writing!'

Aleister Crowley - *The Book of the Law*

I'M WALKING THROUGH CAIRO MUSEUM in a culmination of a thirty year journey. A loud multi-national hubbub of noise throbs around the enormous high-ceilinged interior as a great tumult of life bustles everywhere around me. Egyptian guides compete to make themselves heard, instructing international groups clustered by the mind-shattering exhibits whose imagery has so deeply permeated western consciousness. Arab art students sit in groups on the floor, girls in Muslim headscarves, guys in western attire, chatting, laughing, comparing pictures on their mobile phones, whilst sketching assorted antiquities. The backdrop of sound blends with synthesiser droning, wind, thunder, tambura, tablas, chanting, and twelve-string electric guitar coming from my headphones. I've started to notice something. Amidst all of this movement the artefacts of Ancient Khem convey a profound stillness.

Moving slowly, savouring every moment, past huge stone figures, up the stairs to the second floor, I'm coming into the vicinity of the most famous archaeological find in the world. An ever denser crowd gathers around the exquisite death mask of Tutankhamun and I will certainly be joining them. I have far greater preparation to appreciate its beauty than when I last saw it as a schoolboy at the British Museum in 1972. I haven't come just to see the boy king though.

My main reason for being here is a noon appointment marking the anniversary of a perplexing event. It's with another nearby item that receives far less attention. Large elliptical and rectangular openings on the second floor look down upon the first. Pillars support a balcony walkway which in turn has arched entrances to smaller enclaves. Section 23 is flanked by large figures of the goddesses Isis and Nephthys, standing with arms outstretched, in glass cases. Passing through between them, and looking immediately to my right, in the fourth level of a cabinet full of wood and stucco funerary stele, I see for the first time the object of my quest: exhibit 9422 commemorating Ankh af na Khonsu, an obscure twenty-sixth dynasty priest.

The stele is about 21 inches high and 11 wide. A card from its previous home in the now defunct Boulak Museum numbered 666 gives a hint of why I am here. More brightly colourful than its companion pieces and of more accomplished artistry, it attracts some of the young people to sit in front of it and draw. A plaque on the wall labels the room's contents as New Empire Funerary Furniture. Panning back out and around from my initial focus on the stele I now notice some of the other items displayed. There's a cabinet full of wooden hawks, another full of haunting golden-faced busts with nemyss headdresses, all manner of different sized figures, such as dog-headed Anubis, that, in combination with the ebb and flow of synthesiser drones and deep surging sounds that could be mellotron cellos, help to create an outstanding ambiance.

There's a sound from my headphones now like an extended rumble of thunder from what one commentator likened to a storm in the desert at dawn as I listen to the conclusion to the twenty minutes of music Jimmy Page composed for occult filmmaker Kenneth Anger's *Lucifer Rising*. I feel fortunate to have finally tracked down a bootleg recording of this legendary piece and that a musician friend was able to clean it up in his studio. It has assisted superbly in setting the necessary mood, also giving me a further sense of full-circle as it was Page's interests that helped begin this journey for me decades ago as well.

There's a little red book in my pocket and it's not the *Thoughts of Chairman Mao*. I take it out as noon approaches. *The Book of the Law* is supposed to be a text dictated by a non-human intelligence announcing the onset of a new era. The stele was of central importance in its creation, Ankh af na Khonsu being an alleged past-life of its twentieth century scribe, the legendary Aleister Crowley.

★ ★ ★

THE MYSTERY OF HISTORY

'From the perspective of "science" what matters in a myth is whatever historical elements can be extracted from it. From the perspective that I adopt, what matters in history are all the mythological elements it has to offer.'

Julius Evola. *Revolt Against the Modern World*

I was born in 1959. My parents were of the generation involved in the Second World War. I came to consciousness in the sixties with a growing awareness of an amazing contrast between two decades only twenty years apart. I have very early memories of Beatlemania. In 1967, as the Summer of Love unfolded, I can remember *San Francisco* on *Top of the Pops* and some vague sense of Flower Power. During the same period I developed a passion for history, looking at picture books about the world wars.

I had a modest awareness and knowledge of many of the tumultuous events of 1968. I remember waking up on my birthday and playing with a new toy car on the living room floor as the news came on the radio that Martin Luther King had been murdered the day before. I remember Robert Kennedy as well and the Grosvenor Square demonstration actually shown live on TV. I was aware of Russian tanks in Czechoslovakia, even if only because it was so important that an early episode of *Dad's Army* was cancelled to make way for a documentary on it. I recall the Mexico Olympics Black Power salutes and the Apollo Christmas moon orbit with its iconic Planet Earth photo.

There was a new unknown world that was confusing my parents' generation. The excitement of the space race and a dark unsettling feeling that seemed to surround the subject of drugs sat alongside the family tales of the war. My father and his brothers, who were all in their early twenties in 1939, had their fundamental imprints from their experiences during that period, some of which had assuredly been quite horrific. It was strange to be surrounded by 1939 adults in a 1968 world.

I was an early sci-fi fan, having seen the very first episode of *Dr Who*, going on to become a dalek obsessive. *The Invaders, Star Trek*, and early viewing of classic movies such as the fifties' *Day the Earth Stood Still* and *War of the Worlds* helped shape my mindset and made me aware of the UFO phenomenon which was a significant part of the sixties blend. I scanned the night skies for flying saucers. In the era of the run up to the moon landings it seemed obvious that the human race might not be the only ones travelling between planets. This predisposed me to an interest in UFOlogy that would eventually happily embrace its profound weirdness.

By the age of ten, I had a sixties jukebox playing in my head. I liked the Beatles and the Stones. I recognised that they had considerably changed their appearance and sound over the years and gone a bit weird. I got up early to watch the moon landing, an event obviously at the very edge of modern possibilities but I also had a totally clear chronology of the still recent past, primarily the two wars, firmly established. 1936: Remilitarisation of the Rhineland. 1938: German union with Austria and then the Czech crisis, Munich and Neville Chamberlain. 1939: the invasion of what remained of the Czechs, Poland, Britain and France declaring war. I could tell you the whole sequence of major invasions and battles that followed. I became a history obsessive. This wasn't simply dull pub-quiz nerdism though. I was on fire about this stuff.

The Nazis perplexed me. Film footage of the gigantic Nuremberg rallies brought me out in goose pimples. Hitler was totally strange. There simply wasn't anybody else remotely like him. The British culture of the time, which I somehow took to be represented by the George Formby and Will Hay movies that were still regularly shown on TV, and the old songs that my father and uncles remembered with nostalgia, *The Lambeth Walk* and so on, was completely different.

The theme of the ongoing mystery of the two diverse decades continued to intensify for me. In 1973 I watched the whole of the stupendous *World at War* documentary series. I wouldn't like to say how many times I've seen it since. I subscribed to a multi-volume magazine work, *Purnell's History of the Second World War*. I also repeatedly read Lord Russell of Liverpool's account of Nazi war crimes, *The Scourge of the Swastika*. In that same year I bought *Sgt Pepper*. I had also become a Beatles obsessive. In order to appreciate their greatest moments I investigated the sixties in far greater depth. Before long that extraordinary decade had become another life-long study to put alongside the war and in particular, the Nazis.

It began to dawn on me that history felt like a mighty weird affair. I read top historians and took on board arguments for economic, sociological, and technological determinants but for all the growing mass of data and ideas that filled my head something that felt like it ought to be cohering wasn't. Yes, if you look at what was happening in Germany following their defeat in the First World War, their treatment by the Allies with the Treaty of Versailles and the economic troubles of the twenties, a resurgence of an aggressive nationalism seemed inevitable. That doesn't account for the strangeness and severity of form it took.

With the sixties, it is possible to point to a number of economic and technological factors that made the emergence of some sort of youth culture highly likely. That doesn't really explain why it turned out to be such an outrageous party. The drugs certainly made a difference but they simply can't bestow talent on mediocrities. How remarkable that as Hitler, Himmler, and their associates reached the climax of their endeavours at Stalingrad and Auschwitz, so the grouping that included John Lennon, Bob Dylan, Jim Morrison, Jimi Hendrix and Mick Jagger, were coming into incarnation.

It seemed to me that the main players of the Nazi nightmare and the swinging sixties were rather specialised groups. They were uniquely over-qualified for the situations that they were born into. The group of characters who were available to take the whole thing to the limit and beyond seem to have been assembled by a brilliant casting agency. The usual ways of looking at history didn't satisfactorily explain to me why it all turned out to be quite so hideous, quite so ridiculously brilliant. I felt there was a deeper mystery trying to reveal itself.

CROWLEY AND THE AEON

The first time I consciously heard Aleister Crowley's name was at the age of fifteen in 1974 when I'd bought David Bowie's *Hunky Dory* album. He was mentioned on a track called *Quicksand*. It didn't tell me anything about him though other than to put him in the same song that mentioned *'Himmler's sacred realm of dream reality'*. An article by Mick Farren in the *New Musical Express* on cults and general weird mystical shit gave me some minimal info for starters.

In May 1975 I saw Led Zeppelin during their epic series of gigs at Earls Court in London. Sitting in my £1.50 seat (yes, £1.50), reading the programme whilst waiting for the rock gods to appear, I learnt that guitarist Jimmy Page owned a former home of the man known as the Great Beast on the shores of Loch Ness.

It was the centenary of Crowley's birth in October that year and

BBC Radio 4 featured a programme on him that I went out of my way to listen to. I was astonished by his multi-faceted personality. Regardless of his evil reputation, I was sure he was a phenomenon worth studying. The first real account of his life that I read was in Colin Wilson's *The Occult* in 1978, and although it wasn't exactly a hymn of praise, it fuelled my interest still further.

One night in early spring 1980 I dreamt that I was in the company of an imposing bald-headed man, in a darkened room. My immediate thoughts on waking were that it was Colonel Kurtz, as portrayed by Marlon Brando in the movie *Apocalypse Now*, which I had recently seen twice. It had profoundly affected me. That morning I found myself browsing in a second-hand bookshop. My attention was suddenly transfixed as I discovered a copy of *The Great Beast*, John Symonds' biography of Crowley. On its back cover was a picture of him wearing a pointed magician's hat that displayed an Egyptian Eye of Horus design. It was accompanied by the words,

> '*I am the Beast, I am the Word of the Aeon.*
> *I spend my soul in blazing torrents that roar*
> *into Night, streams that with molten*
> *tongues hiss as they lick.*
> *I am a hell of a Holy Guru.*'

I would have grabbed the book and immediately devoured it anyway but the thought that, perhaps, it was Crowley who I had dreamt of the night before, added to the sense of excitement.

Symond's work is entirely unsympathetic, expressing scorn, mockery, and contempt for his subject wherever possible. Nonetheless it did nothing to diminish my fascination. I soon purchased Crowley's masterful tarot deck with its accompanying *Book of Thoth*. It was perfectly obvious to me that it was a work in a class of its own. I barely retained anything of what I read there but the numinous images spoke to me in a language I seemed to already know but had somehow forgotten. Later on in the year I tackled the enormous autobiographical *Confessions* and found far more intelligence, wisdom, and above all, humour, than in most of his critics. An enduring fascination with the man and his work became an ongoing feature of my life.

Finally, with Crowley's concept of the Aeon of Horus, I had a metaphor and a model by which to look at the two diverse periods that obsessed me with a perspective that satisfied that part of me that had always been somehow agitated with the sense of something missing that needed to be found.

This is the information age. We have access to more data in a shorter space of time than could ever have been imagined even a few decades ago. That still leaves us with the issue of what we choose to look for and why. Kids leave school today without being able to recount any details of Auschwitz or Hiroshima. A teenager asked for a response after seeing *Schindler's List* at the cinema derided it as boring. Nothing really happened in it. The passion, intensity, and brilliance of popular music in the sixties have become all but unknown to new generations. There are hippy kids in Glastonbury with hardly any real knowledge or interest in the sixties upheaval. On one level, I can't understand that at all. On another, seen from the perspective of the idea of Gurdjieff's sleep-walking humanity and James Joyce's nightmare of history from which we need to awaken, the Gnostic prison of the *Matrix*, I can.

As far as I'm concerned this whole thing, the twentieth century, with it's Nazi and psychedelic eras, this time that Crowley has called the dawning of the Aeon of Horus, is so mind shatteringly heart-bustingly compellingly interesting and important that at times I feel like I'm straining with every nerve to take on board every last nuance in order to maintain the altered state of gnosis necessary to comprehend it. In that comprehension is ecstasy and terror, *'the flame that burns in every heart of man, and in the core of every star'*.

I don't expect everyone to be as passionately intense as I am about knowing all of the names, dates, and places, the connections and lineage. I do feel that my peculiar temperament, which combines the ability to remember lots of information as well as a feeling for magic and mysticism, actually places some kind of responsibility on me to ensure such sensibilities do get an airing and save some people the time and trouble of spending decades looking for certain combinations of data. I would like to think that maybe a few readers might get their heads set on fire and their personal journeys in some way enhanced by this work.

Most of the material here originated from a series of lectures. *The Enigma of Aleister Crowley* was initially presented to Andrew Collins' Essex *Earthquest* group in 1989. It was expanded and subsequently aired on a number of occasions in Glastonbury when it was recorded and distributed for a while by the *Isle of Avalon*

Foundation. The Psychedelic Era and the Aeon of Horus, UFOs and Occultism, The Rebirth of Witchcraft, and *The White Goddess and the Lady of Shalott* followed in 1996. The material on Nazi Occultism was featured in another 1989 *Earthquest* lecture delivered to commemorate the fiftieth anniversary of the start of the Second World War. This in turn derived from a dissertation I had done towards my degree in the Study of Comparative Religion in 1983. Some of it was also included in *War in Heaven: Glastonbury and the Occult War against the Nazis,* first presented in Glastonbury on Dion Fortune's birthday in 1995 and likewise taped by the IOAF.

When I began writing a Glastonbury focused autobiography, *Avalonian Aeon,* in 1999, a work with a strong Thelemic theme, it was originally intended to include the entire contents of the Crowley based lectures. The publication of Gary Lachman's *Turn Off Your Mind: The Dark Side of the Mystic Sixties* in 2001 had initially caused me some concern due to possible duplication of material. All of the usual suspects were present: Crowley, Parsons, Leary, Manson etc. I really loved the book and have made some use of it here for minor details but I was happy that I was putting a more distinct Thelemic spin on events and that my ongoing undertaking remained worthwhile.

Avalonian Aeon features an extensive account of my adventures in psychic questing, including the legendary Seven Swords saga and Andrew Collins' experiences in Glastonbury. During the course of the writing, previously lost relevant archive material of his came to light that had never been in print and was so spectacular it could not possibly be excluded. The bulk of *Aeon* continued to increase until it was obvious it had become top-heavy.

My first book *Mysterium Artorius* saw a siphoning off of some material to become a separate work that stood in its own right. *Aleister Crowley and the Aeon of Horus* is another. The final form of *Avalonian Aeon* will still include material that features in both of the separate works but in a context that hopefully deepens appreciation still further. All three works will complement each other.

I would also like to acknowledge the late Gerald Suster's work, variously known as *Hitler and the Age of Horus, Hitler the Occult Messiah,* and *Hitler: Black Magician.* Although published in 1981, I first read it in 1985, after completing my dissertation. I was gratified to see how much the historian and occultist confirmed much of my existing understanding. I've made some use of Suster here and I do heartily recommend the book but he makes no mention of Jung and in my opinion has misunderstood Gurdjieff and thereby missed at least some pieces of the puzzle that I feel I have managed to put into place.

It has also been extremely useful that Richard B. Spence's *Secret Agent 666* appeared during the course of this writing. Crowley's espionage background and connection to Ian Fleming and the Rudolf Hess mystery is a topic that has been circulating for decades and I was already featuring but Spence supplied a wealth of detail previously lacking that I am happy to make use of and acknowledge.

I am obviously sympathetic to the view that conventional history does not tell us everything about the past but I do respect the need to anchor speculations in consensus data of names, dates, and places. This is not an academic work but it is sufficiently referenced to enable the interested reader to expand their studies further.

As part of the culmination of this writing project, *The Book of the Law* was recited aloud in front of what Crowley called the Stele of Revealing on the relevant days and times of its initial reception. My thanks to Andrew and Sue Collins, Rachel Blake, and Daniel Gallagher for helping that to happen.

Paul Weston.
Cairo.
April 8th - 10th 2009.

'*A feast for the three days of the writing of The Book of the Law.*'

INTRODUCTION – THE ENIGMA: BEYOND THE LEGEND OF INFAMY

'What Einstein did for physics and Joyce for the novel (and Picasso for painting, and Pound for poetry, and Wright for architecture), Crowley did for the mystic tradition.'

Robert Anton Wilson.
Introduction to Israel Regardie *The Eye in the Triangle*.

I BELIEVE THAT Aleister Crowley was the most comprehensive prophet of the twentieth century in all of its diverse, ecstatic, terrifying glory. There are immediate problems in trying to understand why that might be the case.

Crowley has accrued around himself a remarkable legend of infamy. In the nineteen-twenties, during his lifetime, the British press described him as the *'wickedest man in the world'*. *'A man we'd like to hang'*. Here was the King of Depravity. A bisexual drug addict who practised the worst forms of black magic. Since his death the reputation has expanded still further until it's easy to find accounts describing him as a practitioner of human sacrifice.

One particular quote seems to represent the hardcore of the legend of infamy. It's in Crowley's 1928 book *Magick*, from a chapter entitled *"On the Bloody Sacrifice"*.

'For the highest spiritual working one must accordingly choose that victim which contains the greatest and purest force. A male child of perfect innocence and high intelligence is the most satisfactory and suitable victim.'

In a footnote Crowley then says *'he made this particular sacrifice on an average about 150 times a year between 1912 and 1928.'* The quote is thrown up again and again in exposes by Christian authors and even allegedly serious occult writers. The very last sentence of Crowley's *"Bloody Sacrifice"* chapter says *'you are likely to get into trouble over this chapter unless you truly comprehend its meaning.'*

So let's think about this one. We're being asked to take this passage as evidence that Crowley murdered 150 children a year from 1912 to 1928. That's 2,550 of them. This would make him unique in the annals of crime. It's strange how he got away with it really. Rather odd that we have no record of any of the victims. No witnesses. No evidence. Although expelled from some countries and refused entry to others, he was never arrested for any offence, let alone served a jail sentence. Some of his books were banned, even burned as pornographic. He lost a libel action in Court. The little matter of those 2,550 child murders seems to have been ignored.

Crowley was a great jester who loved to write in code in a way that only those with commitment to the subject could understand. He didn't mind being shocking in some of his poems but *Magick* was a serious work which he hoped would reach a wide audience. He had seen himself condemned in a cultural climate that was making works like James Joyce's *Ulysses* and D. H. Lawrence's *Lady Chatterley's Lover* unavailable through their use of material related to sex. Crowley's magickal practices involved sex. The 'blood' was semen. He was referring to ejaculation in the context of 'the sacrifice of oneself spiritually', one's creative power, without 'lust of result', as a further footnote explained. The *'male child of perfect innocence and high intelligence'* was likewise clarified as 'the perfect understanding of the magician', the aim of the process. It was an unfortunate choice of metaphors however and substituted an even more controversial topic for the original.

As a human being he had many failings which rendered him sometimes a sad tragic figure and often showed him as reprehensible in his relationships. He inherited a fortune that would be valued in the millions today and was able to live a superb romantic life for over a decade. A complete lack of functional intelligence, which he readily admitted to, meant that he entirely squandered his resources and was reduced to becoming in effect a ruthless beggar who thought nothing of wasting the generous gifts of friends on high living whilst those close to him starved. And he did suffer himself. Two of his young children died. The loss of his fortune and the lack of commercial success and acclaim of his literary work, along with the unprecedented vilification in the press and his prolonged slide into a wretched heroin addiction with an attendant long-term weakening of his general health, was assuredly a major test of his gigantic egotism. Through all this nonetheless, he did demonstrate a stoic determination to disseminate his ideas and this never failed him, even in his last frail days in a Hastings boarding house.

Yes he did, here and there in rituals during his career, kill an animal, and I personally don't approve of that.

He didn't however, as another persistent story states, kill his 'occult son', named Macaleister. The tale is that, at some point in the nineteen-twenties, Crowley had a 'magickal' son who he had named Macaleister. The two of them performed a ceremony to raise Pan. Something went horribly wrong and Macaleister was found dead the next morning. Crowley, reduced to the level of a naked, gibbering idiot, ended up in an asylum in Paris.

I first came upon this tale in an introduction by Dennis Wheatley to an edition of Crowley's novel *Moonchild*. The story gets retold in many shallow surveys of the occult and variations of it continue to circulate and expand. It may seem strange that this dramatic episode is absent from the works of his principal biographers. Surely the hostile John Symonds could have created a damning chapter out of such lurid material? Basically the whole story is a complete fabrication. Macaleister never even existed.

It has often been suggested that, towards the end of his career, he was perhaps insane, at least senile, and basically a spent force. The fact that he was undeniably dependent again on heroin during his later years is usually taken to imply a complete decline. In reply to this I would simply suggest taking a long hard look at the work he produced during that time. *The Book of Thoth* remains to this day perhaps the greatest of all Tarot decks. It's creation involved six years of work with artist Lady Frieda Harris. That represents a tremendous amount of application.

It does rather seem that the legend of infamy may be some kind of smokescreen of nonsense. What lies behind it?

Crowley was a poet hailed in numerous literary journals as a genius. His work was included in the *Oxford Book of Mystical Verse* but he was also responsible for what has been considered to be some of the vilest pornography in the English language.

★ ★ ★

Crowley has also been considered to be either a monstrous degenerate or pioneer of sexual freedom for the endless lovers, both female and male, that he had throughout his life.

At one time he held some of the world mountaineering records, having climbed higher in the Himalayas than anyone else.

He played chess to a standard approaching that of a Grand Master and was able to simultaneously manage two games whilst blindfolded, thus displaying extraordinary abilities of visualisation and concentration.

Crowley was one of the first westerners to fully immerse themselves in the study of eastern religion, having travelled extensively in Arab countries, India, and China. Beyond the studies of the many translators of the time, in the first decade of the twentieth century, he practiced physical and mental yoga with great dedication. Many works that later became famous in the West were familiar to him such as the *I Ching, Tao Te Ching, Bhagavad Gita, Dhammapada* and Patanjali's *Yoga Sutras*.

He was the first person of any note in the West to systematically experiment with the full range of consciousness expanding drugs ie, cannabis, mescaline, ether, cocaine and heroin. For better or for worse, the psychedelic revolution of the sixties was inspired more by him than anyone else.

First and foremost though, Crowley comes down to us as the magician. A member of the most famous occult group of the nineteenth century, the Hermetic Order of the Golden Dawn, he went from there to believe he had received in 1904 a communication from a non-human entity, an angel for want of better terminology, who dictated to him a scripture for a new age or *Aeon*. This work was *The Book of the Law* and it contains the phrase which is most strongly associated with him, '*Do what thou wilt shall be the whole of the Law.*' He came to refer to himself as the Great Beast 666 thus guaranteeing the horror and hostility of many Christians. What did he really mean by this?

We find in the book things that seem to be fascinatingly prophetic of the Nazi era and the psychedelic sixties. There are also early indications of themes later to become increasingly visible in New Age and pagan circles; the return of the goddess and the deities of Egypt. A case can be made for Crowley's influence in the mid-twentieth century rebirth of witchcraft that has proved to be a crucial aspect of the ever-expanding general pagan revival.

One of the most distinctive oddities of the years since the Second World War has been the UFO phenomenon and the culture that has arisen around it. Here again, remarkably enough, his presence can be discerned.

His influence can be seen in the life of a military theorist who inspired the Nazis, a rocket scientist who had a moon crater named after him, the founder of the most controversial and powerful recent new religion, and the psychedelic psychologist who helped turn on the sixties flower children.

This was one man. And this is the enigma of Aleister Crowley. Picture the effeminate homosexual side of Crowley and Crowley the pornographer. Can we then see this man 22,000 feet up the Himalayas without oxygen? Can we see the junkie likewise? Could we picture Quentin Crisp or Sid Vicious in that context? As Thelemic writer Gerald Suster clearly stated in *The Legacy of the Beast*, 'debauched degenerates don't set world mountaineering records.' Contrariwise, how about Chris Bonington? Can we see him returning from an Everest trip to write a book of mystical or pornographic verse and proclaiming himself to be Logos of the Aeon of Horus? When, on one occasion, Crowley was camped out on a glacier, he insisted on packing with his climbing equipment leather-bound editions of the great poets. He would retire to his tent to drink champagne and write his own epics. What about some of our recent esteemed poets such as John Betjeman or Philip Larkin? Can we imagine them performing a magical ceremony in the Great Pyramid or rites of sex magick with prostitutes or taking psychedelic drugs? As for yoga, can we imagine some of the sweetness and light types who get attracted to it composing poems such as *On the Delights of Passive Pederasty*, and *Of Dog and Dame*, or going big-game hunting?

This indeed is the enigma of Aleister Crowley. We all have different facets to ourselves but in Crowley they are written large. Very large. Any one of his different aspects would serve most people for a life's work. How can we get to the essence of the man?

Trying to understand Crowley, his ideas and influence and the way he seems to be a prophet of a dawning age, has taken me on an epic journey of discovery that has involved the investigation of numerous diverse and endlessly fascinating topics and necessitated an ongoing personal transformation. I believe I have noticed some important themes that have potential relevance to our personal and collective lives and the paths we walk in this intense modern epoch so I present an Aeon of Horus primer in the hope that something not just of the information but the *feeling* of what I have come to understand might be communicated.

Although I do write on Crowley's ceremonial Magick here, this is not a work on how to perform it but the dynamic in psychology and culture, the nature of the times in which we live, that empower it. The interested reader is referred to Crowley's own *Magick*, *Abrahadabra* by Rodney Orpheus and *The Magick of Thelema* by Lon Milo DuQuette.

I am not a member of any Thelemic group and find my own way through the assorted never-ending controversies of the genre using the principles explained here in *The Psychology of Thelema* as my guide.

FIN DE SIECLE ZEITGEIST

CROWLEY'S LIFE AND WORK did not arise out of a vacuum. He was certainly massively influenced by his early magical training in the Golden Dawn. Israel Regardie's *Eye in the Triangle* exhaustively demonstrates this. The late nineteenth century was a time of a great revival of occultism and mystical thinking. The founding of H. P. Blavatsky's Theosophical Society in 1875, the year Crowley was born, was a fundamental event in bringing eastern wisdom into the blend. I believe that a wider look at the period is also useful in establishing a context for Crowley's psychology and assessing his concept of the Aeon of Horus.

The last decade of the nineteenth century has often been referred to as the Fin de Siecle after a phrase originating in France in 1885 became widely used across the English-speaking world. More attention was given to the idea of potential significance in the coming end of a century than ever before. It was during this time that Aleister Crowley came to adult consciousness, in a culture full of ideas about itself being in a transitional period where a great cycle of history was ending and a dramatic but indeterminate future already unfolding.

Britannia ruled the waves with the greatest empire in history. Although there had been wars in the nineteenth century, there had not been one involving all of the major European powers together since the final defeat of Napoleon in 1815. The unification of Germany had been a powerful and disruptive event, but the royal families of Europe were related and a system of alliances had been forged that seemed to guarantee peace and security. Progress in science and industrialisation had been extraordinary. There was a consensus confidence that all problems could and would be solved. Despite Darwin, Christianity appeared to remain as the centre of gravity of European civilisation. Nonetheless there were social critics who despaired over a perceived decadence and meaninglessness. In Britain some thinkers were troubled by the old Roman concern with decline and fall.

Any voice however suggesting that this whole world would soon go up in flames would not have been widely heeded. Nonetheless, that process would soon begin. The First World War ravaged Europe's morale, leaving it wide open for the Nazi denouement.

Artists and more progressive thinkers had expressed intimations of the forces at work beneath the surface. A dark undercurrent of the time was given iconic expression in the form of Munch's 1893 painting *The Scream*, which in retrospect seems to effectively express raw indefinable angst as if the protagonist has somehow intuited not just the alienated materialist meaninglessness of the age but the horror of the coming half-century.

Darwin had made a powerful case for recognising the animal side of humanity as fundamentally significant. The very end of the century saw the appearance of Freud's *Interpretation of Dreams*. The idea that the human psyche contains powerful, non-rational, internally coherent forces that determine behaviour and may be effectively unknown to the rational mind, would contribute to undermining confidence in many of the forms which held societies together. The horrors of the coming world wars would make the existence of such forces increasingly easy to believe in.

In the world of the arts although the absinthe-addled foppish aesthete became the style model to affect, with the likes of Oscar Wilde and Aubrey Beardsley enduring as icons of that epoch, some were made of sterner stuff. If the artists of that hedonistic time had potentially mystic temperaments they may have felt as the French poet Baudelaire in his *Poem of Hashish* that *'Alas! the vices of man, full of horror as one must suppose them, contain the proof, even though it were nothing but their infinite expansion, of his hunger for the Infinite.'*

From such intuitions, common to the zeitgeist of the time, the astonishing French teenage poet prodigy Arthur Rimbaud evolved a mission and methodology already in place by the Fin de Siecle that would massively influence Crowley and many subsequent kindred magicians and rock and rollers such as Jim Morrison and Patti Smith.

In a legendary 1871 letter to his friend Paul Demeny, Rimbaud stated that, *'The first study of the man who wants to be a poet is the knowledge of himself, complete. He looks for his soul, inspects it, tests it, learns it. As soon as he knows it, he must cultivate it!' 'But the soul must be made monstrous.'*

'The Poet makes himself a seer by a long, gigantic and rational derangement of all the senses. All forms of love, suffering, and madness. He searches himself. He exhausts all poisons in himself and keeps only their quintessences. Unspeakable torture where he needs all his faith, all his super-human strength, where he becomes among all men the great patient, the great criminal, the one accursed – and the supreme Scholar! – Because he reaches the unknown! Since he cultivated his soul, rich already, more than any man! He reaches the unknown, and when, bewildered, he ends by losing the intelligence of his visions, he has seen them. Let him die as he leaps through unheard of and unnameable things: other horrible workers will come; they will begin from the horizons where the other collapsed!'

Here was the poet as shaman magician, stealer of fire from heaven, Satanic rebel, Luciferian light-bringer.

Probably the greatest nineteenth century influence on Crowley was the German philosopher Nietzsche, prophet of the *ubermensch*, the superman, whose ferocious ecstatic Dionysian will to power makes the world in transcendence of the petty slaveries and conventions that religions and moralities have inflicted on humanity.

When still a young man he wrote a poem *To the Unknown God* which carries something of the same feeling of mystical surrender to a higher power which Crowley cultivated in his quest for his Holy Guardian Angel.

★ ★ ★

> '*I shall and will know thee, Unknown One,*
> *Who searchest out the depths of my soul,*
> *And blowest through my life like a storm,*
> *Ungraspable, and yet my kinsman!*
> *I shall and will know thee, and serve thee.*'

As the new century began a powerful theme became apparent. There was an immense expansion of what was considered to be 'reality'. Simultaneous to this came the biggest undermining of the collective understanding of reality yet seen. These coinciding opposites clearly display two of the most fundamental themes and processes of the age: acceleration and dissolution.

The Education of Henry Adams was the classic autobiography of a man born into one of the most distinguished families in America, responsible for producing two presidents. Primarily a historian, he included in the work an essay written in 1904 giving the beginnings of a theory on acceleration as a dynamic force in history that due to scientific developments, particularly in industrial technology, was becoming ever more rapid in an unparalleled manner.

By 1909 he had refined his ideas to speak of a *Phase Change*, an event whereby the acceleration process would alter forever the relationship between technology and the human race. He suggested this event would probably occur within the coming century or at least by 2025. Adams concepts of progressively accelerating periods of history building up to a climactic and transcendent moment have found modern restatements in the 2012 psychedelic apocalypse of Terence McKenna.

The biggest example of the dissolution theme has been with the concept of Matter itself. Nineteenth century physics conceived of a realm that was like a solar system in miniature where solid objects still revolved around central suns even if it was atoms and electrons being discussed. They moved in a space considered to be essentially empty. Einstein's Relativity and the work of the Quantum Physicists mutated this forever. Matter and Energy became inseparable. And space is not empty but full of rays that pass through what only appear to be solid objects.

As well as science, the dissolution of form was a major twentieth century theme in many other fields. In painting, music, and literature, the idea was widespread. One of the most immediate and important outcomes was the realisation in the arts and sciences that looking at things from one point of view only may be a limitation to transcend. Multiple perspectives were necessary. The co-existence of opposites had to be accepted. Light could be considered to be modelled by both waves and particles depending on the nature of the measurement experiment. Uncertainty became a principle. The importance of language as something that in effect creates our world (an idea that magicians appreciate) would come to pervade cultural studies. Boundaries blurred. All previously established rules of how to see the world and behave in it seemed undermined.

The more that absolutes were undermined and relativity became a general climate so potential meaninglessness and alienation became problems and fundamentalisms of all kinds resisted.

In an introductory section to a 1938 edition of *The Book of the Law* Crowley summarised the social characteristics of the emerging Aeon.

> *'Observe for yourselves the decay of the sense of sin, the growth of innocence and irresponsibility, the strange modifications of the reproductive instinct with a tendency to become bisexual or epicene, the childlike confidence in progress combined with nightmare fear of catastrophe, against which we are yet half unwilling to take precautions. Consider the outcrop of dictatorships, only possible when moral growth is in it's earliest stages, and the prevalence of infantile cults like Communism, Fascism, Pacifism, Health Crazes, Occultism in nearly all its forms, religions sentimentalised to the point of practical extinction. Consider the popularity of the cinema, the wireless, the football pools and guessing competitions, all devices for soothing fractious infants, no seed of purpose in them. Consider sport, the babyish enthusiasms and rages which it excites, whole nations disturbed by disputes between boys. Consider war, the atrocities which occur daily and leave us unmoved and hardly worried. We are children.'*

That seems rather good as prophetic social commentary to me.

The superbly educated Henry Adams had felt inadequately prepared to handle living in the new world of constant and increasing change and acceleration. In the century since, the psychology and sociology of how to deal with what Alvin Toffler in 1970 called *Future Shock* remains undeveloped. His mammoth best-seller spoke of the *'information overload'* involved in *'too much change in too short a period of time'* and the many human problems this can bring.

A major modern theme has been the increasing primacy of the individual. *'Every man and every woman is a star.'* We are all unique in our own orbits. Such a new world requires the development of a psychology of fluidity and multiple perspectives. At its very inception Crowley laid out detailed instructions for how to achieve such aims. In *The Psychology of Thelema* we will examine them at length.

THE BOOK OF THE LAW

THE MOST IMPORTANT EVENT of Crowley's life occurred in Cairo in 1904 when he believed that he received a holy scripture for a newly dawning epoch, the Aeon of Horus. The previous year, when on honeymoon with his wife Rose, they had briefly passed through Cairo and spent the night in the Great Pyramid. At that time Crowley was not actively involved in ceremonial magic of the western mystery tradition. He had dedicated a lot of time and energy to work within the Golden Dawn between 1898 and 1900. After that he had put it all aside to climb mountains, study yoga and Buddhism, and play the role of the world traveller and romantic poet. The evocative environment of Egypt and the desire to impress his wife tempted him to perform what he would later refer to as a little '*exhibition game*' of magic inside the King's Chamber. This may have acted as a stimulus for the sequence of events that followed a few months later.

In February 1904, they were back in Cairo. By March, Crowley was involved in Golden Dawn type magic again. His wife began to experience altered states of consciousness and conveyed a message to Crowley that '*they*' were waiting for him. Crowley always stated that, until that moment, she had shown no interest or aptitude in the magical realm. At first he was dismissive of the material but the trance like states persisted and, under his questioning, she began to reveal details that compelled his attention.

On March 18th Rose said that it was the Egyptian God Horus who was '*waiting*'. As a result of this, Crowley performed two ceremonial invocations to him. They were interesting because the ritual details were supplied by Rose and did not conform to Golden Dawn procedures. She went on to state that the '*Equinox of the Gods*' had come. The old world, the epoch of Christianity, had been destroyed by fire on the inner planes. At that crucial time, Crowley was to formulate a link between the solar spiritual force and humanity.

During the whole of this process, Crowley held to a certain attitude of scepticism towards the strange behaviour of his wife. Over a period of a few days he applied twelve tests to verify the genuineness of the communication from Horus. They mainly consisted of him asking Rose to pick out various attributes of Horus, such as the planet associated with him, his weapon, enemy, and Golden Dawn colour and numerical designations. She was entirely successful in every instance. Given her complete lack of knowledge of Egyptology, Crowley considered that the statistical odds against her picking them all correctly by chance were astronomical.

The most spectacular 'proof' came when, on March 21st, he took her to the Egyptian Museum to see if she could identify an image of Horus. She passed by a number, which greatly pleased Crowley, as he was irritated to see his wife seeming to have a melodramatic episode like the kind of fake mediums he despised. However, she then exclaimed *'There he is,'* pointing far ahead to an exhibit amongst a collection from an earlier version of the museum at Boulak. It turned out to be a wooden funerary stele of one Ankh-af-na-Khonsu, a Priest of Mentu, a God of War, dating from about 725 BC. On it was an image of Ra Hoor Khuit, who is a kind of amalgam of Horus and Ra. This was interesting enough but what clinched the matter for Crowley was seeing that the exhibit number was 666. This famous number, attributed to the Great Beast of the *Book of Revelation,* and the happy hunting ground of numerologists and nutters down through the ages, was one that Crowley had already personally adopted as his own. His parents had been members of a fanatical Christian sect and his mother had used the name of the Beast to castigate her young son. He had happily accepted this as a token of rebellion. Today educated pagans consider that it represents the energy of the sun. Some of the other tests could be interpreted as Rose somehow reading her husband's mind. This would be remarkable in itself but not as striking as the idea that an ancient Egyptian God was seeking to communicate. From that point onwards, Crowley allowed himself to go along with the strange adventure.

For a few weeks the pace slowed slightly, as he commissioned a translation of the writing on the stele into French that he then rendered into English poetic paraphrases. Rose then stated that the communications were not directly from Horus but were coming via a messenger of his named Aiwass. Eventually she gave Crowley instructions to enter a specially prepared room at noon on three successive days and be prepared to take dictation for an hour.

All accounts published during his lifetime stated that it began on April 8th. Crowley sat down at a desk, with Rose in attendance, and waited. At exactly noon he heard the voice of Aiwass, seeming to originate from a point over his left shoulder, behind him in the furthest corner of the room. He felt it echo in his heart. The voice *'was of deep timbre, musical and expressive, its tones solemn, voluptuous, tender, fierce or aught else as suited the moods of the message. Not bass - perhaps a rich tenor or baritone. The English was free of either native or foreign accent, perfectly pure of local or caste mannerisms, thus startling and even uncanny at first hearing. The effect was thus as if the language was "English in itself" without any background, such as exists when any one human speaks it.'*

In order to keep up with the pace of rapid dictation, Crowley never turned his back to look in the direction of the voice. Rose was present and could hear it as well. On one occasion she had to confirm the wording for Crowley. In all of the many accounts he wrote of these events it is never mentioned as to whether he ever asked her if she looked and saw anything. I certainly would have quizzed her and, if I'd been in her position, hearing the voice, I would have looked in its direction, but who can really imagine the strange conditions prevailing in this situation? It has been suggested that Rose may have acted as a medium for Aiwass and spoken the words herself. If this was the case it has been kept well-hidden. As it is, Crowley did experience an inner impression that Aiwass was present in a fine body, transparent like a cloud of incense smoke. *'He seemed to be a tall, dark man in his thirties, well-knit, active and strong, with the face of a savage king, and eyes veiled lest their gaze should destroy what they saw. The dress was not Arab; it suggested Assyria or Persia, but very vaguely.'*

Over the course of the three sessions, The Book of the Law was dictated. Aiwass introduced himself as *'minister of Hoor-paar-Kraat'*, elsewhere known as Hor-pa-Kred, and in Greek as Harpocrates. This is the infant Horus, usually pictured with a finger to his lips, making a gesture of silence. In a magickal sense, this represents the sealing of a formula that has been put out into the world. Each chapter contains the words of particular forces pictured on what Crowley came to call the 'Stele of Revealing'.

Arched over the whole scene was Nuit, the Goddess of the night sky. The first chapter is hers. It is ironic to realise, considering Crowley's reputation as misogynist and abuser of women, that the words of Nuit represent one of the first clear indications of the return of the Goddess in the magical literature of the time. If a woman had written such words they might have become a feminist scripture.

(All following quotes from *The Book of the Law* are representative selections from the respective chapters condensed together with verse numbers referenced.)

3. *Every man and every woman is a star.*

12. *Come forth, o children, under the stars, & take your fill of love!*

13. *I am above you and in you. My ecstasy is in yours. My joy is to see your joy.*

15. *They shall gather my children into their fold: they shall bring the glory of the stars into the hearts of men.*

29. *I am divided for love's sake for the chance of union.*

32. *– the joys of my love will redeem ye from all pain.*

41. *The word of Sin is Restriction. There is no bond that can unite the divided but love.*

51. *Also take your fill and will of love as ye will, when where and with whom you will! But always unto me.*

53. *This shall regenerate the world, the little world my sister, my heart and my tongue unto whom I send this kiss. – ecstasy be thine and joy of earth.*

57. *Invoke me under my stars! Love is the law, love under will.*

61. *I love you, I yearn to you. I who am all pleasure and purple and drunkenness of the innermost sense desire you. Put on the wings and arouse the coiled splendour within you: come unto me!*

A winged disc is pictured on the stele. In Egyptological terms, it depicts an aspect of an early predynastic form of Horus, from a cult centre at a place called Behdet. This name was later given to the famous Horus temple at Edfu and other places of his worship. As defender of Ra he would travel the sky as a winged disc hunting Ra's enemy Set. Chapter Two is his words, but his energy is named as Hadit, which is understood as a mathematical metaphysical principle.

★ ★ ★

> 6. I am the flame that burns in every heart of man, and in the core of every star. I am Life, and the giver of Life, yet therefore is the knowledge of me the knowledge of death.
>
> 9. Remember all ye that existence is pure joy; that all the sorrows are but as shadows; they pass & are done; but there is that which remains.
>
> 20. Beauty and strength, leaping laughter and delicious languor, force and fire, are of us.
>
> 22. I am the Snake that giveth Knowledge & Delight and bright glory, and stir the hearts of men with drunken-ness. To worship me take wine and strange drugs whereof I will tell my prophet, & be drunk thereof! They shall not harm ye at all. It is a lie, this folly against self. The exposure of innocence is a lie. Be strong, o man! lust, enjoy all things of sense and rapture: fear not that any God shall deny thee for this.

Powerful and inspiring words but amongst them were some with a more disturbing flavour.

> 21. We have nothing with the outcast and the unfit: let them die in their misery. For they feel not. Compassion is the vice of kings: stamp down the wretched & the weak: this is our law and the joy of the world.

The third chapter gives full expression to such sentiments. It is the voice of Ra-Hoor-Khuit.

> 3. I am a god of War and of Vengeance.
>
> 11. Thou shalt have danger & trouble.– Worship me with fire and blood.
>
> 18. Mercy let be of: damn them who pity! Kill and torture, spare not, be upon them!
>
> 51. With my Hawk's head I peck at the eyes of Jesus as he hangs upon the cross.
>
> 54. I spit on your crapulous creeds.
>
> 55. Let Mary inviolate be torn upon wheels: for her sake let all chaste women be utterly despised among you!

For some years Crowley rejected the work because of passages like these. He considered Chapter Three to be *'gratuitously atrocious'*. The relationship between the three forces came to be understood by Crowley as quite an interesting metaphysic. Nuit represents infinite space. Her body is the whole universe. All possibilities are contained within it. She is the womb of creation that continually supports and sustains all of existence. She can be symbolised by a circle. Hadit symbolises any point of actual manifestation within the body of Nuit. He is a dot in the centre of her circle. *'In the sphere I am everywhere the centre, as she, the circumference is nowhere found.'* Nuit and Hadit are in infinite contact. They can never be separated. Their union creates a child, Ra-Hoor-Khuit. He dictates the flavour of the Universe's manifestation.

There have been previous Aeons, also symbolically presided over by Egyptian deities. Isis ruled the matriarchal epoch of the great mother goddess. Osiris was a dying and resurrected god, typical of the mystery cults of the Mediterranean world. Jesus and Christianity demonstrate the triumph of that form. Horus inevitably partakes of qualities of both his parents but is an individual beyond them. This individuality is perhaps the most characteristic form of what is now unfolding, for better or worse. *'Do what thou wilt.'*

I believe that Crowley was basically honest in his account of how *The Book of the Law* came to be written. There are a few issues that present difficulties however. On one page of the original version of Crowley's handwritten copy there is a grid of squares encompassing the words with a line passing down at an angle across them. It ends with a circle containing a cross. The page (in the third chapter) makes it clear that all subsequent published versions must contain a copy of the original *'for in the chance shape of the letters and their position to one another: in these are mysteries that no Beast shall divine.' 'Then this line drawn is a key: then this circle squared in its failure is a key also.'* There is a sense of a secret cipher that Crowley himself would never be able to crack. It is further prophesied that this would be the work of another, yet to come. In terms of the various accounts of the writing of the text, it is difficult to envisage exactly what was happening as this page was created. It seems likely that Crowley added the grid later as part of an attempt to understand the cipher.

I don't doubt Crowley's basic sincerity in believing that the words were not a product of his own mind. That doesn't mean they weren't. The events surrounding the Stele of Revealing are fairly spooky but what about the text they generated? How can one prove in any way that it can be said to be the work of a discarnate being of higher intelligence? He may not have been able to solve the mystery of the line and the circle (which we shall return to later) but Crowley did find Qabalistic numerical codes within the book that he offered as his main evidence. Some ancient alphabets, most notably Hebrew, had numbers assigned to each letter. This meant that each word had a numerical value. The Hebrew Qabalah has a branch of knowledge within it, known as Gematria, which deals with the mystical interpretation of this. For example, if two words add up to the same number, there will be a link between them that needs to be understood. Some of the key words in *The Book of the Law* were Greek. *Thelema* means 'Will' or the casting of a spell. *Agape* means 'Love'. Both words have a value of 93. A variant spelling of Aiwass as 'Aiwaz' also adds up to 93. When Aiwaz delivers a message about *'love under will'* it invites a deeper investigation.

There are other numerical mysteries within the text. Crowley spent the rest of his life studying them. He stated that it is simply not possible for any human mind to create a piece of work embodying such codes within the body of a generally coherent narrative. There were other works of his that were written in exalted mystical states but he always affirmed that *The Book of the Law* was unique and that he was not the author. The New Age market is full of writings supposedly channelled from discarnate entities. It's ironic that the unending bland platitudes that promise a cotton wool and candyfloss utopia don't have the kind of internal verifications contained within Crowley's infamous work nor have they been followed by events that seem to fulfil them.

I feel that the concept of the Aeon of Horus offers, at the very least, a superb poetic metaphor to help understand the enigma of the twentieth century. Whilst the appalling two world wars were the most dramatic events, many other themes characterised what was clearly a new epoch of some kind.

There has been an explosive unleashing of knowledge and energy, symbolised by Hadit, *'the flame that burns in every heart of man, and in the core of every star.'* Nuit's admonition to *"arouse the coiled splendour within you"* may have seemed obscure in 1904 to all but scholars of arcane Hindu texts, but by the sixties they seemed to sing with prophecy. LSD and the atom bomb, DNA and the space programme, were all examples of our mental horizons being expanded as never before, as the light within matter itself was unleashed.

GNOSTIC REVIVAL

WAS CROWLEY ALONE IN HIS BELIEF in the end of an entire epoch of civilisation in 1904 along with the return of ancient spiritual forces? Did anyone else of note likewise describe stirrings of what we could recognise as the Aeon of Horus?

One man who gave profound expression to undercurrents in the psyche of western humanity during the twentieth century was Carl Gustav Jung. The modern common idea of a collective unconscious derives from him. He played a significant role in inspiring interest and revival in a wide range of mystical topics drawn from the world's traditions. In 1936 his *Wotan* essay showed a deep understanding of Hitler and the Nazis, proclaiming the messianic leader as a shamanic mediumistic figure, who was in effect channelling certain aspects of the archetype of the Germanic deity on behalf of the unconscious of a whole nation. Jung recognised the dangers and spoke a truth about Nazism that no-one else had expressed so clearly. 1958's *Flying Saucers* remains a core text for understanding the bigger picture in which the enigmatic aerial phenomenon arose, the changing of an astrological age with its accompanying signs and portents. Surely such a man would have been aware of at least some of the distinctive flavour of Crowley's Aeon if it really was arising in the collective mind.

In the middle of the First World War, Jung was involved in an astonishing episode with the Gnostic deity Abraxas. Gnosticism could be seen as a blanket label covering a spectrum of distinctive religious beliefs and practices that flourished during the first centuries AD whose adherents would not necessarily have recognised the terminology. The Gnostics included people who considered themselves Christian and others who would be thought of as pagan, ie devotees of classical and Egyptian deities, along with the creators of some unique cosmologies and hierarchies of angelic beings.

Common to most groupings was a belief that the material world was created by a secondary deity who could be considered evil. The highest god stands above and beyond creation. Something of this can be found in the Christian idea of Satan as lord of the world. Some believed that the Old Testament Jehovah was in the same class. A host of entities work for these controlling powers holding the matrix in place. There were various realms, conceived of as emanations of the source. The Qabalah has similarities and its modern form may owe much to the Gnostic period. The material world is a prison that must be transcended. The response to this conundrum can be as diverse as ascetic world rejection or the embrace of ecstasies pursued through sexual means. This dichotomy can be found in today's New Agers. Both approaches seek to cultivate an innate inner star that retains the qualities of its divine source. A direct experience of it is required and the purpose of Priests and Priestesses is to facilitate this rather than keep aspirants apart from it. Somewhere in the creation cosmology, usually between the true source and the jailer, was a feminine energy that promised salvation.

Gnosticism flourished at the same time as Hermeticism, another important influence on the modern magical revival. What is Hermeticism? In the early centuries AD, Alexandria surpassed Rome as a multi-cultural centre. People from all over the empire and beyond gathered there. Its gigantic library was legendary. Indian 'Gymnosophists' and Persian Magi met with Jewish Mystics, Greek philosophers, Egyptian magicians and Gnostic Christians in a climate of cross-fertilisation and tolerance. Works from the ancient cult centres of Babylon and Assyria were available for inspection. Extraordinary mixtures resulted. Much of the foundations of the whole western magical tradition were laid there. Beliefs that later resurfaced during the Renaissance and in the Golden Dawn can be traced back to Alexander's fabulous city.

The Egyptian god Thoth and the Greek Hermes had become identified with each other. They were both associated with communication between the human and divine realms, and with writing and magic. The figure of Hermes Trismegistus, the thrice-great, emerged from this. He came to be seen as someone who had lived as a human being but been divinely inspired to reveal mysteries to the human race. In some versions, he attains immortality. A number of authors wrote works in his name, which are collectively known as the *Corpus Hermeticum*, on mystical, magical, and philosophical themes, often featuring Egyptian deities. They tend to emphasise the harmony and inter-relationship between all of creation. The mysterious art and science of alchemy also developed from the same mix of influences.

Another crucial religious form was the Mystery Cult. They included both public ceremonials and more selective initiations focused on seasonal dramas of death and resurrection featuring gods and goddesses. Deities such as Sumero-Babylonian Tammuz and the Phoenician-Greek Adonis are examples of beings intimately linked with the seasonal drama, veritable vegetation deities, infused with the spirit of life. The ceremonies of these cults, which often involved participants experiencing transformations that induced identification with the deities involved, also inspired the Golden Dawn and the general occultism of the time.

From this incredible cultural blend the figure of Abraxas appeared. He is usually depicted as having a human body with a rooster's head and legs like serpents. Sometimes he has a hawk or a lion's head. He tends to hold a whip and a shield. Abraxas rides in a chariot drawn by four white horses. The sun and moon may both be shining above him to indicate his embodiment of opposites. He is associated with one of the leading Gnostics, Basilides, who flourished in Alexandria around about 120-30AD. Basilides made use of numbers in a way reminiscent of Pythagoras. The name Abraxas is an example of the kind of Gematria familiar to us from Crowley. It adds up to 365 and is therefore taken to refer to the solar year in some way. From the supreme God emanated seven attributes or powers that had their correlations in the seven days of the week. There were likewise seven similar forces in every realm of the spiritual world. The complete total was 365.

From this reverence for Abraxas derives the 'Abraxas gems'. These come in the form of gems, plates, or tablets of metal. They are mainly inscribed with the word *Abraxas*. They are not exclusively associated with Basilides. Of those that are, some depict Egyptian god-forms with inscriptions such as *Abraxas* and *IAO*. Most interestingly of all from my point of view, some depict the infant Horus seated on a lotus flower, forefinger raised to his mouth in the magical gesture of silence. This is none other than the same Harpocrates who features in *The Book of the Law* and is shown on Crowley's *Aeon* tarot trump. Some have Jewish words like Jehovah and Adonai. There are images of a cock, a lions head with the word *Mithras*, monstrous forms, sphinxes and apes, and many Egyptian deities. The phrase "solar-phallic," which Crowley used to refer to the Thelemic current, sums up their general attributes.

Sometime between the summer of 1916 and February 1917 (there are variant dates in different accounts), over three consecutive evenings, Jung had a *Book of the Law* experience, writing *Seven Sermons to the Dead*. The episode was heralded by strangeness in the family home. Jung's children saw and sensed ghosts. One had a serious dream featuring an angel and a devil. Jung himself felt a powerful atmosphere building. On a Sunday afternoon, the doorbell started ringing. No earthly visitor was responsible. The apparatus could be clearly seen moving on its own. The air in the whole house seemed so thick with spirits that it was difficult to breathe. Jung cried out, *'For God's sake, what in the world is this?'* A chorus of voices replied, *'We have come back from Jerusalem where we found not what we sought.'*

With the barriers between the worlds broken, Jung settled down to write a stunning text. Its authorship was attributed to Basilides, the location, *'Alexandria, the city where East and West meet.'* We don't have as many details on the process of composition as there are with Crowley. There is still conjecture over whether or not Jung was mediumistically channelling dictation from a source he believed to be Basilides or expressing some part of his own psyche through the form of a Gnostic teaching.

Basilides sets out to instruct the dead, who seem to be crusading knights who failed to find fulfilment in Jerusalem, in other words, through conventional Christianity. Their god concept gets a makeover through encountering Abraxas who,

'is undefinable life itself, which is the mother of good and evil alike.'
'He is the brightest light of day and the deepest night of madness.'
'He is both the radiance and the dark shadow of man.'
'Abraxas generates truth and falsehood, good and evil, light and darkness with the same word and in the same deed. Therefore Abraxas is truly the terrible one.'
'He is the monster of the underworld, the octopus with a thousand tentacles, he is the twistings of winged serpents and of madness.'
'To fear him is wisdom.'
'Not to resist him means liberation.'

What was Jung the psychologist doing having a full-on occult episode like this? There are some who think he was perhaps as much a Hermetic magician as a psychologist. Abraxas did not exactly arrive unheralded. The figure of Aiwass was of central significance in Crowley's *Book of the Law* experience. Jung had his own daemonic angel who helped open the portal for the *Seven Sermons*. In 1913 he had begun to deliberately cultivate visionary experiences through what is now known to Jungians as active imagination. A figure appeared who he knew as Philemon, an impressive white-bearded robed sage with multi-coloured kingfisher wings.

Jung described him as having '*an Egypto-Hellenistic atmosphere with a gnostic coloration.*' In an event typical of what he would later come to call synchronicity, the initial contact was followed by Jung's discovery of a dead kingfisher. The bird was all but unknown in the vicinity of his Swiss home and he never saw another in his remaining decades there. Philemon became a guru to Jung, guiding him through times of visionary experiences that verged on psychosis. This wise old man aspect of his psyche, who some occultists might designate as an inner plane contact, later served as the conduit for the incoming Basilides-Abraxas transmission.

The 1913 visions were undoubtedly shaped by Jung's extensive reading on the mystery cults of antiquity, in particular Mithraism, which had an enduring fascination for him. During the peak of the Alexandrian Hermetic era, Mithras had become tremendously successful in the Roman world. In the syncretistic manner of the time, his form mutated. A complex of kindred god-forms blurred and blended. Mithras, Abraxas, Aion. A variant spelling, Meithras, adds up to 365 like Abraxas. Crowley claimed that the correct name of the idol supposedly worshipped by the Templars was Baphometr which meant "Father Mithras."

The Golden Dawn had a technique known as the assumption of a god-form. It involved powerfully imagining oneself in the appearance of some deity. One might sit with a particular posture that the chosen form has been depicted in. If it was an Egyptian god for example, it might also mean imagining oneself to have an animal head of some kind. Various artefacts might be visualised as being held. Crowley had often taken on the form of Horus during his Golden Dawn days. He later felt that this had helped to predispose him towards the Cairo revelation that led to his proclamation of himself as Logos of the Aeon.

The climax of Jung's visionary experiences has only recently become more widely known, primarily through *The Aryan Christ* of Richard Noll. One night in December 1913, in a state of active imagination, he started to experience a snake wrapping itself around his body. As it did so, he found himself taking on a crucifixion pose and his head changing shape into that of a lion. Jung had assumed the god-form of the Mithraic leontocephalic (meaning lion-headed) cosmocrator (ruler of the cosmos), Lord of Time, Aion. He achieved such intensity as to experience total identification, in his own words,

'*Deification.*'
'*In this deification mystery you make yourself into the vessel, and are a vessel of creation in which the opposites reconcile.*'
'*So Aion, the lion headed god with the snake round his body, again represents the union of opposites, light and dark, male and female, creation and destruction.*'

It was essentially an initiatory experience. The scene was set for *Seven Sermons*, where Jung was the vessel of the Mithriac Aion's kindred Abraxas, unifier of opposites.

Remember those Abraxas gems? The one featuring the infant Horus Harpocrates seated on a lotus, forefinger raised to his mouth? Abraxas is sometimes depicted with a hawk's head. It's fruitful to compare the *Seven Sermons* with *The Book of the Law*. It's now accepted that Jung's text was of fundamental importance for the future of his work. It was as defining a moment in his life as was Cairo 1904 for Crowley. Crowley and Jung's true-self concepts were personified by kindred Gnostic god forms, both associated with time cycles.

At the time of the reception of *The Book of the Law*, Crowley stated that the old world had been destroyed by fire, at least on the inner planes. In the ancient world, some Stoic philosophers, believed to have heavily influenced Mithraism, expounded a concept called *ekpyrosis*. Vast cycles of time come to an end either through flood or fire. When it came to flame, it was a kind of alchemical process whereby all of the energy of the universe was transformed into fire. This ending was also a beginning of a new world. Mithras became the presiding deity of this process. The Mithraic Aion was the turner of the zodiacal wheel, the mover of the cycles of the heavens. I tend to feel that the Cambridge educated classically literate Crowley would have had the concept of ekpyrosis somewhere in the back of his mental filing cabinet in 1904. He obviously readily used the term *Aeon* to refer to a cycle of time.

Seven Sermons wasn't published until after Jung's death in 1961. Not many of his followers had even known of its existence. A small number of copies had been distributed amongst a select few. There's a hint that Herman Hesse may have seen it and been stimulated in the production of his own *Demian* that features Abraxas. Crowley had no knowledge of it. Compare this passage however, from *Liber VII*, one of his later holy books, to Jung on Abraxas.

*'O all ye toads and cats rejoice! Ye slimy things,
come hither!
Dance, dance to the Lord our God.'*
Crowley

*'He is the lord of toads and frogs, who live in
water and come out unto the land, and who sing
together at high noon and at midnight.'*
Jung

The *Hermetic* Order of the Golden Dawn had roots as strongly in Alexandria as those of Basilides. Some of its members, including Crowley, were as enthusiastic students of mystery cults and Gnosticism as Jung. The most magically significant example of this is the mileage got from an obscure mid nineteenth-century academic work, *Fragment of a Graeco-Egyptian Work upon Magic from a Papyrus in the British Museum* by Charles Wycliffe Goodwin. It featured an *Invocation of the Headless One*.

Golden Dawn chief Samuel Liddell Macgregor Mathers had made use of it as a general preliminary invocation in a translation he made of the medieval grimoire, the *Lesser Key of Solomon* that became known in the order. It featured a sequence of what's become known to magicians as "Barbarous names of Evocation," weird, seemingly meaningless words that carry a feeling of archaic strata of humanities' religious consciousness. Part of their effectiveness may stem from their very unintelligibility and the strange emotions stirred by intoning such stuff aloud. Some would avow however that amongst the medieval theatrics may lie authentic fragments with a history that goes back to Alexandria and beyond. If you call out with heightened emotion to weird deities they may come, even if you don't realise that's what you're doing. Hence this stuff is generally considered to have a bit of a government health warning attached.

As Kenneth Grant explains it in *The Magical Revival*, 'The Headless One was a name given by the Gnostics to the Sun in Amenti, ie the Light in the Underworld. — In other words, the headless one typified the hidden god submerged below the horizon: in terms of psychology, the subconsciousness, the subliminal Will.' Crowley adjusted the translation from Headless to Bornless, 'to indicate the fact that the True Will is subject to neither birth nor death, its vehicles alone are subject to these twin phases of activity in the phenomenal world. The *invocation of the Bornless One therefore forms the practical basis for contacting the most hidden of all gods or daemons – the Holy Guardian Angel.*" It begins -

> '*Thee I invoke, the Bornless One.*
> *Thee, that didst create the Earth and the Heavens.*
> *Thee that didst create the Night and the Day.*
> *Thee, that didst create the darkness and the light.*'

Crowley's adaptation found its final form as *Liber Samekh. Theurgia Goetia Summa (Congressus Cum Daemone)*, a hefty section within the great masterwork, *Magick*. This included the barbarous names Qabalistically adjusted, elucidated, and translated into English. He considered it to be his definitive manual for the invocation of the Holy Guardian Angel.

Crowley advised in his explanatory notes for the ritual that it would involve a sequence of '*assuming the form and the consciousness of the Elemental God of the quarter.*' With fire in the south, this would be '*a solar phallic lion*'. Jung knew all about that. The barbarous name Abrasax (a variant spelling) is interpreted to mean, '*of the Father, the Sun, of Hadit, of the spell of the Aeon of Horus!*'

Perhaps the most famous of all magical incantations, Abracadabra, derives from the name of Abraxas. *The Book of the Law* contains the important Thelemic variant *Abrahadabra*, a magical formula explaining the nature of the union of Nuit and Hadit. '*In the sphere I am everywhere the centre as she, the circumference, is nowhere found*'. It also refers, as Kenneth Grant explains in *The Magical Revival*, to '*the two faces, or the dual aspect, of HAD, as the solar twins, – Set and Horus (Hoor-Paar-Kraat and Ra-Hoor-Khuit).*' This calls to mind the duality of Jung's Abraxas.

The magickal mystical group that Crowley came to be the head of, the Order of the Templars of the Orient, generally known as the OTO, had come into being during the late nineteenth century bringing together a blend of influences both western and eastern. Its founder Carl Kellner had encountered Sufi and Hindu adepts as well as being experienced in the full range of European Masonic based occultism. Theodor Reuss collaborated with Kellner in the formation of the Order and succeeded him as head.

In 1908 Reuss met some French Gnostic revivalists, including the notable occultist known as Papus, who had founded a church that considered itself to be Christian, however heretical in form.

Reuss was consecrated into their order and created a new branch of it, the Gnostic Catholic Church, which subsequently became independent of its source and a part of the OTO.

Reuss introduced Crowley to the OTO in 1910, conferring upon him authority to create and lead a British version in 1912. On a trip to Russia in 1913, Crowley was inspired by a Greek Orthodox Church ceremony to write a Gnostic Mass for what he referred to as the *Ecclesia Gnostica Catholica* (EGC), which the OTO Gnostic grouping subsequently came to be known as. It soon became their official rite. The obvious difference from its Christian source is the presence of a Priestess who conducts the rite in harmony with the Priest. The OTO came to accept *The Book of the Law* and their Gnostic Church likewise. The two groupings were essentially inseparable.

Crowley and Jung appear to both be expressing something very similar. The question now arises as to whether we can say that the Aeon of Horus is part of a Gnostic revival or the other way round? I would say they are intimately related and that will become even clearer when the Babalon Working is examined. The study of one very much helps understanding of the other. Both can also be seen to be part of a bigger picture of things stirring in the greater life of the world. This is strongly indicated by hints from another titanic spiritual figure of the time.

GURDJIEFF, TIBET, AND THE KALI YUGA

GEORGE IVANOVITCH GURDJIEFF was perhaps the most mysterious, haunting magus figure of the twentieth century. Like Crowley, he has been reviled as a charlatan. Others have seen him as a superhuman ambassador of Central Asian esoteric schools. Born some time in the eighteen-seventies in the multicultural melting pot of Armenia, he claimed to have spent decades on a quest for living sources of ancient wisdom. His overwhelming charisma and unusual knowledge and abilities convinced many he had succeeded. He came to prominence as a teacher of esoteric knowledge in Tsarist Russia. The revolution forced a departure to Europe. In the early twenties he established a base in France in a large house with extensive grounds. Many people of a high level of culture and breeding joined him there.

Gurdjieff wrote a gigantic and difficult to read work entitled *Beelzebub's Tales to his Grandson* which included much material that seemed to be autobiographical, including a strange account of events in Tibet at the time of the dawning of Crowley's Aeon of Horus.

During the late nineteenth century Britain and Russia engaged in what's been called the "Great Game" in Asia. India was the jewel in the imperial crown. Russia had expanded across the continent. Spheres of influence were contended. Afghanistan and Tibet became places where political intrigues were played out as the two superpowers vied for position. One result of this involved a British expedition entering Tibet in 1903 led by a man named Francis Younghusband. It was not a full-blown invasion but the group was primarily military and its intention was to force Tibet into opening up more fully to British influence.

Gurdjieff was supposedly in Tibet during this period. *Beelzebub's Tales* gives an account of the history of a particular esoteric group, always numbering seven people, which had been founded by a divine messenger named by Gurdjieff in his typically idiosyncratic style as Saint Krishnatkharna. This is generally taken to refer to Krishna. This group endured and adapted through the time of Buddha and the arrival of his teaching in Tibet with its adoption by Saint Lama who can be thought of as Padmasambhava, founder of Tibetan Buddhism. The group were extremely powerful and played a mysterious role in the balance of global forces.

They were still active when the Younghusband expedition entered Tibet. Their leader was present when a kind of national assembly discussed how best to meet the challenge. He advocated a pacifist approach which was subsequently adopted with him accompanying a group sent out to meet the British. This went horribly wrong when the great adept was shot dead.

The dynamic of the group of seven which had lasted for millennia was fatally compromised. There were detailed instructions handed down from Saint Lama concerning the transmission of the teachings by the leader which were determined by the spiritual preparedness of the other six. The leader was on the verge of becoming the divine messenger of the age. At the vital point the survivors were on the threshold but the process was incomplete. They took a hardcore esoteric option, attempting to communicate through the corpse of their leader with what might be termed his spiritual energies. Gurdjieff used a variety of complex terminology to describe the process. For such an undertaking to be successful it should have been started whilst the leader was still alive.

Sufficient to say the gamble catastrophically failed. Some kind of negative alchemy occurred resulting in a huge explosion referred to by Gurdjieff as the "Sobrionolian contact." The remaining group were killed and all of the texts and relics of their tradition were destroyed. This disaster meant that planetary conditions as a whole immediately deteriorated. To what extent the story is meant to be taken literally is difficult to assess. Nonetheless Gurdjieff is clearly pointing to a time and place where he believed that a crucial shift had occurred.

The most notable event in the Younghusband expedition could well be the one referred to by Gurdjieff. On March 31st 1904 British and Tibetan forces faced each-other at point-blank range in a situation that seemed to offer possibilities of peaceful resolution. Discussions were in progress when a shot was fired. The Tibetans, hemmed in and armed with antiquated muskets, soon suffered somewhere in the region of 700 fatalities. Himalayan mountaineer Crowley was already in Cairo. A few days before, he had been informed that the old world was in the process of disappearing in flames. The usual accounts state that barely a week later, he took dictation of *The Book of the Law*. This fits together very interestingly.

There is another Tibetan flavoured strand of evocative data independent of Gurdjieff that also gels intriguingly with the Thelemic mythos. *Gods, Beasts and Men* by Ferdinand Ossendowski was published in 1922. It was an account of Central Asian travels and the author's encounters with a tradition of a secret kingdom where the true rulers of the planet reside. Shambhala is the most well-known name for this fabled realm. It represents a living and vital reality for the Tantric Buddhists of Tibet and Mongolia, who believe it to be the home of a system of secret wisdom. Some of this is embodied in the teachings of the Kalachakra, which means "Wheel of Time," a system widely taught by the current Dalai Lama. Its origins are believed to predate Buddha, who visited Shambhala himself to be initiated in its mysteries. On the one hand it has a tangible physical location but also strange qualities which can hide it from the profane, making it all but invisible to the outside world. Its pilgrims are somehow summoned by subtle inner means.

In some versions, this kingdom has a connected underground realm called Agarttha. Ossendowski related that an awesome being known as the "King of the World" lives there. A remarkable story tells of how he actually appeared above ground and visited a Mongolian monastery in 1890. He uttered a series of prophecies concerning a time of warfare and tribulation that was soon to come upon the world and would usher in *'a new life on the earth, purified by the death of nations.'* After this, the underground super-beings of Agarttha would rise up and claim the world. One obvious problem here is that the account was published after the First World War and the Russian Revolution so cynics can wonder if the traveller created a retrospective fiction.

Beyond Ossendowski, during the twenties, there was a powerful belief in Central Asia that a time of an earthly kingdom of Shambhala was near. There were elements that a westerner could recognise from Christian millennial enthusiasms over the coming of the New Jerusalem. In a time of profound uncertainty in Asia following the Bolshevik revolution and the increasing power of Japan, Shambhala focused nationalist aspirations. A warrior lord was expected to lead the process. He was Gesar Khan. This hero of Tibetan and Mongolian myth cycles may have lived in the 8th century AD. A champion of righteousness, he had disappeared with a hint of return. I rather feel that something of this idea of a coming Shambhalic epoch presided over by a warrior and involving *"the death of nations"* has resonances with the Aeon of Horus.

Blavatsky's Theosophy introduced to a western audience the vast Hindu time cycles known as Yugas. There are four of differing lengths during which planetary conditions range from paradisiacal purity down through a declining spiral to a dense darkness of unrighteousness. We are currently in one of the final *Kali* Yugas and therefore surrounded by things likely to induce a general fear and desperation and the sense of a world that is ending. The great French esotericist and expounder of the Yugas, Rene Guenon, cautioned against what is in the bigger picture a false perspective. Ends are inseparable from beginnings. The golden age follows the greatest darkness. Regardless of planetary upheavals, humanity survives the Kali Yugas.

The different ages call forth particular religious forms. One primordial wisdom tradition remains functioning on varied levels of visibility. Many groups lack a true connection with it and therefore serve only as often debased expressions of temporary conditions. Guenon believed that most of the occultism and Theosophically inspired eastern influenced beliefs of the current times are typical Kali Yuga manifestations and did not serve true spirituality.

In *The Lord of the World* published in 1927, Guenon linked Agarttha with the Yugas. He depicts it as the spiritual axis of the planet, the true source and centre of the primordial tradition. During the Kali Yuga it is hidden from sight and its connections to religious groups weakened or broken. Now, as we experience the greatest darkness, we are also near to the ending of the cycle with the hope of change to come. Agarttha emerges again and the presence of its mysterious ruler who has both material and spiritual power is discernable.

This raises questions concerning Crowley's magick, and the Aeon of Horus. Is it a transient and debased cultus or does it link with the primordial wisdom tradition? Are there other links between Crowley and Gurdjieff? And what of the vexed issue of the so-called Secret Chiefs who allegedly govern the great occult and mystical groups down through the ages? These are themes that will be examined in *Extra-Terrestrial Gnosis*.

For now it is sufficient to register that the two most significant magus figures of the twentieth century both stated that a cataclysmic new epoch had been unleashed upon the world. Not only that, they both dated it's beginning to exactly the same obscure period of time that had been generally unheralded by astrologers and other prophets.

So yes, Crowley was not eccentrically alone in his intuition of the dawning of a new spiritual epoch and its characteristics. Two major figures of the time, Jung and Gurdjieff, had things to say which take on a very peculiar flavour when placed alongside the Aeon of Horus idea.

It might seem problematical to think of different conceptions of time cycles together. We have the Aeon of Horus, the transition from the astrological age of Pisces to Aquarius, Kali Yuga, Kalachakra and so on. Can they all be true? Do we need advanced multiple perspective skills to deal with this? Once we turn our attention to it, we begin to realise that most of us are comfortably living with a large number of different time and calendrical associations that give structure and meaning to our lives. We may have three hands on our time pieces to give us seconds, minutes and hours. There is morning and afternoon time, days, weeks, months, years, decades, centuries, millennia, and so on. Within that set of co-ordinates we may orientate ourselves through the individual significance we attach to how old we are, the birthday thresholds of thirty, forty, fifty etc, how long we have been in a relationship, when our children were born and their changing age, how long ago our parents died, and we have lived in different homes. We have the financial year, football season, cricket season, agricultural year, cycles of Olympic Games, World Cup, political elections. Many people also pay attention to lunar and astrological heavenly cycles. It is possible to live with all of this data quite easily.

ABSOLUTE ELSEWHERE: THE MORNING OF THE MAGICIANS

PROLOGUE

PART OF THE PROCESS of the opening of the doors for the new world involves the opening of other doors that let back in archaic strata below the surface of the dissolving consensus of Christian civilisation, hence Egyptian deities, Mithras and Abraxas, and, as we shall see, Wotan, and various forms of the divine feminine. To reiterate, the Aeon of Horus concept as presented by *The Book of the Law* seems to me to provide at least an excellent poetic model with which to appreciate and perhaps better understand the diversity.

The Aeonic process can be considered to be entirely neutral but its effects on the life of the world vary. Two immense historical cultural phenomenon demonstrate the full range of distinctive twentieth century forces at work and seem to strikingly manifest qualities expressed in *The Book of the Law*, from the Goddess Nuit calling us to return to her as she arched over the Summer of Love, to the ferocity of Ra Hoor Khuit as he presided over Auschwitz and Hiroshima. These mind-shattering opposites were part of a law of nature, the general flavour of a dawning epoch, which was inescapable. The full spectrum of the incoming Aeonic energies need to be understood and integrated. We do have a choice as to where we go with it but the old forms are falling.

Hadit's second chapter of *The Book of the Law* gives the overall backdrop present throughout the great upheaval. The apparent diversity of the two periods masks a greater unity. They were both part of the same underlying process involving the breaking down of old forms. It could be argued that the Nazis destroyed western civilisation. They manifested so many of its governing ideals in hideous forms that, for many people, patriotism, patriarchy, strict self-discipline, respect for authority and love of one's country with it's history and traditions, could never be the same again. The Nazis seemed to embody and amplify things that were present in the whole of European culture. They revealed something horrendously rotting at the heart of civilisation. The post-war baby boomer generation instinctively sensed that rot and had no desire to recreate the pre-1939 world.

It has been suggested that Hitler was the first rock star. Swooning female multitudes wept before him in religious sexual abandonment in much the same way that their daughters' generation would later submit to the Beatles. Some evangelicals have tried to brand popular music as inherently evil because of the mass Nuremberg Rally consciousness it seems capable of stirring up. Something of that eerie but exhilarating force does sometimes appear to be present, but Woodstock and Live Aid were the triumph of a different kind of will.

Looking more closely at the Nazi and psychedelic eras, puzzling and disturbing features become apparent. There are some Summer of Love manifestations in Germany and some murderous distorted strangeness in the sixties. The sense of relationship between the two periods becomes increasingly enigmatic.

HIPPY REICH

We have noted the powerful inner life and sensitivity of Jung. Through his intense interest in the Gnostic Hermetic Mystery cult era he had experiences that registered the stirrings of the same forces Crowley tapped through his Golden Dawn and Cairo magic. Jung's insights into Hitler and Nazism were briefly mentioned. The story of the cultural background to his understanding opens up the incredible truth of the real roots of the hippies in Fin de Siecle Germany.

The general sense of Germany in the period leading up to the First World War conjures up visions of the vainglorious Kaiser in his pompous parade uniforms reviewing spike-helmeted marching multitudes prepared to challenge Britain for a 'place in the sun' and ready to plunge Europe into the carnage of the trenches. There's a good deal of truth in that but a lot more was happening as well.

In the closing years of the Nineteenth Century what came to be called a *German Youth Movement* came into being. This rapidly expanded into something quite extraordinary involving the mid-teens in their tens of thousands. The youth of the Reich spontaneously went walkabout. Sometimes taking on the appearance of medieval minstrels, woollen caped, guitar playing dudes wandered the countryside singing old folk songs round fires whilst camped out in the woods. They gathered in ruined castles. Both sexes were involved. The spirit of Woodstock came early with nude bathing in rivers and lakes.

Before long some of these groups might disappear for a month at a time, covering hundreds of miles. Camps were created in the countryside available to anyone. The youth worked at their own expense to build them. The Youth Hostel network actually came into being in 1907 as a result of this phenomenon.

They came to be known as the *Wandervogel*, meaning migratory birds. There was a definite pagan mysticism about them, enamoured as they were with their landscape and its historical and mythological traditions. In this they partook of another German cultural movement of the time known as *Volkisch*. This was a blood and soil affirmation of the folk, the people, with this increasingly tending to be focused on race.

At first it all seemed supremely idyllic. Sun-worship was a powerful theme. It had a romantic connotation connecting back through to an ancient past. There is a photo dating from 1926 that has become quite well-known of a group of young naked people with arms raised in such a ceremony. The most notable German sun symbol of the time was the increasingly visible swastika.

The Wandervogel embraced a huge spectrum of alternative thinking that really does call to mind the later hippies and particularly their green sensibilities. Accompanying the archaic pagan revival with its landscape mysticism, rune enthusiasm, and nudist sun worship, was vegetarianism, health food, and the kind of concerns with the soil that would influence Steiner and today's organic movement. All sorts of social ideas went along with the blend, including what we would term sexual, female, and animal liberation.

In an amazing strand of forgotten social history some of the Wandervogel types emigrated to America and found their way to California. There, in the first decades of the twentieth century, they mixed with the diet and lifestyle experimenters already present in the 'New Thought' movement, adding a distinctive long-haired, bearded barefoot appearance, often living in the wild, hanging out with Native Americans, playing guitars, the basic hippy package, but generally without drug use. They came to be known as 'Nature Boys', advocating a raw food, fruitarian, yoga approach. Some of these characters can be traced in the connections and ideas they engendered down through to the sixties.

The European scene had its own Esalen. At the southerly point of the wandering, in Ascona, Switzerland, a superbly scenic mountain by a lake was renamed in 1900, *Verite,* Truth. Buildings served as a gathering place for a dizzying mix of the whole of European progressive culture. Over the next few decades the guest list was impressive.

Hermann Hesse, Rudolf Steiner, D. H. Lawrence, the legendary dancer Isadora Duncan, Lenin (yes, Lenin the primary figure in the Russian Revolution) and Jung only represent a sample. The place had the pulling power of Haight Ashbury in summer 1967 but the dream endured for years rather than months with hordes of people sleeping outdoors, hiking around, and experimenting with all forms of diet and lifestyle. The social experiment there became a major think-tank and all kinds of ideas spread out.

As early as 1903 an anarchist newspaper in San Francisco published a large article about Ascona thus making perhaps the first connection between the American West Coast and the European alternative culture.

During the First World War, OTO head Theodor Reuss established enclaves of the group in Switzerland. This proved to be an important bit of Thelemic history. In August 1917 he put on the grandly titled *Anational Congress for Organising the Reconstruction of Society on Practical Cooperative Lines* at Ascona. It included readings of Crowley's poetry and a performance of the Gnostic Mass. This clearly indicates that Crowley and the OTO were not working in isolation but were involved in the general mystical culture of the time.

Jung profoundly absorbed Volkisch and Wandervogel culture. The hugely influential Eranos Foundation of which he was a major early mover was created directly out of the Ascona ambience, being based along the same Swiss lake. Jung's concept of the collective unconscious helped him to feel the powerful return of long-buried Germanic archetypes. He felt that Christianity, which had come later to Germany than most of Europe, was a thin psychic veneer that needed to be penetrated for Germans to connect with deeper strata to give them wholeness. The most powerful deity involved was the Norse pantheons' Odin, or Wotan to use his German name. The multi-faceted god had many inspirational qualities but also potentially a dark frenzy known from his Viking elite troops whose very title, the Beserkers, has given the English language a distinctive concept. Jung's knowledge of this helped him to an awareness of Hitler that enabled him to sound a warning of what might be to come. Indeed, such was his understanding of the Nazis he has been accused of being too much a fellow traveller.

The end of the Wandervogel dream was poignant and tragic. After the First World War, despite the ghastly wounds in the nation's psyche, the movement continued. Before long though, the idealism and dynamism were exploited, manipulated, and eventually appropriated by the Nazis until the Hitler Youth movement had the copyright on the whole package. The joyful wandering out in nature, the songs around the campfire and camaraderie had been the hook. At that point the paganism and lifestyle reform were jettisoned as a generation were groomed to become racist killers.

BANALITY OF EVIL?

Many historians have characterised Nazism as a materialist totalitarianism not unlike Soviet Russia. The many triumphs of German science during the war, demonstrated by the likes of the first jet fighter and the V1 and V2 rockets, give the sense of a thorough grounding in consensus reality.

When the Nazi bureaucrat primarily responsible for the logistics of handling the Holocaust was captured by Israeli agents from his hiding place in Argentina and put on trial in Jerusalem the world watched in stunned amazement. Adolf Eichmann was not a monstrous sadist but a mediocre clerk. He was just following orders. Here was horribly demonstrated what Hannah Arendt in her account of the trial memorably termed 'the banality of evil'. The implication was that when the force of a state apparatus sets something in motion, many people will not resist and might perform horrific actions if an authority figure commanded them.

American social psychologist Stanley Milgram was inspired by the Eichmann controversy to create a classic experiment to test the conformity and obedience hypothesis. Volunteers were introduced into a scenario that was not what it appeared to be. They were to ask a person seated opposite them a series of questions. A button enabled them to administer electric shocks of increasing power in response to wrong answers. The process was administered by a white-coated scientist figure providing the 'authority'. There was no electricity. The scientist and subject were actors. When the fake shocks produced increasing screams of pain, the volunteers obviously became uncomfortable and questioned the procedure, always being told to continue. Some eventually refused but a disturbingly high percentage carried on, even through strangulated screaming and protests from the subject about a heart condition. Normal people can easily become the vehicles for evil deeds.

Why do I mention this? Firstly, it's a major modern theme, an essential part of the twentieth century tumult. We have seen totalitarianism and ideological slaughter on an unprecedented scale. This has required the conformity and obedience of what Gurdjieff called sleepwalking humanity to accomplish. There is a dynamic tension between this and the Thelemic ideal of what constitutes the fundamental imperative of the age, of unique individuality, *'Do what thou wilt'*, so in response to the horror of the situation, we have also seen the expression of diverse acts of protest and resistance and the quest for all types of freedom.

HITLER THE OCCULT MESSIAH

It would be very comforting to be able to state that the most important figure of the twentieth century was Gandhi or Einstein or someone like that. Unfortunately I do not believe that to be true. A strong case can be made for Hitler being the pivotal figure of the age. His was amongst the most extraordinary careers in history. He shaped the tangible destinies of millions and the course of world politics decades beyond his death.

One thing that is immediately obvious is that Hitler was a uniquely unusual being. There was clearly something messianic and mystical about him. In many ways he was unremarkable, certainly in terms of intellect, and pathological by most standards of psychological evaluation, but he displayed an extraordinary charisma and relentless will, obviously compelled by some vast vision that helped him to become a builder and above all, a destroyer on a gigantic scale. The Nazis made full use of mythological themes and motifs in every aspect of the state cult. The war against Russia had the fervour of a medieval millenarian crusade.

In *Hitler: a Study in Tyranny* his first major biographer Alan Bullock stated that *'Hitler's power to bewitch an audience has been likened to the occult arts of the African medicine-man or the Asiatic Shaman; others have compared it to the sensitivity of a medium, and the magnetism of a hypnotist.'*

Jung spoke of Wotan as the primordial archetype possessing

Hitler. '*He is the god of the storm and frenzy, the unleasher of passions and the lust of battle; moreover he is superlative magician and artist in illusion who is versed in all secrets of an occult nature.*' In his famous 1936 essay Jung went on to prophecy, with words that would soon ring horribly true, that with Nazism '*Things must be concealed in the background which we cannot imagine at present, but we may expect them to appear in the course of the next few years or decades.*' In the anthology *C. G. Jung Speaking: Interviews and Encounters*, he said that '*Hitler as a man scarcely exists*', '*he disappears behind his role.*' He was a '*medicine man, a form of spiritual vessel, a demi-deity or even better, a myth.*'

The idea of some kind of Nazis occultism has entered popular culture and gained impetus through the Indiana Jones movies. The topic has become a whole genre of literature.

Two works have been of primary influence in the dissemination of this mythology. Trevor Ravenscroft's *The Spear of Destiny* can be readily acknowledged as a classic of sorts. The legend of the Spear concerns the weapon that pierced the side of Christ on the cross. The Roman soldier responsible for this act supposedly held the fate of the world in his hands as his act prevented the legs of Christ from being broken to accelerate his death. If he had been thus injured it would have messed with a Jewish messianic prophecy telling about no bones being broken on the body of the chosen one.

A spearhead now housed in a Vienna museum has been believed to be that very artefact and thereby partakes of formidable mystical power. Its verifiable history does include ownership by some major historical game-players stretching back as far as Charlemagne. Forensic work on it appears to push its story back even further.

In Ravenscroft's presentation it seems to serve as a potential portal to a kind of Time Spirit that could see history in its totality, the rise and fall of empires, monarchs, and messiahs. Access to the Time Spirit seems to provoke the revealing of previously hidden or neglected historical tales from a new perspective.

Ravenscroft's major source for his tale was allegedly the Anthroposophist Walter Johannes Stein, a noted mystic and author of a notable work on the Grail. His psychic awakening, as Ravenscroft recounts it, began in earnest when he was studying the famous Grail romance *Parzival* by Wolfram von Eschenbach. In a strange space between sleeping and waking, he found himself reciting words in the original old German dialect of its composition.

Writing them down on waking, he was perplexed to discover their verbatim accuracy with the original text further on from where he had already read. This led him into a lifelong study of the Grail mysteries. A faculty of 'Higher Memory' developed, whereby detailed visions of historical events unknown to him led to research that seemed to confirm their truth and unfold a coherent narrative.

Being in the presence of the Spear in the museum significantly moved the process along. Stein's greatest achievement was his book *The Ninth Century*, which expounded a theory connecting events of that time with the later composition and contents of the Grail romances.

Stein had apparently met the young Hitler in Vienna before the First World War after coming into possession of a copy of *Parzival* annotated by him that the penniless mystic had been forced to sell. The notes revealed to Steins horror an adept in the process of initiation onto a very dark path indeed. This included experiences with mescaline. Hitler likewise encountered the Spear in the museum and tranced-out with a dark destiny-download. He moved slowly towards taking possession of the Spear which he finally managed when Germany united with Austria in the Anschluss of 1938.

According to Ravenscroft, Stein and his mentor Rudolf Steiner also psychically picked up on hideous magical rites practised by Nazi occultists in the early days of the movement and tried to counteract them. The story is lurid in a Dennis Wheatley *Devil Rides Out* style, full of demons, human sacrifice, and ectoplasm. It basically portrays Hitler, at least in his early days before becoming Fuhrer, as a ceremonial black magician whose inner vision and powers were awakened through brutal methods by a cabal of demonically inspired adepts.

I would readily rate *Spear* as a ripping yarn. Unfortunately there are considerable problems about its material. A lot of the details are shot full of holes. Ravenscroft thoroughly buys into the Crowley legend of infamy and tries to place him on the same team as his Nazi Satanists. Walter Johannes Stein was on record as saying that the first time he heard Hitler's voice was on the radio. This makes the account of his extensive meetings with the future Fuhrer more than a bit suspect. His connection to clandestine intelligence work on behalf of the British government in the early part of the Second World War is a matter of public record though. It is not entirely unreasonable that he would not have publicly revealed an early association with Hitler or its mystical context. The story supposedly told to Ravenscroft was only revealed after the war. The extent to which he had contact with Stein is also problematical.

It does seem that the young Hitler did absorb a wide range of mystical magical literature and occultist concepts. There are however accounts of his disdain towards volkisch Ariosophical types and even Himmler's predilections in the SS. He seemed to consider most mystics as ineffectual. Nonetheless all through his career his belief in the power of the Will seemed to go beyond the psychological into the realm of the magical, such was the extent of his faith in its ability to affect reality. That does not mean he was ever an actual member of any working group. Hitler as black magician in the Dennis Wheatley sense is definitely case unproven.

Nonetheless *Spear* does still work as a mood piece. The most evocative aspect of that mood for me is the Anthroposophical theme much propagated by Rudolf Steiner that particular groups of people reincarnate together at various crucial historical moments. Evil powers can make use of this and the karma involved to blind people to the true nature of their deeds. Walter Johannes Stein supposedly uncovered strands of such reincarnational identities himself with the most dramatic example concerning his belief that Hitler had been one Llandulf of Capua, portrayed as a notorious necromancer, based in ninth century Sicily who had allegedly provided the model for the wicked sorcerer Klingsor in *Parzival*. It's not a case of specifically believing particular stated cases but more a willingness to be open to possibilities. We will return to this theme with a look at another Ravenscroft work a little later in the narrative.

FANTASTIC REALISM

The Morning of the Magicians by the Frenchmen Louis Pauwels and Jacques Bergier, published in 1960, was a major contribution to the occult revival that swept through the decade. It contained a mind-blowing mix of subject matter including an extensive section on Nazi occultism. The whole genre virtually began there.

I feel it is important to approach the book in the right way. In terms of historical data it is also full of material that has yet to be validated or is just plain wrong. For example, there's a tale that has been widely repeated that the corpses of a thousand men '*of Himalayan origin*' in German uniform were found by the Russians in the ruins of Berlin in 1945. I'm not aware of any sources for this story earlier than *Magicians*. This notable event, which one would imagine might have generated a few photographs and controversy, does not find its way into the accounts of historians. I would classify it as occult gossip.

There's no point in getting too hung up about detail with Pauwels and Bergier so what are their merits then? Why do I consider *Morning of the Magicians* to be a classic work in general and still the best introduction to the topic of Nazi occultism, especially considering the more recent appearance of a work like the academically sound *The Occult Roots of Nazism* by Nicholas Goodrick-Clarke? It's another mood piece but one that's immensely more sophisticated and successful than *Spear of Destiny*.

The authors were very much products of a distinctly French mystical culture. Pauwels had studied Guenon and been involved with a Gurdjieff group. He had known the founder of the Surrealist movement, André Breton. Bergier had a background in atomic physics and had survived a concentration camp. Together they gathered an enormous body of strange ideas and information that they shaped to propound an approach they called *fantastic realism*. This involved not an escape from reality but an attempt to see it from a higher perspective where many puzzling oddities could be understood and reconciled. To that end they incorporated the new physics, alchemy and other ancient mysteries, and material at the furthest edge of psychology in a relentless blend that served the same purpose as Breton's Surrealism, to subvert consensus reality and assert the primacy of something else, what we can understand here as '*the flame that burns in every heart of man, and in the core of every star*'.

The dawn of the atomic age was considered to be a moment of immense importance. The dangerous knowledge that the alchemists had guarded through their obscure symbolism was now unleashed. All kinds of other knowledge held by select groups in ancient civilisations pertaining to altered states of consciousness was also being released. A constant theme in *Magicians* concerns evolutionary mutants, portents of a super-humanity to come who are appearing in ever-greater numbers. This is an idea that obsesses magical schools of all persuasions.

Pauwels and Bergier state that '*The rise of Nazism was one of those rare moments in the history of our civilisation, when a door was noisily and ostentatiously opened on to something "Other".*' A virtual parallel universe was set up in Nazi Germany so radically different from the rest of western civilisation that we just haven't come to terms with it yet. To justify this claim they list some of the unusual people and beliefs circulating during that time that actually influenced state policy.

Already familiar with the conventional history of the Nazi era when I first read *Magicians* in 1981, I was inspired to make a sustained investigation of their material myself, culminating in a dissertation on Nazi Occultism towards my degree in 1983. This helped me to cultivate my own perspective.

THE DEMONS OF HOUSTON STEWART CHAMBERLAIN

One of the leading inspirations for the Nazis was actually an Englishman. Houston Stewart Chamberlain became a naturalised German and was Wagner's son-in-law.

Although categorised primarily as a pseudo-intellectual he had considerable occult leanings. William Shirer in the *Rise and Fall of the Third Reich* gives fascinating details of how his fundamental 1898 work *The Foundations of the Nineteenth Century* came to be composed.

Chamberlain was *'given to seeing demons'* that *'drove him relentlessly to seek new fields of study'*. In 1896 a powerful dream forced him to abandon a train journey and *'shut himself up in a hotel room for eight days'* producing *'a biological thesis'*. As with most of his books, he wrote *Foundations 'in the grip of a terrible fever, a veritable trance, a state of self-induced intoxication'* and, observing the results, *'was often unable to recognise them as his own work'*.

Race and history were Chamberlains obsessions. Part of *Foundations* concerned the Aryan credibility of Jesus and recounted the story that he was *'a blond blue-eyed Aryan illegitimate offspring of a liaison between a Galilean woman and a Roman soldier'*. He believed that the German mind should guide the Aryan race to world domination. Chamberlain felt that mysticism was the ultimate Aryan achievement and that every mystic was inevitably anti-Semitic.

It's a bizarre twist of history that a man born British became accepted by the German Kaiser and wielded an encouraging influence over his war-mongering Prussian pride. In Chamberlain's later years he would hail Hitler as the messiah Germany awaited and Hitler in turn acknowledged him as a founder-figure of Nazism.

GUIDO VON LIST AND THEOSOPHY

By the start of the twentieth century there were many occult groups in Germany. This was not unusual in the Europe of that time. In Britain, France, and Germany, there was a certain common ground amongst magical groups. The mythology of the Golden Dawn stated that its material and authority derived from a German group. The OTO emerged out of Central Europe. A few of the German strands had distinctive elements though that set them apart.

Guido von List was an enthusiast of the history and mystical traditions of the German tribes, rune lore and the like. He was passionate about the sacredness of nature, in particular his homeland, and spent much time absorbed in solitary treks that included alpine mountaineering. He was an early example of the Wandervogel mentality. In the big occult year of 1875, when Crowley was born and the Theosophical Society formed, List and some friends visited an ancient Germanic site in commemoration of what they believed to be the exact 1500th anniversary of a victory over the Romans. The occasion was celebrated by burying wine bottles in the shape of a swastika.

When Blavatsky's *Secret Doctrine* was translated into German in the early years of the twentieth century, List eagerly absorbed it. Part of its teachings included an alternative version of the world's history featuring the concept of *Root Races*. The current form of human being is part of an evolutionary process that has taken in earlier forms, starting from initial ethereal beings, through what would ultimately be a sequence of seven races of ever greater power and accomplishments. These races have flourished at different stages of a long history of shifting and sinking continents, Hyperborea, Lemuria, Atlantis. The fifth race was the Aryan and its particular symbol of power was the swastika. Eventually a highly evolved super-humanity would predominate possessing all of the paranormal powers spoken of in magic and mysticism.

A comment in *The Secret Doctrine* stated that the Jews '*constitute an abnormal and unnatural link between the Fourth and Fifth Root Races*'. This may not have been particularly noticed when the work first appeared in 1888 but it looks a lot different now. This idea landed well with mystical Germans already inclined towards anti-Semitism. In the early days of the Holocaust before the industrial efficiency of the gas chambers, special units of SS killers known as *Einsatzgruppe* roamed the Eastern Front shooting Jews. The leader of one such group was Otto Ohlendorff, a man responsible for overseeing 92,000 deaths. He was known for his interest in Theosophy and one wonders if the *'abnormal and unnatural'* concept helped him to justify his behaviour?

List's investigation of Theosophy was soon followed by a powerful process when, following a cataract operation, he was forced to wear bandages over his eyes for nearly a year in 1902/3. During this ordeal he experienced an increasingly intense inner vision which he believed enabled him to penetrate the mysteries of the runes and also to become aware of a previously hidden history of an elite clairvoyant German Priestcraft known as the Armanen with whom he was in psychic communion and their last descendant. Names of various hills, rivers, and villages recalled its meeting places. The similarity of his experience to the mythology of Odin who lost an eye in order to obtain the knowledge of the runes was not lost on List. In certain respects he was a proto-Earth Mysteries hippy. Where he differed, and where some of the Wandervogel movement took a tragic wrong turn was his increasingly virulent racism and in particular, anti-Semitism.

As Crowley was receiving his mandate for a new humanity and Gurdjieff was observing events in Tibet, so List was coming back out into the world as newly empowered occult prophet of a Germanic paganism that was now powerfully conceptualised as, above all, Aryan in designation. He would soon join forces with another unusual character.

THEOZOOLOGY AND THE NEW TEMPLARS

Jorg Lanz von Liebenfels was expelled from a Cistercian monastery. Drawing on his biblical studies he published in 1905 the astounding *Theozoology or the Science of the Sodomite Apelings and the Divine Electron*. For anyone who has problems with Blavatsky's *Secret Doctrine* or Gurdjieff's *Beelzebub's Tales*, *Theozoology* puts true perspective on mystical derangement. Unfortunately, events that occurred forty years later prevent a contemporary audience from laughing quite as loudly at it as they otherwise might.

Liebenfels was obsessed with race and sex. Strangely inspired by Blavatsky's Root Races he believed that the Bible and other ancient literature contained coded references to a range of peculiar entities, bird-men, fish people, and of course, sodomite apelings. These beings were physically real and a different strand of creation from the pure Aryans made in god's image, possessors of the Divine Electron. Sexual relations between the two produced other lower and dark races, ie the whole human race apart from white Germans. The original monsters died out but the bastard mongrel hordes they helped create live on and pollute the Aryan remnants.

Theozoology had a unique take on the crucifixion. The usual stuff about being nailed to a cross and whatnot is a misunderstanding. '*The passion of Christ was a struggle with Sodomite monsters.*' Jesus was '*outraged by the Sodomite hobgoblins*'. After this ordeal '*The bites of wild sodomite beasts were viewed by the Christians as the most excellent bodily decorations.*' Phew! One shudders to think of what might have happened to Liebenfels during his stay in the Cistercian monastery to lay the foundations for such a mindset.

There are a few echoes of the third chapter of *The Book of the Law*. '*Away with false and suicidal brotherly love which was invented by the Sodomite apelings and their pastors in order to strangle us.*' '*We must arm ourselves against pity*' is perhaps the most succinctly prophetic of the nightmare to come.

Liebenfels launched a magazine called *Ostara* to propagate his views. It anticipated in many ways the later infamous *Der Sturmer* of rabid Nazi Julius Striecher with its persistent theme of blonde women violated by caricatured Jews. It has been reliably recorded that Hitler was aware of *Ostara* during his early years in Vienna. After the *Gotterdammerung* of the Thousand Year Reich, Liebenfels (who escaped prosecution and lived on until 1954) claimed a direct meeting with the young Hitler at a time when such a boast wouldn't exactly have helped him much.

Liebenfels admired List and helped found a Society in his name. In 1907 he set up his own Order of New Templars and acquired a castle at Werfenstein in Austria from which a swastika flag was flown. His intense racial theories blended with medieval revivalism. The List and Liebenfels blend came to be called Ariosophy, a heavily Aryan Germanic spin on Theosophy.

Their prescription for society was a tough one. Strict breeding laws were recommended, involving total discrimination in favour of Aryan men, whose infringement would be punishable by death. Families would keep records detailing their racial purity. Women were to become breeding machines. Other races would be little better than slaves. Enforced sterilisation and extermination were considered acceptable options. These outpourings would only have been noticed by a small group at the time but within barely a quarter of a century they would have become the law and helped set the scene for the horrors of the Eastern Front and the Holocaust.

List created a magical group using the Qabalistic Tree of Life as its grade structure. He managed to get round the fact that the Qabalah is famously Jewish by claiming it was originally a Germanic teaching that in a bizarre medieval circumstance had briefly been entrusted to the Jews who then blagged it for their own. It also seems likely that List was inspired by the Golden Dawn system in this respect, thus indicating the extent to which the magically inclined of the time were aware of each other's existence.

THULE: POLAR GNOSIS AND POLITICS

The most potent aspect of the myth of Nazi Occultism concerns the Thule Society. An enormous amount of occult gossip surrounds this group and its membership. They seem to have come together during the First World War. Their emblem was a swastika on a dagger.

Baron Rudolf von Sebottendorff was barely a month younger than Crowley. He had been initiated into a Masonic group in Egypt, spent time in Turkey becoming closely involved with Islamic Sufi mysticism, and cultivated existing Rosicrucian and Odinist sympathies. He was likewise strongly racist with a particular detestation of the Jews. No stranger to small secretive esoteric and political groups, he became the focal figure in the Thule Society.

Thule was a kind of arctic Atlantis, the earliest home of the human race. List and Liebenfels also both favoured a northerly origin for the Aryans. Thule itself can be connected to the famous classical land of Hyperborea that lay beyond the north winds. The Norse mythology with its Tree of Life and Valhalla blends in with this powerful archetype that is not just the domain of Nazi enthusiasts.

The existence of a northern polar gnosis in the background of European occultism, a distinct strain separate from Judeo-Christian culture infused the work of two of the twentieth centuries most erudite esotericists, Rene Guenon and Julius Evola. They both advocated the concept of a northern polar centre that existed during an epoch when the climate there was conducive to a life that subsequent mythology has rendered as paradisiacal.

The fall came with a pole shift axial displacement resulting in a cultural drift to the south and west. The Agharrta Shambhalic centre lay to the south. What became known as Atlantis reflected the westwards dispersal. Both of those subsequent centres influenced European culture from separate directions but the origins of both lay in the polar original. Far-fetched as this may seem, there is evidence indicative of fundamentally different climate and conditions once existing in arctic regions that could have made the sustaining of an advanced culture there feasible.

The Thule Society have been portrayed as a group with an inner core of serious magical practitioners. Ever since Blavatsky the notion of the Secret Chiefs had become indispensable to magical mystical groups. Even if these characters were alive in physical bodies somewhere they could communicate in various ways at a distance. Usually a psychic mediumistic type would be the vehicle of messages which directed the group. Crowley and his wife in Cairo with Aiwass is an example of such a procedure. Golden Dawn chief Mathers made use of his wife Moina's abilities in creating some of the material in the Order. We will come to speculate on just what is involved in such cases later on but for now it seems a safe bet that, considering the experiences of Chamberlain (mediumistic and compelled by demons to write) and List (in psychic communion with ancient German druid-types), the Thule group would have believed themselves to be in communication with spiritual forces probably not dissimilar to Blavatsky's Himalayan Masters. More than likely they were from Thule and therefore probably had some strange things to say.

Quite what mystical practices the hardcore Thulists engaged in is difficult to determine. A lot of new material continues to surface, often allegedly coming from elderly German veterans. The modern versions now include the excellently bizarre Nazi UFO mythos. The most important thing about them was the willingness of at least some of their members to engage in tangible political action.

In the closing days of the war, Germany descended into chaos. Communist groups attempted to follow the lead established recently in Russia and spread revolution. They were fought by army veterans. One such uprising was centred on Munich, the base of the Thule Society, and involved an attempt to declare the whole of Bavaria an independent state. Ultimately a Socialist republic was set up.

The Thulists were allowed to hold meetings as they were classified as an antiquarian organisation carrying on studies reminiscent of List.

They allowed themselves to become an umbrella for racist nationalist groups, published a newspaper, collected weapons, stirred up anti-communist and race-hate feelings and encouraged violent activities. Their members included a police chief, Justice Minister, and assorted aristocrats. Only those who could prove Aryan ancestry and looked the part through their fine physical condition were admitted.

A man refused admittance due to Jewish ancestry decided to prove his German credibility by assassinating the leader of the new republic, Kurt Eisner. Months of bloodshed ensued. A Soviet communist republic was proclaimed. Armed resistance in which Thulists were involved failed. Eisner's murder led to investigation of the group and eventually seven members, including some aristocrats, were shot by communists in April 1919. Outrage over this prompted a popular uprising. A huge force of army veterans who marched under a swastika banner arrived in time to join in. The communists were defeated.

Peter Levenda summarises the surrealism nicely in *Unholy Alliance* stating that

> '*an occult organisation – a secret society based on Theosophical, runic, and magical concepts (a kind of redneck Golden Dawn with guns) – had fought an armed conflict in the streets of Munich against the purely political forces of a Soviet state... and won. Today, this would be considered the stuff of science fiction or, at worst sword and sorcery fantasy. But in Munich, in 1919, it was reality.*'

Most Thulists were fairly financially comfortable despite the privations of the war. Their meeting place was a plush hotel. To spread their agenda, a new subgroup was created to hopefully appeal to the working classes who were being snared by the nefarious communists. This German Workers Party would soon develop into the Nazis, having attracted an early member in the form of Adolf Hitler.

Hitler had enthusiastically fought in the German army, taking on the difficult task of running messages between trenches. His physical bravery was undeniable and he was duly awarded the Iron Cross. He narrowly avoided death on so many occasions that he came to believe that something was definitely looking out for him. In the closing days of the conflict he was temporarily blinded in a gas attack and left in bandages like List. It was whilst in this condition that a massive inner experience convinced him it was his destiny to lead the German people. Coming into contact with some of the machinations of the Thule group was the final preparatory element necessary for the Nazi party to come together.

A vital game player in the early blend which created the Nazis from the Ariosophical Thule influences was Rudolf Hess, a man dedicated to many forms of mystical thinking such as astrology, herbalism, yoga, and Steiner's Anthroposophy. Hess was one of Hitler's earliest associates in the party and famously went to jail with him following the failure of an attempted coup based in Munich in 1923. He had assisted in the creation of *Mein Kampf* in prison. The most controversial aspect of this was his introduction of Karl Haushofer into the situation. Haushofer is primarily known to history for a school of thought named Geopolitics he advocated. He believed in a potential destiny as global super-power for Germany but this was dependent on it acquiring *lebensraum*, living space, in the east, in territory primarily part of Russia. These ideas seem to have been introduced to Hitler by Haushofer in prison and found their way in to *Mein Kampf*, ultimately inspiring the war against Russia.

This ideological legacy of Haushofer makes him an extremely important figure. Thanks to Pauwels and Bergier he has also become an occult legend. According to them and an increasing number of enthusiasts for the myth, Haushofer was a major initiate in a whole bunch of powerful secret societies spanning from the west to the Far East. They place him in the centre of the Thule action.

Hess would go on to become the second most powerful person in Germany and find himself at the centre of perhaps the most enduringly enigmatic episode of the entire Second World War, a story in which Crowley seems to have had at least some involvement.

HIMMLER: THE GRAIL AND ANCESTRAL HERITAGE

The fulfilment of the dynamic represented by List, Lanz, and Thule came with Himmler. People can argue about the extent of Hitler's occult interests and their effect on his career but with the SS chief, there is no doubt of the matter. On taking control of the small elite group in 1929 he moulded them into his vision of a modern chivalric order after the manner of the medieval Teutonic Knights. With the massive resources of the state to fund him and slave labour to do the work Himmler was able to take Liebenfels' New Templar vision, with its castle and swastika flag to another level. He took control of a Schloss at Wewelsburg in Westphalia and lavished immense time and resources into turning it into a Grail castle for his SS.

Wewelsburg was a place for their elite. It was a shrine to German history. There was actually a circular table there around which twelve men would gather. Ceremonies took place in the crypt that one can only speculate upon. Processes of a meditational, ritualistic, and occult nature were probably engaged in, at least occasionally, over a period of years. We don't have to go as far as Trevor Ravenscroft in *The Spear of Destiny* as to see Himmler as some empty shell manipulated by demonic forces, but the man's track record speaks for itself. Wewelsburg was his spiritual base. It was believed that many ley lines passed through it. This was where he and his buddies like Reinhard Heydrich recharged their batteries. The thriller writer Duncan Kyle wrote a novel about Wewlesburg. It's a tale of espionage rather than occultism but its title evokes the magical reality: *Black Camelot*.

Further funding was allocated for the propagation of the *Ahnenerbe*, a wide ranging 'Ancestral Heritage' study group under the general control of the SS through Wolfram Sievers. These guys went out on archaeological Guido von List style field trips in Germany, and when the war began, into the newly occupied territories, looking for signs of ancient Germanic culture. On one level their studies were not unlike the English ley line pioneer Alfred Watkins or his later sixties followers like John Michell. Recovering astronomical knowledge hidden in Norse texts, looking for landscape alignments and reviving old pagan customs sounds quite appealing but the Ahnenerbe were always politicised and following a clear Nazi racist agenda. If one could find supposed evidence of ancient German settlement in Eastern Europe for example, it could be considered justification for invasion on the basis of it being part of an original German homeland.

The Ahnenerbe also immersed themselves in a huge number of unusual studies covering the complete spectrum of mystical magical weirdness. Pauwels and Bergier stated that *'plurality and incoherence seem to be most typical of this subterranean Germany'*. Before *Magicians*, Hugh Trevor-Roper in *The Last Days of Hitler* had mentioned briefly that the Ahnenerbe had investigated occult aspects of the top hats worn at Eton, and alleged magical powers of some church bells in Oxford. Assorted dowsers and diviners were on the case for all kinds of tasks.

The Ahnenerbe ranged far and wide on a quest to investigate Theosophical Root Race ideas and also to try and validate another very strange Nazi mystical prophet.

In 1894, at the age of thirty-four, Hans Horbiger had a vision that explained the working of the universe to him. The result was the *Welteislehre* (World Ice Theory) presented in his 1913 book *Glazial-Kosmogonie* (Glacial-Cosmogony). Inspired by Norse mythology, Horbiger postulated a universe in which two fundamental principles, Ice and Fire, interacted like the Chinese Yin and Yang. In the beginning, two huge masses of ice and fire collided and the solar system came into being. He believed that the moon was made of ice and the Milky Way significantly glacial. Planet Earth has periodically attracted by gravitational pull ice bodies that become moons and then inevitably crash into the Earth setting off Atlantis and Biblical flood scenarios. There are intervals when there is no moon at all.

One of the Theosophical Ariosophical aspects of the theory was that the varying gravitational conditions caused by the rhythm of the process of the falling moons led to races of giants and mutant beasts. Yes, of course, the giants were Aryans, the mutant beasts Jews.

What makes Horbiger's theories different from the kind of weird cosmologies that crank visionaries have been creating for centuries was his ability to widely and aggressively disseminate it and its subsequent adoption by people in positions of considerable political power such as Himmler. Horbiger put out propaganda belittling the 'Jewish science' of Einstein and lauding his own theories as appropriately Aryan. Although dying in 1931 before the Nazis came to power, Horbiger's ideas became so widely known in the Third Reich that they formed part of the overall backdrop, the ambience of that society. Horbigerians presented all kinds of tables and graphs in support of the theory, giving it the appearance of science. Pauwels and Bergier state that a bizarre Horbigerian weather-forecasting bureau was consulted concerning likely conditions in Russia for the winter of 1941 and the prognosis was mild. This influenced the disastrous decisions involved in failing to provide the necessary clothing for German troops.

The Ahnenerbe travelled to the haunting South American ruins at Tiahuanaco, thought by some to be far more ancient than conventional history would accept. There are many who believe this still. A combination of alignments and inscrutable inscriptions was interpreted by Horbiger's leading follower H. S. Bellamy to be a calendar

that only made sense in terms of one of the falling moon cycles.
One of the earliest accounts to come out of Nazi Germany concerning this bizarre occult underworld came from rocket research pioneer and later successful science writer, Willy Ley, who fled the Reich for the USA. A 1947 article *Pseudoscience in Naziland* mentioned a *Wahrheitsgesellschaft* (Society for Truth) that had existed in Berlin dedicated to something called *Vril*. The word was central to an 1870 proto sci-fi novel *The Coming Race* by Edward Bulwer-Lytton. It described a race of giants living in vast underground caverns who are masters of a powerful life-force energy. The day grows ever nearer when they will appear and take over the world. It was a tale that struck a cord amongst some mystics. Blavatsky was enthusiastic. Ley suggested that the German group believed in the force if not necessarily the subterranean giants. Vril power has now been incorporated into just about every nook and cranny of the Nazi occultism mythos.

A strong Nazi interest in Shambhala/Agarttha has often been suggested. The tales tell that it may have begun with Thule and Haushofer but was certainly in full swing by the time of Himmler and the Ahnenerbe. As usual, we can look to *Magicians* for the main impetus for these ideas. The thousand *'Himalayan'* corpses have already been mentioned. There's also an evocative tale of a clairvoyant Tibetan, prone to wearing green gloves, who was present in Germany from the twenties onwards as part of the mystical Nazi team. He has sprung from the pages of *Magicians* to take on a life on the internet as the subject of baseless occult gossip.

Some Nazi mystics supposedly saw themselves as mystically connected to the King of the World and his master race who have taken on something of the flavour of Bulwer Lyton's Vril adepts. Attempts were made to make contact with the Central Asian masters. There was certainly an SS expedition to Tibet shortly before the war and this has helped to fuel the rumours. Considering the debt owed to Blavatsky with her Secret Chiefs and swastika mythos it's not unlikely that some Nazis in Ahnenerbe circles would have sought to cultivate such connections.

There's a dark denouement to the Ahnenerbe story. The SS Tibet expedition spent a lot of time making face-masks, measuring people's skulls and suchlike to check out Aryan physiognomy. In 1941 Sievers brought Tibet expedition veteran Ernst Schaefer to Dachau concentration camp to observe as part of his scientific work murderously brutal medical experiments on prisoners. In 1943

Sievers set up Bruno Beger, who had made face masks of Tibetans, on a mission to Auschwitz. He was acting on behalf of a Profesor Hirt of the University of Strasbourg who had a renowned anatomy collection that was unfortunately lacking good Jewish specimens. Beger selected a group of what he considered to be interesting types and took face masks of them. They were then killed and their skulls sent on to the Professor. For his active role in the process, Sievers was sentenced to death at the Nuremberg trials.

It's vital to realise that the Ahnenerbe were not just a bunch of mystical weirdos and amoral potential killers. Their ranks included top academics, Professors and so on, in a wide range of studies. After the war a lot of them returned to respectable university careers. As well as archaeology, there was considerable interest in Eastern religion and culture, including Hinduism, Buddhism and Islam. It would be a mistake to denigrate their work in its entirety. The Grail enthusiast Otto Rahn for example has undergone something of a rehabilitation in recent years with the translation of his works into English. This makes the entire Ahnenerbe story all the more difficult to understand and assimilate into the consensus data-bank.

The power of Pauwels and Bergier's fantastic realism comes through them touching something deeper than rational historical reality. I'm sure they would never have intended to help generate a mutated form of esoteric Nazism but that is exactly what has happened. Their surreal parallel universe did not die in the ruins of Berlin. Many of its elements have survived and developed further. Nicholas Goodrick-Clarke's *Black Sun* provides a comprehensive entry into that zone for those inclined to investigate further. What's intriguing is the compelling nature of this strange Thule Agarttha SS axis that is resistant to standard historical analysis. It's possible to understand intellectually that it is not rooted in real events but it still feels as if some truth is lurking in the background. That doesn't imply an endorsement of esoteric Nazism however. The power may well be because it activates the polar gnosis archetype. Joscelyn Godwin's masterly study *Arktos* best evokes it.

We can now better appreciate the feelings of Pauwels and Bergier that a radically different world had arisen in Nazi Germany. If we think of the Britain of 1939 with Neville Chamberlain as leader, a man of whom it was disparagingly said that he would have made a good mayor of Birmingham in a lean year, and George Formby and Arthur Askey as icons of popular culture, and contrast this against the messianic Fuhrer, the Nuremberg rallies, the Ahnenerbe, falling moons, hidden masters of Thule and so on, one gets their point. This world came into being, played out an epochal drama resulting in the deaths of tens of millions and was reduced to rubble during pretty much the exact timescale of the adult life of Aleister Crowley.

ILLUMINATION

In *Book Four*, that would eventually become the introductory part of *Magick*, Crowley mentions the mystery of how previously normal people undergo some extraordinary experience that permanently mutates them, allowing access to a power-charged state of consciousness through which they are able to affect great change in the world. The definitive example remains Saul on the road to Damascus who was suddenly overwhelmed by light and 'converted' into St Paul, the major figure in the creation of Christianity. Maybe he was epileptic. The debate continues. If he was, we could say that the seizure served as a vehicle for a transformational process that would have world-historical significance. One therefore hesitates to limit its source to nothing more than random internal physiology. Buddha, Christ, Moses, and Mohammed are also discussed by Crowley. His contention was that science would come to understand what occurred in such cases. The aim in formulating his magickal order the AA was to be able to produce such illumination to order.

We have been looking here at a group of people who experienced major life-changing altered states of consciousness during the same period from the Fin de Siecle to the First World War. Firstly, of course, there is Crowley himself with the Cairo Revelation and its fundamental text, *The Book of the Law*. Jung had his Mithraic Aion experience which predisposed him to *Seven Sermons*. Houston Stewart Chamberlain, Guido Von List, and Hitler have now been put along side them. I would again venture the suggestion that there may be some kind of unity behind the apparent diversity here. All of these people are involved in the same process.

★ ★ ★

IN DEFENCE OF BLAVATSKY AND STEINER

The occult heavyweights of the early twentieth century have all found themselves accused of varying degrees of complicity in the Nazi era. We will soon examine Crowley in some detail. A few words need to be said on behalf of the other notables as their cases have a certain typicality in the occult gossip defamation genre.

Theosophy and Anthroposophy were banned by the Nazis. As organisations and spiritual movements they were considered inimical to the party. That some of their ideas may have been deemed useful within certain contexts does not in any way mean that they can be considered Nazi in themselves.

Helena Petrovna Blavatsky was one of the most remarkable women in history. Surrounded by scandals, as so many adepts often are I am certain that she worked for the good of humanity and although some of her statements on race are now tainted by the horror they bred I am sure she would have detested what the Nazis made of her work.

She did have something of a political programme that may have provoked some of the hostility against her from British sources in her lifetime. The championing of Indian spirituality by the Theosophical Society was a factor in the growing strength of the independence movement. It's a very strange irony of history that Gandhi was first introduced to the *Bhagavad Gita* by a Theosophist in London. According to controversial commentator on the early days of Theosophy, Paul Johnson, the Secret Chiefs Blavatsky worked for were in some cases flesh and blood individuals with an agenda that did not support British imperialism. Some had a sense that Eastern ideas were overstepping a certain balance as they arrived in the west. Rudolf Steiner broke with the group to found his own primarily for that reason. On the other hand, Rene Guenon thought that Theosophy served the interests of British espionage.

Otto Ohlendorff and his family were likewise enamoured by Rudolf Steiner's work as indeed were many Nazis including Hess, Himmler, and a surprising number of SS men. This tended to be focused on ideas like biodynamic gardening as there was a bit of an eco-hippy contingent in the party. This extended to the grotesque horror of herb gardens cultivated by Steiner techniques attached to concentration camps. *Spear of Destiny* has a tale concerning the utilisation of a kind of homeopathic pest control Steiner had devised to cope with rabbits being used at the war's end when ashes from Jewish corpses were spread across Europe to prevent them returning. We know that *Spear* is profoundly unreliable but the story has more likelihood than much of the other material.

There are some seemingly disturbing ideas scattered through Steiner's work that are his own slant on the Root Race concept. Some of his statements about Jews and blacks do look decidedly dubious. The issue here is what one really means by such ideas and above all what you *do* with them. To jump from this to portraying Steiner as part of the same ilk as List and Liebenfels is extreme and unjustifiable.

Spear portrays Steiner as the Nazis early spiritual nemesis. In this we can believe it. Steiner had been Europe's greatest occult superstar at the time of the outbreak of the First World War. He was, as *Spear* rightly attests, a spiritual confidante of Helmut von Moltke, a mystically inclined soldier with a vital role in the German High Command. Moltke was responsible for the smooth running of the military master-plan on how to quickly win a war against France. After a few seemingly minor problems in its execution the plan failed and the stalemate of trench warfare ensued. Moltke took the blame for this and died in 1916.

After the war Steiner promoted a plan for economic and social regeneration based on spiritual principles. It was widely discussed and not just in Germany. People of importance were interested. As early as 1921 Hitler himself wrote an article against Steiner in a Nazi newsletter linking him and his plans with the hated Jews. It would not have been unknown to the early Nazis that Steiner had been an influence in the German military. Hitler had attracted General Ludendorff, one of the most important soldiers of the First World War, as an early follower. Ludendorff had been right there with Moltke during the crucial moments in 1914. A repetition of such influence would have been considered an outcome to avoid.

An astonishing episode occurred in May 1922. Steiner was booked for a lecture engagement at a Munich hotel. Unfortunately this was the home turf of the Thule Society. To his great credit, when he learned the reality of the situation Steiner did not cancel. The resulting ruck got a mention as far away as the *New York Times* though without the Thule angle. Worlds collided as Steiner spoke on the *Vitalization of Thought* to an audience apparently comprised mainly of women and *'long- haired Theosophists'*. Thankfully he did have a security team. The lights were suddenly switched off as firecrackers and stink bombs announced a storming of the stage and general punch-up. After the police cleared the building the Nazis carried on a commotion in the streets for some time.

Steiner and his followers were engaged in building an extraordinary edifice called the Goetheanum as a kind of Anthroposophical temple. The whole process of its creation and the nature of its elaborate design incorporated the full range of Steiner's detailed esoteric Christian cosmology. On New Year's Eve 1922/3 it was destroyed in a fire. It has often been stated that the Nazis were behind this. A second building followed which stands to this day but Steiner's energies were depleted by the struggle and he died in 1925.

An enduring controversy concerns Steiner's alleged early membership of the OTO. He did have connections with Theodor Reuss before Crowley came on the scene. It was part of a complex situation involving the passing on of the right to use particular Masonic type rites. Steiner seemed to be clear he was following his own path from the very beginning and kept a definite distance from Reuss. Mystery cults were as important to Steiner as Jung and Crowley and he did create ceremonial dramas for Anthroposophy but the elaborate theory behind them was very much an expression of his own style.

In many respects one would imagine at first glance that Crowley and Steiner were worlds apart and this is assuredly the case. Steiner was the great esoteric Christian, devoted to the Archangel Michael and the mysteries of the *Book of Revelation* and Crowley was the man who had deliberately cultivated the persona of the Beast but there is some significant blurring of distinctions in a few notable cases. Lady Frieda Harris, the artist who worked with Crowley over long years to create the *Thoth* tarot deck was sufficiently immersed in Steiner's work to have taken some of his theories on art and colour into the creation of the Thelemic masterpiece. Pat Doherty actually mothered Crowley's last child when he was in his sixties and was present during his final days. She had likewise been an Anthroposophist. These details are mentioned to show that many disparate groups were all involved in the bigger picture of the world-historical drama and did not function exclusively in isolation or in simple rivalry.

★ ★ ★

BEELZEBUB AND THE BEAST

There are tales that Gurdjieff may have been one of the Secret Chiefs behind Nazism. The idea is mentioned, for example, by Gerald Suster in his generally excellent *Hitler and the Age of Horus*. Works in the Nazi occult genre will state that Gurdjieff knew Haushofer, perhaps in Tibet, and remained in touch with him. Another important early mystical Nazi theorist, Alfred Rosenberg, has been described as a student of Gurdjieff. I would classify all of this as yet more occult gossip. Louis Pauwels has a lot to answer for here. He wrote a long critical work against Gurdjieff after having been involved with one of his groups although never meeting the man himself. The Nazi ideas began there and filter into *Magicians*. They do not stand up to any scrutiny. Pauwels later admitted that his Gurdjieff book was deeply flawed.

There is also a further old chestnut stating that Gurdjieff had another identity as a character known in Tibet as Lama Dorjieff. This bit of intrigue gets stirred in to the Nazi Tibetan pot. Photos of Dorjieff looking obviously like an entirely different person have not been enough to dissipate this story. Gurdjieff was a master of the art of changing his appearance it is said. This went way beyond a wig and dark glasses. He could use a mysterious 'art of plastics' to reconfigure his very body! James Moore's Gurdjieff biography ought to be enough to clear up the Dorjieff issue for most people.

Finding potential connections between Crowley and Gurdjieff is a fascinating topic. We began with the bigger picture of their separate identification of 1904 as a turning point in history. The two are usually thought of as being in opposition to each other. Crowley the black magician is contrasted by Gurdjieff the white. Both men, with a certain humour and knowledge of the probable consequences, took on the persona of anti-Christian demonised deities, Beelzebub and the Beast. They both created controversial communities, dedicated to some sort of spiritual practice, in Europe in the twenties. It is known that they both slept with many of their female students and fathered children upon them. Both suffered immense negative publicity when a person died whilst visiting them (Katherine Mansfield and Raoul Loveday).

There are schools within Sufism that have come to be known as the 'Way of the Blameworthy'. Some individuals are required, as part of their own development, to participate in difficult public work involving the bigger picture of the world historical process.

All kinds of hassle will come their way. In fact they may even be required to deliberately create some. They will inevitably suffer but it accomplishes something for the greater good. Crowley and Gurdjieff have been suggested as possible candidates for such a destiny. In recent times Rajneesh may be another.

Advocates of Gurdjieff generally buy into the legend of infamy surrounding Crowley, whilst seeing the similar reputation of their own magus as an obvious example of media-fuelled fear and stupidity. The most obvious source for the idea of a fundamental opposition between them comes from what is known about an occasion when they actually met and had lunch together at Gurdjieff's French institute during the twenties. Crowley's diaries make favourable references to Gurdjieff and his followers, calling him '*a very advanced adept*'. One eyewitness, C. S. Nott, states however, that eventually Gurdjieff slung Crowley out, telling him in no uncertain terms that he was a scumbag. John Symonds repeats this story.

When studying the meeting of two such mysterious characters, it's worth noting that the protocol may be a bit unusual. For example, when Meher Baba first met Upasani Maharaj, he was greeted with a tirade of abuse and a stone thrown at his head. He departed, bleeding from the wound. It happened to hit him directly on the third eye area however, and brought a profound yogic process he was undergoing to a conclusion. Maharaj later extolled Meher Baba as Avatar of the Age. It's difficult to assess such inscrutable events. It may well be that in the bigger picture of things, Gurdjieff and Crowley could never be publicly seen to be connected in any way. A more prosaic possibility will be looked at shortly. Hints of deeper mysteries will surface again later.

To set the record straight on the Nazi Secret Chief, during the Second World War he remained in occupied Paris. It *is* intriguing that in a climate where numerous mystics and members of Masonic and occultist groups were persecuted and imprisoned across Europe that Gurdjieff, who was not exactly unknown, was left alone. When in May 1942 the Germans ordered all Jews to wear a Star of David, he urgently advised those close to him to go underground or try to flee the country. Gurdjieff arranged for the welfare of Jewish members of his followers who chose to hide in Paris, thus putting himself at great personal risk. The prescience of his decision was validated by July, when the Jews of Paris were rounded up. Over 100,000 French Jews ended up in Auschwitz. 1,500 survived. When the war was over, and France was ablaze with recriminations over collaboration, Gurdjieff emerged unscathed.

The unknowable enigma was supremely pragmatic and able to handle himself in all kinds of situations that most floaty mystics would have floundered in. It may be very difficult to establish any truth about his activities prior to his emerging as a public figure in Russia. Tibet remains contentious. Perhaps he was involved in the Great Game between Britain and Russia, perhaps not. He did marry a lady in waiting to the Tsar. Material circulates claiming that he knew the young Stalin who may have lodged with his parents. From this morsel occult gossipers have made Mr G the occult teacher of both Hitler and his arch-enemy Stalin thereby making him the truly evil agent of some nefarious global Illuminati scene.

A story told by Ouspensky in his masterpiece *In Search of the Miraculous* probably serves as a reality-check here. Gurdjieff had to take a group of followers on a dangerous journey across Russia during the time of the revolution when opposing armies ebbed and flowed back and forth and life was cheap. Meeting up with a group who thought of you as sympathetic to the opposing side could easily result in death. Gurdjieff arranged to have forged papers made out for his people granting safe passage with both sets of protagonists. When encountering any soldiers, secret hand signals gave the tip-off as to which papers to produce. This shows Gurdjieff as beyond the mechanical conflicts of sleepwalking humanity, acting with practical intelligence and above all, saving the lives of those around him. He understood how the world worked. I don't think it's at all out of the question that he may have participated in espionage of some kind at various stages of his life if he considered it to be expedient action. I also do not believe that in any way denigrates the 'Work' he brought to the west.

CROWLEY AND THE NAZIS

THERE IS ONE DEFINITE LINK between Crowley and Hitler that makes an interesting case-study for those who believe occultists are deluded ineffectual people unable to really influence the world. It comes through the unique career of Major-General John Frederick Charles (commonly JFC) Fuller, known as Boney. I first came across Fuller when I was a twelve-year-old history obsessive. He was the author of *The Decisive Battles of the Western World and their Influence on History*. I owned a two-volume paperback abridgement that I repeatedly read. I later discovered that he had been one of the Beast's most ardent followers, writing a book, *The Star in the West*, that praised him as a god. It's a work of immense verbosity that is nonetheless hugely entertaining. For example, he referred to Jesus Christ in passing as, '*that unfortunate fakir*'. Fuller executed some excellent magickal artwork for Crowley's publication *The Equinox* such as designs for the decoration of a temple. Best of all is a superb painting of Baphomet. Like many other of Crowley's associates he eventually fell out with him but communication lines between them were not completely severed.

Fuller went on to develop revolutionary theories concerning the possible applications in war of tank forces. The British army showed limited interest but the Germans were more enthusiastic. Fuller has the dubious distinction of being credited as an inspiration behind Blitzkrieg. In April 1939 he was one of only two British guests to attend Hitler's fiftieth birthday celebrations. Fuller had accepted *The Book of the Law*. Crowley passionately believed that its reception and publication had ushered in the immense events that followed.

During the twenties Crowley had increasing business in Germany. In 1925 he attended a gathering of OTO associated occultists having staked a claim to be the head of the Order. Shortly afterwards he met with Erich Ludendorff. Remember, this was not exactly an insignificant person. He had been perhaps the most important military figure in the German army during the First World War. He became an early supporter of the future Fuhrer and was involved in the 1923 Munich uprising. Ludendorff ran for president in 1925 and failed. He later changed his mind about Hitler and apparently had considerable misgivings when he became German chancellor. The man was a stern humourless German military type. What on earth was he doing meeting up with someone with a continent-wide reputation as debauched Satanist? The Beast had been very visibly expelled from Mussolini's Italy only a few years previously. Crowley later recalled discussing *'Nordic theology'* and the esoteric symbolism of the swastika with Ludendorff.

There are occult rumours that Hitler was familiar with *The Book of the Law*. A German Thelemite named Martha Kuntzel was a strong admirer of the Fuhrer and sent him a German translation. That is a long way from any kind of proof that he actually read it. Rather a lot of mail was addressed to Hitler. A team was involved in handling it. Items considered to be significant were then brought to his attention. What is curious is that when the Nazis came to power and occultists of all kinds were persecuted and ended up in concentration camps (and this included members of the OTO) Kuntzel did not experience any problems.

A more vexed issue concerns the extent to which Crowley could be considered to be pro-Nazi. There's no doubting the aristocratic fascist tone of some of *The Book of the Law* and of much of Crowley's other writings but that's a long way from endorsing Hitler despite what much internet material suggests. It is possible to find anti-Semitic remarks scattered through the Crowley corpus. It's very difficult in the post-Holocaust era to find an appropriate response to this kind of thing, bearing in mind it had been endemic to European culture for nearly two thousand years. Such sentiments can be found in innumerable other writings of the time. That doesn't excuse them. Crowley's remarks are worthy of our contempt but do not put him alongside those who systematically cultivated what ultimately became genocidal hatred.

In 1930 Crowley tried to open up a direct line of communication with Hitler using JFC Fuller. Nothing came of it. Does that somehow prove Crowley was a Nazi sympathiser? During exactly the same period he was also writing to Stalin. Crowley had a number of associates who were communist sympathisers. On one level it could be simply that he believed the triumph of Thelema would have to come initially through its adoption by a powerful nation already predisposed to move beyond the old Christian forms. Germany and Russia were the obvious candidates. The great upheavals in those countries were enough to validate Crowley's prophetic feelings about the birth of the New Aeon. He could also be seen as an inveterate and somewhat sad publicity seeker. Beyond such considerations, his list of contacts and knowledge was potentially quite a resource for Intelligence agencies. He could serve a number of purposes simultaneously as we shall see.

THE MAGICAL
BATTLE OF BRITAIN

THE 1588 HERMETIC
ESPIONAGE MATRIX

'*ONCE, THE WORLD WAS NOT AS IT HAS SINCE BECOME. It once worked in a different way than it does now; it had a different history and a different future. Its very flesh and bones, the physical laws that governed it, were other than the ones we know.*'

'*Whenever the world turns from what it has been into what it will be, and thus earns a different past and a different future, there is a brief moment when every possible kind of universe, all possible extensions of Being in space and time, are poised on the threshold of becoming, before all but one pass into nonexistence again; and the world is as it is and not as it was, and everyone in it forgets that it could ever be or has ever been other than the way it is now.*'

'*And just as the world is thus turning from the what-has-been into the what-is-to-be, and all possibilities are just for a moment alight and one has not yet been chosen, then all the other similar disjunctures in time (for there have been several) can become visible too.*'

'*I discern the shadow of another story and another world, symmetrical to it, and yet as different from it as dream is from waking.*'

Aegypt, John Crowley

IF BRITAIN EVER PRODUCED A REAL MERLIN it was John Dee. A true Renaissance prodigy, excelling in many disciplines, he was one of the most influential figures of the Elizabethan age. Mainly known today as an occultist, it is generally considered that Shakespeare used him as the model for Prospero in *The Tempest*. He may well have been involved in the circulation of underground mystical ideas that spectacularly surfaced in Europe as Rosicrucianism. Dee was a political figure who, inspired by Arthurian tales, believed that Britain had a role of global destiny to play.

He actively encouraged the growth of its empire and did this in a practical manner by recommending to Queen Elizabeth the creation of a powerful Royal Navy and providing maps for many of the great seafarers.

Dee will make a number of appearances throughout this work primarily through his legendary Enochian angel magic, a whole system of interacting with non-human entities famously resorted to by Crowley. It is important to realise that he would have felt that his many interests were the expression of a fundamental unity. For now, we shall note one of the most multi-levelled events of his life involving the great national drama of the Spanish Armada in 1588.

In May 1583, early on in the strange mediumistic sessions he engaged in with his notorious sidekick Edward Kelly (who Crowley claimed as a past life), material appeared that seems to be startlingly prophetic. Dee asked the archangel Uriel the meaning of a vision Kelly had reported from the night before involving *'the appering of the very sea, and many ships thereon, and the cutting of the hed of a woman, by a tall blak man'* Uriel, through Kelly, stated that *'The one, did signifie the prousion of forrayne powres against the welfare of this land: which they shall shortly put into practice. The other, the death of the Quene of Scots. It is not long vnto it.'* Mary Queen of Scots was beheaded in 1587. The Armada arrived in the following year. It was possible in 1583 to spot that things stood a strong chance of ending in tears for Mary and trouble with Spain was likely. Nonetheless there's an uncanny atmosphere about that Dee Kelly session.

A larger context is needed for better appreciation. Dee dates from the earliest days of the British Secret Service. He was closely involved with Sir Francis Walsingham who is usually considered to be its founder. Under his direction Dee carried out extensive espionage missions at the direct instruction of the Queen. He was actually involved in the monitoring of Mary that led to her beheading. During his European travels he relayed all manner of information about Spain. Does this somehow invalidate the psychic session? I don't believe it does.

Dee studied weather forecasting and advised the British authorities that severe weather was likely in the summer of 1588. He made further use of that forecast by creating and circulating prophecies from his base in Prague concerning the defeat of a powerful nation in the context of terrible storms. It was clear that Spain was being referred to. These ideas were circulated throughout Europe by Dutch almanac makers. The prophecies also reached the Vatican. It seems a definite intention of Dee that this material reached Spain and was part of what could be called magical propaganda. It has been suggested that the morale of the Spanish navy was negatively influenced by this ploy.

The great storms did appear, playing a big role in the real events of the Armada. The fleet was forced, by a combination of the naval action of Sir Francis Drake and bad weather, beyond the English Channel and into the North Sea necessitating a dangerous journey back to Spain around the top of Scotland. Many vessels were lost. It was not a huge defeat in military terms but the geopolitical ripples were immense. The Spanish king lost his credibility. Britannia came to rule the waves thereafter. Occult legend has Dee actually conjuring up the storms that bedevilled the Spanish.

Astrology was used in the context of espionage and propaganda in Tudor times. It was very much part of the collective mindset. Queen Elizabeth trusted Dee enough to get him to choose the date for her coronation. At one point, when it appeared she may have been on the verge of marrying either of two French aristocratic brothers, Dee was sent to France to investigate their suitability. He drew up horoscopes for both men. Walsingham was opposed to any such union and there are hints that the horoscopes may have had a certain artfulness to their conclusions. No marriage occurred.

Cryptography was the central concern of the Elizabethan espionage agents. Dee proved to be a great adept of the art. Occultism provides a mindset that readily thinks in terms of correspondences. We have seen from Gematria how letters and numbers can signify each other. This is the essence of the secret code. The most puzzling aspect of this is how Dee's occultism was able to serve a cryptographic purpose. He was exhilarated to discover during one of his continental trips a manuscript of a legendary text, the *Steganographia* of Abbot Trithemius. The book only circulated in manuscript form and was sought after by people offering huge sums of money. Its initial publication faltered amidst rumours of the text being demonically inspired. The German mystic had flourished in the early part of the century and been a teacher of such heavyweights as Cornelius Agrippa and, it is often stated, Paracelsus.

Steganography is a term referring to a text which completely hides an encoded hidden meaning in distinction from Cryptography where a hidden meaning is known to be present. Trithemius was a master of the art. His great grimoire is assuredly a kind of manual on the subject. It can be used for espionage purposes. Dee wrote to his spymasters full of excitement for his find purely in terms of its coding potential. Does this mean that the magical side of the text is therefore a hoax of some kind and not to be taken seriously by the student of the occult arts?

The relevance of the question concerns Dee's use of his own angelic messages to convey espionage information. Any occultist who has given the Enochian corpus a modicum of attention, particularly those who have actually worked magic with it are likely to attest to an exceptional strength and power that conveys a sense of otherworldly realms and their denizens in a manner few other systems are able to. How can it possibly work? How can some kind of interdimensional grimoire also serve the purpose of encoded espionage?

This is a conundrum. If the reader feels drawn to try and resolve it I would recommend deep immersion in the works of Frances Yates for a prolonged period of time. The fundamental point is that the Renaissance was imbued with magical Hermetic thought to an extent that is so much at odds with the modern world as to represent almost another reality altogether. The occult arts were envisaged as a path of high mysticism that potentially led to an understanding and experience of divine unity. The systems of correspondences were a kind of philosophers stone that when fully comprehended worked great alchemical transformation on the adept and the world around them. Something of this is present in the way Crowley understood his reception of his holy scripture and the way it changed the world. It's there with Dee, his sense of mystical British politics, angels, and espionage. He did exert considerable influence on how the British Empire came into being.

Dee's case shows the willingness of the early British Secret Service to make use of the unusual talents of a man with a reputation as some sort of necromancer who inspired fear and a legend of infamy. During an absence in Europe a mob burned down Dee's house which included a library considered to be the equal of Oxford and Cambridge universities. For centuries after his death he was generally considered to be deluded or demon-driven and his role as a scholar and political visionary neglected.

Dee engaged in long-term magical workings that brought through the Enochian system but he didn't really use the system itself. He waited on the angels themselves to tell him to do so but the instructions never came. Part of the material was integrated into the Golden Dawn by Mathers and became familiar to all adepts who reached the appropriate grades who would indeed have made some practical use of it. It was Crowley who became the first person to get a major result. There is a sense that the entities were concerned with an apocalypse very much in keeping with *Revelations*. It's entirely appropriate that, as if following some arcane timescale, Crowley would be involved in its fuller activation.

The basic point here is this: the events of 1588 created assorted national archetypes which the threat of invasion in 1940 seemed to automatically activate. 1588 also constituted one end of a set of historical co-ordinates relating to the British Empire of which 1940 provided the balance. Somewhere in all this lies something very mysterious that occasionally surfaces to our awareness like a fragment of a dream, carrying strange nuances hinting at another narrative altogether. Dee and Crowley were agents of this process and parts of it can be deciphered in the unfolding of particular events.

A hint comes with the numbers 007 that vast numbers of people today know as the code designation for the world's most famous fictional spy, James Bond. John Dee was the original 007. He signed his letters from Europe to his Tudor spymasters with two zeros that indicated he was acting as the eyes of the Queen. A larger seven lay to their right, its bar over-reaching them. Why did Ian Fleming use Dee's signature? What might we uncover if we pursued such a line of enquiry?

SPOOKINESS

Crowley had a long history of German connections dating from his induction into the OTO. One of the most controversial episodes of his life was played out when he was living in the United States during the First World War. He cultivated the company of German propagandists and began writing pieces advocating their cause. After the war he claimed to have been secretly working on behalf of the British by publishing material so absurd as to undermine German credibility. The home press used this 'traitor' aspect to fuel the legend of infamy.

The question of the extent of Crowley's involvement in espionage has come into increasing prominence in recent years, having been featured by Peter Levenda and Dave Evans, and represents yet another aspect of his multi-faceted life. Richard B. Spence's *Secret*

Agent 666 comprehensively shows that Crowley was in constant contact for decades with large numbers of people connected to Intelligence agencies. It really does look as if he was broadly telling the truth about the period in America.

The 1925 Ludendorff meeting is a good example of something that could have served a number of purposes at the same time. Crowley would always have been looking to cultivate important people with mystical inclinations with a view to making himself and the concept of Thelema and the New Aeon known. He was consolidating his position as head of an order largely based in Germany at that time so the fact that the politics of the country was in turmoil and the messianic Hitler with his swastika bearing cohorts clearly on the rise would have been of considerable interest to him. He had a great chance to use his apparent pro-German sympathies to his advantage.

Any information gathered would have been considered useful to British Intelligence. The twilight world of German secret societies that the Nazis seemed to have appeared from needed to be understood. Crowley's meeting with Ludendorff would have been one of the most unusual opportunities to gather data available at that time. His earlier visit to Gurdjieff may not have been unconnected with British suspicions he was a Russian spy. That doesn't mean Crowley didn't use the situation for other purposes.

Back in Britain in the mid-thirties, Crowley came into contact with Dennis Wheatley. The man who would achieve fame through his occult horror novels had cultivated Crowley ostensibly as a source of material for his interests. Decades later the Hammer movie *The Devil Rides Out* based on Wheatley's novel would introduce a new generation to a villain inspired by the legend of infamy.

Wheatley was not just a writer. He moved in espionage circles and was responsible for introducing Crowley to Maxwell Knight, an important figure in MI5 who would become one of the inspirations for the character "M" in Ian Fleming's James Bond novels. Knight was another bewilderingly multi-aspected character. Alongside his espionage career he found time to be a Jazz musician, fisherman and cricketer. He was also a Naturalist who authored such classics as *Frogs, Toads, and Newts in Britain*, broadcasting with the BBC in such a capacity.

Knight's espionage speciality was the infiltration of groups considered potentially dangerous to British interests. A measure of the ambiguities of this world was the fact that he had been a member of the British Union of Fascists before being recruited to MI5. It seems that in the twenties the fascists were considered useful in fighting communism. A decade later, as Germany and Italy formed an alliance, the connections were exploited with different intentions. Inter-war espionage was a game much like the later Cold War with double-agents and bewildering layers of subterfuge.

Knight and Wheatley both shared an interest in the occult and had convivial dinner dates together with Crowley before the Second World War. The Beast's general demeanour at that time was that of a well-bred Oxbridge don and he was renowned as an excellent conversationalist. His notorious biographical background wouldn't exactly have been unknown to Knight who would also have been aware of the many spooks Crowley had been in the proximity of and undoubtedly would have known about his more obscure exploits in that respect.

Knight told his nephew Harry Smith that he and Dennis Wheatley together actually became novice magickal students of Crowley on a *"purely academic"* basis. Wheatley later became a member of a secretive Intelligence group directly linked with Winston Churchill whose remit included full application of the art of deception. The novelist always maintained a façade of distance in his public pronouncements on the level of his occult involvement but in the world of the Intelligence operative nothing is ever quite what it seems. The magical glamour of illusion as a tool is one of the fundamental espionage talents.

It was quite possible for one group in Whitehall to be in possession of documents suggesting Crowley was indubitably dodgy whilst the people in the office next door were actually making use of him. This seems to be essentially what was happening. Richard B. Spence has made a strong case suggesting that Crowley seems to have regularly supplied information on communists and fascists throughout the twenties and thirties. He probably continued to work as a kind of double-agent with the Germans before the Nazis came to power. Whatever the case, as Britain faced its greatest challenge, we have the astonishing situation of one of the most important people in British Intelligence having the world's most notorious occultist as his occasional agent, dinner guest, and magickal mentor. Here are strange resonances with John Dee.

★ ★ ★

FINEST HOUR

The myth of the Finest Hour is perhaps the fundamental item in the story Britain likes to tell itself about its role in the world and national character. I may be about to suggest some disquieting things that indicate other levels of the game at work but I believe it all leaves Finest Hour essentially intact.

I'm not someone who looks at Winston Churchill through rose-tinted glasses. I believe however that he was, for all his considerable faults, including not only some bad decisions but ruthless dodgy dealing, an epic hero who was brought forth by some national spirit of Arthurian energy at precisely the right moment in a manner that no conventional view of the world-historical process can do justice to. Just like Crowley and a number of other people featuring in this work I believe that seeing him solely in terms of his failings is hugely limiting and in the case of a man of such achievements and general sensibilities, grotesquely inappropriate.

I consider it most interesting to contemplate the extent of Churchill's escapes from death and how they helped instil in him a feeling of destiny. He came to feel that *'Over me beat invisible wings'*. An accident at the age of 18 saw him fall 29 feet down through fir trees onto hard ground, where he ruptured a kidney, was unconscious for 3 days, and bed-ridden for 3 months. He was fortunate not to drown in a Swiss lake. A Great War dugout was destroyed by an explosive shell shortly after Churchill leaving it. This is very similar to Hitler's experiences in the trenches. He was lucky not to be killed when hit by a car in 1931.

That Churchill was a member of a druid order alongside a whole bunch of other strange sounding groups is not something I would make too big a deal about. This was not unusual. Plenty of aristocrats and politicians did likewise alongside the usual Masonic affiliations. I do feel though that Churchill was in many respects a natural magician himself, using his bardic eloquence to inspire and often to effectively create reality.

In 1938 at Munich, Britain allowed Czechoslovakia to be dismembered by the Nazis essentially because we weren't militarily ready to confront them. When we finally did go to war, seemingly on behalf of Poland, we actually did nothing to help them as they were defeated and horribly brutalised. None of this looks particularly noble. Nonetheless, I still subscribe to the basic tenet of school history books. The Nazis were the bad guys. Britain continuing to stand against them in 1940 was the greatest moment in our history and prevented a descent into a catastrophic barbarism that would have been worse than any of the wretchedness that characterises the modern world.

A British occult response to the Nazis had certainly begun in 1940 during the mythic days of the Dunkirk evacuation, Churchill's legendary speeches, and the Battle of Britain. The nation's second most illustrious occultist, the redoubtable Dion Fortune, mobilised her nationwide associates through the use of weekly letters giving instructions for visualisations using Glastonbury Tor and its mythical hollow interior as a focus. The resulting images rapidly took on a life of their own and soon became structured on the Qabalistic Tree of Life, featuring a Rose Cross and including Arthurian imagery. Fortune used it to stir up powerful archetypes of national warrior protection and also got her groups to strongly picture angels holding flaming swords and suchlike standing guard along the coast.

It doesn't appear that there were any obvious official connections to this undertaking. One of Fortune's pre-war close associates Charles Foster Seymour was a military man but the dynamic seems entirely inspired by the mystical sensibilities of Fortune herself. Her methodology was the opposite of the secretive world of espionage. In fact it was quite a moment in the history of magic, effectively democratising it so that previous grade levels in magical organisations did not dictate who participated.

I have covered this episode in *Mysterium Artorius*, including modern inspiration I have derived from it. Gareth Knight's collection of Dion Fortune's wartime letters *The Magical Battle of Britain* gives the full details. Something that I have noticed is how apt it was that Glastonbury, with its Arthurian associations, acted as the focus for the British magical Grail knights bearing in mind the existence of Himmler's Wewelsburg which was actually unknown outside Germany at that time.

There is a photo that has been increasingly circulated in recent years that has Crowley striking an obviously Churchillian pose with a bulldog expression and big cigar. One senses a little bit more behind all this.

A few days after war began in September 1939 Crowley's diaries record that he had filled in a form for NID (Naval Intelligence Division). He then listed some names with no explanation. Sir Percy Harris was one of them. He was the husband of Lady Frieda, the Anthroposophically inclined artist who would later paint the *Thoth* tarot. Percy was an MP and would be part of Churchill's wartime circle. Crowley was soon invited for an interview and from minor details concerning departments and phone extensions it seems he was seen by people specialising in interrogation.

The Director of Naval Intelligence, Admiral John Godfrey, would soon come to make use of astrologer Louis de Wohl. It was believed that astrology had some influence in the Third Reich and knowing the kind of advice that may have been circulating could prove useful in anticipating future developments. Ellic Howe would later claim a modicum of fame for his accounts of his own role in using astrology for psychological warfare purposes against Germany. A lot of long-term concerted energy and application went into these projects and one spectacular result ensued as we shall see.

The Germans also made use of astrological propaganda. They skilfully manipulated material that appeared in America to put subtle spins on the idea of a German victory and the desirability of Britain making peace. Both sides created their own versions of the prophecies of Nostradamus. Leaflets were dropped by aeroplane. Similar ideas are on record as early Crowley suggestions to his Intelligence contacts. His strategies were officially turned down but still seem to have been made use of. Whether or not others had independently created their own versions is hard to determine. All of this is strangely reminiscent of Tudor times. It is certainly odd to contemplate its use in 1940.

Crowley claimed to have introduced the 'V for Victory' sign, so strongly associated with Churchill and used in occupied Europe from 1941 onwards, inspired by a Golden Dawn grade gesture made with two arms upraised in a V shape. This is not an accepted piece of history but he specifically wrote about it and the inevitable denial of his input six months before it was adopted, supposedly following an idea by a Belgian working for the BBC.

Crowley also wrote a short book of poetry, *Thumbs Up*, that blended straightforward patriotism with magickal lore. The optimistic gesture of the title was also derived from ritual. It wasn't exactly a best-seller but there may have been more subtle intentions behind it. Perhaps it was intended to be seen by a target audience that was not entirely domestic. The odious traitor William Joyce, known as Lord Haw-Haw, who broadcast Nazi propaganda in English, on one occasion made mention of Crowley celebrating a Black Mass in Westminster Abbey showing that the old man had not exactly been forgotten.

There is yet another tantalising fragment suggesting a tip of an iceberg when we find that Dion Fortune was corresponding with Crowley during the war and even met him a few times towards the end. One letter from her to him, dating from January 1942 mentions *Thumbs Up* in a way indicating it had been mentioned before. She also states, '*I am afraid my Biblical knowledge has grown rusty and I cannot follow the reference to Daniel and the Apocalypse with regard to Mr Churchill*'. This was followed humorously by '*Is Mr Churchill to be conceived of as crowned with the stars, or does his tail draw the twelfth part after him?*' There is a clear indication here of topics already under discussion. One wonders what else they may have shared? Unfortunately their correspondence seems to have been destroyed in a bizarre and disturbing context that will be noted later.

Amongst Himmler's apparently more fanciful ideas was his belief that Rosicrucianism was a branch of the British Secret Service. If he had later discovered that British occultists had been visualising a Rose Cross inside the interior of Glastonbury Tor during the Battle of Britain he would probably have felt his suspicions were confirmed. The best was yet to come.

GOLDEN EYE OF HORUS: THE SPY WHO FED ME MEXICAN BRAIN POISON

The Rudolf Hess mystery sees an outbreak of fantastic realism onto the wider world stage. It's obvious that something damned peculiar occurred and a strong feeling of suppressed information hangs in the air. Delving a little beneath the surface one encounters that weird mix of surrealism and magic that serves to undermine the consensus leaving behind the unsettling sense that the world is not at all as it appears to be and we have been told a story about it that is not true. The trickster spirit of mercurial Hermes seems present in the labyrinthine complexities of a plot that possibly no single individual ever entirely understood.

Rudolf Hess, as Deputy Leader of the Nazi party, was officially the second most powerful person in Germany. This status primarily stemmed from his early close relationship with Hitler that included the time spent in prison when *Mein Kampf* was written. It's difficult to get the measure of the man. We have already noted his passion for the mystical. Compared to Himmler, Goebbels, and Goering he doesn't seem to be the type to play the ruthless games of power politics or to have that element of sadism about him. An insightful glimpse of him can be seen in Leni Riefenstahl's notorious documentary covering the 1934 Nuremberg Rally, *Triumph of the Will*. Hess gives a speech praising the Fuhrer where he states with religious devotion *"Hitler is Germany"*.

Hess was portrayed as a decent sort of chap and the conscience of the party. The idea that the Nazis, the guys who made Jews pay for their own train tickets on the journey to Auschwitz, might have had a conscience is enough to raise a few contemporary eyebrows. One interesting example is enough to show what that meant in relation to Hess. He had a legal power that placed only Hitler above him. He could make judgements in individual cases that found in their favour even if they were in effect contrary to the law. Hess was the man Germans could appeal to. Steiner's biodynamic farming came under attack from makers of chemical fertilisers. Early on in the history of the regime, in 1933, a local minister banned biodynamic products. The Anthroposophists turned to Hess for help. Notwithstanding that he was happy for the movement itself to be banned, he opted to assess this individual aspect of it on its own merits and set up a series of trials. They lasted for four years and produced entirely positive results. The war and other political factors intervened and that was how the matter ended but it indicates the enigma of Hess. He has also been portrayed as an idealistic Thulist who tried to keep the original mysticism behind the Nazis intact.

It must not be forgotten that Hess had participated in some brutal street fights in the early days of the party. He was considerably involved in the creation of the Nuremberg Laws of 1935 which effectively made anti-Semitism state policy. When the Nazis invaded Poland his hand can also be seen in the processes creating an appalling apparatus of violence and degradation as the defeated nation was ethnically cleansed.

The basic narrative of the Hess mystery is simple enough. In May 1941, with the invasion of Russia imminent, he flew solo to Scotland on a mission to broker some kind of peace deal between Britain and Germany. He actually landed by parachute. The entire episode appeared to be a fiasco in as much as his overtures were rejected and he was imprisoned and sidelined. The initial impression is that he had no authority to negotiate and therefore nothing real to put on the table. Hitler immediately denounced his old comrade stating that if he returned to Germany he would be shot. The obvious fear was that he would ruin the surprise attack on Russia. Interestingly enough, astrologers were blamed for his questionable undertaking. A purge of the remaining such elements in the Reich rapidly ensued.

What on earth was Hess up to? He must have strongly believed he could get a result to be willing to take such a huge risk. In trying to disentangle the complexities we come up against what appear to be conflicting versions of reality that may ultimately be part subsumed in a greater whole where they can exist side by side.

In one version it seems he was the victim of a spectacular sting primarily engineered by James Bond creator Ian Fleming who was also working for the Department of Naval Intelligence and knew Maxwell Knight and his ability to improvise strategies for endlessly unusual situations.

Fleming came up with an interesting scheme and was allowed to run with it. Sir Barry Domville had been a former Director of Naval Intelligence during the twenties. He had formed an Anglo-German cultural association called the Link. He and his associates, who included JFC Fuller, were monitored by Knight after the Nazis came to power and proved to be a bit too sympathetic towards the German cause. When war broke out Domville was interred and the group effectively ceased to exist. Fleming thought it could be useful to use espionage techniques to make the Germans believe that the Link still existed and had gone underground harbouring new and extremely influential people who had the capacity to usurp Churchill and negotiate peace. The ultimate aim was to trick a member of the Nazi leadership into a meeting that would result in their capture and a huge propaganda triumph. Extreme artfulness was needed because there really were many highly-placed people who were hoping for a deal with the Nazis. If the operation was handled properly they could be made visible and out-manoeuvred as well.

Rudolf Hess was selected as target for a number of reasons. He spoke English and was a known Anglophile. He himself had set up a group to cultivate Anglo-German relations. One of his main agents was Kurt Jahnke who had known Crowley in America during his First World War German propaganda phase. Jahnke was a classic espionage figure who seemed to be a double-agent and somehow navigated safely between dangerously conflicting influences for decades. This all meant that there were existing potential lines of communication between Hess and the British via the neutral countries Switzerland, Spain, and Portugal. It became known that he had a strong interest in securing peace.

Fleming cultivated astrologers in order to better set the bait for a man known to be devoted to matters mystical. This particular strategy was not widely known. Fleming had a mysterious contact in Switzerland who was aware of what appeared to be an extensive deepening interest of Hess in astrology and the people he was consulting. It seemed he was contemplating some big issue where timing was vital. Fleming's plan was to use astrology to bolster the idea of the Link and its usefulness for Hess.

Hess had been fixating on the idea of a flight to Britain to promote peace from as early as the immediate aftermath of the fall of France in 1940. He was well aware that the timing and logistics had to be spot-on. The plan crossed a threshold when the Haushofer family became involved. Karl's son Albrecht would later be executed for his involvement in the plot to kill Hitler in 1944. Somewhere along the line he obviously felt that things had taken a wrong turn. Whether this was already the case in 1941 is one of a whole batch of conundrums in the Hess case. Albrecht was very knowledgeable about astrology and Hess consulted him over the material he was being fed.

The name of the Duke of Hamilton was fed into the disinformation circuit. Hamilton was Lord Steward of the King's Household and was thereby associated with the highest level of the British establishment. He lived on an estate in Scotland and was head of an RAF squadron stationed nearby. A credible picture of a possible landing area with the promise of no interference could be suggested. Hamilton had briefly met Hess at the 1936 Berlin Olympics. He was put forward as the focus of the peace proponents. Hamilton became involved in manipulated correspondence with Hess via addresses in neutral Portugal. This culminated in an invitation to meet at his home in Scotland with the assurance of a welcome and an auspicious outcome.

It was fortunate for the plotting that a heavenly event presented itself as an ideal focus to bring the plans to fruition. May 10th 1941 was a full moon where six planets would be in Taurus. Astrologers were already giving it a lot of attention. Hess apparently was also brooding on Hitler's own horoscope believing that the Fuhrer had some seriously bad aspects indicative of possible death and that he needed to personally do something to take some of the bad energy away from his beloved leader. One detail of interest is that it was a dream Hess had that convinced him he was on a winner. He was in a large aristocratically furnished building walking along great halls heading for a significant meeting.

The subtle task of the disinformation astrologer was to plant ideas into the Hess circle hinting that a journey for peace was well-aspected, Scotland a potential location, and the Duke of Hamilton the man to seek out. This would need to be accomplished through material that was astrologically credible, vague but enough for the Haushofers and Hess to see the signs of their already existing plans.

We have seen how in one Whitehall office we can have an anti-Crowley faction with a file full of data to back their opinion whilst next door another group have a different file altogether and are making use of him. It's also possible to have one little group working a deception on Hess to lure him to Britain on the basis of a fictional peace party whilst another group are effectively inviting him with the knowledge of what in effect was a real peace party. It's possible for a whole bunch of apparently contradictory stories to all be simultaneously true and happening under the same broad umbrella of British Intelligence. Those curious for more details would do well to consult *Double Standards* by Lynn Picknett, Clive Prince, and Stephen Prior. There are some considerably grey areas in establishing the true narrative.

When Churchill wrote his wartime memoirs he spoke of the dark days in 1940 following the fall of France.

'Future generations may deem it noteworthy that the supreme question of whether we should fight on alone never found a place upon the War Cabinet agenda. It was taken for granted and as a matter of course by these men of all parties in the State, and we were much too busy to waste time upon such unreal, academic issues.'

Here we can definitely see him using his words and the weight they carry to create a certain reality because this simply isn't true. It's a mistake to think that Britain represented a unity at that point. There were highly placed factions who did want peace with Germany, including a few royals. Others centred around Churchill were having none of it and sought to put a spanner in the works.

The coming German attack on Russia was not exactly a total surprise to the British. Gigantic military resources were being grouped in Eastern Europe. This had involved taking them away from positions in France where they might have been involved in an invasion of Britain. With spies and resistance movements communicating to Britain from across Europe it was obvious what was coming. Churchill even directly warned Stalin but wasn't believed.

Despite the successes of the Battle of Britain, by spring 1941 opposing factions still existed. Peace was still desired by influential people. The Russian situation put Churchill in an extremely difficult position. Communism was widely hated and feared by the British establishment. The agency that became known as MI6 had battled Russian espionage since the earliest days of the Bolsheviks coming to power. They were in no doubt that it represented an insidious threat and that whilst various British intellectuals idealised the communist system the grim reality was that Stalin was killing millions of his own people and keeping the rest oppressed under the grimmest of totalitarian regimes.

A lot of people felt that it would be a wise move to let the Nazis and Russia slug it out leaving Britain in a better position at the end whatever the outcome. Sir Stuart Menzies who was Head of MI6 advised Churchill that the best option was to allow the Nazis a free hand. This makes it clear that there was a strong Intelligence faction that would have been happy to extricate Britain from a war that had not been going at all well and would show no sign of improvement for some time to come.

There are still advocates of Menzies' position in the present day. Going to war with Germany over Poland did not really serve our national interests. Keeping it going when we had a number of chances to extricate ourselves resulted in the premature dissolution of the empire and a permanent reduction in our status as a global power. In 1941 this was already a predictable outcome.

All of that is probably true but it neglects the most vital point of all. The Nazis were not ordinary adversaries. Regardless of any occultist considerations they conducted their business with comprehensive savagery. Letting them get on with it would probably have resulted in the completion of the Holocaust, in other words the death of every single Jew in occupied territories. That would only have been the start of the matter. Russia suffered over twenty million fatalities. Weigh that against Britain's death toll of half a million soldiers and forty thousand civilians and one begins to get a perspective on the scale of the war in the east. If Germany had concentrated its full resources against Russia it could ultimately have led to double the body count.

Such were the extraordinary world-historical tensions in the background of the Hess mystery. If the outcome had varied in any of a number of potential ways the war and the subsequent configuration of the world could have turned out very differently.

So we have what appears to be a supreme espionage triumph. In a magnificent sting Hitler's best friend is enticed to Britain and captured. A puzzling story becomes even more puzzling when what follows is significantly underwhelming. One would have thought there were many options for exploiting the Hess situation. The propaganda possibilities of showing a split in the Nazi leadership would have been a modest beginning. Hess instead was comprehensively sidelined and his case buried.

It is possible that he could have revealed details of potential British traitors that would have caused many problems considered to be best left hidden. If he had been used for propaganda purposes perhaps the Nazis could have hit back with some material that could not have been ignored. The mythology of the Finest Hour was already in place and it served many purposes to keep it unsullied.

Churchill seemed to have handled the situation to his advantage. In one version of events his operatives get to Hess and take him out of the picture before others who had hopes riding on the mission were able to fully play their cards. After that Churchill could hold potential allegations of treachery to keep certain opponents silent. A measure of his studied nonchalance over the whole scenario is that on hearing confirmation that he really did have Hitler's deputy under lock and key he refused to cancel an earlier arrangement to watch a Marx Brothers movie.

Occult mythology strongly links Crowley to the Hess case. Self-proclaimed son-of-the-Beast Amado Crowley has written of a huge ritual in Ashdown Forest involving his father and a large cast of extras drawn from the army projecting some powerful psychic force to compel Hess to come to Britain. This does not strike me as at all the style of the great magus and I am inclined to entirely disbelieve it.

What is a matter of historical record is that Ian Fleming had the great idea of using Crowley to interrogate Hess. Within four days of his arrival Crowley wrote to Fleming. *'If it is true that Herr Hess is much influenced by astrology and magick, my services might be of use to the department'.* This letter became a prize possession of Fleming. In later years it has been suggested that a little something of Crowley went into the characterisation of the first classic Bond villain Le Chiffre from *Casino Royale*.

Crowley and Hess together in an interrogation room is an irresistible concept. If it didn't happen it damn well ought to have done. It has tremendous scope for an art-house one-act play. Maxwell Knight apparently decided against it. Or did he? A German POW claimed to have seen Crowley and Hess at a military base called Ham Common which was a top secret interrogation centre where things were known to get a bit rough. The two were allegedly together for a few weeks. It cannot be said that there is any real substance here but the idea that one Intelligence faction could secrete Hess away with Crowley whilst others who knew much of the details of the case and Crowley's proximity were unaware is not unrealistic given the extraordinary nature of the espionage game.

In a realm of impenetrable rumour and subterfuge where the definitive truth may never be confidently known it is appropriate to mention another evocative piece of gossip. During his early captivity Hess complained to Red Cross officials that he was being fed *'Mexican brain poison'* that was causing him to hallucinate. It is easy to gallop away with this one and assume it must be mescaline and that a man with considerable knowledge of it has been shown to be somewhere in the vicinity. As we shall later come to see, there is more than one rumour linking Crowley and mescaline to a famous person.

After being imprisoned for over four years Hess appeared in public at the Nuremberg war crimes trial. He had been assessed as fit to stand trial but seemed considerably dissociated. There are speculations that range from his brain having been fried by drugs in extreme interrogation scenarios to the person on trial not even being Hess at all but a hapless zombie double, the genuine article having died in assorted scenarios after capture. Picknett, Prince, and Prior have some controversial material about the death of the King's brother, the Duke of Kent in a plane crash. They believe that the real Hess was on board and sabotage machinations in which Churchill may have been involved finally destroyed the plans of a real peace party. If indeed a double was put on trial at Nuremberg he took one of history's great bum raps by spending forty years in jail before his death in 1987 over which the same level of controversy is present. Was it suicide or murder?

Hess may have left the scene before the Holocaust began but he clearly supported the war against Russia. One of the few aspects of the mysterious flight that appears straightforward is that Hess was seeking peace with Britain in order to free Germany up to fully engage in the coming campaign. It's because of this, it's generally stated, that the Russians insisted on keeping him imprisoned, eventually as the only inmate of Spandau. Remembering the extent of Russian suffering it's understandable why they felt that the only leading Nazi left alive and in captivity needed to be made an example of. Against that it has been claimed that with the advent of the Gorbachev era the Russians were ready to release him but the British resisted.

Hess is like a man from another dimension who has somehow blinked into view during one of those disjunctures in time when a whole bunch of parallel realms become visible. He hardly seems to belong in our world, surviving under the magical umbrella of his beloved leader but entirely out of place alongside Churchill, Stalin, and Roosevelt. He lingered, gradually fading away in a strange half life like a ghost or indeed a figure in a dream but he was flesh and blood, rather brave and idealistic, and he did somewhat suffer for those virtues. What can be said is that Hess came as a sincere unarmed peace envoy, albeit of a genocidal regime, and was effectively locked up with the key thrown away forever. His appearance on the world-stage of the Aeon of Horus is indeed a considerable oddity.

Pauwels and Bergier sing the praises of the entirely ordinary people who defeated the elitist magical reality of Nazism and quite rightly so. Nonetheless, in the Magical Battle of Britain, one gets the feeling that a clash of two fantastic realisms is being observed. Crowley the full activator of the Enochian apocalypse took on the aspect of the John Dee type figure somehow needed to play a certain role and enable particular buttons to be automatically pressed. Alongside some of our other mysterious timescales, the British Empire effectively began in the time of John Dee and reached its culmination in the time of Aleister Crowley. The entities behind the Enochian apocalypse, so intimately linked with the Aeon of Horus, were not just concerned with the British Empire however.

THE BABALON WORKING

*'Here is Wisdom. Let Him that hath
Understanding count the Number of Our Lady; for
it is the Number of a Woman; and Her Number is
An Hundred and Fifty and Six.'*

Aleister Crowley
Waratah Blossoms. The Book of Lies

APOCALYPTIC ALCHEMY

THE HISTORY OF SCIENCE can depict a cumulative path of knowledge and application leading to the moment of the first atomic explosion. People with particular predispositions might also have intuited that immense mystical spiritual forces were at work in the world.

Perhaps one of the most evocative scene-setting accounts comes from an episode in Trevor Ravenscroft and Tim Wallace-Murphy's *The Mark of the Beast*. There are the same problems with this work as with *The Spear of Destiny*. I do not by any means endorse the entirety of the Christian Steiner-influenced tale which has been created through the same mix of historical data and visionary psychic information but once again it does conjure a certain mood I feel is appropriate.

Refugees fleeing the Byzantine emperor Justinian's closing down of the old pagan academies in 529 were welcomed by the Persian monarch who set up a centre for them at Jundi-Shapur near the foothills of Afghanistan. The area is steeped in spiritual history. In nearby hills Zarathustra preached from a cave on the cosmology of the constant struggle between Ormuzd and Ahriman, principles of light and dark. In the early centuries of the Christian era the Gnostic Mani was martyred there for preaching his own version of dualism.

Assorted heretics and mystics from throughout the Middle East soon joined the exiled Byzantines. Science and medicine were given considerable attention and the old Greek wisdom mixed with Arab and Indian material.

The Mark of the Beast dwells on the man the authors claim was the founder of the academy, Joshua ben Jesu. He had allegedly been exiled from the Nestorian Christian community for *'developing an unnatural form of clairvoyance through black magic'*.

He and his family *'secretly perceived the god Behemoth and their motive was to replace Christianity with the worship of this mighty evil being who was none other than Sorat, the two-horned beast of the apocalypse'*. Supposedly the study of science at Jundi-Shapur was pursued by spiritually dangerous visionary methods that enabled the Great Beast to directly download knowledge in advance of its time into the minds of the academy. If things had gone according to this evil plan the science of the twentieth century could have arrived a thousand years earlier with humanity unable to emotionally assimilate it. The result would have robbed us of our spiritual possibilities, leaving us adrift and enslaved in a materialistic wasteland. Unsurprisingly, things really got going during the year 666.

The diabolic plan was thwarted with the advent of Islam. An invading army severely culled the academy despite (so Ravenscroft and Wallace Murphy state) a fierce magical resistance involving the projection to visible appearance of terrifying demonic thoughtforms. The ruling ben Jesu family managed to escape unhindered and other survivors manoeuvred themselves into the retinue of the Caliph of Baghdad. The main impulse of the enterprise had been busted but something of the transmission remained in the Islamic world, subtly trying to spread its influence into Europe.

A great twist of the karmic spiral later saw scientists who had been exiled from their homelands due to Hitler, just as their distant predecessors had been expelled by Justinian, gather together for the atomic bomb project.

'All of the teachers and pupils involved in the community of the academy in Jundi-Shapur have reincarnated or will soon reincarnate once more – They are the leading atomic physicists! Their new Jundi-Shapur was the research facility of Los Alamos in New Mexico.'

Blinded by the abstract beauty of science they worked towards a terrible goal without sufficient emotional connection to its reality. Once they had witnessed the first ever atomic explosion in July 1944 in the desert a number of those involved awoke to the immensity of what they had unleashed and tried to persuade the military not to use it. This was, sadly, futile. Oppenheimer, one of the crucial figures in the saga, famously quoted from the *Bhagavad Gita*, *'Now we have become death, the destroyer of worlds.'* A natural gut-level response to the great mushroom cloud was surely awe and terror.

LIVING FLAME

Crowley considered himself to be Logos of the Aeon, meaning he was able to embody and thereby help manifest in the human realm the start of the dawning era. The power and extent of the new energy to break down old forms, matter itself being the best example, had revealed itself by the wars' end. Crowley by then was old and dying. Perhaps in the midst of this chaos it was again necessary for someone to take on board something of the whole matrix personally and embody it, direct it.

In the second chapter of *The Book of the Law*, Hadit says

'I am the flame that burns in every heart of man, and in the core of every star. I am Life, and the giver of Life, yet therefore is the knowledge of me the knowledge of death.'

These powerful words, so evocative of the summer of 1945, serve as a suitable introduction to the life of the next Thelemic superstar.

John Parsons aka Jack was born on October 2nd 1914, a day when the Jehovah's Witnesses believed the world would end. This was perhaps prophetic of his later life. By 1945 he was a prodigiously precocious explosives expert and innovator in rocket technology, having helped to found the Pasadena Jet Propulsion Laboratory that still contributes to the space shuttle programme. He stood at the very beginning of America's space programme, later having a crater on the moon named after him. Among his associates were people with peripheral involvement in the A Bomb project. Here was a man with a tangible role in the scientific events that shaped the century.

Tall and Hollywood handsome, Parsons was also a bit of a playboy and wildman with a passionate mystical intensity about him. He claimed to have successfully invoked Satan to visible appearance at the age of thirteen. Although admitting that the result had terrified him, it proved to be the start of a path that would lead him to become a Thelemite ritual magician. It's amazing to think of him actually reciting Crowley's *Hymn to Pan* when launching experimental rockets.

Parsons found in Crowley's work a libertarian ethic that expressed his deepest feelings. As far as this can be made into a political formula it states the basic credo that the *sole* function of the State is to safeguard the rights of the individual. Parsons' writings on these ideas, the exhilarating exhortation *Freedom is a Two-Edged Sword,* feel like a prophetic call to awakening that later resounded through the sixties. In a filmed interview Robert Anton Wilson called it *"one of the greatest statements of libertarian philosophy ever written"*. One of its strongest points has perhaps not been fully heard yet. The other edge of freedom's sword is responsibility. The one demands the other. Those who have come across Parsons in the increasingly dense occult conspiracy genre and seen him portrayed as some kind of evil antichrist would do well to peruse *Freedom* and get a feeling for the passionate idealism that drove his rebelliousness.

Just as Crowley had legendary lairs at Boleskine on the shores of Loch Ness and the Abbey of Thelema in Sicily, so Jack held court at the building that came to be called the Parsonage. 1003 South Orange Grove Ave Pasadena was a three-storey mansion set in twenty-five acre grounds in an opulent area known as "Millionaires' Mile" where the streets were lined with palm trees and the gardens full of magnolias.

The builder of the house had been Arthur Fleming, a fabulously wealthy philanthropist. During the first great phase of Cal Tech during the thirties, when Einstein had visited the campus, he had dined at the mansion. Fleming had a unique Aeon of Horus motif in his life. The armistice in the First World War had been signed in a railway dining carriage. He later bought and renovated it, donating it to the French government. When Nazi Germany defeated France in 1940 Hitler had enjoyed a moment of exquisite revenge on behalf of an entire country by getting the surrender signed in the carriage again and then destroying it. The elderly Fleming died a broken man shortly afterwards.

The 1929 Wall Street Crash had impacted in the area. Lavish properties drastically declined in value. Parsons was able to lease the house in 1942 from its new owner who was not unaware of what kind of man he was dealing with. Jack converted rooms into apartments and sought out unusual characters to rent them. A Fortune Teller and a cinema organist from the silent movie era were fairly typical types. A large upper room served as both Jack's own and a temple for the Agape Lodge of the OTO. Crowley's Gnostic Mass was regularly celebrated and ongoing serious magickal work undertaken.

Whilst the sixties rock deities came into incarnation and the death camps got into full production the Parsonage became the centre of an extraordinary social scene where the different aspects of Jack's life converged. He was the successful rocket fuel innovator, having helped the Allied cause with his major contribution to the development of JATO (Jet Assisted Take Off) involving fuel canisters which could be attached to conventional planes to give them a boost during take-off that reduced the length of runway needed. This led to him associating with various characters in the defence industry and the inevitability of having an FBI file. Science Fiction was understandably a favoured form of literature for many in the field. Parsons attended and later hosted gatherings of figures from the Golden Age of early sci-fi including Robert Henlein, Ray Bradbury and A. E. van Vogt. Crowley, whose literary tastes were formed at Cambridge University during the eighteen-nineties was critical of Parsons' reading in this respect. Jack became the leading figure of the Agape Lodge and was likewise playing host to their meetings. He made considerable financial contributions to the cause and to Crowley personally during this period.

Wild parties became the norm where people from these different areas might meet. Parsons liked to recite *Hymn to Pan*. There was dancing around bonfires in scenarios that often had a definite pagan ritualistic ambiance. It was a booze, sex, and drugs scene in the era before rock 'n' roll. Inevitably the neighbours noticed. All kinds of rumours circulated. The police were often called. Parsons' status in the war effort was just about enough to prevent trouble.

ENTER LRH

A crucial turning point came in August 1945 with the arrival of L. Ron Hubbard at the Parsonage. Ron has achieved the considerable feat of surpassing Crowley in the legend of infamy stakes and has become the recipient of more vitriolic hatred on the internet than has been directed at some genocidal dictators. The mere mention of his name seems to press people's buttons to a remarkable extent. He is, of course, responsible for founding the new religion of

Scientology, an enterprise more successful in the material realms than anything Crowley was ever able to manifest. An appendix will deal more specifically with the mystery of his role in the events that followed. It is sufficient to say here that, unlike virtually every writer who has tackled the subject of the legendary Babalon Working, I am not a Ron hater.

In late 1945 Hubbard had an already spectacular CV. He had been a successful writer of pulp fiction whilst still in his twenties during the nineteen-thirties. He hung around on the edge of the Hollywood scene and moved into the fledgling genre of Science Fiction. He had been a daredevil glider pilot, travelled widely, becoming a member of the Explorers Club, and served in the navy during the war. An intense interest in the magical and mysterious had been present in him from a young age. This much is agreed upon by even his most hostile biographers.

Ron became the centre of attention from the moment he first appeared at the Parsonage, dominating the scene with his story telling and general charisma. Some felt his ripping yarns were too good to be true. People were generally extremely polarised in their response to him. He and Jack soon settled into an intense interaction. Hubbard spoke of some kind of higher intelligence he called the Empress that he believed himself to be in touch with. Jack felt this to be a kind of Holy Guardian Angel. Parsons libertarian principles were soon severely tested. He believed in free love and encouraged his partner to not be hung up about monogamy. When Ron became intimate with her within weeks of arrival this messed him up considerably. Nonetheless Parsons wrote to the aging Crowley, praising Ron as *'the most Thelemic person I have ever met'*.

THE HOLY WHORE

Pondering on the nature of the Aeon of Horus, Parsons concluded that,

> *'This force is completely blind depending upon the men and women in whom it manifests and who guide it. Obviously it's guidance now tends towards catastrophe. The catastrophic trend is due to our lack of understanding of our own natures. The hidden lusts fears and hatreds resulting from the warping of the love urge which underlie the natures of all Western peoples have taken a homicidal and suicidal direction. This impasse is broken by the incarnation of*

another sort of force called BABALON. The nature of this force relates to love understanding and Dionysian freedom and is the necessary counterbalance or correspondence to the manifestation of Horus.'

In *The Book of the Law* Ch1,V22, it is written, '*I am known to ye by my name Nuit, and to him by a secret name which I will give him when at last he knoweth me.*' The secret name was later revealed by Crowley as Babalon. The difference in spelling to the usual "Babylon" was Qabalistic. Crowley's version adds up to 156. The name of the ancient city meant "Gate of the Sun". The most important entrance into Babylon was named after their major Goddess, Ishtar. Babalon can be understood as a channel of solar force through her gate in sexual terms. She could be considered to be the true form of the archetype later corrupted in the mass mind by the Christian Whore of Babylon from the *Book of Revelation.*

In many ancient cultures, most famously the Babylonian, there was a form of sacred prostitution. The Hierodules, as they were known, were Priestesses of the Goddess. Ishtar was Goddess of love, sex, magic, war, and plenty else besides, in a time when it was accepted as perfectly natural that a woman could harmoniously embody all these things. Christianity has been responsible for a disastrous fragmentation over this. We can see it quite clearly in *Revelation* where the Whore is depicted as in conflicting opposition to the woman clothed with the sun, a Queen of Heaven type later identified with the Virgin Mary. The Babylonians could accept them as one and the same. Something of the esoteric tradition of the sacred hierodule has remained in eastern Tantric sects where a woman can be the vehicle of the force of the Shakti, the energy of the divine feminine. Crowley was attempting to restore this back into the western mysteries.

Parsons had an intense devotion to Babalon. He felt that this force needed to be brought into tangible manifestation. With L. Ron Hubbard available to help, a magical working to achieve that end was devised on Parsons' own initiative, primarily from OTO and AA (Crowley's other magickal order) material but with distinctive individual aspects. The idea was firstly to attract a woman of particular magickal elemental qualities who would then, in a further series of workings conceive a moonchild, a kind of babe of the aeon with a soul from beyond, a child to embody the new era of the baby boomers. A female messiah. Babalon incarnate.

The legendary *Babalon Working* began on January 4th 1946 to a soundtrack of Prokofiev's *Violin Concerto No 2*. A significant amount of the magical techniques used came from John Dee's Enochian system. Edward Kelly's psychism had brought through over an extended period of time detailed instructions for communicating with a previously unknown group of entities. It has been stated that the new language produced in the sessions is internally coherent in following the rules of language and for an individual to create such a corpus is virtually impossible.

Enochian magic was used by Crowley in one of the most famous magickal episodes of his whole career. He walked across the Algerian desert with his disciple and lover, the mystical poet Victor Neuberg in 1909, entering in a visionary state into a series of zones known as Aethyrs which form the geography of the Enochian realms. He experienced apocalyptic visions worthy of *Revelation* and performed a ritual to confront the mighty demon Choronzon, guardian of an Abyss that Crowley had pledged himself to cross. In purely Jungian terms it was a major encounter with the Shadow side of the psyche. Crowley believed that the process was successful. A number of critics have doubted this and wondered if he did irreparable damage to himself. Neuberg undoubtedly was traumatised for the rest of his life by what occurred. The full record is in Crowley's astounding *The Vision and the Voice*. Israel Regardie gives a good account in *The Eye in the Triangle*.

It was during this epic Enochian episode that Crowley first really encountered Babalon. She was what lay on the other side of the Abyss. A successful crossing necessitated complete surrender to her, symbolised as giving up ones blood into her chalice. A new state of Being, beyond the play of opposites, as a Master of the Temple awaited.

Crowley saw on one occasion a *'column of fire is dancing – the fire is but the skirt of the dancer, and the dancer is a mighty god.'* She said,

'I gather up every spirit that is pure, and weave him into my venture of flame. I lick up the lives of men, and their souls sparkle from mine eyes. I am the mighty sorceress, the lust of the spirit. And by my dancing I gather for my mother Nuit the heads of all them that are baptized in the waters of life. I am the lust of the spirit that eateth up the soul of man. I have prepared a feast for the adepts, and they that partake thereof shall see God.'

'This is the Mystery of Babalon, the Mother of Abominations, and this is the mystery of her adulteries, for she hath yielded up herself to everything that liveth, and hath become a partaker in its

mystery. And because she hath made her self the servant of each, therefore is she become the mistress of all.'

After the Babalon Working began, Enochian style invocations were performed on a daily basis. The full details are available on a number of web sites. John Carters' Parsons' biography *Sex and Rockets* gives a good summary. On Jan 18th Parsons and Hubbard went out into the Mojave Desert to complete the first sequence of ceremonies.

On their return red-haired, green-eyed Marjorie Cameron had arrived at the Parsons household. Many accounts of the Babalon Working tend to imply that she appeared unheralded and unknown at a spookily appropriate moment in the magickal proceedings. This is not entirely true.

Her family had moved to Pasadena at the war's end. There she met someone she had known in the navy who was living at the Parsonage and suggested she might be interested in checking out the *'mad scientist'* and the social scene around him. She visited in early January 1946 and briefly met Parsons, each registering strong resonance with each other. The date for this is unclear. It may have been after the Working had begun. One account clearly indicates that her credentials for inclusion were immediately recognised with Jack and Ron urgently demanding of her old navy friend that he get her back to the Parsonage.

Born in 1922 during a thunderstorm during which her father had attempted suicide in the mistaken belief that her mother was dying, from an early age Cameron had manifested a powerful individuality that led her to readily identify with the archetype of witch. Her red hair was enough to convince a devout grandmother of her infernal nature. She soon developed natural visionary abilities and an aptitude for art. At seventeen the suicide of a close friend prompted a number of attempts of her own which seemed to further develop her psychism.

During the war she served in the navy and was involved in drawing maps for military operations. She later came to feel a sense of talismanic sigil magic was involved that somehow connected her to soldiers that died as a result of their deployment in accordance with the plans she had been responsible for manifesting. At one point she briefly met Winston Churchill.

The timing of her return to the Parsonage was indeed perfect as was her willingness to immediately engage in what was essentially a sex magick marathon without any real idea of exactly what it was all about. It was only after the whole operation was completed that Parsons explained it to her.

Cameron appeared to exactly fit the requirements of a being capable of both embodying Babalon and conceiving an aeon babe. There is some confusion as to whether she was Babalon herself or simply a kind of elemental force that could birth her and therefore the child would be Babalon. Cameron herself eventually came to feel she was Babalon incarnate. Parsons wrote on a number of later occasions of the advent of Babalon still in the future tense.

The three protagonists got down to some intense magickal business. Hubbard served as the scryer, meaning that he used his developed faculties of psychic vision to commune with the forces invoked by their rituals.

On February 28th Jack went back out into the desert alone to invoke Babalon. The result was the transmission of *Liber 49*, which he considered to be a further chapter of *The Book of the Law*. Quite how he received it, whether through hearing a voice, or as automatic writing for example, is unclear. Considering his dedication to Thelema and Crowley personally it may seem surprising that he could have thought that the holy scripture could be in any way incomplete. His reasoning is interesting. The famous Hebrew name for God known as the Tetragrammaton has four letters usually rendered in English as YHVH. This has been the foundation of a vast amount of Qabalistic lore. The letters have been designated as symbolic of father, mother, son, and daughter. In Golden Dawn tarot teachings expounded by Crowley they are depicted by the King, Queen, Prince, and Princess cards. Parsons believed that the three chapters of *The Book of the Law* corresponded to YHV and that *Liber 49* completed the daughter H. This has not been generally accepted by Thelemites. Although *Liber 49* is a strange and powerful document it is not considered to be on anywhere near the level of inspiration of Crowley's text.

Returning from the desert he discovered that Ron had experienced a vision of '*a savage and beautiful woman riding naked on a cat like beast*' who wanted to deliver a message. This seemed very similar to the image of the *Lust* card from Crowley's Tarot deck that is a representation of Babalon. For those who think Ron was surely familiar with the imagery and therefore using his writer's imagination to make up suitable details, what followed, regardless of a *Vision and the Voice* flavour, and especially in the hindsight of events

occurring six years later, should give pause for thought.
Against a background soundtrack of Rachmaninoff's *Isle of the Dead*, ritual details emerged from Ron.

'She is flame of life, power of darkness, she destroys with a glance, she may take the soul. She feeds upon the death of men. Concentrate all force and being in our Lady Babalon. Light a single flame on her altar, saying Flame is our lady, flame her hair. I am flame.'
'Dedicate thy soul to her for she shall absorb thee and thou shalt become living flame before she incarnates.' He added, *'For it shall be through you alone and no one else can help in this endeavour. It is lonely, it is awful.'*

The *Vision and the Voice* had served as a foundation for the Babalon Working. Quotes from it were incorporated. The process also seemed to further form a link with the system's Elizabethan creators. Parsons and Hubbard were not exactly lightweights. Any weirdness arising between them was likely to be a bit intense. They got into a very strange space indeed that seemed to echo an episode from Dee and Kelly's life when they had indulged in a spot of wife-swapping at the behest of the Enochian angels whilst investigating a magical zone presided over by a distinctly Babalon-esque female. Cynics would suggest it was all down to the swindler Kelly indulging himself. Hubbard has generally been portrayed as a scoundrel after an episode involving a large sum of money and Parsons former partner. It's worth noting that in conversations with author Peter Moon towards the end of her life, Marjorie Cameron, who had later married Jack, expressed no ill-will towards Ron at all and recalled how the two men were like brothers.

Parsons kept Crowley informed of the working with a series of letters. The Beast became increasingly suspicious and ultimately flabbergasted by the unfolding tales. Other American followers were writing to him with considerable doubts about Hubbard and the clarity of Jack's thinking. Ultimately Crowley wrote Parsons off as a failure.

★ ★ ★

NAG HAMMADI PLASMATE

Alongside the big 1945 nuclear backdrop to the Babalon Working there is another evocative set of influences that we can again cross-reference with Jung for greater appreciation. By the end of the year, Hubbard had sufficiently impressed Parsons for him to lay plans for the rites which began in January 1946. In December 1945, one of the greatest ever discoveries of historical literature was made by a peasant at Nag Hammadi in Egypt. A stunning stash of Gnostic texts emerged including items which have since had major impact in the rehabilitation of Christianity's holy whore Mary Magdalene and studies of the divine feminine in the west in general. These works took decades to translate. Parsons would never have seen them. Following on from the initial general Gnostic revival that we have seen both Jung and Crowley expressing, this represented a major new impetus in the process so the timing, in conjunction with a major Thelemic event, is interesting.

A great visionary thinker had a unique take on Nag Hammadi. Philip K. Dick is best known as the sci-fi writer whose stories were made into the movies *Blade Runner* and *Total Recall*. In the mid-seventies he had an extended experience that could be seen as a breakdown or a breakthrough. One result was his classic novel *VALIS* in which he incorporated some of the details. A pink beam of light repeatedly manifested, seemingly downloading all kinds of data into his head. For a while first-century Rome became transposed with 1974 California. He felt himself to be in both with equal vividness simultaneously. In Rome he was an early Christian called Thomas. He could hear languages he couldn't speak but wrote down phonetically and were later identified as the Greek of the time. Very weird shit went down. He was given specific medical information concerning his young son and an undiagnosed potentially fatal condition that required immediate attention. The details were entirely correct and arrived in time to save the boys' life.

Dick wrote an 8,000 page document concerning his experiences. The major theme concerned the Gnostic Christians and their world-view. The world has been created by a crazy cruel deity and is essentially a prison. A higher level of divinity intervened in the form of Christ. *Living information* that Dick called the *plasmate*, and is generally known as the Holy Spirit, came into contact with human consciousness. When a recipient was suitably receptive the force could enter and crossbond, creating a hybrid *homoplasmate*.

Dick stated *'This annexes the mortal human permanently to the plasmate. We know this as the "birth from above" or "birth from the Spirit."' 'As living information, the plasmate travels up to the optic nerve of a human to the pineal body. It uses the human brain as a female host in which to replicate itself into its active form.'* The whole world could potentially be converted. This energy was the key to escape from the prison and achieve some kind of eternal life.

The emerging church establishment and the Roman authorities acted as antibodies for the body-politic and hunted down and destroyed any person or thing showing signs of the plasmate. The last remnant of the energy of living information was contained in the texts stashed at Nag Hammadi. In one sense real history stopped at that point. *'In dormant seed form, as living information, the plasmate slumbered in the buried library.'* When the material was rediscovered something was let loose into the world again.

It has been noted that the *meme* concept of Richard Dawkins has similarities to the plasmate. If ideas and their transmission are observed from the perspective of similarities to genetics fruitful comparisons can be made. Ideas replicate and mutate and sometimes die, depending on the vehicle of transmission and communication. Just as genes group together in chromosomes so memes cluster in a memeplex. The difference seems to be that the plasmate seems like an airborne virus that can work over a distance with no obvious route of transmission.

When the Egyptian shepherd Mohammed Ali Samman lifted the lid of the first jar full of manuscripts he discovered he was fearful it might contain some kind of evil spirit. Apparently a golden mist rose from within. In consensus 3D terms this was likely to be dust particles disturbed by the sudden rush of air. Dick felt differently. This was a sign of the plasmate stirring. It's an evocative idea to wonder what ripples may have been felt in California long before Dick's 1974 experiences?

Jack Parsons was particularly attuned to the Gnostic aspect of the Thelemic current. He was devoted to Crowley's Gnostic Mass. The Babalon Working made use of the Priest's call from that ceremony. This includes mentions of Abraxas and Mithras.

Jung personally played a role in ensuring that the pace of translating and disseminating the Nag Hammadi material was accelerated so that the kind of controversies that accompanied the same process with the Dead Sea Scrolls did not occur.

★ ★ ★

PERFECT MIND

Here are a few verses from *Liber 49*.

'*I am the Bride appointed. Come ye to the nuptials - come ye now!
My joy is the joy of eternity, and my laughter is the drunken
  laughter of a harlot in the house of ecstasy.
All your loves are sacred, pledge them all to me.*'

And a taster of Parsons' passionate poem, *The Birth of Babalon*.

'*She has clothed her beauty in robes of sin
and pledged her heart to swine
And loving and giving all she has
brewed for saints immortal wine.
But now the darkness is riven through
and the robes of sin are gone,
And naked she stands as a terrible blade
and a flame and a splendid song
Naked in radiant mortal flesh
at the Birth of BABALON.*

*And her whoredom is holy as virtue is foul
beneath the holy sky,
And her kisses will wanton the world away
in passion that shall not die.
Ye shall laugh and love and follow her dance
when the wrath of god is gone
And dream no more of hell and hate
in the Birth of BABALON.*'

The most notable Nag Hammadi material containing feminine spirituality is generally known as *Thunder: Perfect Mind*. It has become increasingly well known in recent years. Interesting comparisons can be made with the Abraxas of Jung and the Babalon mysticism of Crowley and particularly Parsons.

Here are a representative series of extracts from *Thunder*.

'*For I am the first and the last.
I am the honoured one and the scorned one.*

*I am the whore and the holy one.
I am the wife and the virgin.*

I am the silence that is incomprehensible.

*You who deny me, confess me,
and you who confess me, deny me.
You who tell the truth about me, lie about me,
and you who have lied about me, tell the truth
about me.*

*For I am knowledge and ignorance.
I am shame and boldness.
I am shameless; I am ashamed.
I am strength and I am fear.
I am war and peace.
Give heed to me.
I am the one who is disgraced and the great one.
Give heed to my poverty and my wealth.*

*But I, I am compassionate and I am cruel.
Be on your guard!*

*I am the one whom they call Life,
and you have called Death.
I am the one whom they call Law,
and you have called Lawlessness.*

*And take me to yourselves from places that are ugly
and in ruin,
I am the union and the dissolution.'*

Remember that Parsons and Hubbard ran into problems when thy entered an Enochian zone where the Elizabethan occultists had encountered a female force very reminiscent of Babalon. Edward Kelly described her appearance. *'All her attire is like beaten gold; she hath on her forehead a cross crystal, her neck and breast are bare unto under her dugs: she hath a girdle of beaten gold slackly buckled unto her with a pendant of gold down to the ground.'* Her words look rather extraordinary when placed alongside *Thunder* and the Babalon material.

'I am the daughter of Fortitude, and ravished every hour from my youth. For behold I am Understanding and science dwelleth in me; and the heavens oppress me. They cover and desire me with infinite appetite; for none that are earthly have embraced me, for I am shadowed with the Circle of the Stars and covered with the morning clouds. – My garments are from the beginning, and my dwelling place is in myself. – I am deflowered, yet a virgin; I sanctify and am not sanctified. – I am a harlot for such as ravish me, and a virgin with such as know me not.'

TANGENTIAL RIPPLES

So what was the result of this great magickal undertaking? It could easily seem that the Babalon Working was a failure. Cameron did not give birth to a moonchild. Kenneth Grant's concept of Tangential Magick may be useful here. Sometimes the consequences of a magical working do not appear to match the consciously intended outcome. In fact they may seem to have no obvious connection or even be so much at variance as to suggest major error or outright failure. Nonetheless, as the ripples spread out and time passes, it can be seen that the results are clearly connected with the magical impetus and, although the conscious ego couldn't initially see it, are in accordance with the True Will of the participants.

I believe that the Babalon Working was immensely powerful and has sent out ripples on many different levels ever since. Not long after its completion Parsons and his carnival crew had to vacate the mansion. It was soon demolished to make way for another building. A copy of *The Book of the Law* was found in the rubble. Marjorie Cameron later stated that the house remains in an astral realm as a permanent temple. It's almost as if the voltage generated by the magickal coming together of the uniquely powerful trio of Parsons, Hubbard, and Cameron was enough to blow the place to pieces. That was just the first ripple.

The connection with the return of a distinctive type of feminine spirituality, synchronous with the uncovering of *Thunder: Perfect Mind* and various Magdalene themed material at Nag Hammadi as part of a mysterious Gnostic revival is another. Further ripples will be explored in the rest of this work.

Towards the end of 1947 Parsons advised Cameron to go and

meet Crowley in England. He was sure that the Beast would finally understand and forgive when he met the extraordinary Scarlet Woman. A sad twist of magickal destiny determined that it was not to be. Cameron got as far as France and was preparing for the final part of the journey when she learnt that Crowley had just died.

BLACK PILGRIMAGE

Jack Parsons' Babalon odyssey had not yet finished. In the following years his material life went into a nosedive. His finances had been wrecked through Hubbard. Security clearance was revoked. At one point he was making ends meet by working in a petrol station. He and Cameron separated but were later reunited.

At Halloween 1948 another magickal intensive began. This led to some kind of dream experience where he encountered Babalon and was instructed to perform an astral working. It involved a

> 'Black Pilgrimage – into the night past accursed and desolate places and cyclopean ruins, and so came at last to the City of Chorazin. And there a great tower of Black Basalt was raised, that was part of a castle whose further battlements reeled over the gulf of stars.'

Chorazin is located in Israel near the Sea of Galilee. Its buildings were notably constructed of black basalt. The place is mentioned in the gospels of Matthew and Luke as somewhere Jesus had been rejected despite performing *"mighty works"*. As a result of this he cursed it. This led a few obscure writers to believe that the Antichrist would be born there. Parsons seemed to have found this idea in M. R. James's story *Count Magnus*. The phrase *'Black Pilgrimage'* had already featured in *Liber 49*. 'Yea, thou shalt take the black pilgrimage, but it will not be thou that returnest.' As if to fulfil such a prophecy, after the return from astral Chorazin, Parsons 'swore the Oath of the Abyss, having only the choice between madness, suicide, and that oath. – having passed the ordeal of 40 days I took the oath of a Magister Templi, even the Oath of Antichrist'.

It was during the Chorazin experience that Parsons came to believe that he had been the Gnostic Simon Magus in a past life. This controversial figure features briefly in the *Acts of the Apostles*. Other Christian apocryphal material expands on him considerably. He has come to be known as the "first heretic" and a rival to Christ, in a certain sense the first Antichrist figure, before *Revelation* had even been written. Simon flourished during the time of the Emperor Claudius and became honoured in Rome as a living deity with a statue erected in his honour. He had a female partner, a former prostitute named Helen. An elaborate mythology explained their interaction. God's first thought had been female. She created assorted angels and demigods who in turn created the Earth at her behest. They rebelled and imprisoned her in the material world. This led to a long series of incarnations, including that of Helen of Troy, during which this divine female was tortured and humiliated, until finally she became Helen the prostitute. Simon as God incarnate came to rescue her.

There are accounts of philosophical teachings, paranormal powers, and ultimately a fateful magical battle with the Apostle Peter in Rome in which, after levitating high into the air, Simon was dashed to the ground and horribly injured, retiring a spent force.

The followers of Simon and Helen apparently engaged in sexual rites involving sperm and menstrual blood. Although later Christian heretic busters were fond of attributing all kinds of controversial behaviour to their opponents it doesn't seem that unlikely. G. R. S. Mead had produced an essay on Simon published by the Theosophical Society in 1892 containing such allegations. I'm inclined to feel that Parsons could have been familiar with it prior to the Babalon Working and it may have helped inspire some of the details that most definitely did involve such Tantric substances. The final identification with Simon Magus was possibly the culmination of a long process.

If these ideas seem a tad odd, they're not unique. Another Gnostic text, known as Pistis Sophia and published during the nineteenth century, has Jesus coming to rescue Sophia, who is linked with Mary Magdalene.

In some brief fragments on Gnosticism included in *Freedom is a Two-Edged Sword* Parsons wrote that

'The Holy Ghost is the feminine counterpart of Christ – the Sophia. God is manifest in the union of Christ and Sophia.' 'Let us celebrate in singing and in dancing, in friendship and in lovemaking, and in all manner of joyous and bountiful and beautiful things that are fitting to the love and worship of God, who made all things. Let us put away fear and envy and hatred and intolerance and all thought of guilt and sin out of our hearts, that we may worthily *celebrate our brotherhood in joy and love. In the name of Christ, that is the Son of God, and of Sophia, that is the Daughter of God, and of their union that is God, Amen.' 'Formal Christianity has distorted, perverted, and misinterpreted the teachings of Christ. Mankind can only find happiness by rejecting the false doctrines of sin, guilt, fear, hatred and intolerance: and in accepting the gospels of Love.'*

It is in the context of such sensibilities that Parsons Antichrist material must be assessed. Much has been made of him deliberately taking on the role and vowing to spread the Law of Thelema throughout the world in the name of the Beast 666. Despite Israel and Chorazin and a general *Revelation* ambiance we're not talking about an *Omen* movie here. A brief sample of his *Manifesto of the Antichrist* may hopefully restore some perspective.

'An end to the pretence, and lying hypocrisy of Christianity.
An end to the servile virtues, and superstitious restrictions.
An end to the slave morality.
An end to prudery and shame, to guilt and sin, for these are of
  the only evil under the sun, that is fear.
An end to all authority that is not based on courage and
  manhood, to the authority of lying priests, conniving judges,
  blackmailing police, and
An end to the servile flattery and cajolery of mobs, the
  coronations of mediocrities, the ascension of dolts.
An end to conscription, compulsion, regimentation, and the
  tyranny of false laws.'

Babalon is attributed to the Qabalistic sphere of Binah. Sophia, the principle of Wisdom is appropriate to Chokmah. Both spheres are above the Abyss. This is very much in keeping with the concept that the first thought of God was female. The current form of the Qabalah does seem to owe something to the climate of the Gnostic era. It's interesting to look back on the Babalon Working with such information. It further adds to the feeling of the powerful Gnostic theme present throughout.

Hubbard's *"flame of life"* became eerily prophetic when on June 17th 1952 Jack Parsons was killed in an explosion in his home by some of the alchemical substances he had worked with. It appears to have been a bizarre accident although it is inevitable that when such a man dies in dramatic circumstances conspiracy theories arise. His was a truly extraordinary life. One of his last poems had these lines:

> '*Go free, star, go free*
> *Seek the dark home*
> *On the wild sky*
> *Good bye, star, good bye.*'

Marjorie Cameron (who referred to herself by her surname only) went on to walk a suitably unusual unique personal path slightly off the consensus radar. She memorably appeared in Thelemic film-maker Kenneth Anger's *Inauguration of the Pleasure Dome* in 1954, of which more later. On the underground film circuit she met the young Dennis Hopper. Not one to do things by halves, she married Sherif Kimmel, a man of intensely varying mental states. Over the years Cameron developed a strong reputation as artist and powerful witch woman, before dying in 1995.

Although no physical child resulted from the Babalon Working, magical lore suggests that all such activities produce a child on the inner plane. If such a higher dimensional Aeon baby had been brought into being, it would have reached it's coming of age in 1967. Cameron later went on to say that she felt that the sixties hippies were in some sense her children.

In 1950 an event occurred that Jung noted as a significant moment in the collective unconscious. The Catholic Church's attitude to the Virgin Mary has always been intriguing. The gradual increase in her official status has been a response to grass roots impetus, to spontaneous devotion that could not be ignored. To some observers it had seemed as if the Church had wanted to keep her earthbound in sorrow. Mary's seven sorrows were like Innana/Ishtars seven levelled ordeal in the underworld. Stories that Mary had not died in the usual way but been taken bodily into heaven had been circulating since the last days of the Roman Empire. In 1950 following the presentation of an immense petition it was finally made doctrine. This may have been helped by the spectacular Fatima event of 1917 and the sense that it might be actually encouraging the *Revelation* End Times to manifest. Now the underworld ordeal was officially transcended. Mary, and with her the whole archetype she'd absorbed, were restored as Queen of Heaven, as Nuit.

The fifties began. An apocalyptic generation had been born into a new reality. Unknown objects were seen in the sky. Babalon the Scarlet Woman Gate of the Sun and Mary, the woman clothed with the sun, had taken up their positions in the heavens as per the *Book of Revelation*.

THE REBIRTH OF WITCHCRAFT

> *'We are the Witchcraft. We are the oldest organisation in the world. When man was born, we were. We sang the first cradle song. We healed the first wound, we comforted the first terror. We were the Guardians against the Darkness, the Helpers on the Left Hand Side.'*
>
> Jack Parsons. *The Witchcraft.*

THE FIFTIES seem at first glance to have been the most monochrome and miserable of decades. Future historians will obviously highlight the Cold War as the predominant theme that dictated the flavour of pretty much everything else. Nonetheless it might be argued that the arrival of rock music was an event of gigantic cultural import providing a catalyst for incredible rapid change. The fifties also saw the full manifestation of the uniquely bizarre UFO phenomenon, of which plenty more later. Complementing these two Thelemic war engines was the rebirth of witchcraft. The level of Crowley and Jack Parsons involvement is an ongoing controversy. A double-take soon makes it clear that in fact the fifties were a damned strange decade indeed.

I get a strong feeling that witchcraft was hanging in the airwaves waiting to happen in accordance with a special timescale and a number of things were set up in readiness. In the section *Modern Pagan Witchcraft* by Ronald Hutton in Volume 6 of the *Athlone History of Witchcraft and Magic in Europe* a wealth of detail shows how many of the characteristic elements were present in the nineteenth century, expressed through poets and folklorists alongside the widespread existence of secret societies of various kinds who took structural inspiration from Freemasonry. I am not going to cover such extensive ground but will selectively focus on particularly striking influences present during Crowley's lifetime that went with his own work into the alchemical cauldron that produced the unique magnificent blend that is Wicca.

THE SABBATH OF THE GOAT

'Come, O come!
I am numb
With the lonely lust of devildom.
Thrust the sword through the galling fetter,
All devourer, all begetter;
Give me the sign of the Open Eye
And the token erect of thorny thigh
And the word of madness and mystery.'

Aleister Crowley. Hymn to Pan.

'Io Io Io IAO Sabao Lord Abrasax Lord Meithras Lord Phallos, Io Pan Io Pan Io Mighty One, Io Deathless One, Io immortal One, Io IAO. Hail Phallus, Hail All-Devourer, Hail All-Begetter. Holy, Holy, Holy, IAO.'

Aleister Crowley. The Gnostic Mass.

Modern witchcraft venerates a male and female polarity of god and goddess embodied by the priest and priestess. The nature of the forces invoked is controversial. We have already pondered links between Babalon and the general return of the divine feminine. This theme will be expanded later in connection with the witch goddess. It is time now to look at the complementary force.

During the Middle Ages witches were accused of worshipping the Christian devil and died in large numbers on that basis. The standard iconography of horns and cloven hooves substantially derives from the Greek goat-footed Pan, wildly lustful fertility god of shepherds and their flocks, groves, untamed landscapes, hunting, and haunting rustic music. Some mystics during the classical and later Renaissance eras, inspired by the same kind of syncretism that lay behind the blending of Abraxas, Mithras and co, believed that he was a notable cosmic force. Pan and Dionysus sat quite well together. During the nineteenth century, inspired by the Romantic poets' love of nature and an increasing appreciation of the classical era, Pan became popular again. By the Fin de Siecle era he was the subject of innumerable poems.

Here is another immense archetype that returned to consciousness as the New Aeon began, one that both Crowley and Parsons were devoted to, and known today to witches and pagans in general as the Horned God. Pan powerfully embodies a form of the divine masculine as equally intimidating to those fearful of the flow of life as the sacred whore. There are definite similarities between Pan, Wotan, and Abraxas. They are all associated with a wildness that has a hint of danger, unpredictability, a blurring of the usual boundaries between light and darkness. Pan could give inspiration, rapture, and also fear and madness. The word *panic* has passed in to the English language as a token of this. William Blake's famous statement that '*the lust of the goat is the bounty of god*' shows how Pan could easily become an icon for those who were excited by the territory mapped out by Freud.

For all of the obvious significance of Egyptian deities in his life, Crowley is often remembered for his devotion to Pan. In the masterwork *Magick* it is the *Hymn to Pan*, his best-known poem, which takes pride of place in the introductory section rather than any invocation to Horus. The *Thoth* tarot deck has a devil image that is thoroughly goatish and deliberately allusive to Pan. One of the most widely circulated photos of Crowley shows him sitting at a table with raised hands that have the thumbs deliberately facing out and up to signify the horns of Pan. Jack Parsons' party-piece was the passionate recital of the *Hymn to Pan*. For all the playfulness, this was a sign of a deep devotion.

Other occultists such as Dion Fortune with her novel *The Goat Foot God* and Arthur Machen with *The Great God Pan* gave fine expression to his inspirational and disturbing character. Victor Neuberg published a volume of poetry *The Triumph of Pan* not long after the epic events in the Algerian desert which had included him taking the role of Pan in an act of homosexual magick with Crowley. It was probably the Beast and Parsons though who gave over most completely to the force.

The mystical understanding the two men came to was not unlike some of the Hindu realisations inspired by their archaic god Shiva who has many points of connection to the western horned god. In some etymologies Pan means *All*. This may not reflect the true origin of the name but it suited Crowley's purpose, enabling him to characterise Pan as thereby both creator and destroyer. The dance of Shiva simultaneously creates and destroys the universe.

The *"Night of Pan"* was a topic of considerable importance in Thelemic mysticism. Pan was linked with Babalon in *The Vision and the Voice* in a way that was later given further expression in *The Book of Lies* that featured the succinct formula *'PAN: Duality: Energy: Death'*. As part of the process of crossing the Abyss and experiencing a death of the ego by giving up one's blood into the chalice of Babalon, the male adept becomes a babe in her womb, impregnated by Pan waiting to be born on the other side of the Abyss. This darkness, which is ultimately supremely fertile, is the Night of Pan. The panic arises from the necessary dissolution of ones' previous sense of identity which may come about in an entirely uncomfortable manner.

Crowley wrote of a mystical formula for this process that he called NOX, which is a Latin word which if it is generally known at all is in reference to a classical goddess of the night known as Nyx in Greek. Crowley used the component letters to weave his usual Qabalistic explanations, writing in *The Book of Lies 'NOX adds to 210, which symbolizes the reduction of duality to unity, and thence to negativity, and is thus a hieroglyph of the Great Work.'* Jack Parsons magickal motto was a phrase *"Thelema Obtentum Procedero Amoris Nuptiae" TOPAN*. This indicates his feeling of the central importance of Love under Will. The initials rendered into Hebrew added to 210 which enabled the NOX formula to be incorporated. This high mysticism of Pan can serve as an inspiration to all who have heard the call of the piper at the gates of dawn regardless of their opinion of Crowley in general.

THE GOLDEN BOUGH

'No poet can hope to understand the nature of poetry unless he has had a vision of the Naked King crucified to the lopped oak and watched the dancers, red-eyed from the acrid smoke of the sacrificial fires, stamping out the measure of the dance, their bodies bent uncouthly forward, with a monotonous chant of "kill, kill, kill" and "blood, blood, blood"!'

Robert Graves. *The White Goddess.*

A good starting point for a consideration of the wider cultural background that helped prepare the necessary conditions for the rebirth of witchcraft is J. G. Frazer's *The Golden Bough*. This *'Study in magic and religion'* was greatly helped by its author being a brilliant writer. It inspired many readers to, in Ouspensky's phrase, '*think in other categories*', opening up a whole new world of potential meaning in myth, folklore, and ancient religion. A number of unusual thinkers produced extraordinary works of their own after absorbing its material.

Frazer's initial background was in classical studies. He became fascinated by a puzzling custom from the Roman era. On the northern shore of Lake Nemi in Italy lay a grove sanctuary of Diana of the Wood. She was thought of there as a fertility-bestowing huntress. Flaming torches decorated her shrine during her mid-August feast. At the grove's centre was a special tree. A figure known as the King of the Wood kept guard around it with a drawn sword in as perpetual a vigil as he could manage. At any hour of the day or night a runaway slave might appear and try to break a branch off the sacred tree. This would entitle him to challenge the incumbent in a fight to the death for the title. This was how the succession was passed on.

In the manner of a typical Victorian encyclopaedist, vast amounts of data from the world's religious history and folklore, alongside contemporary material, was gathered to elucidate Frazer's explanation of the mystery. The first version of *The Golden Bough* was published in 1890. It would eventually extend to a dozen volumes. A nine-hundred page abridgement published in 1922 achieved wide circulation.

The fundamental fact of life to early cultures was the seasons. Good hunting and a good harvest were essential. Without them catastrophe was never far away. The most basic issue that religious beliefs had to face were how to understand the forces involved and somehow placate them.

According to Frazer, the sun which ensures a good harvest and fertilises the earth became focused in the figure of the king. A kind of vegetation deity lived within him. He and the land were one. If he were healthy and virile the land would thrive. When he waned the land would suffer, so the simple answer was to ritually kill him when he started to droop a bit and get some young stud instated in his place. The land is the goddess, his consort. The seasonal festivals are the story of the birth of the sun god and his battle with the old sun, his marriage to the land, and his inevitable demise, only to be reborn. The religions of ancient Babylon, Egypt, Greece and Rome, the mystery cults, all tell this story to some degree with dying and reborn gods. Christianity's early success was helped by its incorporation of some of these themes.

An early example of Frazer's influence was Freud's 1910 *Totem and Taboo* which began with the words famously translated into English as *'In the beginning was the deed'*. Freud dragged his own obsession with the Oedipus Complex back to the Stone Age using *The Golden Bough* to back him up.

Crowley was inspired to produce *Golden Twigs*, a collection of short stories dating from 1918 during his stay in America. It included a charming tale of a modern cult devoted to the formidable goddess Cybele, whose most noteworthy form of worship involved male devotees working themselves up into a total frenzy that climaxed with self-castration and the flinging of the offending items onto a ritual fire. This particular practice has been thankfully largely absent from the subsequent pagan revival.

Arthurian scholar Jessie Weston was reminded of the recurring theme of the wasteland in the medieval Grail tales. The important figure of the Fisher King seems to be a Frazerian monarch in decline. When the questing knight Perceval finds him in his castle he is languishing with a mysterious wounding through the thighs that is often taken as a euphemism for impotence. His whole kingdom suffers with him. In *From Ritual to Romance*, published in 1920, she argued that romance literature derived from myth, and because Frazer believed that myth derived from ritual, the stories could have some kind of foundation in ancient ritual. There may have been a direct continuity linking ancient fertility rites with the Grail romances.

Weston's theories don't have much credibility amongst Arthurian scholars today but their cultural impact has been strong. T. S. Eliot's *The Wasteland* was one of the most significant poems of the twentieth century. Its structure was shaped by *From Ritual to Romance*. My own favourite movie, *Apocalypse Now*, has many levels of narrative. Hints of its depths come when Colonel Kurtz's book collection is shown to contain Weston. He himself is a Fisher King figure in the midst of a wasteland, and knows it. The "King and the land are one" theme was also used to great effect in John Boorman's *Excalibur*.

ARADIA

A work that was little noticed when it was first published in 1899 would prove to be of immense significance in the modern re-imagining of witchcraft. *Aradia, or the Gospel of the Witches* by Charles

Godfrey Leland is one of those outstanding works that inspire and divide people, exerting fascination and irritation on a long-term basis and thereby demonstrating they have a peculiar quality that transcends the usual criteria of credibility. When dealing with the rebirth of witchcraft we shall encounter a number of similarly controversial items.

Leland was an American folklorist who had spent a long time in Italy investigating traditions that supposedly dated from before the Romans. He claimed to have discovered a living cult of witchcraft dating from the classical era via the Christian Middle Ages and reflecting its influence. His information was provided by a woman he referred to as Maddalena. She made available to him extensive material including a manuscript that was a kind of sacred book of the local witches.

Leland used the text and his own research to outline a kind of cosmology of the group and the magic it employed. The Queen of the Witches was the Roman goddess Diana, generally associated with hunting and the moon, who is portrayed as a more universal force who divided herself into light and dark. The light was her son and brother Lucifer. When Diana saw his beauty she yearned to be reunited with him. This led to the bizarre scenario of her descending to earth and taking the form of his cat in order to gain access to his bed and then seduce him. Thus was a witch saviouress named Aradia conceived.

She came to live amongst medieval peasants to teach magical practices to help them resist the oppression of the church and feudal system. The earliest witches were escaped slaves. Her help proved so successful that there remained in the late nineteenth century entire villages where the cult was predominant.

Leland considered it notable that regardless of the powerful figure of Lucifer, the fundamental source of the witches' power and indeed the whole cosmos was the great goddess Diana. It's certainly true that she became considerably revered in the classical world. St Paul had a major task at her cult centre in Ephesus to establish his church. The subsequent triumph of the Virgin Mary cult needed to assimilate Diana and Ephesus into its mythology before she could be theologically proclaimed there as Mother of God.

Most of *Aradia* consists of the details of assorted spells and rituals for the usual sort of thing such as winning the love of a desired person and what was needed for a feast dedicated to Diana. It's not a big surprise that most of *Aradia* has been doubted and denigrated. The most extreme interpretation holds that Leland invented the whole thing.

Half a century after its publication one particular passage from *Aradia* went on to achieve a circulation and influence that Leland could probably never have anticipated. Included in the text were some poetic words that served as a message and instruction for the witches from their Queen. Part of the sequence stated:

> '*And as the sign that ye are truly free,*
> *Ye shall be naked in your rites, both men*
> *And women also: this shall last until*
> *The last of your oppressors shall be dead.*'

THE MARGARET MURRAY CONTROVERSY

We come directly from Frazer to witchcraft with the case of Egyptologist Margaret Murray. When staying at the Chalice Well, Glastonbury's cauldron of Morgan, in 1915, she became involved in a conversation concerning the idea that the witch cult suggested by the medieval trials was an authentic pagan survival. This was not an entirely new idea and it is not out of the question that Murray, who was also a member of the Folk Lore Society, might have heard it before but something about the timing and her preparedness produced a powerful inspiration to investigate it further.

From that starting point she developed the hypothesis featured in her first book on the subject *The Witch Cult in Western Europe*, published in 1921. The stories of the devil appearing at witch gatherings were distorted by people who either didn't want the truth to be known or didn't actually know it. It wasn't really the devil but a man with antlers on his head wearing a costume. He was a representative of a principle in nature, perhaps best remembered through Pan, acknowledged as far back as the Stone Age where depictions of shamans wearing antlers were painted on cave walls. This figure is not simply the Christian devil and the forms of devotion to the ancient practices were not deliberate parodies or blasphemies of the church. The whole thing was a fertility cult. This may not seem too startling a proposition today but in Murray's time it was scarcely believed that witches had ever existed at all because of the way the trials had been written up full of outlandish paranormal events.

Murray linked these ideas with *The Golden Bough*. The goddess who seemed to be most mentioned in the records of European witchcraft was Diana whose cult was Frazer's starting point. Murray attached more significance to the horned god who is a fertility figure like Frazer's central protagonist the divine king, expounding on the topic in *The God of the Witches*. She also stated that beliefs concerning him, his link to the fertility of the land and the laws concerning his sacrifice were held by the monarchs of Britain during the Middle Ages. William II, supposedly a notorious pagan, was a willing sacrifice, dying at the time of the great August Lammas festival so the land would thrive. The famous death of Thomas Becket was as a willing substitute victim for Henry II.

Perhaps Murray's most evocative idea was her treatment of the Robin Hood stories. She stated that in the records of the trials the head of many a group was known as Robin or some slight variant. He wore a hood. Marian also appeared and amongst the revellers at the witch gatherings was often a defrocked or heretic priest. Murray concluded that Robin Hood was not a name but a title. Marian was the Priestess. The Greenwood gatherings were witch cult meetings. Friar Tuck was the defrocked priest. The whole amalgam of diverse legends which eventually formed around Robin contained a series of folk memories of the old religion.

This concept eventually manifested in popular culture with the eighties *Robin of Sherwood* TV series. Main writer Richard Carpenter depicted Robin as horned god Herne the Hunter's son. In the light of solar reason this may be historically total rubbish but it is incredibly evocative stuff and to plenty of people stirs deep feelings of recognition. In some sense, in our emotions, in the collective mind, it is true and therefore these are ideas to work with.

Such is the case with the whole of Frazer's work and the people such as Jessie Weston and Margaret Murray who he inspired. Frazer was considered to be a social anthropologist but he was very much of the old school and his approach has zero credibility today. All of his data was gathered from an armchair through endless reading and wide correspondence with far-flung missionaries and such-like. The idea of field work, going and living with one of the tribes he wrote about, learning their language and engaging in their customs, would never have occurred to him. His fundamental concept of the widespread killing of the divine king has few believers today.

Margaret Murray seemed to have academic respectability for a while. Her ideas on the medieval monarchs were never likely to gain consensus adherence but her basic conception of the true nature of witchcraft was widely accepted. Successive editions of the *Encyclopaedia Britannica* carried an article by her on the subject. There were some rumblings of discontent however. Eventually a real intellectual heavyweight came along to put the boot in.

Norman Cohn's most famous work, *The Pursuit of the Millennium*, detailed religious and social upheaval in the European Middle Ages inspired by the *Book of Revelation*. It's an astounding work, full of barking-mad crusading utopian visionaries and the bloodbaths surrounding their bizarre careers. He also investigated Anti-Semitism from the starting point of the infamous *Protocols of the Elders of Zion*. This forged work was widely circulated at the start of the twentieth century in Russia, and later in Nazi Germany. It purported to reveal an international Jewish conspiracy aimed at world domination. With *Europe's Inner Demons*, Cohn turned his attention to the witch trial mania. He noted continuity with discoveries in his earlier studies.

Throughout European history, groups of people have been vilified and demonised. They are often accused of strangely similar crimes. The earliest Christians were believed to indulge in the grossest of orgies. They were supposedly cannibals with a particular taste for babies. They had no respect for the existing social status quo and were happy to see it collapse. Some sought to actively encourage the process. Once Christianity triumphed, the Jews came to be considered guilty of the same kind of activities along with various heretics. The witch-burning era saw the whole syndrome in its most extreme form. Cohn argued that, because the early Christians and Jews were never guilty of any such non-existent crimes, we should look very carefully at the witch trials as well.

Europe's Inner Demons systematically trashed Margaret Murray's work. It was very clear that her use of source material was selective, biased, and distorted to such an enormous extent that it left her hypothesis ruined, at least as far as the way she had presented it. Cohn came to believe that because what was said against the Jews and Christians was untrue the accusations in the witch trials were untrue and there were no real witches. That last part of the argument doesn't seem to hang together. That the accusations were untrue doesn't mean that some of the people being accused didn't exist as followers of some practices that didn't conform to the social norm. The Jews and early Christians obviously existed as deviators from the consensus even if the virulent mythologies used against them were corrupt.

The great theorist of comparative religion Mircea Eliade presented other possibilities. There's a kind of checklist that witch-busting inquisitors would tick off that featured a fairly standard catalogue of crimes. Orgies, incest, human sacrifices, cannibalism, consumption of bodily fluids and waste, were all taboo breaking behaviour. Cohn showed that the early Christians were accused of exactly the same stuff and went on to shift it on to the heretics and later witches. In his essay *Observations on European Witchcraft*, Eliade turned his attention to the Tantric cults of the east, often devoted to Shiva, and discovered a whole bunch of *'eccentric Indian sectarians'* who were actually quite happy to boast of engaging in the full gamut of such behaviour, often because they actually did. He looked at the early Gnostics and the medieval witches and saw notable similarities. The possibility of some level of direct connection between such disparate groups is raised. It is not absolutely out of the question and gives endless scope for fear-filled evangelicals to indulge their Satanic paranoia. The horned god of the witches and Shiva have presided over the riotous Sabbath of the collective imagination in both dreams and reality.

Medieval witchcraft is a vast study and perspectives regularly change. Certain aspects of Murray's work concerning the persistence of archaic magical folklore practices look better today when removed from the context of her faulty methodology. It seems possible that the pressures of the inquisition warped out some of the adherents of fertility practices until they did indeed became hostile sorcerers. Sufficient to say it's a field full of controversies and strongly held opinions. Nothing is set in stone although some might pontificate as if it is.

I am very aware that Frazer, Jessie Weston, and Margaret Murray have more credibility in terms of how they have inspired artists, writers, occultists, and mystics rather than academics. I reiterate: these ideas affect some people very deeply. They inspire extraordinary outbursts of strange creativity in a liminal zone where their power demonstrates how in some way they do contain truth, vital truths that feed the imagination and spirit. With such an attitude established we can better approach perhaps the most spectacular of all the Frazer influenced works.

★ ★ ★

THE WHITE GODDESS

Robert Graves was a poet and novelist. He is best known as the author of *I Claudius* but it may well be *The White Goddess* that is his most important work. The story of how it came to be written and published is a strange one that can be profitably placed alongside the 1904 events in Cairo and other cases of illumination we have noted. Comparing and contrasting Graves with the racist patriarchal case of Guido von List could be a whole study on its own. It backs up the idea that something deep in the collective mind was trying to re-emerge.

Graves was living in Devonshire during the Second World War and in the process of completing a novel about Jason and the Argonauts by matching their mythic journey against a map of locations associated with it. On his desk at the time was a small brass box with a design on the lid. On the box was a figure of a humpbacked man playing a flute. Ten years later these items came to seem like potent signs of what was to come when he discovered that the design on the box was the African triple moon goddess Ngame and the flute player a herald of a Queen mother of an African state who claimed direct descent from her.

Graves found himself suddenly massively sidetracked from his Argonaut map. He'd been reading a nineteenth century edition of the *Mabinogion* translated by Lady Charlotte Guest, a work much read by the Pre-Raphaelites. It's a collection of early medieval Welsh tales full of undoubtedly earlier themes and material that find their way into the later Arthurian sagas. This version contained the *Song of Taliesin* which is not really part of the corpus and now generally published separately. Its strange style has become relatively well-known.

> 'I have been in many shapes before I attained a congenial form –
> I have been a drop in the air, I have been a shining star –
> Enchanted for a year
> in the foam of water
> I have been a poker in the fire –'

And so on.

Nobody knew what all this stuff was about and people are still arguing now. The nature of the language made it the domain of nutters, mainly Druidic types, to work out the most obscure interpretations possible.

Graves suddenly knew that the work was a series of riddles which he, although not a Welsh scholar or medievalist, knew the answer to. He also knew that it was linked with a Welsh tradition of a Battle of the Trees occasioned by a lapwing, dog, and roebuck from the other world and won by a god who had to guess the name of his opponent.

What he believed he'd uncovered in the tree battle were the letter names of an ancient Druid alphabet. Linking this with the Taliesin material he believed it was possible to work out a story of a struggle between two rival priesthoods in Britain for control of national learning. According to Graves the Druids had used a tree alphabet which also served as a calendar. The vowels stood for equinoxes and solstices and it was all associated with the worship of a triple moon goddess.

This whole thing Graves described as *'a sudden overwhelming obsession'*. In three weeks he had written a 70,000 word book which he was calling *The Roebuck in the Thicket*. It didn't stop there.

After the war was over he returned to his main home in Majorca. An antiquarian neighbour had died and left a few bits and pieces to Graves. One was a mummy like figure with a single eye which was later discovered to be an African Okrafo priest, a substitute sacrifice to the White Goddess. A carnelian ring given to Graves by a friend who knew nothing of his current interests had a seal showing a stag, a moon, and a thicket. He discovered that they had been clan totems in the Argonauts saga. Ngame's group had moved to Nigeria across the Sahara from Libya and were racially linked to the early Athenians, Jason's people. The synchronicities went on and on. Eventually it all coalesced as *The White Goddess*, published in 1948.

The White Goddess has been criticised as a work of historical scholarship. I am more concerned with it's analysis of how myth is conveyed by artists and why we respond to some forms of art in a different way to others. Graves drew the distinction between "muse" poetry and (to him) purely intellectual "classical" poetry. Dionysian and Apollonian as Nietzsche would have it. To Graves, Muse material is the only genuine manifestation of poetry and its production is the true test of a poet's inspiration. He asserts that there is only one real subject for poetry.

'The theme briefly, is the antique story, which falls into thirteen chapters and an epilogue, of the birth, life, death and resurrection of the God of the waxing year; the central chapters concern the God's losing battle with the God of the waning year for love of the capricious and all-powerful Threefold Goddess, their mother, bride and layer out. The poet identifies himself with the God of the waxing year and his muse with the Goddess – All true poetry – celebrates some incident or scene in this very ancient story – the main characters are so much a part of our racial inheritance that they not only assert themselves in poetry but recur on occasions of emotional stress in the form of dreams – The Goddess is a lovely, slender woman with a hooked nose, deathly pale face, lips red as rowan berries, startlingly blue eyes and long fair hair; she will suddenly transform herself into sow, mare, bitch, vixen, She-ass, weasel, serpent, owl, she-wolf, tigress, mermaid or loathsome hag. Her names and titles are innumerable. In ghost stories she often figures as "The White Lady" and in ancient religions from the British Isles to the Caucasus, as the "White Goddess" – The test of a poet's vision, one might say, is the accuracy of his portrayal of the White Goddess – The reason why the hairs stand on end, the eyes water, the throat is constricted, the skin crawls and a shiver runs down the spine when one writes or reads a true poem is that a true poem is necessarily an invocation of the White Goddess – Sometimes, in reading a poem, the hairs will bristle at an apparently unpeopled and eventless scene described in it, if the elements bespeak her unseen presence clearly enough: for example, when owls hoot, the moon rides like a ship through scudding clouds, trees sway slowly together above a rushing waterfall, and a distant barking of dogs is heard; or when a peal of bells in frosty weather suddenly announces the birth of a New Year.'

The material had taken over Graves. The book wanted to be published. The first publisher he took it to rejected it and died of heart failure soon afterwards. A second not only rejected it but sent a rude letter saying he couldn't make head or tale of it and doubted if anyone else could either. He was found in his garden, hanging from a tree, dressed in women's underwear! The third publisher approached was T. S. Eliot's Faber and Faber. He probably thought his reputation as the centuries' greatest poet might suffer if a similar fate befell him and it was best to publish the goddamn thing. He got his money back and received an Order of Merit award in the same year.

Graves was already an established literary figure so his work impacted across a wider spectrum than specialist mystics. His fundamental theme after all was the nature of poetry. *The White Goddess* has had powerful life-changing effects on a lot of people over the years and can be considered to be a major source text of the pagan revival.

Decades later Graves came to ponder the potential advent of a complementary Black Goddess. He had been aware of the enigmatic Black Madonna statues across Europe and some of the mystical currents associated with them. Wisdom has sometimes been characterised as black like the night. The stirrings at Nag Hammadi and the furnace of the Babalon Working in many ways contained much of what Graves felt lay ahead and it had already been activated all but simultaneously to his *White Goddess* illumination. This represents a comprehensive divine feminine package.

We'll come to note how some LSD mystics believed that the timing of its appearance in 1943 was connected with the new nuclear age and showed some complex alchemy that needed to be understood. I would place this stirring of the multi-faceted goddess, the Isis of 10,000 names, fully into the same alchemical cauldron. In Thelemic terms, Nuit would inspire the coming Love-Ins.

PRIESTESS

One crucial imbalance in Graves' exegesis came from his suggestion that the White Goddess primarily serves the purpose of being a male muse and that women tend to lack poetic gifts. With him the powerful interlinked archetypes of witch and priestess are undeveloped. The great tides that were returning the divine feminine nonetheless ensured that they were able to powerfully surface as well.

Numerous models have existed for the male magician magus-type. From the Middle Ages to Crowley, there was a certain way of being, a particular style that the would-be-adept could take on board. For women it was different. The Burning Times had left unfavourable archetypes associated with witches. If the figure of the Priestess was to return, she needed to be rehabilitated, restored to the fullness of her functions. People had to have an idea in their heads of what such a figure would be like and how she might feel and behave in the modern world.

It is entirely appropriate that Margaret Murray's initial stimulus should arise at Glastonbury, a location associated with Britain's most famous sorceress, Morgan Le Fey. Half-sister of Arthur, she is characterised in the early medieval Arthurian literature as Queen of the faery realm of Avalon in the Celtic otherworld. She is a shapeshifting sorceress and healer, learned in starlore and mathematics, a female Merlin Druidess. By the time of Malory at the end of the Middle Ages, her character had been thoroughly assassinated. Helen Mirren's portrayal in *Excalibur* typifies her general depiction as a scheming manipulative malevolent figure, largely responsible for the doom that befalls the King.

Dion Fortune, who had a home in Glastonbury and wrote a poetic book, *Avalon of the Heart*, extolling its unique charisma, wrote two occult novels set in the thirties, *The Sea Priestess* and *Moon Magic*, that featured the character Vivien Le Fey Morgan, who became Lilith Le Fey Morgan. The names combined two notorious women of the Arthurian romances. Vivienne had led Merlin to imprisonment. Fortune's portrayal of the characters expressed a good deal of her own idealised magical personality, in the process embodying the qualities of the Arthurian sorceresses, but in a way that revitalised their mystery, expanding what they represent and opening up vistas that speak of a lineage of profound antiquity. Both works featured poetic fragments of evocative rituals full of the ebb and flow of moon and tides.

Crowley was endlessly driven by the quest for the Scarlet Woman. So many of his female magickal partners burned out and departed. The only women he was ever able to find who were capable of the kind of trance states his magickal work required were often emotionally unstable and needed powerful combinations of sex and drugs to get them going. Only a few Thelemic women demonstrated any staying power. Cameron was certainly an authentic witch woman but she was so intense and individual that her role never extended to working with groups. Dion Fortune was more successful in reinvigorating the archetype and all subsequent Wicca and Goddess adherents owe her a debt of gratitude.

Two of Dion Fortune's magical associates, Charles Seymour and Christine Hartley, performed a series of workings during the late thirties. Alan Richardson's *Dancers to the Gods* gives a fine account of what transpired. One of their sessions (which tended to involve a lot of eyes-closed meditation-visualisation) has become increasingly well-known. In June 1938 Hartley reported feeling *'extremely desirous of being a witch.'* She soon began seeing *'little pictures of Ishtar worship through the ages, the most common being one of silhouetted witches in pointed hats and ragged skirts dancing round a fire. Then it seemed to focus a little more steadily and I was aware of the goddess standing before us mistily veiled.'* Ishtar spoke to her of the need for love and celebration and lamented how she had been turned into the Virgin Mary which was not, *"the fullness of her worship."* Ishtar enfolded Hartley with her veils and began to ascend with her to the threshold of the *"Fields of Ishtar"* but an inner resistance curtailed the process. The lineage of the witch goddess had been taken further back from the Diana of Leland and Murray to the very dawn of civilisation thus enabling all of the goddess cults of antiquity to be potentially included in the returning archetype. Seymour and Hartley were a long way from Crowley in their general demeanour and approach but Ishtar and Babalon are strongly connected.

GERALD GARDNER
AND THE WICCAN MYTHOS

In Britain in 1951 an antiquated law that made witchcraft illegal was repealed. It's probably not a big surprise that people claiming to be witches soon surfaced and the mock-prurient sensationalist press enjoyed regularly featuring stories about them for decades to come. The witches seemed to enjoy prancing about naked and occasionally donning robes to worship scary deities that would have got Old Testament prophets fulminating fire and brimstone. It all had an edgy vibe about it that was disturbing to many and attractive to some. The very word "Witch" carries quite a psychic charge full of extraordinary history and mythology.

One man stood very much stage centre in the early days of legality. Born in 1884, Gerald Gardner's early life was unusual but not exceptional. Taking advantage of the opportunities provided by the British Empire he had been a rubber planter in the Far East and a government inspector in Malaya. He wrote a book on local weapons and on returning to England in 1936 became interested in Naturism. In a moment of destiny he and his wife moved from London to the outskirts of the New Forest in Hampshire.

Gardner already had serious interests in the occult and witchcraft. He came into contact with a Rosicrucian group whose membership supposedly included witches from a coven in the New Forest. They apparently recognised a connection with him from past lives and in September 1939, just a few days after war was declared, Gardner was initiated into their group by a woman known as Old Dorothy. This scenario has been much debated with varying levels of historical analysis and acrimony concerning its validity. Some entirely disbelieve in the existence of the coven. With each passing decade more angles of enquiry present themselves.

Following the initial Margaret Murray effusions here was the first indication that something called witchcraft was being practiced rather than just written about and possibly had been since the Burning Times.

Novelist Louis Wilkinson, who was a long-term associate of Crowley, claimed to have also met up with a New Forest witch group in the late thirties who contained a wide social spectrum from intellectuals to 'local peasantry'. They apparently made use of hallucinogenic mushrooms.

The idea of the New Forest witches links in with another piece of occult folklore concerning the Magical Battle of Britain that has been circulating in various forms for decades. It states that in the summer of 1940 a coven of witches performed an outdoor ritual aimed at preventing German invasion. This was a group accustomed to working naked and the oldest member deliberately neglected to cover their body with the usual magical ointment thus exposing themselves to the elements and a voluntary death to add power to the rite. Some versions name the New Forest coven under the direction of Old Dorothy as responsible.

A similar procedure, so the story goes, had been undertaken by their predecessors in the time of Napoleon and further back still with the Spanish Armada. In this witch version of the 1588 matrix Sir Francis Drake is a member of the old religion and the man responsible for conjuring storms rather than John Dee.

The most elaborate depiction of the 1940 witch workings can be found in Katherine Kurtz's Murray-inspired 1983 novel *Lammas Night*, which brings in a fictional member of the Royal Family to become a willing Frazerian sacrifice in the war against occult Nazism. Hitler is depicted as a Thule adept and the group portrayed as sacrificial Satanists. A central past-life theme has the royal prince as reincarnation of William II and Thomas Becket. The main protagonist, an intelligence officer who had also been Drake the witch-initiate, had slain him on both occasions. A coalition of every type of occultist is brought together to put out the basic idea to the

Nazi leader that he simply can't cross the channel. There are brief references to Dion Fortune in Glastonbury and the voluntary death in the New Forest group. Dramatic scenes worthy of Trevor Ravenscroft's wildest imaginings occur on the night of the old Lammas festival in August when Rufus was killed. A robed Hitler presiding over an evil ritual is confronted magically and physically. A few weeks later the prince goes willingly to his death as the invasion of Britain is cancelled. There are no versions of the 1940 event in print that predate Gardner's arrival on the public scene but a few people have claimed some level of involvement. It's another measure of how much mileage and inspiration these ideas can generate.

Crowley had given some thought over the years to the desirability of generally reviving paganism. He knew that the Golden Dawn tradition was elitist and demanded a lot of time and energy. Larger numbers were needed to help usher in the Aeon. He mentioned the topic in correspondence in 1914. *'The time is just ripe for a nature religion. People like rites and ceremonies, and they are tired of hypothetical gods. Insist on the real benefits of the Sun, the Mother-Force, the Father-Force and so on... In short be the founder of a new and greater Pagan cult.'*

During the seventies a series of articles were published in *The Wiccan* periodical linking Crowley to witchcraft at an early part of his career. This formed part of a larger mythology advocating the major status of George Pickingill, a nineteenth century East-Anglian Cunning Man, an archaic term for a type of male witch that persisted in rural communities as figures of status and fear beyond the Burning Times. Pickingill allegedly founded nine covens, one of which Crowley joined in 1899. This was just after his induction in the Golden Dawn and before the Cairo Revelation. His general demeanor soon got him expelled.

Once this material had circulated it became a kind of truism of occult gossip. I have major doubts about it. Crowley wrote extensively on his experiences in all kinds of different practices. He took oaths of secrecy with the Golden Dawn and then broke them, happily appearing in Court against his previous chief after publishing ritual details. There is no good reason why he would entirely neglect to mention such a potentially interesting episode as involvement in a witch group.

Francis King in *Ritual Magic in England* claimed that Gerald Gardner paid Crowley to create the rituals of Wicca. Doreen Valiente, an early priestess in one of Gardner's groups and later to develop into a major figure on the Wiccan scene, felt this was unlikely purely on the basis of Crowley being a spent force in his later years and therefore incapable of producing such material. Although this is not at all true the point is irrelevant anyway. It can readily be demonstrated that material clearly originating from the Beast was present in the early days of Gardnerian witchcraft and it came from writings dating from decades earlier. Establishing context and meaning for this has been a lingering controversy.

It is generally accepted that Gerald Gardner first met Aleister Crowley on the appropriate date of May 1st 1947. Within weeks he had been initiated through a number of OTO grades and given a charter to set up a group which at that time would have been the only OTO enclave in Europe. Gardner paid Crowley for all this and one must therefore assume that it had some level of importance to him, at least at that time. This would appear to be where the payment story originates and witchcraft was nowhere on the recorded agenda.

A crucial period in Gardner's development followed for which the details are frustratingly scanty. In 1947, not long after the documented meetings with Crowley, Gardner travelled to America. When he returned his interest in the OTO seemed to rapidly wane. It doesn't seem that he practiced their rituals but wasn't averse to later displaying his charter in an early witchcraft museum. The full-blown witch was soon to emerge.

A novel entitled *High Magic's Aid* was published in 1949. Following the change of the legal status of witches and Gardner's increasingly public role *Witchcraft Today* appeared in 1954 and *The Meaning of Witchcraft* in 1959. Margaret Murray wrote an introduction giving her approval. She and Gardner had actually known each other in the Folk Lore Society and produced a joint paper on a witchcraft topic back in 1939.

In common with Murray, Gardner presented witchcraft as part of the old religion of the British Isles and thereby part of a spectrum that included Druidism and input from various middle-eastern travellers. The different categories tended to blend. He accepted, for example, the idea that a huge terrestrial zodiac had been fashioned in the Glastonbury landscape by Sumerian travellers and that motifs that were passed down through the witch cult can be found in minor aspects of its designs. Unfortunately he tells the reader he is bound by oaths not to reveal the details. A number of his authorities would not be considered credible today but his books are potent and establish a mood receptive to the flow of inspiration and magic.

Gardner stated that the knowledge and rituals he received from the New Forest coven were in a fragmentary form and he felt the need to add other elements he deemed appropriate. Freemasonry was a huge influence on most secret groups during the nineteenth and early twentieth centuries, from the ceremonial magicians to some early Trade Unionists. Three degrees, initiations that involved binding and oaths, an altar, working tools, and the designation of the *Craft* are all present within Gardner's witchcraft. From what is known of its early form, there are considerable borrowings from Crowley.

Gardner had a personal book in which he appeared to compile relevant material for his enterprise. *Ye Bok of ye Art Magical* contains a significant amount of Crowley material drawn from the likes of *The Book of the Law*, the Gnostic Mass and various poems. All of this could have been extracted from just two works where they were found together. It is also possible that their presence in *Ye Bok* precedes Gardner and Crowley's meetings. Whatever the case it is clear that Crowley was considered to be the most useful template available from which to make a start.

Things changed when Doreen Valiente arrived. She had a gift for composing poetry and soon created a number of works for the ritual corpus that were so successful they became "traditional" overnight. Valiente cautioned against association with Crowley who had recently again become notorious through the 1951 publication of John Symonds' biography. Gardner was ambivalent about Crowley in print, sometimes referring to him as a harmless charlatan but clearly mindful of the power of his reputation. Valiente's own poetic output began to replace the Crowley material but some remained and that probably gives a better indication of Gardner's real feelings on the status of his work.

The main initiatory rite of Gardner's witchcraft was the Third Degree which is clearly sexual in content. It featured readings from a text that was essentially identical to a section of Crowley's Gnostic Mass which in turn had included quotations from *The Book of the Law*.

Some of the words of Nuit are indeed as prophetic of the rebirth of witchcraft as anything else from the preceding century or so. Wicca has proved to be a potent vehicle of the larger general return of the divine feminine. Gardner's witch covens were notable for the important role of their priestesses. If there could be said to be such a thing as Wiccan scripture it would be what is generally known as the Charge of the Goddess. This consists of a kind of policy statement and list of attributes of the divine feminine recited by the priestess, ideally in some kind of altered inspired state of consciousness, on behalf of the one great goddess who is behind all of the variant forms.

The words used by Gardner's early groups have been preserved and it is therefore possible to see the process of their creation. It does rather seem that he simply copied out some existing words that seemed appropriate and joined them together. They have primarily come from two sources. One was *Aradia*, the other, *The Book of the Law*. Valiente adjusted it, producing a poetic and then prose version which was widely adopted. Despite her objections to Crowley some of the words of Nuit and other phrases that seem directly inspired by her still remain. Today versions of the Charge have been created by a number of Wiccans. Some feel that the words can be the base for a spontaneous trance outpouring and are therefore not fixed.

Here is one version of it, and for all of its blending of Leland and Crowley it is assuredly a thing of beauty in its own right.

'Listen to the words of the Great Mother; she who of old was also called among men
Artemis, Astarte, Athene, Dione, Melusine, Aphrodite, Cerridwen,
Cybele, Arianrhod, Isis, Dana, Bride
and by many other names:

Whenever ye have need of anything, once in the month, and better it be when the moon is full,
then shall ye assemble in some secret place and adore the spirit of me,
who am Queen of all the witches.
And ye shall be free from slavery; and as a sign that ye be really free,
ye shall be naked in your rites;
and ye shall dance, sing, feast, make music and love, all in my praise.
For mine is the ecstasy of the spirit, and mine also is joy on earth;
for my law is love unto all beings.

*I am the gracious Goddess, who gives the gift of joy unto the heart of man.
Upon earth, I give the knowledge of the spirit eternal;
and beyond death, I give peace and freedom and reunion with those who have gone before.
Nor do I demand aught in sacrifice; for behold,
I am the Mother of all living, and my love is poured out upon the earth.*

*Hear ye the words of the Star Goddess;
I who am the beauty of the green earth, and the white moon among the stars,
and the mystery of the waters, and the desire of the heart of man, call unto thy soul.
Arise, and come unto me. For I am the soul of nature, who gives life to the universe.
From me all things proceed, and unto me all things must return;
and before my face, beloved of Gods and of men,
let thine innermost divine self be enfolded in the rapture of the infinite.*

*Let my worship be within the heart that rejoiceth.
All acts of love and pleasure are my rituals.
And therefore let there be beauty and strength, power and compassion, honour and humility, mirth and reverence within you.
I have been with thee from the beginning;
and I am that which is attained at the end of desire.'*

There are a number of particular themes that the pagan revival in general has in common. Perhaps the most fundamental is the acknowledgement of the solar seasonal festivals, the equinoxes and solstices and the cross-quarter days known widely again by their old names such as Beltaine and Lammas. Gardner began with a partial observance of the sequence but his early witches were enthusiastic to restore them all and this was done by 1958. A number of groups such as assorted druids had celebrated some of the dates but the real restoration of what has come to be called the wheel of the year spread out from Gardner.

With this he performed a great and timely service as study of the festivals and their associations inevitably draws one into an increased awareness and affinity for nature and the psychology of the ancestors, the lore of the land. This rootedness with its accompanying feeling of a return to reality has proven to be a healing process amidst the alienation of the technological world. There is much folklore linking witches to stone circles and other ancient sites. Many have sought to act out the myths and make them real. This created more ripples from the point of origin, connecting with the growing field of the so-called Earth Mysteries, the concepts of ley lines and so on. Having been reborn in the hibernation-gestation fifties the ancient archetype could fully emerge in the coming spectacular decade.

On a magical and spiritual level it is entirely appropriate that Crowley has played a part in what I would consider to be one of the strongest signs of his New Aeon. Gerald Gardner deserves huge credit in his own right. He can be readily acknowledged as a true magician because he ushered something of peculiar power into a world that was clearly waiting for it. The rate of its expansion is the measure of the needs it has met. To unravel the source material Gardner used and wonder about the historical veracity of his foundation myth is a fascinating and important study but it carries the risk of missing the point.

JACK PARSONS AND "THE WITCHCRAFT"

'And she shall wander in the witchwood under the Night of Pan, and know the mysteries of the Goat and the Serpent, and of the children that are hidden away.' 'Gather together in the covens as of old'. 'Gather together in public, in song and dance and festival. Gather together in secret, be naked and shameless and rejoice in my name.' 'The work of the image, and the potion and the charm, the work of the spider and the snake, and the little ones that go in the dark, this is your work.' 'This is the way of it, star, star. Burning bright, moon, witch moon.' 'You the secret, the outcast, the accursed and despised, even you that gathered privily of old in my rites under the moon.' 'You the free, the wild, the untamed, that walk now alone and forlorn.'

Liber 49. The Book of Babalon.

The Book of Babalon dates from 1946. It is remarkable how much it carries a very strong feeling of what later became known as Wicca. The question is whether there are any direct connections or if it is a case of Jack Parsons being prophetically in tune with something that expressed itself similarly and all-but simultaneously through other people as well? Alongside his Gnostic leanings, Parsons had a passion for the idea of witchcraft. Towards the end of his life he was very keen to try and instigate a revival of the old paganism and set up a group he called "the witchcraft". His basic policy statement from his writings on the subject has a familiar tone.

'We are on the side of man, of life, and of the individual. Therefore we are against religion, morality and government. Therefore our name is Lucifer. We are on the side of freedom, of love, of joy and laughter and divine drunkenness. Therefore our name is Babalon.'

Although there is no direct evidence that Jack Parsons was familiar with *Aradia* a few motifs in his work are strongly suggestive of its influence. Firstly there is Lucifer as god of the witches. A number of contemporary Wiccans prefer to avoid this topic as it brings in the possibility of a Biblical ambiance that might not take too much development to bring in Satan and the whole Burning Times mythological package they are trying to erase. Others have eloquently defended what could be termed the Luciferian gnosis and affirmed it to be a thing of beauty that no fundamentalist Christian could ever understand. It is now more generally accepted as part of the greater Wiccan mythology that Luciferic covens have long been part of the scene.

Liber 49 also seems to echo *Aradia* with an instruction for the would-be witch to *'Be naked and shameless'* . One of many excellent phrases that Gerald Gardner assembled and passed into general Wiccan use is *sky clad*, meaning nude. His groups assembled thus. Later critics have pointed to his predilection for Naturism as an indication that he used *Aradia* as justification for bringing his personal tastes into what was simply a cult of his own invention. Regardless of whether that point is fundamentally accurate or not the practice has a history that sits very well with what one could term Wiccan mythology.

Throughout the Middle Ages and beyond, groups of Christian heretics appeared who decided to emulate Adam and Eve before the fall and live naked. Across the planet numerous sects have done likewise or at least gathered temporarily in such a manner.

Their intentions have much in common if we can accept the theories of Mircea Eliade. All of these nudists were seeking a return to an imagined primordial paradisiacal state before a fall into history began. If we look at Gardner's witches they were hoping to partake of something as old as the Stone Age, something from the very dawn of humanity, a time of a purity and oneness with nature that has since been lost. That state could be regained. Parsons may well have been similarly motivated.

Modern Wicca has often tried to get away from the popular mythology of witches as practitioners of malevolent sorcery. This was what led to the murderous persecutions and it's understandable that modern adherents want to rehabilitate the archetype. There's no getting away from the basic theme of spells and magical battles and suchlike throughout witchlore. A big difference between Jack Parsons and the adherents of Murray and Gardner is that the Thelemic wildman was fascinated by phenomenon of manifestation that would scare the crap out of most people, and above all, the image of witch woman as being attractive in proportion to her potential dangerousness.

Parsons's concept of Babalon was significantly advanced by his reading of Jack Williamson's novel of lycanthropy and witchcraft, *Darker Than You Think*. The lead character is enthralled by a red-headed, green-eyed witch named April Bell who he soon discovers is guilty of sorcerous murder which does nothing to diminish her attraction. There is a memorable scene that was depicted with pulp-art finesse on the cover of early editions where the hero has transformed into a sabre-toothed tiger and the witch-woman rides naked on his back. This is very reminiscent of Crowley's Babalon (with which the author was unfamiliar).

Gerald Gardner made his largely undocumented trip to America in 1947. He had just been initiated into the OTO and there was only really one functioning group there at the time. There is a possibility that he may have met with members of the Agape Lodge, even Parsons himself. A number of internet sources state this as if it was an established fact. It isn't. Parsons had been expelled from the OTO and was out of favour with Crowley by then. He was still in contact with some of his old associates but wouldn't have been an obvious person for Gardner to seek out.

The American occultist Allen Greenfield, who we will meet again in a UFOlogical context, took an interest in the Jack Parsons aspect of the mystery. He corresponded with Doreen Valiente who was well aware of *Liber 49* and Parsons specific witchcraft writing. She acknowledged the striking similarities with what was brewing in Britain and wondered if there had been more direct connections. The problem is that we can find no clear quotes from Parsons in Gardner or indeed any mention of him in extant personal material. A direct meeting between Parsons and Gardner has to remain as no more than an excellent occult rumour. The nudity theme may well be another indication of powerful ideas that were in the airwaves then. Parsons deserves to be noted as a prophetic figure is this context and the rebirth of witchcraft to be a phenomenon influenced by tangential ripples from the Babalon Working.

KING OF THE WITCHES

Gerald Gardner was shy and retiring in comparison to the man who walked out onto the paisley-patterned red carpet that the psychedelic sixties rolled out for witchcraft. Alex Sanders told tales that were even more flamboyant and unreliable about his background. A touching story related how at the age of seven he had come upon his grandmother standing naked in a circle drawn on a kitchen floor. Realising the game was up she ordered the boy to strip and join her. An initiation was conducted that climaxed with Sanders bending down to touch his toes whilst granny drew a knife across his scrotum. At the age of ten the old woman took the boy to see Crowley in London who buggered him senseless and tattooed a magickal sign on his hand.

The witchy granny appears to be a fact although the initiation tale is likely to be a ripping yarn only. It's a fairly harmless conceit but the Crowley element has had unfortunate consequences in helping to further fuel the legend of infamy. Sanders' tale doesn't fit any known data on Crowley. Christian fundamentalists have found it and spread the idea that Crowley was a paedophile. From such reliable sources the new breed of darkly paranoid occult conspiracy theorists have taken their own information on Crowley with predictably uninspiring results.

During the sixties Alex Sanders and his wife Maxine were the prime media witches. Any British newspaper or magazine article or TV feature on the subject was likely to feature their usually naked group. There's no question that he loved publicity, was a born showman, and sometimes enjoyed being shocking for the sake of it.

In terms of a flamboyant public persona that revelled in notoriety he clearly activated the archetype created around Crowley. Sanders had proclaimed himself as independent of Gerald Gardner and his covens and a separate "Alexandrian" strain of witchcraft was promoted.

For all of the elements of charlatanism present in his attention-hungry persona Sanders was nonetheless passionately committed and entirely sincere in his long-term dedication to the Craft. He was naturally mediumistic with an oft-attested ability to produce tangible physical manifestations. An early use of his talents to cultivate a certain amount of power and wealth he later characterised as essentially black magic. His sister had died during this period and he considered that to be a negative complementary outcome of his unlawful use of the force.

During the time of Sanders' greatest fame in the sixties he spent considerable time engaged in healing. He was hugely generous with his time and energy. His Notting Hill home was constantly heaving with a wide spectrum of people from academics and journalists to hippy seekers and assorted unclassifiables from all over the world. Alex Sanders held them spellbound with his charisma and knowledge. It was a microcosm of the sixties upheaval with a few notable differences. Drug use was actively discouraged. Despite the inevitable frequent nudity involved in the witchcraft it was not a zone of orgiastic activity. Sanders himself was openly bisexual but the covenstead was kept in order through the presence of his remarkable wife.

Maxine Sanders was still in her teens when she was first photographed in a Sanders witch ritual and hounded by the media. Although Alex was the obvious centre of gravity she was always strongly visible in the proceedings. It was far from just being a case of a naked bodacious blonde being good copy to get press coverage (although it definitely helped). Maxine was quite a force in her own right having studied for years in a Gurdjieff group and been initiated into an Egyptian order by the time she was only fifteen.

It was discovered that Sanders had been briefly connected to a Gardnerian group and much of his basic magical material was derived from it. This seemed to undermine the credibility of his claims. Nonetheless he clearly introduced many innovations. His initiated witches received a level of comprehensive magical training that could stand comparison with many more well-established groups. Herb and starlore were extensively studied. The Qabalah and tarot were involved. Egyptian deities were sometimes featured. Healing and personal development became important themes.

Books by Crowley were part of an increasingly extensive library and Sanders was happy to hold forth on their contents thus clearly bringing the Beast into his witchcraft blend. Unlike Gardner, Sanders never wrote any books although lecture notes remain but the Alexandrian tradition has been a most fruitful one on both sides of the Atlantic. A number of distinguished creative witches such as Janet and Stewart Farrar and Vivianne Crowley emerged from it.

In the bigger picture of the magical dream drama of the sixties a strange set of motifs surface with the involvement of Alex Sanders as an advisor on the subject of witchcraft for the 1966 Hollywood movie *Eye of the Devil* (sometimes known as *13*). A strong cast headed by David Niven and Deborah Kerr play out a story that seems inspired by the *Golden Bough* via Margaret Murray. Niven portrays an aristocratic landowner who returns to his family home in France when the grape crop seems set to fail. His ancestors have conformed to a heretical divine king type tradition that demands a sacrifice so that the crops can thrive. It's an odd movie. Filmed in black and white it would probably not impress new generations of horror fans who are looking for blood, gore, monsters, and special effects rather than subtlety. If it is known today it is because of a rising starlet in her first major role playing a local malevolent witch. Both Alex and Maxine later reported that Sharon Tate had expressed sufficient interest in the Craft to become initiated during the making of the film. It could be said that the sixties was book-ended by two ritual sacrifices. JFK was the first and Tate would become the second. We have jumped ahead to the heart of the sixties. How did it all get so intense and weird? Time to return to the larger narrative from a Thelemic hawks-eye perspective.

OPENING THE DOORS: THE PSYCHEDELIC EXPERIENCE

'*Turn On, Tune In, Drop Out.*'
Timothy Leary.

'*The word of sin is restriction.*'

'*Come forth, o children, under the stars, & take your fill of love!*'

'*Also, take your fill and will of love as ye will, when where and with whom you will!*'

'*To worship me take wine and strange drugs whereof I will tell my prophet, & be drunk thereof! They shall not harm ye at all. It is a lie, this folly against self.*'

'*Be strong o man! lust, enjoy all things of sense and rapture: Fear not that any God shall deny thee for this.*'
The Book of the Law.

'*Feed your head.*'
Jefferson Airplane. *White Rabbit.*

'*Break on through to the other side.*'
The Doors. *Break on Through.*

RETURN OF THE SACRAMENTAL MYSTERIES

'I will put a live coal upon your lips, and flowers upon your eyes, and a sword in your hearts, and ye also shall see God face to face. Thus shall we give back its youth to the world, for like tongues of triple flame we shall look upon the Great Deep - Hail unto the Lords of the groves of Eleusis!'

Aleister Crowley. *Rites of Eleusis.*

IN 1910 ALEISTER CROWLEY was at the peak of his powers. He had just returned from the epic magickal journey in Algeria. His fortune had not yet dissipated. He was going through a time of considerable creativity thanks to his interaction with his closest associates, Victor Neuberg and the Australian violinist Leila Waddell. The group sparked off each other and enabled Crowley to create a unique spectacle and experience for the London scene. He and Leila had been experimenting with the Mexican hallucinogen peyote. Crowley was one of the first Europeans to do so. He would compose and recite invocatory verses to her violin accompaniment. Neuberg was capable of dancing himself into a frenzy where he seemed to be possessed. This led to the creation of a series of rituals to the seven planets honoured by the ancients (which include the sun and moon). They became collectively known as the Rites of Eleusis and were publicly performed to paying customers in London.

This was no cheapo publicity stunt to grab some cash. The ceremonies were complex, drawing on all of Crowley's Golden Dawn background and his extensive knowledge of literature and world religion. His stated aim was to induce some kind of mystical ecstasy in the audience. The mood set by the ritual combination of dim light, incense, costumes, music, dancing, and poetry would probably have been very effective to those with the right temperaments. It's likely that most of those who attended weren't expecting a night of music hall vaudeville entertainment. To help things along at a first experimental performance the punters were offered a bowl to drink from that prefigured the Electric Kool-Aid Acid Test by containing fruit juice and a mild dose of mescaline! This was a brave move fraught with peril. Even with a mild dose a stampede of freaked-out moustaches and crinolines onto the streets of 1910 London could have occurred.

There is no question that these performances were astonishing for the time. It was a huge departure for the occultism and theatre of the day. The rites would have still blown a lot of minds in the sixties and we shall come to examine the cinematic work of Kenneth Anger to see when the zeitgeist caught up with Crowley. One motif that I find of considerable interest for what was to come is the combination of mystery cult and psychedelic sacrament

The Eleusis reference links to the most famous of the classical mystery cults. The Greeks had established a centre dedicated to the myth of the goddess Demeter and her daughter Persephone who was kidnapped by Hades, the Lord of the Underworld. A deal was made where it was agreed that Persephone would stay with her abductor for a third of the year. It's primarily a seasonal drama but all manner of mystical meaning was found within it.

The cult endured for two thousand years. Some of the proceedings were conducted in public but such effective secrecy surrounded the central core that despite a huge number of people being initiated over such a long period nobody ever gave away the secret. Whatever happened must have been extremely powerful. It was generally known throughout the ancient world that secrets of life and death were somehow revealed in a way that transformed the participant forever. It seems a safe bet that the full range of Greek theatrical skill was brought to bear but the key speculation surrounds a beverage known to have been consumed. There's a good case to be made for the drink having contained a powerful psycho-active chemical.

The press gave attention to the Crowley performances. There were a few good reviews. They were outweighed by features that really began the legend of infamy. The rites were characterised as blasphemous with hints of sexual irregularity. Anything from Crowley's past that could be dug up and used against him was printed or insinuated. Nothing was quite the same for him from then on. The attempt to induce non-Christian religious experiences though the combination of music, lighting, dance and drugs would cause problems for a few other people a bit further down the line as well.

GOODBYE TO BERLIN, HELLO SGT PEPPER

There are some events that can retrospectively assume a power and poignancy impossible to anticipate. A personal favourite of mine, where context and ever-widening perspective are crucial, seems to form part of a dream-like mythic loop linking events from the Nazi to psychedelic eras.

In October 1930 Aleister Crowley had dinner with Aldous Huxley in Berlin. Crowley was briefly living in Germany and displaying some of his colourful drug inspired expressionist paintings at an exhibition in the city. According to Martin Booth in *A Magick Life*, Huxley had even been the subject of one of them.

In *Sexuality, Magic and Perversion*, the noted occult historian Francis King stated that

'Aldous Huxley was first introduced to mescaline in pre-Hitler Berlin by Aleister Crowley and one of his disciples. Curiously enough Huxley made no mention of this fact in his Doors of Perception.'

This evocative fragment has been widely circulated but proof has remained elusive.

Huxley had made his name in the twenties by satirising the shallow foibles of the same lost generation who Crowley had chronicled in *Diary of a Drug Fiend*. In 1932 he would move into a new phase with his prophetic fable *Brave New World*. His futuristic slave society was kept passive with the drug *Soma*. It's not at all unlikely that pharmacology could have been a topic of conversation with Crowley. The wild paintings would have been an obvious starting point. Whether that actually means that Huxley physically tripped-out in Crowley's company or was given some substance by him that he later ingested is another thing altogether. What does seem a safe bet is that Huxley would never have met anyone before with the visionary background of Crowley who could have given him such comprehensive accounts of the effects of various drugs from a mystical perspective.

I'm inclined to doubt the mescaline story. When psychedelic archivist Michael Horowitz was assembling the anthology of Huxley writings named *Moksha* he had the opportunity to question a number of people who had known Huxley well, including his wife, about the Crowley rumour. They all disbelieved it on the basis that they had never heard Huxley even hint at such a thing. One would have thought that he might have at least mentioned such a major piece of biographical information to his wife. There is still something about the matrix of that Crowley Huxley meeting which has the most evocative resonances, the most suggestive nuances, rippling across space-time though. The initial context is powerful enough to begin with.

From a starting point in autumn 1930, Christopher Isherwood's *Goodbye to Berlin* chronicled the ambience of the poignant cusp of the decline of the artistically sexually free Weimar republic era and the coming to power of the Nazis. It would be superbly recreated in the movie inspired by his book, *Cabaret*. Isherwood knew Crowley during that period and likewise dined with him.

March that year had seen the German premiere of Bertolt Brecht's opera *The Rise and Fall of the City of Mahogany*. Its savage satire on the belief that *'money makes the world go around'* contained *Alabama Song* with its English lyrics sung by prostitute characters.

'Show me the way to the next whiskey bar.
Oh, don't ask why, oh, don't ask why.'

At the start of 1930 a Nazi who had written the words for an increasingly popular marching tune was killed in a street fight with communists. From that point on, Horst Wessel's song became increasingly prevalent, eventually enshrined as a second national anthem.

'Already millions are looking to the swastika, full of hope;
The day of freedom and bread is dawning.'

Or, as *Cabaret* would put it, *'Tomorrow Belongs to Me'*.

This was the world outside of the room where Crowley and Huxley, two extraordinary men of destiny and refined mystical sensibilities, sat down to eat and talk. Both of these great prophetic thinkers would have been stunned to catch even a glimpse of what lay ahead.

Huxley began his literary career as an advocate of rationalism but read widely in mysticism and would ultimately be best remembered for his later writings on the subject. The shift began in the mid-thirties and came to fullness when he went to live in America. Assembling the beautiful anthology and commentary *The Perennial Philosophy* in 1945 was superb preparation for his legendary mescaline experience recorded in 1954's *The Doors of Perception,* possibly the most significant single stimulus to the psychedelic era. The title, taken from the visionary poet William Blake, was certainly inspirational to Jim Morrison and Ray Manzarek in naming their new rock band just over a decade later.

Of all the many people inspired by Huxley, perhaps the most important was Francis Crick, the scientist who in an epochal intuitive moment in 1953 caught a glimpse of *'the coiled splendour within'* that is the double-helix form of DNA. Crick had been taking occasional small doses of LSD long before the sixties and even before *Doors of Perception*. Rumours circulated that he had been under its influence at the moment of his DNA breakthrough. After his death investigation of his personal papers revealed this was true. He had been a founder member of a group called *Soma*, named after the drug featured in *Brave New World* and dedicated to the cause of legalising cannabis. He was one of the signatures on the famous full page advertisement for the cause published in *The Times* in 1967.

Huxley's last novel *Island*, published in 1962, was a presentation of his vision of an ideal future society to place against his *Brave New World* nightmare. His primary concern was the freedom of the individual to pursue their inner inclinations and how a society would need to work in order to best realise that. Crowley would have recognised vital Thelemic issues in the story. Set in a Balinese-type paradise, the community in question are embodiments of what Huxley took to be the best of eastern and western thought, believing in being life-affirmingly present in the world with full-meditative attention. Work and play are both forms of yoga. Sex is entirely positive when freed from the Christian guilt-trip. Science and religion are in harmony. The narrative eventually depicts the harsh realities of an emerging new world order of big business and the military destroying the dream.

Island featured an extended consideration on the death process and the many negative factors in western Christian culture surounding it. Huxley first demonstrated a serious concern with the topic when his first wife died in 1955. He recited affirmations to her as she lay dying in the hope of making it a more harmonious process. In 1963, as Huxley himself went into terminal decline he made a brave decision. He asked his new wife to inject him with LSD. She recited words to him inspired by the *Tibetan Book of the Dead* concerning going towards the light. It was a superb affirmation to demonstrate that *Island* was not just a novel of ideas, a head trip. It was possible to live and to die by those ideas and that was what he wanted people to take on board.

Not many literary or even mystical figures make such a powerful exit. Stranger still, in this sequence of dream-like events, when Huxley's wife left his bedroom to get the LSD she was perplexed to see the other people present in the household sitting in front of the TV. This was surely not granting the occasion the dignity it deserved. In fact they can be forgiven for a few hours earlier that day President Kennedy had been murdered. This would prove to be a massive event in the collective psyche of the USA and one of the most potent accelerating on-buttons for what was to come.

JAILBREAK FROM THE CONSENSUS PRISON

'No we will not forget who we are
Our wild souls still beat
Our muscles strain against the bonds
When tides of ancient energy surge within
We tremble
We sit trembling in our cages
It is hard for the proud wild to be captive
We will not forget who we are
We pray that you, beloved, do not forget who we are.'

Timothy Leary. Prison 1970

The life of Timothy Leary was a classic twentieth century tale that if told solely as a work of fiction or presented as a movie would never have been believed. He managed to polarise opinion in such a way as to engender huge love, affection, and respect in some and hatred and contempt in others. A decade after his death, two disparate biographies gave ample proof of that. John Higgs' *I Have America Surrounded* approaches the subject with sufficient affinity to give the reader a good feeling for why Leary is a much-loved legend to many. Robert Greenfield's *Timothy Leary* can be compared to John Symonds' *Great Beast*, Russell Miller's L. Ron Hubbard biography *Bare Faced Messiah*, and Albert Goldman's *Lives of John Lennon*. These writers certainly had considerable real data at their disposal but used it in a one-sided manner to trash their subjects, entirely failing to convey what made them so charismatic and popular in the first place.

Their whole approach got underway in the nineteenth century and proceeded apace with the advent of Freud. Books came along categorising genius as disease and applying a reductionist ethos to understanding the Leonardos and Mozarts of this world purely in terms of infantile factors in their psychology. There are plenty of egotistical, petty, angry people. Many of them accomplish little of merit. It's clear what my attitude here is to Crowley. I'm not denying his failings but I consider it to be a major error to allow them to exclusively define him for us. It means we miss out on a lot. Whilst it may be important to acknowledge such factors in a persons' total psyche, exclusive focus is clearly unbalanced. What's actually far more significant is how someone is able to manifest genius with such baggage on board. It is possible to have a creative and spiritual relationship with what Jungians would term the Shadow. This process may be one of the most vital studies of our time.

Timothy Leary was a compulsive rebel and attention seeker. He was certainly not a successful family man. Academics and quieter mystics may curse him for his pied piper role that was probably the major factor leading to the cessation of all research into psychedelic substances and their criminalisation. Leary was occasionally confronted by people blaming him directly for cases where friends or family members had died in scenarios linked to acid. Terence McKenna described him though as *'a guy who's probably made more people happy, arguably, than anybody else in history'*. I will come to argue that Leary confronted his Shadow side in an unprecedented initiatory ordeal that ultimately stands as the real measure of the man and that a strong Crowley influence is discernable on that journey.

Born in 1920, Leary travelled what seemed a respectable path to a distinguished career as lecturer and theorist in clinical psychology at Harvard University but some stranger destiny was already showing signs of its presence. Inducted as a cadet at West Point, a rebellious streak saw him drop out after an alcohol related Court Martial controversy. Indeed throughout his life he would repeatedly clash with many forms of authority. In 1955 he went through an intense rite of passage when his wife committed suicide on his birthday. This event may well have helped to cut him loose from identifying with the American consensus society of the time.

Leary first sampled hallucinogenic psilocybin mushrooms in Mexico in 1960 and was permanently mutated. His first inclinations were to attempt to apply this powerful new tool to his existing trade. He soon entered into a cordial interaction with Huxley who helped to feed Leary's head with what could be termed high culture.

It wasn't just the rock deities who were born during the Second World War. In 1943, as the tide of the war turned against the Nazis, in 'neutral' Switzerland, on April 16th, Sandoz chemist Albert Hoffman had the first experience with his newly synthesised LSD25.

Just over a year later, the first atomic bomb was detonated. When Timothy Leary first ingested LSD it was as if an atomic bomb had been detonated inside his head.

There can be no doubting the psychotherapeutic possibilities of LSD when applied with the vital criteria Leary came to advocate of appropriate set and setting, broadly meaning ensuring its ingestion occurs with adequate mental preparation and a supportive environment and company. Just what constitutes success in such undertakings is open to debate. Beyond the transformation of particular traits in emotion and behaviour lies the issue of the rehabilitation and adjustment of the entire human being necessary for such changes to endure. Any school of therapy carries assumptions of what the nature of a healthy sane human consists of.

Freud kept the bar fairly low. Stopping people from indiscriminate rape and murder and conformed to the societal norms necessary for that were really about as far as he went. The split with Jung ultimately derived from their radical differences over the upper levels of human possibilities. Psychedelic drugs soon bring out any latent mysticism that might be lurking inside. People begin talking in terms that sound religious and at this point outside observers get uncomfortable.

Religion has looked like a profoundly negative repressive force in the life of the world for good reason. That's exactly how it has so often worked down through the ages and its worst manifestations can be readily observed in the modern world right now. No wonder the likes of Richard Dawkins have felt the need to sound-off against it.

Crowley experienced evangelical idiocy throughout his childhood and railed against it with venom but went on to proclaim a new religion himself. He enthusiastically cultivated as wide a knowledge and experience of the world's sacred traditions as he could and encouraged his students to do likewise. Huxley the rational cynic became Huxley the mystic. Some would say he addled his brain and lost the plot. Others would say he *evolved*. He used his intellect to see what was false in the world as it is found and developed a critical intelligence to integrate a higher level perspective into his original understanding.

Island is not just a hippy-dippy drug utopian fantasy, it's also a savage indictment of the modern world. '*Onward Nazi soldiers, onward Christian soldiers, onward Marxists and Muslims, onward every chosen People, every Crusader and Holy War-maker. Onward into misery, into all wickedness, into death!*' Huxley brought both sides of his life-long vision together. Huxley and *Island* were huge early influences on Leary that endured throughout his life. However spaced-out he may have increasingly appeared in the media-consensus reality he also kept a clear critical intelligence for the way of the world, continually presenting an ongoing critique of its failings and looking for the signs of what in the emerging future could be cultivated to best effect.

It's that Gnostic theme again. The priests of the world's religions have come to stand between the people and their experiences of something that transcends the consensus reality. Whether we consider that something to be simply expanded brain function or a doorway to realms that are external, the point remains the same about what stands in the way. The priests, whether of religion or scientific materialism, have become jailers. If anyone demonstrates signs of actually having any of the experiences discussed in the great scriptures, the local branch of the inquisition will bust them. Death has often been the result. What begins with the life of an adept who has charismatically demonstrated illumination, spoken words like fire, and set great transformation in motion soon becomes a prison. This is the great trick the demiurgic intelligences that work on behalf of the jailer god have managed.

As recently as 1957 the heretical psychologist Wilhelm Reich had died in an American prison after the authorities burnt his books and papers in a public incinerator. This was a disgraceful fate to befall a man who had been forced to leave Nazi Germany and made a home in the land of the free. Reich had developed profound psychotherapeutic work concerning the *Emotional Plague* that afflicts the inhabitants of the consensus prison due to the *Character Armour* of rigid musculature reflecting rigid personality caused by the unhealthy constriction of sexual life-force energy. He went into complete taboo territory by claiming to have discovered a universal power he named *orgone*, the energy behind orgasm, and became interested in the UFO mystery. The creation of a device that could pump-up what scientific authorities deemed to be a non-existent energy was the start of his path to death in prison. Even for those who don't buy into orgone the extreme form of Reich's treatment might suggest forces other than objective scientific rationality were at work. We are not necessarily talking the usual conspiracy rap here.

Reich hadn't just channelled some occult cosmology. He had volumes of experimental work to back up his theories. Experiments that could be checked by repeating them. Robert Anton Wilson's *The New Inquisition* gives a great account of how it became essentially a policy of the scientific establishment to discourage anyone from attempting to check Reich's work and to ignore or vilify those who did and found in his favour. Watch the movie *Pleasantville* for a parable on the issues involved when the monochrome shallow fantasy of American fifties consumer soap-opera reality becomes disrupted by the stirrings of technicolour sexuality and freedom. The busting and suppression of Reich were the last time that the lid was effectively kept on. Something was already in place to blow it off. LSD and mass communication could not be controlled like the comparatively small scale work of Reich.

The CIA had been experimenting with acid during the fifties, often on unprepared subjects. Mind control was their aim. The substance seemed to have an agenda of its own though. In various medical sessions where volunteers were sought all kinds of tangents developed. Ken Kesey tapped his creativity and saw the psychiatric sights that led to his arrival on the literary scene with *One Flew Over the Cuckoo's Nest*, a passionate portrayal of individual integrity against the psychiatric abuse that attempts to suppress it. Kesey used his new fame and money to gather a motley crew in a painted bus and take it on a legendary odyssey across America, dispensing acid in public gatherings that were the ancestors of modern raves. It was an anarchic complement to Leary's work. Tom Wolfe's *The Electric Kool-Aid Acid Test* is the essential record of that incredible journey to destination *Further.*

Timothy Leary took his first mushroom trip only three years after Reich's death in prison. He was well aware of the case. Leary carried through the impetus of Crowley and Parsons and found himself instigating a new millennial mystery cult. When he famously playfully suggested in a *Playboy* interview that it was possible for a woman to have literally hundreds of orgasms during an LSD session Doris Day fifties America felt the presence of a new public enemy number one. Sex, drugs, and mysticism. The time-honoured ultimate heretical package.

The fervour of those times may seem difficult to comprehend. A few factors are crucial to understanding. First of all, in case anyone hasn't heard, LSD is an extremely powerful substance mindwise. To experience it just after the drab fifties was a bit of a shock to the system to say the least. Those who were a tad disturbed by 9/11 would do well to ponder the Cuban Missile Crisis of October 1962. This was the most intense episode of the Cold War. It might just have been the most intense episode not just of the Cold War but the whole of recorded history in as much as a nuclear war was genuinely an imminent strong possibility. Short version: Russia started setting up nuclear missile bases on Cuba within close first strike proximity to the USA whilst stating that they were doing no such thing. America found out and said stop doing that or there will be trouble. An invasion of Cuba and nuclear strike on Russia were seriously planned for. Bombers were loaded and ready to go. For a few weeks global stress levels rose to unprecedented highs. A deal was struck and the missiles removed.

It was as if the enormous collective alchemy stirring since 1945 was reaching a crucial transformative stage. Just over a year later Kennedy was killed as Huxley exited on LSD. Some of the early acid heads felt that LSD and the Bomb were like a kind of yin and yang of the new epoch that needed to be balanced out. Was there some kind of mysterious timing that had revealed such power in the realms of the sub-atomic and the energy field of consciousness all but simultaneously? The world had nearly destroyed itself, the divine king of Camelot (as Kennedy's presidency came to be known) had been sacrificed. Unless the world caught up in the inner wisdom game very rapidly the final catastrophe could be horribly near. War mongering madmen riddled with Reich's emotional plague, armoured against the free flow of love and sexuality, ruled the world. Give them some acid and chuck them in a pool full of dolphins and they might just sort it all out. They would probably be at least a bit less inclined to want to kill each other.

THE MOST DANGEROUS MAN IN AMERICA

A parade of luminaries experienced psilocybin and acid in the early 'therapeutic' Leary sessions. Many were wildly enthusiastic. Of those that weren't perhaps the most perceptive comment came from the Beat Generation's literary deity Jack Kerouac, already fading and on the road to alcoholic decline and an early death. *'Walking on water wasn't built in a day.'* The Harvard authorities became increasingly concerned about the scientific work that seemed to be taking on the semblance of a religious cult. By May 1963 Leary and his team, who included Richard Alpert, later to establish considerable fame, credibility, and affection as Baba Ram Dass, author of *Be Here Now*, had left.

After a period of wandering and uncertainty, rich patrons intervened and the Leary crew were set up in a now legendary mansion in enormous grounds at Millbrook in the New York area. Jack Parsons would have been impressed. Indeed in some respects it seems like the Parsonage and Crowley's Abbey of Thelema had reconfigured on another twist of the spiral. The Millbrook period was the peak of Leary's sixties work.

With Alpert, and his other main associate Ralph Metzner, he had already investigated one of the great treasures of the wisdom tradition of humanity, the text generally known as *The Tibetan Book of the Dead*. The material in question was recited to a dying person, continuing for forty nine days beyond their transition, a period believed to mark the timing of movement through intermediate zones prior to either reincarnating or ideally escaping from the wheel of birth and death into the white light of the void. Jung had helped bring the work to wider attention by providing an introduction to an edition.

If a dying Christian sees Jesus, Mary, and hordes of saints and angelic beings appear they are likely to be well chuffed rather than simply regard it as an initial manifestation of consciousness that should pass and not be identified with. The psychology is quite profound and can readily serve as a guide for the living as well. It basically involves the attempt not to identify with what arises in consciousness regardless of whether it be attractive or repulsive. This helps the cessation of the desire that binds one to the karmic wheel of birth and death with its inevitable suffering. All of these manifestations of mind arise from a greater white light that ultimately outshines them all and can be realised in the present moment with the necessary preparation and perspective.

Leary recognised that the text had enough parallels to the process of a typical LSD session to serve as a potential guide. *The Psychedelic Experience* was the first major publication from him and his team. It set the mood for the early days at Millbrook and soon influenced the growing LSD culture.

Millbrook started to seem like the centre of a mystery cult. Leary and the early pioneers obviously became interested in the role of mind-manifesting substances throughout history. This is a topic that goes back to the Stone Age. The Mexican mushrooms that started Leary on his journey had a whole culture of shamanic sorcery around them. This would soon prove to be fertile ground for the works of Carlos Castaneda. Millbrook looked to the east for higher consciousness guidance but the mystery cults of the classical world were also an inspiration. It was as if an archetype had been activated. Mystery Cult. Gnosticism. Trippers seemed to be talking the same kind of language. Maybe the ancients were doing mushrooms? Before long, even though LSD was still legal, its enthusiasts were starting to see the world in a similar way to the old beliefs. Acid was increasingly regarded as a sacramental substance. It was no longer a scientific investigation but the race to bring down the Holy Spirit before nuclear end times.

John Lennon found a copy of *The Psychedelic Experience* in the recently opened *Indica* book shop in London on a visit with Paul McCartney. He apparently took the contents on board and tripped-out in that reality-tunnel. A particular line lingered. '*Whenever in doubt, turn off your mind, relax and float downstream.*' Such was the inspiration for the Beatles first psychedelic track *Tomorrow Never Knows* that appeared on their 1966 *Revolver* album. This was one of the most radically experimental musical compositions of the sixties. The basic sound of it was unlike anything heard before. It's a candidate for the accolade of being their greatest moment, even beyond the coming triumphs of *Sgt Pepper.* A basic Indian-style drone and processed hypnotic drum beat had backward tapes of guitars, cymbals, and strange tape-loop sounds overlaid to form an appropriate soundscape for Lennon's double-tracked vocals that seemed to chant as much as sing the lyrics.

John Lennon's journey was one of the most remarkable of all sixties examples of how far things could move in a short period of time. In 1964 he had been singing, '*I want to hold your hand.*' A mere two years later he was encouraging his listeners to,

> '*Lay down all thought,*
> *Surrender to the Void,*
> *It is shining*
> *It is shining.*
>
> *That you may see*
> *The meaning of within,*
> *It is being,*
> *It is being,*
>
> *That Love is all and*
> *Love is everyone,*
> *It is knowing,*
> *It is knowing.*'

Within another year it had come to,

> *'Limitless undying Love which*
> *Shines around me like a million suns,*
> *It calls me on and on, across the universe.'*

After a chat with Marshall McLuhan, the great sixties media analyst and prophet of the communication age global village where the medium is the message, Timothy Leary was advised that he himself was a vital part of the package he was hoping to disseminate. He needed to cultivate an endlessly positive persona. This wasn't too difficult for him. He also needed a snappy soundbite slogan for the media advertising age. *'Turn on, tune in, drop out'* would resound down through the decades to Leary's good and to his detriment. It became the equivalent of Crowley's *'Do what thou wilt'* and took precedent as a legacy over Leary's preferred *'Think for Yourself. Question authority'*.

1967 rapidly manifested events typical of its mythic status. There had already been sizeable stirrings of what would become recognisable as hippieness. Something was building and the need was felt for a larger scale event that could expand it further. Talk of the coming Age of Aquarius was in the air. A date in January was chosen for astrological reasons suggestive of well-aspected communication. Golden Gate Park San Francisco hosted the *Human Be-In*, *'a Gathering of the Tribes'*. Mysticism and politics met as chants to Shiva led by Beat poet Allen Ginsberg shared the stage with anti-Vietnam war diatribes and rock music. Leary, fully prepared by McLuhan, now manifested his full acid guru persona, dressed in white and intoning for the first time to a sizeable audience his *'Turn on, Tune in, Drop out'* mantra. The 30,000-strong crowd smoked plenty of spliffs, tripped-out, and felt generally excited and empowered to see just how many of them there already were. Leary had been the star of the show.

I can forgive Timothy Leary his grandiloquence in trying to save the world with LSD. I will cut him some slack for what in hindsight was irresponsibility in encouraging a generation to drop out and thereby facilitating a westward flow of innocents like some children's crusade that would soon overwhelm the Haight-Ashbury scene and be exploited, abused, and leave some very real human tragedies in its wake. The clinical pre-requisites for a good trip of set and setting would not always be available for some of these unfortunates. We shall examine the more gruesome outcomes of that shortly. In the sixties the sense of how far it was possible to take something dissolved. The space race was the best indicator of that. Huge developments in the history of the human race were occurring in rapid succession. The sky was no longer the limit. If we can put a man on the moon within a decade of deciding we want to do it who says we can't transform the consciousness of humanity in a similar period of time? Such was the incredible spirit of the age.

On June 1st 1967 the most legendary of all rock-pop albums was released. With each passing decade perspective on the relative merits of the Beatles' *Sgt Pepper* change. A few things remain constant. Some of it has always seemed brilliant and probably always will. Some of it is a bit weak. Other tracks people are changeable about. Maybe it's not even the Beatles' best album. It does carry a quite extraordinary atmosphere with it that snapshots a stunning period of time and always evokes it. The cover was an important part of the whole charisma of the album as it featured the band lined up in the company of rows of faces of famous people from different fields they had selected. This is where the dream-like thread of narrative that has taken us from the Berlin of 1930 has led.

John Lennon arranged for Aleister Crowley to be among the group featured on the cover. The famous shaven-headed image can be seen along the top row on the left. Early on in the project he had wanted to include Jesus and Hitler as well. Along with Mahatma Gandhi, JC and the Fuhrer never made it to the final version. There's little to indicate that Lennon really knew much about Crowley at all, beyond his reputation as drug pioneer and general wild man. Just below the Beast, slightly to his right, is Aldous Huxley. It's like Crowley is standing behind him looking over his shoulder. There they both are at the peak of the Summer of Love in a manner their most psychedelic visions and social prophesying could never have imagined.

A few weeks later, on June 25th, in a major moment for McLuhan's new communication age global village, the Beatles represented Britain in an unprecedented satellite TV link-up called *Our World*, performing the specially-composed *All You Need is Love* to an audience estimated at 400 million. McLuhan himself actually appeared in the Canadian section of the broadcast. The global sensorium was thoroughly massaged. It was the peak of the great wave. Other vibrations were arising that would wither at least some of the flowers.

In October 1966 LSD had been made illegal in the USA. This made a particular trajectory fairly inevitable. Leary became the most bustable person in America. G. Gordon Liddy, who later masterminded the Watergate break-in, was an early nemesis, raiding Millbrook in 1966. Leary seemed to become more politicised. He famously appeared, alongside his wife of the time, Rosemary, with John and Yoko for the recording of *Give Peace a Chance* in a Montreal hotel two years to the day after the release of *Sgt Pepper* in June 1969. Leary flamboyantly decided to seek election as Governor of California, running against incumbent Ronald Reagan. The campaign slogan was *"Come Together"* and Lennon started writing a song to promote it. Strangely enough this was when the attempts to thoroughly bust Leary peaked with various sentences for a few minor offences being strung together so that he eventually faced an astonishing twenty years in jail for possession of a small amount of marijuana.

SYMPATHY FOR THE DEVIL

'Thou shalt have danger and trouble.'
'Worship me with fire and blood.'
'Damn them who pity! Kill and torture,
spare not, be upon them.'

The Book of the Law.

'I am Abraxas, the son of God, the son of Darkness, and I stand behind ALL the courts of the world.'

Charles Manson. 1986 payroll hearing.

STRANGE DAYS

'Strange days have found us,
Strange days have tracked us down.
They're going to destroy
Our casual joys.'

The Doors. *Strange Days*.

I FEEL IT'S SIGNIFICANT that perhaps the two most notable rock tracks from the year of the Summer of Love carried a mood somewhat at odds with Flower Power. The Beatles *A Day in the Life* is the final moment of *Sgt Pepper* but it seems to almost celebrate bleakness and alienation with stupendous intensity. The Doors provide another motif from the Crowley Huxley Berlin 1930 dream as they brought Brecht's *Alabama Song* forward into 1967 with a version on their first album. The closing track, *The End* presented an unsettling oedipal psychodrama set to music that seemed to be an appropriate soundtrack for a primal ritual. This was understood by Francis Ford Coppola who would later make use of it in the climactic moments of *Apocalypse Now*. Jim Morrison found *'weird scenes'* and *'danger on the edge of town'* as he travelled the *'highway to the end of the night'*, a rider on the storm of the *'snake'*, Dionysus inciting the maenads to sacrifice him. Fiercely literate and cultured, Morrison saw something else that was stirring. If the great ceremony was about to begin and the gods and myths of the ages be reinvented then sex and death might meet at the *'feast of friends'*. The enduring success of the Doors music and Morrison's status as mythic icon indicates he helped express feelings that others shared.

When a two thousand year reality tunnel breaks up, things are not necessarily going to run smoothly. During the sixties the tensions between contrasting generations produced extremes of response amongst the young. There were Nuit's Love-ins and psychedelia but that was not all. In the heady cocktail many different forms of magic and mysticism flourished. In California in '67, if you looked beneath the surface there were a number of groups who seemed to be taking their lead from Ra Hoor Khuit. Vietnam dramatised a lot of the issues. The repression brought down on the hippy drug culture created a lot of anger and then hatred. Not everyone was into Gandhi and putting flowers down soldier's rifle barrels as protest.

On April 30th 1966 the Church of Satan had been founded by Anton Szandor LaVey. He was a remarkable character with a mythic biography worthy of film noir. Onetime circus lion tamer and cinema organist, he had allegedly been an early boyfriend of Marilyn Monroe. Working in Las Vegas he met the gangster Bugsy Seagal. A student of criminology, he later found employment as a photographer for the San Francisco Police Department which inevitably meant him seeing some unpleasant things. In the middle of this busy schedule he found time to become a psychic investigator and delver into all things magical.

LaVey considered that the natural energies repressed by Christianity should be released and celebrated. He seemed to consider Crowley to be a wimp and was into Nazi regalia and the study of their occultism. H. P. Lovecraft, and Enochian magic were incorporated into his fiercely Nietzschean blend, *The Satanic Bible.*

Fading Hollywood sex-goddess Jayne Mansfield had a serious interest in the philosophy. Not all of her associates shared her enthusiasm. Contention arose. A curse was cast. LaVey warned Mansfield to stay clear. She didn't. The famous result: virtual decapitation in a car crash. Satanism was hip in '68. One of the big movies of the year was Polanski's *Rosemary's Baby*. For a while the Church was a big media deal, fading in the seventies through the usual schisms and making a comeback in the eighties and nineties.

LaVey hated the hippies. His film noir sensibilities despaired of the aesthetic polluting of his beloved San Fransisco by those he considered to be terminally unstylish. I can understand why Frank Zappa had proclaimed that, *'flower power sucks'*. There had been a lot of fluffy bleatings by cultureless freeloading dorks at the time. During the Summer of Love some of LaVey's Black Masses involved crushing a sugar cube soaked in acid, urinating on some cannabis and hanging a picture of Timothy Leary or some eastern guru upside down.

Perhaps the most interesting manifestation of the powerful, apparently opposing forces, working through the sixties was the Process Church of the Final Judgement. It began when Robert and Mary Anne DeGrimston met in London in 1963 whilst studying Scientology. Robert was a former cavalry officer, militaristic, tall, athletic, well-dressed. Mary Anne was once the wife of boxing champion Sugar Ray Robinson, and a runner of a prostitution service linked to the Profumo scandal. They left Scientology to create their own system of psychotherapy called Compulsions Analysis, soon attracting wealthy and influential types. Things started getting weird. Some kind of group mind seemed to be emerging. Just as Dianetics had developed into Scientology, so Compulsions Analysis begat the Process Church of the Final Judgement.

The transition from psychotherapy to religion was affected when the core of the group went off for a profoundly strange episode at the ruined Mayan site of Xtul. It was idyllic until hit by a massive hurricane. Somehow they escaped unscathed. Experience of such extremes crucially affected the fledgling cult's worldview. Robert DeGrimston produced *The Xtul Dialogues*. It became a case of

Apocalypse Now presided over by God and the Devil as one and the same being in its diverse aspects of Jehovah, Lucifer, Satan, and Christ.

Back in London they soon acquired a reputation as weirdo Nazi brainwashers. Championing Hitler and showing films about '*War, Degradation, Violence, Despair, Power, Lust, Fear, Hate, Sin and Horror*' probably didn't help much. They wore a kind of uniform consisting of black robes and silver swastika-like crosses. Many of them had Alsatian dogs.

The group folded in the seventies but their strange sensibilities seem increasingly contemporary. Maybe in some parallel dimension they carried on. In Britain they might have become bigger than the Church of England, as their Jesus enclaves raised millions for charity, presided over by some Luciferian in a limo, some John Lennon in an Armani suit. Maybe.

One notable influence on the nasty side of west coast occult counter-culture was the Solar Lodge of the OTO. With a base in the desert it was run by Jean Brayton, generally depicted as an unpleasant racist. An odd sequence of events led to them being the final resting place for what I consider to be one of the great lost occult treasures of the century: the correspondence between Dion Fortune and Crowley. A child began a fire that destroyed them. He was punished by being kept in a small wooden container outdoors in the high desert temperatures. Some appalled visitors informed the police and the whole scene was busted. The Lodge was an offshoot of Jack Parsons Agape group. He, as a Libertarian, would have been appalled to see such developments.

HELTER SKELTER

The most important product of this matrix of influences was Charles Manson. During time in jail he had come into contact with Scientology and adopted some of its ideas along with paranoia about the potential magical powers of its adherents. He was also impressed by the Beatles, getting serious about singing and guitar playing. Released into the Californian Summer of Love, his jail psychology was brought into contact with drugs, sex, and the whole occult underground.

The original version of Ed Sanders' *The Family* is the most entertaining exposition of the '*sleazo input*' available to Manson. The Process Church was considered to be a strong contender for influence. Complaints about their depiction led to subsequent editions being adjusted. The OTO Solar Lodge allegedly had crossover points with the large grouping that loosely clustered around Manson. Charlie himself was a big fan of Robert Henlein's cult sci-fi novel *Stranger in a Strange Land*. Henlein had known Jack Parsons and allegedly absorbed Crowley via him. This inspiration filtered through into the novel. All kinds of general witchiness was rife.

Manson, for all his jail background, seemed on the surface to be a loved-up kind of guy. He made a strong favourable impression on lots of people, soon attracting a free-floating community around him who came to be known as the Family. His immediate mission seemed to be the promotion of his music. To that end he cultivated as many connections as possible. Beach Boy Dennis Wilson was the most famous long-term convert. The band actually recorded a Manson song on a B side. Even a rock heavyweight like Neil Young stated that Charlie was a major talent. And that's part of the fascination with Manson. There was something unique and brilliant about him, some extraordinary charisma. Despite decades in the prison system there still is. He was clearly a sorcerer of sorts and possessed of an unusual kind of intelligence despite sometimes adopting an almost hillbilly persona. Charlie is now touted as some kind of an eco-warrior.

Something was also horrifically wrong and has stayed wrong. It was intuited early on in the legend by those who claimed he was both Jesus and Satan, a blending also being promoted by the Process Church. There's no getting away from that other side of Manson. He was a big admirer of Hitler and violence in general, managing to put the fear into plenty of people long before he became Public Demon Number One. He also kept the mediocre psychology of the pimp, hustler, and thief, alongside that of the rock star, guru, and sorceror.

1968 was a year of riots, revolutionary agitation, the Rolling Stones' *Street Fighting Man* and *Sympathy for the Devil*. Acid was being replaced by heroin. The Vietnam situation deteriorated. A sense of apocalypse was building. Away from the cities, based out on a ranch and in the desert, Manson and the Family, fuelled by drugs and sex, fed on sleazo input of paranoia and violence. The mood turned bad.

On the night of 8/8/69, Anton Szandor LaVey had performed a ceremony named the 'Rising Forth' to trash the hippies he despised. '*Beware you psychedelic vermin! Your smug pomposity with its thin disguise of tolerance will serve you no longer! We know your mark and recognise it well. We walk the night as the villains no longer! Our steeds await and their eyes are ablaze with the fires of Hell!'* Later that night a group of Manson's associates set out for the home of Roman Polanski and his wife the actress Sharon Tate. There's no direct connection between LaVey and the murders but he clearly expressed in a most spooky manner something of the dark side of the zeitgeist that night, especially considering his own connections to Polanski's *Rosemary's Baby*. A baby was about to be murdered.

If trial prosecutor Vincent Bugliosi is to be believed, Manson had created a bizarre acid psychosis apocalyptic worldview named Helter Skelter after his warped interpretation of a Beatles song on the White Album. He and his followers believed in an imminent race war that only an elite would survive. Charlie intended to help things along by actually committing some murders that could be blamed on black revolutionaries. Manson advocates are contemptuous of this. Something however prompted a group of people around him to feel motivated to engage in the most extreme of acts. Speculation that the killings weren't as random as they initially appeared, that bad drug deals and a whole lot of other factors were involved may have some truth. None of the additional angles of enquiry explain the type and mood of violence involved.

The arguments go back and forth about the extent of Manson's involvement in the atrocities that followed. He did not commit any of the murders and was not in the same room at the time when they happened. The degree to which he may have ordered or influenced them remains contentious. It is certain though that he knew what was happening and could have stopped the events if he had wanted to. And this is the bottom line for fans of the Family. Over two nights, a bunch of people including an eight months pregnant woman and her unborn child, were horribly murdered, and no amount of sophistry on the planet can justify or excuse that.

The anti-matter Woodstock that put the final full-stop to the sixties, *'the day the music died'*, occurred on December 6th 1969 at Altamont in California. It's totally appropriate to the mythology of the time that the Rolling Stones were the eye of the hurricane.

Hell's Angels were hired by the Stones as 'security' for a huge gig they were playing. Some of the bikers proceeded to get violent with the audience throughout the whole course of the day. The vibes got very bad. *Sympathy for the Devil* saw the Stones essentially carrying out an invocation without realising what they were doing.

The event was captured on film in *Gimme Shelter*. A little way into the track the band had to stop as violence spilled over onto the stage. Jagger tried to handle the situation but failed. The title track of that movie contains lines that express the tensions of the time as well as any.

> '*Storm is threatening*'—
> '*Rape and murder,*
> *it's just a shot away.*
> *Love, sister,*
> *it's just a kiss away.*'

A young black guy near the front of the audience was foolish enough to pull a gun. He was instantly stabbed to death by Security in full view of the Stones. Jagger had lost control of the forces the band had romantically dabbled with. This was a defining moment for them. They had been at one with a powerful aspect of the period, wielding an energy and charisma that virtually no other rock bands could hope to match but nothing would ever be the same. For a few years they continued to create great music but before long it just didn't matter any more. From Woodstock to Altamont was barely four months. It did rather seem that an acceleration principle was at work.

LUCIFER RISING

A lot of music expressed the Thelemic side of the sixties. One film-maker was second to none in invoking it on screen. Kenneth Anger had featured as a small child in the classic 1935 movie production of *A Midsummer Night's Dream*. This helped him to cultivate his fascination with the bizarre mythic world of the twentieth century's most distinctive art-form and to later produce his legendary literary expose of that era, *Hollywood Babylon*. He also became an underground experimental movie maker, bringing to his work his uniquely individual style, being both gay and a passionate advocate of Aleister Crowley. He saw the art of film-making as potentially a form of spell-casting. His major works do function as rituals of invocation. The general style of rapid editing image blending with striking surreal juxtapositions, often of emotionally intense material, has been cited as inspirational to the likes of David Lynch and many rock videos.

An early sign of things to come was 1954's psychedelic

Inauguration of the Pleasure Dome. It featured Marjorie Cameron as Kali Babalon and Anais Nin as Astarte. The sixties were Anger's decade. He recognised the massive Thelemic manifestation and encouraged it wherever he could.

Inspired by a short Crowley poem to the light bringer, Anger conceived of *Lucifer Rising* in 1966. One famous line caught the spirit of the time. '*The Key of Joy is disobedience*'. The process that would bring the film project to completion would be a long tortuous one.

Bobby Beausoleil was a charismatic musician who hung out on the West Coast scene before the hippy hype and saw out the Summer of Love and beyond. He had been in an early version of the band that came to be called Love with Arthur Lee. His most ambitious project was the Orkustra, a wildly eclectic improvisational combo who played electrified world music. In the midst of a full-on performance during the heady daze of 1967 he was seen by Kenneth Anger who introduced himself by cutting right to the chase with '*you are Lucifer*'. Beausoleil was into the idea of starring in and providing the soundtrack for an experimental occult movie. The initial collaboration soon concluded acrimoniously after a public autumn equinox musical ritual theatre event imploded through malfunctioning machinery and Anger's ill-advised consumption of acid.

Beausoleil's karma steered him into a dangerous matrix of destiny when he came to move in social circles that included Charles Manson and his Family of wild women and increasingly intense young men. When some hardcore bikers arrived on the scene a chain of events were unleashed that would lead to unimaginable horrors. In common with many of the counter-culture of the time, Beausoleil romanticised the Hell's Angels as noble barbarians. In an attempt to gain kudos he set up a drug deal on their behalf that went badly wrong when the substances were claimed to be duff. Forced to try and regain the bikers cash or suffer likely death himself, Beausoleil found himself in an escalating situation in which Manson himself became involved that led to him stabbing the dealer, a man he had once shared a house with, to death.

It has been claimed that one factor in the motivation of the Tate LaBianca murders was an attempt to set up a copycat scenario that would exonerate the arrested Beausoleil of the earlier murder. Whatever the case, it led him to be associated forever with Manson, although the two men had significant differences. Death Row followed and then years in prisons where gang violence was rampant.

Anger had been in London in 1968, hanging out with the Rolling Stones, later claiming to have inspired *Sympathy for the Devil*. Connections established then were apparent in his most intense creation, 1969's *Invocation of My Demon Brother*. It was described by its maker as '*The shadowing forth of Our Lord, as the Powers of Darkness gather at a midnight Mass. The dance of the magus widdershins around the Swirling Spiral Force, the solar swastika, until the Bringer of Light - Lucifer - breaks through.*' It was only eleven minutes long. Mick Jagger supplied a constant minimalist moog synthesiser soundtrack backdrop to a rapid series of images centred around a ritual scenario. Anger himself was the magus. Footage shot in 1967 for the original *LuciferRising* project was used. Bobby Beausoleil is heavily featured. LaVey appears with a swastika flag. There are images of the Vietnam war and the Rolling Stones' Brian Jones commemoration concert in Hyde Park, including glimpses of Hell's Angels present that day.

The film appeared as Beausoleil was arrested for murder and the Manson horrors began. It seems to encapsulate the intensity of 1969 and to somehow invoke the later conclusion at Altamont. Anger had wanted Jagger as Lucifer and maybe in some sense his film-making spell-casting did manifest that result but in a tangential way.

In 1970 work restarted on *Lucifer*, filming in Egypt with Marianne Faithfull. Anger met Crowley enthusiast Jimmy Page who agreed to do the soundtrack. This was at the busy peak of Zeppelin's career and only 28 minutes of music had been created by 1976. Anger's frustration at this led to a falling out between the two men and left the door open for an extraordinary karmic twist.

In prison Bobby Beausoleil's fundamental musical creativity won through in the end. He was able to set up a music project using donated instruments and through designing his own increasingly complex experimental electronic gizmos. Contact was re-established with Anger. A brief listening to some music composed in prison was enough to convince Anger to replace Jimmy Page. Amazingly, prison authorities were convinced to allow Beausoleil and his Freedom Orchestra to record a soundtrack album. The project took a long time as prison lockdowns following violent gang clashes disrupted the schedule. The musicians saw some film footage at the start of their project and improvised from there. At no point was the music able to be synchronised with the visuals which makes the final result all the more remarkable.

The finished film is barely half an hour long. There is no dialogue. The visuals call to mind the meeting point between magic and surrealism which was perhaps the fundamental dynamic behind the great sixties upheaval. It has to be acknowledged that Beausoleil's music is extraordinary stuff and some kind of triumph of the spirit for a man who has lived an indubitably dark strange odyssey. Jimmy Page appears very briefly, seen sitting in profile, holding a replica of the Stele of Revealing in front of a framed photo of Crowley. The rock connection is stronger via the Satanic Majesties, the Rolling Stones. Jagger's famous sixties consort Marianne Faithfull plays Lilith and Anita Pallenberg, onetime partner of both Brian Jones and Keith Richards, has a strong role in the visual proceedings. Donald Cammell, who directed Jagger in the masterpiece psychodrama movie *Performance* and later shot himself in the head, plays Osiris. The visuals move between an erupting volcano, the Sphinx and the Temple of Karnak in Egypt, the German Externsteine, Avebury, Stonehenge, and the brooding psychedelic den of a group of magicians. Finally, a UFO light disc of some kind appears at Karnak. It may refer to Crowley's poem where the body of *'sun-souled Lucifer'* is a *'blood-ruby'*.

It wasn't until 1980 that the film was completed. Anger has said that just as the final version was set to premiere in New York, one Mark Chapman attended a screening of his films in Hawaii. He approached the director afterwards and questioned him about Mick Jagger, Keith Richards, Anita Pallenberg and finally, John Lennon. After shaking Anger's hand he gave him a couple of bullets saying *'these are for John Lennon'*. Such was the backdrop to the appearance of the masterpiece of the artist who more than anyone else was plugged into the Thelemic backdrop of the sixties.

A MAN SURROUNDED BY A WHIRLWIND OF SAND

'There is no figure from the second half of the twentieth century who has a better claim on the continuation of Crowley's 'Great Work' than Dr. Timothy Leary.'

'The High Priest and the Great Beast'
Sub Rosa article adapted from
I Have America Surrounded: The Life of Timothy Leary. John Higgs.

AS THE DECADE CONCLUDED, Crowley's fame and influence increased. 1969 saw the publication of a new edition of the enormous autobiographical *Confessions*. Israel Regardie's positive study *The Eye in the Triangle* followed in 1970. Sixties psychonauts found Thelemic contexts and perspectives to enhance their understandings.

A prime example concerned Timothy Leary and the appearance of a motif that would come to have increasing significance. The mythological disastrous Altamont concert occurred sixty years to the day after the Choronzon ritual. Leary had actually been present, flying in with Mick Jagger, and had been sitting at the side of the stage with Rosemary. It was a long way from the Human Be-In.

On initially entering the prison system Leary was amused to find himself taking psychological evaluation tests he had designed himself. He made sure the results indicated a conformist with a fondness for gardening and was duly assigned to a minimum security prison. On September 12th 1970, barely a month away from his fiftieth birthday, he escaped. The former Harvard academic climbed a tree to get onto a roof, crawled along a telephone wire and dropped down over a fence. Waiting accomplices whisked him away to a reunion with his wife and a subsequent flight in disguise with a false passport to Algeria. It's no hyperbole to say this was a mind-blowing event. It struck a mythic note by seeming to dramatise what the whole LSD thing was all about. Leary's living legend status increased exponentially with this extraordinary exploit. The American authorities were not exactly best-pleased.

A bizarre period followed that saw the Leary's in the company of the radical political Black Panther group. Things soon soured as leader Eldridge Cleaver got increasingly denunciatory about the revolutionary credibility of psychedelia as a force for social change. He held the Learys captive but they got away and were able to secure the protection of the Algerian government.

Strange destiny intervened in a manner that would eventually cause Leary to wonder just what forces were really at work in manoeuvring him across the world to Algeria.

When the news spread that Leary had surfaced an English writer named Brian Barritt made a long journey specifically to try and meet him. The two men shared some biographical traits including absurd military careers that had both ended in Court Martial and drug-related time in prison. Most importantly, Barritt had done a lot of acid, had occultist leanings, and was the author of *Whisper*, a freeform Beat piece that had drawn favourable comments from William Burroughs. Leary would soon describe him as *'a fucking genius'*.

The pair were drawn into a strange event in the Algerian desert that I feel partakes of similar haunting qualities to the Babalon Working in terms of a gradual decades-long process of greater levels of meaning being revealed. What ensued gradually filtered out in the seventies, mentioned in Leary's *Confessions of a Hope Fiend* and Robert Anton Wilson's *Cosmic Trigger* but the most detailed account didn't appear until over a quarter of a century later in Barritt's own powerful poetic *The Road of Excess*.

The Easter weekend of 1971 saw Leary and Barritt take their first LSD trip together. The chosen location was Bou Saada on the edge of the Sahara desert, a place known for the beauty of its setting, hence the meaning of its name: *City of Happiness*. Having ingested the acid they drove a little way into the dunes, eventually stopping at a dried up riverbed to watch the sun set and a full moon rise as the drug began to take effect.

Barritt saw in his head *'the image of a man surrounded by a whirlwind of sand, the dust devil spinning a thin shroud around his figure, and from out of nowhere the name Doctor John Dee and the impression of a scrolled manuscript.'* It was as if the sky was on fire. There was an intense feeling of the presence of an enormous timescale where the ancient past was simultaneously present.

'The throbbing earth-beat pulsing through my blood grows louder, powered by the clapping hands and stamping feet of all the

ancestors who have gone before me.' 'I stand a mile high, time is wrapped around my ankles causing flurries in the atoms of sand, spinning universes around me, building galaxies, creating microcosmic stars.'

'Golden vessels with the faces of Egyptian Gods on their prows glide between life and death.' 'Through a window a woman with the face of an angel and the body of a spider is chatting me up with her eyes. I am climbing up the rungs of a vertical ladder leading to the entrance of her flying saucer' – 'it's the face of the moon I am climbing towards. At the top of the dune the moon is so big it blocks out the rest of the sky.'

Whilst Barritt was experiencing this he was also aware of Leary walking up and down, as if engaged in some ritual performance, repeatedly reciting *"Solve et Coagula"*, an alchemical phrase broadly referring to a process of separation followed by a new joining together.

The next morning saw the pair

'watch the sun rising in all its glory on one edge of the horizon as the full moon sets on the other, with Venus, Mars and Jupiter (I think) spanning the arch between them. Behind the planets the stars have laced themselves together into fantastic complexities that spin off Catherine wheels of vibrations that stream across the solar system right down to Tim and myself, standing with arms spread soaking them up through the palms of our hands. It's Easter Sunday.'

They returned from the trip feeling pretty damn good and with a mysterious feeling that something big had gone down.

Time passed. A typical series of Leary adventures saw him relocated to Switzerland under the protection of a fabulously wealthy totally dodgy business man who was, amongst other things, an arms dealer. A contract was created ensuring he got a sizeable proportion of any money coming from future Leary publications in exchange for keeping him out of jail and enabling him to live a very comfortable lifestyle. Despite his delicate international status an American company were prepared to front a sizeable sum for the jail escape saga. Faced with writer's block Leary persuaded his patron to fly in Brian Barritt to assist.

A colossal sustained drug binge followed. Barritt started reading a copy of Crowley's *Confessions* that someone had left lying around. When he got to the account of the great Algerian desert extravaganza with Victor Neuberg, the Enochian epic most fully recorded in *The Vision and the Voice* that had been of such central significance in the Babalon Working, the mood rapidly changed. It started with a kind of double-take, shortly followed by Barritt feeling like someone had just walked over his grave.

To begin with, Crowley and Neuberg had been in the vicinity of Bou Saada for their desert magick. The centrepiece of the whole undertaking was of course the legendary encounter with Choronzon. Crowley had been wearing a black hooded robe and his description of the demon mentions myriad forms that *'swirl senselessly into haphazard heaps like dust devils'*. Barritt had used the exact same phrase. The manuscript associated with John Dee put the matter beyond doubt.

'I have been moved like a chess piece from London to Bou Saada without being aware of the real cause, my instincts had been told what to do and all the in between actions were only the rationalisations of my intellect.' As for Leary, *'The mysterious force that brought Tim to Bou Saada had to get him out of prison in the States first, fly him across the Atlantic and drive him out of Algiers itself by using Eldridge Cleaver.'*

The Choronzon event has already been briefly alluded to in the section on the Babalon Working. It's worth going into a little bit more detail in order to better appreciate just why it's an occult legend and Barritt and Leary might have got a bit freaked-out to find themselves in synch with it.

According to Crowley he and Neuberg did not initially travel to Algeria with the intention of performing Enochian magic. It was the kind of spiritual retreat in a primal landscape that the world-traveller mountaineer resorted to in order to recharge his batteries. He had just divorced Rose following her descent into alcoholism. He also saw an opportunity to toughen up his student Neuberg. A few days after arriving Crowley heard the same voice that had dictated *The Book of the Law* instructing him to go into the desert and work magick. It was then that he intuited what would be involved. As a man who always carried assorted notebooks with him he had the relevant Enochian material at hand.

In terms of mood and visual aspects the whole undertaking was unsurpassed. Crowley and Neuberg presented the appearance of a walking tableau from the *Arabian Nights* as they wandered across the desert. The Beast was indubitably the great sorcerer, generally dressed in Arab clothing, bearded but with his head shaved save for a phallic forelock, sporting an enormous ring, and during one part of the procedure repeatedly reciting a verse from the Koran with a prostration on the sand to accompany it. Neuberg was fashioned into a vision of Crowley's familiar spirit or some kind of djinn. Already strangely gnome-like in general appearance, he now had his head shaved with the exception of two tufts of hair that were dyed red and twisted into horns. He was occasionally kept on a lead.

Most of the Enochian Aethyrs were explored by Crowley staring into a topaz stone he had fixed to the centre of a cross. He would see visions inside it and report the details to Neuberg who served as scribe. There were a few variants including the creation of a makeshift stone circle on a hill where Neuberg sodomised Crowley.

John Dee wrote briefly of a *Coronzon*, describing it as *'that mighty devil'*. It appears to occupy a role similar to the serpent in the Eden story, at least as far as the church portrayed it, a force that exploited the lower wilfulness of humanity. Crowley adopted a variant spelling which due to the fame of his association has carried through. He categorised Choronzon as *'Dweller in the Abyss'*. He has also become known as the Demon of Dispersion, associated with fear, insanity, lies, malice, and restriction. This force, says Crowley in his *Confessions*, *'is not really an individual'*. The Abyss is filled with false forms, egoic distortions, and *'each such chance aggregation asserts itself to be an individual and shrieks, "I am I!"'* This is in contradistinction to the True Will informed by Knowledge and Conversation of the Holy Guardian Angel.

At some point in any meaningful individuation process such forces within the psyche must be confronted, hence Crowley's deliberate summoning. What Jungians may accede to is the idea that some unusual people may find themselves confronting a more collective aspect of Choronzon.

The Aiwass voice instructed Crowley on the Choronzon business which was to be a more elaborate affair featuring classic elements of ceremonial magic that the modern western mind has absorbed through horror novels and films. There was a circle of protection in which Neuberg sat holding a consecrated dagger. A little beyond that in the sand was a triangle into which would be conjured the mighty demon. The blood of some sacrificed pigeons would provide the energy for manifestation. Although Crowley's accounts of the proceedings deliberately left details out to discourage the foolhardy from attempting repetition most commentators have discerned a controversial innovative procedural point whereby Crowley would be sitting in the triangle himself, dressed in a black hooded robe, offering himself up for possession. Neuberg was under the strictest of instructions not to pay attention to any of the pleading and trickery that the demon would inevitably use to try and get released from the triangle.

Sure enough all kinds of malarkey ensued. Crowley became aware of Choronzon from within the topaz stone when he heard a voice intoning the now famous invocation to open the gates of the Abyss, *'Zazas, Zazas, Nasatanada Zazas'*. The demon's opening lines were memorable. *'From me come leprosy and pox and plague and cancer and cholera and the falling sickness. Ah! I will reach up to the knees of the Most High, and tear his phallus with my teeth, and I will bray his testicles in a mortar, and make poison thereof, to slay the sons of men.'*

The demon took over Crowley and started shapeshifting, appearing to Neuberg as a former lover, a snake with a human head and so on. It pleaded a terrible thirst begging for water. As Neuberg was mesmerised the creature was dropping handfuls of sand over the edge of the restraining protective magical barriers. Suddenly it sprang on Neuberg and, in the possibly humorously overstated account in *Confessions*, *'flung him to the earth and tried to tear out his throat with froth-covered fangs'*. Neuberg bravely flourished his dagger and banished the demon leaving Crowley out for the count. Eventually, by way of conclusion the name of Babalon was written in the sand, the circle and triangle were erased, and a fire of purification lit.

Quite possibly the pair of them were under the influence of some drug that increased the intensity of the visions and general mood but the entire sequence of *The Vision and the Voice* needs to be taken on board for full appreciation of the context. This was the peak of Crowley's career. The magick synthesised all of the traditions he had worked with the incoming Aeon of Horus. As already mentioned the issue of whether Crowley successfully confronted his Shadow and crossed the Abyss remains controversial but there is no doubting that poor Neuberg was ruined by the experience. As Israel Regardie mused in *The Eye in the Triangle,*

> 'This kind of experience, painful and disturbing that it was, is not given to any but a few. Whether they be chosen ones or the damned, is a choice that I do not have to make.'

Brian Barritt felt that he had actually seen Crowley at the time of his possession by Choronzon. This was plenty to be going on with. He and Leary looked carefully at the *Confessions*. Leary was particularly taken by a piece concerning one of the Aethyrs invoked a few days prior to Choronzon. Crowley was given an explanation as to where it was all leading. On the other side of the Abyss, as he became a Master of the Temple, he would leave behind many facets of his previous personas to take on the role of Nemo, the head gardener of planet Earth. He would be responsible for helping other flowers to bloom and eventually take over from him. As recounted in the *Confessions*,

> 'My moral part was to help humanity in Jupitarian work, such as governing, teaching, creating, exhorting men to aspire to become nobler, holier, worthier, kinglier, kindlier, and more generous.'

This idea greatly appealed to Leary who immediately identified himself as the new Nemo and was buzzing with it for weeks afterwards, calling himself Timo and suchlike.

Barritt was initially sceptical but decades later, when writing *The Road of Excess* and moving beyond *Confessions* to *The Vision and the Voice* itself, he found a mention of *'The River-bed near Bou-Sada'* as the specific location for the working. He came to feel *'that on Easter Sat/Sun 1971 Tim inherited Crowley's old job.'*

In Switzerland Leary was handed a deck of the *Thoth* Tarot and decided to test its divinatory capacity. He asked, *'Who am I and what is my destiny?'* Cutting to a single card for his answer, he got the Ace of Discs. In Crowley's deck the design on that particular card is almost a personal signature. It has one of Crowley's magickal names, *To Meta Therion*, the Great Beast, written on it. The qualities he attributes to it are like an idealised self-portrait. Leary felt this was confirmation he was a carrier of the Thelemic energy. In a nice variant on Crowley's most famous designation, President Nixon referred to Leary as *'the most dangerous man in America'*. Something of the legend of infamy and general vilification had certainly stuck to him and worse was to come.

Leary and Barritt didn't think they may have been reincarnations of Crowley and Neuberg. Their lives overlapped datewise. The earlier Dee and Kelly were possibilities even though Crowley himself had already blagged Kelly as a past life. It was more a feeling of being links in a chain of transmission, *'recurring cycles with different representatives each time around'* as Barritt put it. There was also a feeling that with acid, consciousness could become aware of itself functioning on a level beyond the usual understanding of spacetime. The obvious initial thoughts were on the past but I'm inclined to believe the future was just as strongly present.

The book that Barritt had been flown in to help Leary with came to be called *Confessions of a Hope Fiend*, deliberately conjoining two Crowley titles as an acknowledgement of the startling events. In it Leary would state that

'The eerie synchronicities between our lives and that of Crowley, which were later to preoccupy us, were still unfolding with such precision as to make us wonder if one can escape the programmed imprinting with which we are born.'

Having had the hidden Crowley script revealed it wasn't long before Leary's life took another tumultuous turn. An ill-advised trip to Afghanistan led to him being snatched by American agents in January 1973 and taken back to America. His previous problems were as nothing compared to what was to follow.

The following three years or so that Leary spent in jail are perhaps the most problematical in his entire biography. It was very easy for the media to spin the line that he had finally cracked and become a total acid casualty. The reason for this was his sudden interest in outer space. The science section of the prison library helped get him interested in Panspermia, the theory that life originated elsewhere in the universe and was perhaps seeded here by comets, meteorites and suchlike. It was the start of a major new adventure.

During the summer of 1973, Leary and a small group of prison associates engaged in a kind of meditational telepathy experiment to contact Higher Intelligence somewhere in outer space. In response their brains produced what came to be known as the *Starseed Transmissions*. Barely a few pages long, this short passage is sufficient to give their flavour:

'*Life was seeded on your planet billions of years ago by nucleotide templates which contained the blueprint for gradual evolution through a sequence of biomechanical stages.*

The goal of evolution is to produce nervous systems capable of communicating with and returning to the Galactic Network where we, your interstellar parents, await you.

Mutate!
Come home in glory.'

It's reasonably clear that this is not dissimilar to Nuit's '*I am divided for loves sake, for the chance of union*', '*put on the wings and arouse the coiled splendour within you. Come unto me.*' Leary knew *The Book of the Law.* Was he just engaging in a self-indulgent attempt to restate it in more modern scientific terminology?

It was also stated that '*We are sending a comet to your solar system as a sign that the time has come to look to the stars.*' This was a reference to what became the major astronomical event of 1973. A comet named Kohoutek, initially discovered in March, was set to reach maximum brightness by the end of the year. Scientists predicted a visual feast as it approached the sun. It was widely publicised that it was expected to shine as brightly as the full moon.

This was the beginning of a strong interest in ideas of space migration, orbiting cities, and so on. Some would deem it fantasising from a man trapped in prison who wanted to imagine himself free. Others feel there was much of merit there and Leary was only making clear what could have actually been made real with the technology of the time if the world hadn't been investing such enormous resources in the perpetuation of the nuclear arms race and general insanity. The fundamental point for Leary was the evolutionary issue of what purpose does getting high actually serve? The human body does seem built to potentially experience altered states. It may be that as well as a spiritual component they are waiting to fully kick in when we leave the planet and return 'home'.

To Leary the comet was a tangible sign of the starseed phenomenon and an auspicious omen of a new mass consciousness of the idea. He wasn't alone in seeing significance there. The unwholesome Children of God cult saw it as a sign of a *Revelations* apocalypse. In the end, Kohoutek entirely failed to provide the promised spectacle and became a byword for total dud but it did provide a background and mood-setter for some powerful events. 1973 did turn out to be an above average year. Leary's great opponent, the man who had proclaimed him as the *'most dangerous man in America'* progressively imploded. Watergate was probably the one word that dominated American consciousness.

Leary's fundamental problem was how he could possibly get out of prison. He came to believe his only option was in talking to the FBI about the kind of stuff they wanted to know from him about the global LSD network, the people who had helped him escape in 1970 and so on. Leary had been surrounded by people he couldn't trust, informers, double agents and suchlike. The Nixon regime had a sophisticated counter-intelligence operation against the alternative-culture which often meant planting people in various groups who then encouraged extreme action that would undermine them. Leary started talking. Word was carefully leaked to the press and his old associates became paranoid and many vehemently denounced him. This destroying of his credibility obviously suited the government's purpose. He was even moved to a new prison with the false surname of 'Thrush' in an obvious strategy to make him unpopular with other prisoners. This kind of game could have cost him his life.

The story of Leary the nefarious snitch has entrenched itself. A few years after his death files were made more available and the press ran the story as if it was new, eagerly taking the opportunity to make him look bad. All of the relevant details had been aired twenty years before and a group of Leary's friends went on a media offensive to defend him. The positive spin is that he played an elaborate game in which for all of the material he gave them no mass busts and annihilation of the counter-culture ever occurred. The only people he ever directly testified against were unpleasant individuals who deserved it. On the other hand, his lack of foresight in terms of what he was saying helped perpetuate a situation where his former wife Rosemary was forced to live in hiding on the run from the authorities for over twenty years. It is fortunate that this situation was resolved and the pair reconciled before Leary's death.

The acid timewarp in the Algerian desert has been written about on a number of occasions now, primarily by Brian Barritt, Leary himself, his biographer John Higgs, Robert Anton Wilson, and Gary Lachman. The big question is what does it mean? Of all the episodes in Crowley's life that Leary could have made a strange connection to why the legendary Enochian Choronzon magick? I intuit more of the Huxley Crowley dream myth process at work.

Barritt mentions at length Leary's own initial conclusions. On the other side of the Abyss Crowley became Nemo the tender of the garden, the great teacher. That was probably the fundamental point. I tend to believe that Leary did get Crowley's old job. Quite often in the initiatory process though, when something is accomplished and signified on what could be termed a fourth dimensional level, the third dimensional ramifications take a long time to play out. At that point in the 3D timeline, for all his troubles, jail escape and so on, Leary had not encountered Choronzon and crossed the Abyss. This process began in earnest very soon after the full realization of the Crowley link with the Afghan kidnapping.

It has often been speculated that when Crowley confronted his Shadow in the form of Choronzon he may have failed to properly complete the process and subsequently deteriorated, albeit slowly, and failed to integrate aspects of his total being that left him unbalanced and prone to undermining by the more negative side of himself hence his decline into heroin addiction, his problematical relationships and so on.

How's this for an ordeal of the Abyss agenda? During the second jail phase Leary endured periods in solitary confinement, was occasionally held entirely incommunicado, had all kinds of false information spread about him and was set up in such a way as to potentially put his life in danger from other prisoners. His head was shaved and marked as if to indicate preparation for a lobotomy. He was dosed with psychiatric drugs. On one occasion when his wife visited him he was being kept in a strait-jacket. The Californian prison system is not known for being a chill-out zone. Violent factions had their turf wars. All kinds of horrors were everyday scenes. He had no idea if he would ever be released.

The most striking indicator of the nature of Leary's journey happened when, in another candidate for an arthouse play scenario, he briefly found himself ensconced in the same cell-block as Charles Manson. They communicated through the wall between their cells. If we can believe the snippets found in Leary's *Flashbacks* and *Neuropolitique* Charlie had some interesting reading matter on the go, lending Leary Ouspensky's *In Search of the Miraculous* and Castaneda's *Teachings of Don Juan*. Charlie laconically stated he had been waiting for Leary to show up and was curious about why Tim didn't use what he knew to control people. This of course was the exact opposite of the intention of Leary's long-term work. The prison psychiatrist was presented with a brief incredible opportunity to look at two such extraordinary individuals together. Whilst concluding that both were megalomaniacs, Tim was essentially a loved-up guy with his feet on the ground regardless of space migration. Charlie on the other hand had some anger issues and frequent plot losses. Charles Manson could almost be seen as an embodiment of everything that Crowley understood as Choronzon.

I believe that Timothy Leary's entire adult life was a unique comprehensive initiatory process that reached its maximum intensity from the time he was first sent to prison, through his escape, recapture and eventual re-emergence. I believe that in all of the areas that really matter he passed the ordeal of the Abyss with flying colours. This is perhaps best demonstrated by the fearless humorous way he entered into his own death process, spreading love and laughter all around him.

In Thelemic magickal mythical terms Leary was involved in making even larger the hole that had been ripped in the fabric of reality by the Babalon Working. He was at the very heart of the sixties Hadit energy. A measure of this is how peculiar it is that whilst he appeared to be at his lowest ebb he was in fact navigating the Abyss and his great enemy Nixon fell into a defeat and disgrace more immense to future history than any of Leary's failings. This process also sucked in the first man to attempt to bust him, G. Gordon Liddy. All this as Kohoutek loomed.

Leary seemed to be really going into space-cadet territory with *Starseed*. If a case can be made for it being a necessary part of his process as he crossed some kind of Abyss it raises the issue of just what can be said to be really happening when people in altered states of consciousness have a contact experience, whether with a higher aspect of themselves, a Holy Guardian Angel or an apparent external intelligence. It brings us back to Aiwass, Illumination, and a wider examination of the Abyss in the context of perhaps the most bizarre of all twentieth century manifestations, the UFO phenomenon.

EXTRA-TERRESTRIAL GNOSIS

> 'My observation of the Universe convinces me that there are beings of intelligence and power of a far higher quality than anything we can conceive of as human; that they are not necessarily based on the cerebral and nervous structures that we know, and that the one and only chance for mankind to advance as a whole is for individuals to make contact with such beings.'
>
> Aleister Crowley. Magick without Tears.

THELEMIC UFOLOGY AND THE CULT OF LAM

IN *FLYING SAUCERS: a Modern Myth of Things Seen in the Sky*, Jung expressed his belief that the UFO phenomenon was an example of *'manifestations of psychic changes which always appear at the end of one Platonic month and at the beginning of another. Apparently they are changes in the constellations of psychic dominants, of the archetypes, or "gods" as they used to be called, which bring about, or accompany, long-lasting transformations of the collective psyche.'* Ideas that were below the psychic horizon were rising again into consciousness during the transition into the dawning of the new Platonic month or astrological epoch, the Age of Aquarius.

If this concept has any validity, and if the idea of the Aeon of Horus has similar veracity, then the things seen in the sky with their accompanying effects on human consciousness may well not just be indicators of the dawning of the Age of Aquarius but might show some signature signs of the Thelemic current as well. I am rather inclined to believe that is indeed the case.

It's not difficult to believe that the threat of nuclear war produced unique psychic tensions in the general population. As the epoch of warfare is the most characteristic flavour of the Aeon of Horus, any peculiar psychological response to it could be seen as similarly representative of Crowley's vision. Technology had become the new God and the new Devil. Desires for salvation could easily express themselves through a new technological mythology. This does make some sense of UFOlogy but there are far deeper stranger undercurrents emerging from that archetypal matrix that switches on when the ages change. I shall present a contentious take on UFOlogy that reflects that idea.

Debate over the nature of the UFO phenomenon has been intense and diverse. The most well-known interpretation states that UFOs are actual physical spacecraft, piloted by beings from other planets. This is often called the Nuts and Bolts hypothesis. In the early fifties outlandish accounts appeared telling of meetings with aliens and journeys with them in their craft through outer space. These tales were recounted with the definite sense that they referred to physical events. Inevitably such spectacular weirdness became the most noticed aspect of the subject.

Jung was prepared to accept that there was an element of physical reality in some cases but was clear that human consciousness was intimately involved in the process. An extraordinary opportunity to observe folklore in the making had arisen. As Kenneth Grant stated in *The Ninth Arch*,

> *'Whatever one's attitude to such phenomenon – positive, negative or indifferent – there is no just denial of the fact that the wave initiated an era of psychomythology unparalleled since man conceived the idea of the "gods".'*

From the very earliest days there arose groups of people who claimed some kind of psychic communication with the extraterrestrials. This occurred through what was often a recognisable form of spiritualistic mediumship. Psychic contactees developed alongside nuts and bolts physical UFOlogy, eventually developing into the New Age channelling of entities from the Pleiades and suchlike that began to increasingly appear a few decades later.

There are tremendous difficulties involved in assessing the phenomenon. It has seriously occurred to many investigators that there seems to be a built-in invalidation principle whereby anyone penetrating even a little way beneath the surface will encounter details so bizarre as to repel the rational mind. This weirdness factor is side-stepped by the nuts and bolts theorists but relentlessly intrudes nonetheless. As Aeolus Kephas states in *The Lucid View,*

'True paranoia is engendered, then, and becomes essential, on realizing that the source of the UFO mystery – because defined by the very clues that it is providing – can itself never be identified. It will always be obscured and disguised by the very evidence which it is presenting.'

Amazingly enough there are some who believe that Aleister Crowley was perhaps the first alien contactee in the modern sense of the term. A Thelemic ET theme has also been suggested running through the Babalon Working, taking us into the birth of the UFO era. This seemingly wild idea will lead us into a consideration of the Contact phenomenon itself and the manner in which UFOlogical studies can take us into the wider field of the paranormal and occultism. Eventually, after a most extraordinary journey indeed, we shall return to the mystery of *The Book of the Law* and ponder whether it may contain a secret key to the whole process.

Kenneth Grant was just twenty when he met Crowley in 1944. Already well-read in western occultism and eastern mysticism, he embarked on a crash-course magickal apprenticeship whilst serving as the Beast's secretary. It only lasted a few months but ensured that Grant became one of Crowley's literary executors alongside John Symonds. This afforded him access to unpublished material and later involvement in the production of editions of many of Crowley's works.

The leadership succession in the OTO has been a controversial and litigious issue ever since Crowley's death. Rival groups have formed. Grant became the head of one of them, known to history as the Typhonian OTO. As well as a connection to Crowley, he also had the distinction of prolonged close contact with the prodigiously talented shamanic artist Austin Osman Spare. After assimilating all kinds of knowledge and experience over a period of decades he finally published his first major work, *The Magical Revival*, in 1972, an account of contemporary occultism seen from the perspective of the Aeon of Horus.

Grant may well be the most controversial occultist of the second half of the twentieth century. There have been critics who have considered him to be genuinely insane and/or monstrously evil and that his writings are a major distortion of Crowley's legacy. Others consider him to be an awesome genius. It does seem rather remarkable that a person of his potential should meet the dying Crowley at such a young age. For now, we shall focus on the theme of what could be termed Thelemic UFOlogy that runs through nine books by Grant that have come to be called the Typhonian trilogies.

The illustrations in *Magical Revival* include a reproduction of a drawing made by Crowley in 1919 which Grant describes as *'Lam, an extra-terrestrial intelligence with whom Crowley was in astral contact.'* It's important to be clear about the history of this image as so much mythology and contention has arisen around it. In 1918, during a period when he was living in America, Crowley engaged in an extensive six-month long magickal episode known as the Amalantrah Working, primarily with the aid of his Scarlet Woman of the time, Roddie Minor. A combination of sex and drugs helped induce repeated consistent visionary material focused on a being named Amalantrah. Crowley was satisfied that the imagery and names produced were authentic in as much as they met his Qabalistic checking criteria. Towards the end of the written records of the working, Amalantrah made the enigmatic statements *'It's all in the egg'*, *'Thou art to go this Way.'* Unusually for Crowley's magickal records there appear to be details missing during the final phase.

The drawing seems to originate from the same period and depicts a being with an elongated egg-shaped head and no ears. It was publicly displayed in an exhibition of Crowley's art-work in New York in 1919. It also featured as the frontispiece for an edition of H. P. Blavatsky's *The Voice of the Silence* with an extensive running commentary from Crowley. There it was designated as *'The Way'* and given this explanation: *'LAM is the Tibetan word for Way or Path, and LAMA is he who Goeth, the specific title of the Gods of Egypt, the Treader of the Path, in Buddhistic phraseology. Its numerical value is 71, the number of this book.'* It was later stated that the figure was Crowley's *'guru'* and *'painted from life.'* That appears to be all that Crowley ever had to say about it. It is by no means clear that the word *Lam* is a name belonging to the being in the picture.

Unlike *Isis Unveiled* and *The Secret Doctrine*, Blavatsky's *Voice* is a short devotional work of Eastern Mysticism and not loaded with her usual esoteric detail. It tries to evoke the source of consciousness, considered to be a silent void, and the key to its mystical realisation, poetically rendered as experiencing its voice. Crowley's mystical side was entirely in harmony with such sentiments and equated the idea with Harpocrates perhaps implying that Lam, as an image of the Voice of the Silence, could be linked with a complex of associated ideas in the Thelemic system.

Part of Crowley's commentary briefly refers to another 1918

event when he spent time on Esopus Island in the Hudson River in New York State. During that period he claimed to have accessed a number of past life memories that became significant in the emerging Crowley myth. These included the major occultists Cagliostro and Eliphas Levi.

Sometimes overlooked in this catalogue is Ko Yuen, stated to be a follower of Lao Tzu, the author of one of the great masterpieces of the wisdom tradition of humanity, the *Tao Te Ching*. During the Esopus retreat, Crowley produced a version of the Lao Tzu classic full of cross-referencing notes to the Qabalah. In the introduction he states that he was still in '*almost daily communion*' with Amalantrah. '*He came readily to my aid and exhibited to me a codex of the original, which conveyed to me with absolute certitude the exact significance of the text.*' Crowley had travelled across Southern China. Taoism was a big influence on his mysticism. The *I Ching* was his constant companion for decades. The records of the Amalantrah Working show extensive use of it. This 1918 work immediately preceded the Blavatsky commentary and the appearance of the Lam picture. Tao has often been translated as "Way," the actual title of the drawing. This has lead to the suggestion by Alan Chapman in the 2007 *Fortean Times* Crowley special that the figure may actually be Lao Tzu himself as depicted by a reincarnation of one of his followers. Crowley's lack of draughtsmanship skills have simply meant it's a poor depiction of a Chinaman.

After this brief appearance, the picture seems to vanish from sight until Kenneth Grant came upon it during his short stay with Crowley who actually gave it to him which alternatively suggests that it was not particularly important or the exact opposite, with him recognising something of the young Grant's temperament and potential.

Following its dissemination through the three Typhonian trilogies, the image generally known as Lam is probably Crowley's most famous art-work. Its original use as the frontispiece to Blavatsky has been virtually forgotten. The visual archetype of a grey ET has become well-established in popular culture, particularly since the eighties when Whitley Streiber's *Communion* featured a striking image of one on its cover. The resemblance to Lam was enough to establish a conceptual linkage that has since become a widespread internet truism whose mythology has included a number of further connections that critics could consider tenuous.

The Babalon Working was concerned with ripping a hole in the fabric of reality to encourage influences from beyond to enter in. That may seem a pretentious megalomaniacal enterprise but consider the very events that Jack Parsons had been connected with. The science of the time was doing precisely that. After the atomic explosions it was easy to believe that the veil was thin and further momentous events near at hand.

It has been increasingly speculated that, following Crowley's Lam contact, the Babalon Working also opened a larger portal that bore a direct connection to the influx of UFOs the following year during which Crowley died. This idea has been widely repeated outside of Grant's work and is gaining strength with each passing decade. That both portals were opened in America, a major focus for early UFOlogy, has also been deemed significant.

In *Outside the Circles of Time* Kenneth Grant stated that *'Parsons opened the door and something flew in'*. The flavour of that *something* is indicated by a strange episode that occurred in March 1946 at the time of the conclusion of the Babalon Working. Marjorie Cameron saw an unidentifiable aerial phenomenon. She was exhilarated, considering it to be a Thelemic sign, a *'war engine'* mentioned in *The Book of the Law*. This event inevitably predisposed her to be particularly interested in a phenomenon that erupted into popular consciousness the following year.

A passage in *The Book of the Law* stated *'I am the warrior Lord of the Forties: the Eighties cower before me & are abased'*. This seemed to mark the decade as Thelemically significant. Grant instigated a specific Cult of Lam after coming to feel that the portrait was a focus of an increasingly intense extra-terrestrial energy that would be of great importance during that time.

It is worth pausing to consider what "Extra-Terrestrial" may be considered to mean. To most people it will obviously refer to something originating on another physical planet elsewhere in the universe. In this Thelemic context it designates experiences and intelligence not confined to the consensus three-dimensional co-ordinates of planet Earth. Higher dimensional realms coterminous with 3D may well be the spaces these mysteries move through.

Grant is a mystic like Crowley. For all of his exposition of entities and magical realms his ultimate devotion is to the non-dual philosophy perhaps best expressed by Hindu Advaita Vedanta and its peerless modern exemplar Ramana Maharshi. As far as this ET issue is concerned it means the distinction between inner and outer is abolished. It is in harmony with Jung's intuitions. The field of

UFOlogy thereby becomes an aspect of esoteric psychology. Its classic cases represent processes of magical and spiritual initiation for individuals and humanity as a whole, whether understood by their subjects as such or not. There is confusion and possible failure and tragedy implicit in this extraordinary scenario.

The basic Kenneth Grant position, which is now an important aspect of the magick of the Typhonian OTO, is that firstly Lam is a name and image of something that gives access to Extra-Terrestrial gnosis, a state of consciousness. Lam was intrinsically part of the Amalantrah Working which opened a portal of some kind to other dimensions. This makes Crowley the first modern style ET contactee. It also opens up a consideration of what is the real nature of the Secret Chiefs of Occultism and in particular, Aiwass.

In the Cult of Lam as initiated by Kenneth Grant and developed by his closest long-term associate in the Typhonian OTO Michael Staley, Lam is not necessarily a distinct entity but a trans-aeonic portal to gnosis outside of the circles of time. Something about his visual appearance potentially serves to stimulate aspects of consciousness otherwise dormant. He could be a mask for the experience of the Hidden God/Holy Guardian Angel and help serve the purpose of crossing the Abyss.

The basic method of Lam meditation consisted of creating a magickal space by the usual banishings and then sitting silently in front of a copy of the Crowley picture staring into its eyes. The name was then repeated internally in the manner of a mantra. This process was considered sufficient to potentially stimulate an altered state of consciousness. As mood shifted an imaginative attempt would be made to enter into Lam's head, the Egg of Spirit, and then look out from his eyes. Profoundly alien zones might be thus encountered or general mutations of consciousness allowing download access to previously unknown realms of being.

An extension of this procedure formulated by Michael Staley begins with the fact that the name Lam also happens to be a Sanskrit seed syllable featured in some Kundalini yoga systems referring to the base chakra wherein the great serpent power resides that can be raised up the spinal column through a progressive expansion of consciousness until a climactic enlightenment at the top of the head. Staley's development involves visualising a serpent with the head of Lam ascending the spine through the chakras. The process does not directly identify Lam with Kundalini but may produce similar results.

We have established at least one example where, regardless of the particular cases' credibility, there is an overlap between the study of UFOlogy and occultism. Closer investigation soon reveals that this zone of overlap is in fact of considerable size and any account of UFOlogy which ignores it is profoundly incomplete.

THINGS SEEN IN THE SKY AND RUMOURS OF WARS

Although the modern UFO era effectively began in June 1947, when pilot Kenneth Arnold saw nine anomalous aerial phenomenon that a newspaper reporter referred to as Flying Saucers, there is a fifty year prehistory that is in fact a huge study in itself, including airships from 1897, the glowing "Foo Fighters" of the Second World War and the Scandanavian ghost planes and rockets of 1946. These episodes have been examined at length in the UFOlogical literature. Of interest here is what could be called the psychological and mystical fifty year prehistory. Crowley has provided our first case study and as we progress others will come to light where we can distinguish more of his influence at work and the general mood of the coming epoch he prophesied. A few twentieth century events stand out to me as portents of things to come.

We have already looked to Central Asia, in particular Gurdjieff in Tibet and the mythos of Shambhala, to expand our feeling for the bigger picture that the Aeon of Horus is framed within. The Russian mystical painter, explorer, and peace campaigner, Nicholas Roerich led an expedition into Central Asia searching for Shambhala. In July 1927, it paused in an area near the Humboldt mountain chain between Mongolia and Tibet. Roerich constructed an elaborate Tibetan Buddhist style stupa shrine and invited local monks and dignitaries to a ceremony consecrating it to Shambhala. It was a spiritual gesture making his presence and intentions known to the mysterious forces that he believed guarded the hidden kingdom.

Shortly afterwards, on the morning of August 5th, a large black eagle or vulture was spotted flying above the camp in a cloudless blue sky. A number of people began to look at it. One saw something higher in the sky behind the bird and drew everyone's attention towards it. In *Altai Himalaya*, published in 1930, Roerich described it as, '*something big and shiny, reflecting the sun, like a huge oval moving at great speed.*' Initially moving from the direction of Altai in the north to south, the mysterious manifestation changed direction towards southwest. It moved slowly enough to give time for inspection through binoculars. A later account in *Himalayas: Abode of Light* mentions that Lamas in the camp identified it as a '*sign of Shambhala*'.

There's a lot of scope for speculation. Tibetan Buddhist lore is renowned for its accounts of adepts able through magical meditational processes to create visible thought forms. Here we have a possible connection between the re-emergence of Shambhala and the mystery of things seen in the sky. There may be a very high level of energy behind at least some of the manifestations.

One event clearly demonstrates that before 1947 many people were already primed to respond to the idea of visitors from other worlds who might have hostile intent. Perhaps the most famous radio broadcast in history was made by awesome Orson Welles, his co-writer Howard Koch, and their Mercury Theatre Company on October 30th 1938. They presented H. G. Wells classic account of invasion from Mars *The War of the Worlds* in a format that suggested it was really happening in the present moment with music being interrupted by newscasters telling a progressively more apocalyptic tale. Simulated live outside broadcasts depicted sounds of carnage and destruction.

Although the programme was clearly identified at its beginning as fiction and this was briefly repeated in the midst of the story it seems that many listeners, perhaps randomly tuning in from other stations, believed that it was genuine and some kind of mass panic ensued. Real American locations were featured. Grovers Mill in New Jersey was the initial landing site and a commemorative monument there now records the fact, a measure of the magnitude of the event in American folk memory. As New York itself came under attack the outside broadcast was apparently cut off as the reporter succumbed to poison gas.

How many people were affected and to what degree has been debated at length for decades. There is no doubt that in some cases the responses were extreme. Poison gas was smelt. Heat rays were felt. Gunfire was heard. Martian machines were seen. Flames of conflict were visible. Families left their homes to escape.

Things got understandably confused in the town of Concrete, Washington. A power failure at a local electricity station that began with flashes of light left the whole place in darkness. To those who had been listening to Welles up to that point it got difficult to figure out what was happening.

The next day the New York Times carried some impressive details.

'In a single block at Heddon Terrace and Hawthorne Avenue, more than twenty families rushed out of their houses with wet handkerchiefs and towels over their faces to flee from what they believed was to be a gas raid. Some began moving household furniture. Throughout New York families left their homes, some to flee to nearby parks. Thousands of persons called the police, newspapers and radio stations here and in other cities of the United States and Canada seeking advice on protective measures against the raids.'

Quite why the broadcast was able to stimulate such an intensity of response has in my opinion never been satisfactorily explained. The gathering storm in Europe certainly played upon the American psyche. Earlier on in the year the crisis over Czechoslovakia that was resolved in Nazi Germany's favour with the wretched piece of paper brandished by Neville Chamberlain as *"peace in our time"* had seemingly boosted the sale of radios in America to an unprecedented extent. The tensions with Japan that would ultimately lead to war were already present. Okay, so people were a bit stressy about another war. Belief in an invasion from Mars is surely another level of the game.

There are rumours that the whole episode was part of a deliberate mass psychology experiment. It has also been suggested that when UFOs and close encounters started to become widely reported a decade later the authorities adopted a cover-up approach believing it had already been demonstrated what the public response to such news being validated might be. All of this remains difficult to prove. What is clear is the phenomenon of saucer mania did not emerge from a vacuum.

It's worth noting in passing that the 1953 movie of *War of the Worlds* contains one scene that carries some strong Aeon of Horus motifs. An idealistic priest goes out to try and communicate peacefully with the Martian invaders. He recites the famous twenty-third psalm about the valley of death. He is mercilessly killed and this serves as the start point for a futile military assault. The scene has a sense of the death of an old dispensation and is therefore redolent of the disturbing third chapter of *The Book of the Law*, especially considering that the agents of destruction are from the planet attributed to Horus. The climax of the movie backs away from this being set in a church and having the feeling of prayers being answered but the power of this sequence is a thing unto itself.

ADVENT OF THE ETHER SHIPS

Other indications of what was to come were also being felt in profoundly different ways by another intriguing character. Meade Layne was steeped in a wide spectrum of general occult knowledge derived from the likes of the Qabalah and Theosophy. He was a student of the work of one of Crowley's most important and controversial followers, Charles Stansfield Jones, often known by his magickal name Frater Achad, who we shall meet again. Layne also had connections with Dion Fortune's Inner Light group.

In 1946 he was working with a psychic named Mark Probert who was apparently in communication with a group of discarnate entities conveying teachings. Most impressive, or ludicrous depending on one's opinion, was the half a million year old Himalayan adept Yada Di Shi-ite.

The channelled teachings led Layne to believe that visitations from other worlds were imminent. This predisposed him to pay attention to things in a way others might not. In October a strange black torpedo-shaped object had been seen in the sky above San Diego where Layne was based. He considered it to be something sufficiently odd to ask Probert's inner plane teachers their opinion. This marked the beginning of what may well be the first psychic investigation of the UFO mystery.

The initial results were perhaps not that inspiring.

'This ship comes from west of the moon. No, I cannot get the name of the planet. These people have been trying to contact the earth for many years. The earth is now sending forth a strong ray or column of light, and this makes it easier of approach from other planets. Yes, these people come in peace. They are more advanced than you are. Their bodies are similar to yours but much lighter.'

Remember however, the coining of the term Flying Saucer, closely followed by a nationwide obsession that would extend over the period of the Roswell incident still lay in the future. Layne was responding to a number of intimations of what was to come and would rapidly develop a very distinct perspective.

He would eventually publish his theories in 1950 in *The Ether Ship Mystery and its Solution*.

'The aeroforms are thought-constructs, mind constructs. As such,

*they are, in effect, the vehicle of the actual entity who creates them.'
– 'The shapes and vehicles and the entity operating them form one being, just as a human being is a psychophysical mind-body unity.'*

This links in with the Roerich sighting and its accompanying mood. Layne spoke of *Etheria* as the point of origin of the phenomenon. The term came from a remarkable late nineteenth century channelled text named *Oahspe* written by an American dentist named John Newbrough in a long series of trance states on a typewriter whilst overshadowed by angelic beings.

Layne's exposition of Etheria did not depict it as some other place in the sense of another planet in a distant galaxy. It is rather a location that is here and now when we have expanded our understanding of where we actually are and what its true dimensions reveal. For the Qabalist the infinite light of the top of the tree of life is not absent from the consensus world of the four elements but is not generally perceived as being present. Layne described humanity as walking on meshes of a huge net full of great spaces through which all manner of things can easily pass.

'The etheric worlds or Lokas are regarded as spacial and temporal regions of existence which interpenetrate with our world of (more rarefied) matter, and also, in their higher aspects, with the lower levels of the astral. Our physical plane includes the lower and higher etheric, but some four-fifths of this lies outside our normal range of sense perception. In this etheric region there flourish civilizations and cultures, and a race of beings which are born into that world and die there. They are NOT excarnate humans. They have knowledge of our world and can and do penetrate it. Many dwellers on the astral plane are aware of the etheric worlds also, and have the power of visiting them. This ability however, does not seem to be a common and natural endowment, but belongs to persons of a certain degree of development, corresponding to those whom we here call Adepts, or possessed of exceptional psychic powers of projection or clairvoyance. Anyone, in short, can function on any plane for which he is prepared, and astral vision and astral travelling is fairly common because of our interest in the after-death life; but the etheric regions have been little explored. Yet they are in many ways the most important of all, since they hold the key to ALL the phenomena of our earth life, and to the origin and history of our race.'

Inspired by the Root Races of Blavatsky and similar ideas of

Steiner whereby the human race has gradually evolved from rarified matter into greater density of manifestation Layne delivered a radical perspective. *'We ourselves are etherians by ancestry and descent, for Etheria is the home of the human race.'* This again is by no means at odds with Roerich and his signs of Shambhala.

Layne was predisposed to notice one of the more peculiar aspects of a number of early sightings. UFOs sometimes seemed to materialise and dematerialise instantaneously. This suggested to Layne a shifting of frequency between vibrational zones that exist essentially in the same space together.

The most famous mathematical equation of the twentieth century, Einstein's $E=MC^2$, helps us get an idea of how Layne conceived of the different levels of reality. Einstein showed how matter only appears solid on one level of perception. It could be said to be made up of particles that are moving so fast they are effectively solid. It's like an aeroplane propeller or the spokes of a bicycle wheel. Throw something against them when they are in motion and it will bounce off. In the process of acceleration and deceleration the blades and spokes are visible. When UFOs seem to blink in and out of visibility it may well be analogous. The vibrations involved are not the same as simple speed however. Although they remain on one level in the same bigger space they shift dimensions in order to appear and function here. They can be used for interplanetary travel but it doesn't mean they originate on potentially visible planets

Meade Layne founded the Borderland Sciences Research Associates Foundation in 1945. It's still going strong, promoting subtle energy, Radionics, the work of Nikola Tesla, alternative science and health and the expansion of perception.

THE NAZI CONTACTEE
AT THE PORTAL OF THE UFO ERA

William Dudley Pelley was a genuine American oddity who has been labelled a "New Age Nazi" and was a significant influence on early UFOlogy. His career represents an entirely unique trajectory that nonetheless includes all sorts of nuances with which we are becoming familiar.

Pelley had some intense experiences when travelling as a newspaper correspondent in Russia during the time of the revolution.

He saw all kinds of horrors which turned him into a vehement anti-Communist. He also began a fateful association in his mind of Communism with Jews. This was not exactly an uncommon idea at the time. Back in America he turned his talents to writing novels that were modestly successful and then screenplays for some Hollywood movies of the silent era. His burgeoning anti-Semitism eventually drove him away from an industry that he felt was dominated by Jews.

What followed was another of those mysterious illumination destiny episodes that our cast of characters are so prone to. Pelley had an out-of-the-body-experience he would describe in a 1928 pamphlet of the same name as *'My Seven Minutes in Eternity'*. In this *'ecstatic interlude'* he came into the presence of beings of some kind. From that point onwards his consciousness was permanently mutated. A few days later on a night-train journey he was reading a book when

'Suddenly as I turned a page, something happened! I seemed to be bathed in a douche of pure white light on that moving Pullman. A great flood of Revelation came to me out of which a Voice spoke such as I had never heard before. What it said, I prefer to keep permanently to myself. But in that instant I knew that my bungalow experience had not been a dream, or even self-hallucination. Particularly I knew of the reality of that Entity whom the world now designates as Jesus of Nazareth! I knew that He was not a mythical religious ideal. I knew His ministry and career had been a literal actuality and that I had once seen Him when He was thus in His flesh!'

Pelley had returned as a man with a divine mission to promote a millennial Christianity, albeit one that was infused with a bizarre mix of Theosophical style ideas and was above all, rabidly racist.

Pelley's first automatic writing message shortly afterwards came supposedly from a being who did not want to be thought of as a master but an elder brother. He stated that,

'There must be neither tears, nor shadows of tears, in the way of the spirit. All is light, all is joy, all is beauty to those whose eyes have been opened to the radiance. Why should joy bring even the fleeting semblance of that which ye call pain.'

It was a long message and volumes more would follow as Pelley's psychic faculties developed to include clairaudient hearing as well. The contrast of the general feeling of the first message with Pelley's racism and where it would lead is a measure of the enigma of the man.

This transformation was occurring at the time of the Wall St. Crash of 1929 and subsequent Great Depression which Pelley blamed on Jewish bankers. He paid increasing attention to the career of Hitler. When the Nazis came to power in January 1933 he was immediately inspired to found a group he named the Silver Shirts. They are generally labeled as fascist but it's fairly clear that they may as well be called Nazis. They supported Hitler, paraded around in uniforms and promoted virulent anti-Semitism.

Whilst the esoteric background of the German Nazis was kept in the background Pelley had no qualms about promoting a blend of politics and a bizarre mix of his channeled messages with their Theosophical and millenarian Christian tone.

He ran for president in 1936 as a Christian Party candidate, coming to be known as the *"Star-Spangled fascist"*. This was the kind of Christianity that desired segregated Jewish ghettos in America along with the same kind of legislation barring them from public life that had been passed in Germany. He didn't get a tremendous amount of votes. Silver Shirt membership maxed out at around fifteen-thousand.

Once the war began Pelley continued to support Hitler and did not want American involvement. Remarks made against the government led to a trial and jail sentence. He was released as the UFO era got underway on the understanding that he would avoid public political life. Certain opinions did leak out however such as his belief that the newly created United Nations organization was part of a Jewish-communist conspiracy.

Pelley soon became a contactee, writing a book called *Star Guests* in 1950. He was therefore one of the very first in print, helping to set the style for what would come. A new group named *Soulcraft* was created as a vehicle for his UFO material which soon became extensive. He claimed to have seen one in 1953.

Humanity started thirty to fifty million years ago when star guests mated with primates. The different races of our planet were seeded by assorted aliens. The white master race came from Sirius. In a model reminiscent of Blavatsky's Root Races, the Jews are some kind of unfortunate trouble-making hybrid and so on. We are involved in an enormous reincarnational process that includes long periods between human lives spent in other planes being purified. A hardcore of individuals come together as mentors for humanity during crucial times. These are the 144,000 mentioned in *Revelation*. Pelley stuck to a millennial Christian centre of gravity and always considered he was living in the End Times. An interest in pyramidology, the belief that the dimensions of the Great Pyramid and its interior design can be interpreted prophetically, had influenced much of his public career. He believed that Hitler's coming to power in 1933 was a pyramid moment. His eventual prediction for the Second Coming of Christ does look rather interesting now. It was 17th September 2001. It's safe to say there was a bit of apocalypse in the air round about then. Pelley began to believe he was in contact with Nostradamus who actually dictated some new material to him and brought along a host of historical figures for a chat as well.

One of Pelley's ideas on the UFO mystery clearly echoes Meade Layne.

'*The scientific world will not entertain (this theory), no matter how real it concedes Saucers to be. It is the theory that the Saucers are not built of fabricated materials, like our earthly airplanes, and propelled by the use of magnetic currents discovered by denizens of outer planets, so much as thought-form creations from higher octaves of Reality, made seemingly solid by lowering the vibratory rates of the substance of their construction. Intellects that have graduated out of our sensatory world, in other words, may, by taking thought, specify the opaqueness or transparency of the craft.*'

Pelley could be considered to have been ultimately ineffectual in his politics but he has left a definite legacy behind him. The bringing together of anti-Semitism, an encouragement to cultivate military and survivalist skills and a Last Days millenarian Christianity that characterised the Silver Shirts became the template for the extreme American Right. A number of its leading exponents such as Richard Butler of the Aryan Nation group had been Silver Shirts and carried their hate agenda into old age.

How bizarre and disturbing that such a figure can be found right in the middle of the early days of UFOlogy. The problem anyone approaching his work faces is not to reject it wholesale. Just because there is much to repel does not mean therefore that every single idea Pelley ever had is wrong. These kind of difficulties are present in varying degrees throughout the study of the UFO enigma and its major personalities but with Pelley they are blown up on a big screen. So suitably forewarned we can journey into a realm where our normal sensibilities are unlikely to remain comfortable.

MULTI-DIMENSIONAL MOJAVE

On June 24th 1947, something appeared from out of the midsummer gate of the sun when the Kenneth Arnold incident began the flying saucer frenzy. Attention turned to the skies and numerous further sightings rapidly followed generating an immediate mythology. Within a few weeks whatever it was that happened at Roswell had occurred. Although the mystery was certainly a known commodity at the time and speculated on during the fifties it was really only decades later in the eighties that the episode took on the mythic magnitude it now possesses. Roswell is a distinctly nuts and bolts mystery regardless of its true explanation and so does not feature in this narrative.

The 1951 movie *The Day the Earth Stood Still* depicted a representative of a galactic federation visiting us in response to their concern about our development of nuclear energy. The Space Brothers essentially warn us that we are being monitored and we need to get our act together or face major punishment from the federation in the form of total destruction. It has often been suggested that the movie was one of the fundamental stimuli to the shape of the phenomenon in the fifties. Many contactees subsequently produced material with such themes until it became a widespread belief. We do need to recall though that Meade Layne had already intuited something of this flavour.

The fifties was the golden age of the contactees. The most notable amongst them were obviously immersed in all manner of occult and mystical beliefs and this was strongly reflected in what they went on to state about the phenomenon. I have presented the Crowley Lam case as a kind of template. Quite clearly I am deliberately cultivating selective attention of data in order to establish a particular mood but I believe that immersion in that mood can be very useful.

During the course of the Babalon Working Jack Parsons and L. Ron Hubbard ventured into the Californian desert. *Liber 49* was received in uncertain circumstances there. Those who endorse the idea that the veil between the worlds was ripped asunder by the proceedings note that the early days of the UFO era did seem to feature a lot of exceptional strangeness out in the desert as well.

The most famous and notorious contactee was George Adamski, a man still able to polarise opinion. He first surfaces to public view in the thirties as the founder of a Royal Order of Tibet. As the UFO era began he was the owner of a burger stall on the slopes of Mount Palomar, a location that would attract spectacular occult gossip as we shall later see. From a desert vantage point he had observed UFOs through a telescope and started trying to photograph them. It is also telling that he had written fiction on the subject. In November 1952 he claimed to have received a telepathic message calling him to a meeting in the desert with the UFOnauts. Adamski went out with a group into the Mojave, later stating that he had seen a big silver cigar-shaped craft fly by. Asking his friends to stand clear, he moved away on his own to observe a smaller vessel come down and land right in front of him. A tall long-haired male, looking quite human and wearing some kind of ski-suit came out to make contact. Through telepathy Orthon (as the being was known), gave a *Day the Earth Stood Still* rap about nukes. His people were from Venus. Adamski's account of his story with some photos he had taken of the Venusian scout-ship was recounted in the 1953 *Flying Saucers Have Landed,* written primarily by Desmond Leslie. The book was a sensation and launched the contactee on a truly bizarre journey as international ambassador for the peaceful space people. Was Adamski for real or a liar? Opinions on him range from paid CIA stooge to genuine mystic.

Something was stirring in the desert though. Giant Rock was believed to be the world's largest free-standing boulder, looming seven stories high and covering 5800 square feet of ground. Situated in the Mojave Joshua Tree area, it had been sacred to the local Native Americans who once held gatherings around it although only the specially consecrated were allowed directly near it.

By the late nineteen-forties it had acquired a most unusual new guardian in the form of George Van Tassell. A pilot who had worked for Howard Hughes, Van Tassel ensured that a small nearby airport was functional and opened a café. Hughes apparently flew in himself to get a slice of a legendary pie Van Tassells' wife would bake. His presence could probably be viewed in a conspiratorial way in the light of future events by those with sufficient ingenuity.

A predecessor at the rock had dug out some underground living quarters beneath it to escape the desert heat. As Tassell became interested in the UFO mystery the rooms came to serve as a powerful meditational chamber. By 1951 he was talking about having been astrally beamed-up into some giant craft orbiting the planet and making contact with the "Council of Seven Lights".

Things intensified when one night in August 1953 he and his wife were sleeping outdoors to try and get comfortable in the heat when he awoke to find a humanoid in a one-piece blue suit standing by him who introduced itself as *"Sylvanon"* and extended an invite to check out his craft. Unable to wake his wife, Tassell accompanied the being about a hundred yards to where the saucer ship had landed. It looked not unlike the one featured in *The Day the Earth Stood Still*. This is not to imply that Tassell was lying but to at least indicate the potential shapeshifting side of the phenomenon and the way it responds to what is in the collective mind. A guided tour revealed clothes hanging in futuristic wardrobes, furniture that could be brought out of walls, instrument panels and general fifties saucer décor. Van Tassell was politely ushered out and the craft rapidly took off and disappeared.

So began a process of intensified contact which resulted in the receiving of instructions to build a fabulous device that would be known as the Integratron. Its inspiration was the Tabernacle of Moses featured in chapter 33 of *Exodus*, where the cloudy pillar that had been leading the Israelites across the wilderness descended and talked with Moses '*face to face, as a man speaketh unto his friend*'. Van Tassell described his device as '*a machine, a high-voltage electrostatic generator that would supply a broad range of frequencies to recharge the cell structure.*'

The basic frame would be a 38ft high, 50ft diameter, 16-sided wooden dome sited in the Giant Rock landscape according to principles derived from the Great Pyramid and the magnetic field of the earth that would supposedly amplify its power. Its acoustic properties were fundamental to its purpose. The structure was finished in 1959 but the fine-tuning needed to complete it was far more extensive. There were touches suggested by the work of revolutionary visionary scientist Nikola Tesla. Van Tassell sometimes talked of a time machine but this is probably not to be understood in an H. G. Wells manner. The regenerational aspect was paramount. The immense undertaking would consume the rest of Van Tassell's life.

During the initial years of the Integratron project, Giant Rock was the venue for major UFO conventions that featured most of the fifties contactees, including Adamski on one occasion. Enthusiasts came in their thousands via the airport or on long car journeys into the desert. The core of the gatherings involved open-mike trance-channelling slams in the cavernous area at the foot of Giant Rock.

Van Tassell left quite a legacy behind him through his messages which didn't necessarily sound like they were all being transmitted by the same cosmic radio station. He first introduced perhaps the most famous of all ET contacts, speaking of a powerful important figure named Ashtar. Robert Short, also known as Bill Rose, was a friend of Van Tassell and was rather taken by Ashtar to the extent of producing his own material based around the concept of *Ashtar Command*. This led to a falling-out and Van Tassell making it clear that he did not endorse the subsequent results.

The fully developed Ashtar mythos portrays an immense group of ETs, angels, and general light-beings who are working on behalf of humanity, coordinating millions of space-vessels that can be considered both physical and otherwise. They are presided over by Ashtar as representative of a Universal Council of the Confederation of Planets and commander of a formidable galactic fleet, and Sananda, which is the name a certain Jesus Christ now goes by in some New Age circles. Blonde-haired blue-eyed Ashtar has been depicted on numerous occasions in a kitsch type of artwork often used to represent Ascended Masters in a manner occasionally making him look like a kind of slightly camp Nazi. Eventually other channellers starting producing Ashtar material relating to Ascension, light bodies and so on, and the big chief is held in some affection by his modern advocates.

Van Tassell died in 1978 with his Integratron still incomplete. Some believe there may be suspicious circumstances and that a potentially enormous scientific breakthrough was nobbled by the usual vested interests. The building was stripped of assorted gizmos until only the basic frame remained. It is now maintained by people sympathetic to its original intentions and hosts sound healing and suchlike. Magnetic anomalies have supposedly been measured inside it and at the very least the dome is considered to be a mighty fine chill-out zone.

All kinds of conspiracism surrounds the early contactees. The background of cults and strange figures behind the Adamski story is extensive. This was the same period that Jack Parsons went supernova and L. Ron Hubbard began a whole new level of the game. The Cold War was now well underway. Massive paranoia gripped the USA. It's obvious that the appearance of the UFO phenomenon would interest not just the obvious military forces but also the intelligence agencies. When contactees came along preaching universal brotherhood and telling of other planets where classless societies existed it would ring anti-communist alarm bells. These weird groups would need investigating to see if they were fronts for un-American activities.

The extent to which early UFOlogy and the contactee cults were infiltrated and manipulated by the intelligence agencies is difficult to establish but it's a safe bet that anyone with even a modest level of involvement would have had a file on them somewhere. This was certainly the case in Britain even into the seventies.

A doomsday cult established by Marion Dorothy Martin is a good example. Multiple levels of monitoring seem to have been occurring. Firstly, as her messages of impending doom became publicly known, some university academics secretly joined the group as it offered a fine sociological psychological live case study. A famous book, *When Prophecy Fails*, by Leon Festiger, Henry W. Riecken, and Stanley Schachter resulted. It unsurprisingly characterised Martin as delusional in believing she was receiving messages from ET "Guardians" from a planet called Clarion. Nonetheless occasions were witnessed and recorded when she would get phone calls from the Guardians and converse with them and also receive written messages delivered to her home when she was out. Five young men visited, one of whom claimed to be the leader of the Guardians. Martin had a private discussion with them and returned visibly moved as if they had told her something which she found strongly convincing. Who or what were these people? We have here the stirrings of what may have been manifesting elsewhere as the Men in Black phenomenon.

Martin would later become involved with another figure of considerable importance in early contactee UFOlogy who clearly demonstrated the occultist and mystical influences that pervaded the field.

George Hunt Williamson was the kind of person who claims all kinds of academic distinctions and assorted achievements that then prove to be rather difficult to validate. Nonetheless he was an extraordinary and charismatic figure who would come to have a wide influence, albeit often unacknowledged, on the developing New Age movement.

Already a confirmed mystic in his teens, the arrival of the flying saucers immediately captivated him. He met Adamski who was claiming to have photographed them before his legendary close encounter. It has been suggested that the two may have been introduced by William Dudley Pelley. Williamson certainly worked for Pelley's Soulcraft group in 1953, contributing a column in an associated publication named *Valor*. He was actually one of the people with Adamski on the desert excursion although he himself did not claim to have seen the craft.

The Adamski drama really set Williamson off and he soon produced a number of works in quick succession. He clearly absorbed a lot of Pelley, Layne, Theosophy, occultism and the general contactee climate around him. Whilst still in his twenties he tried to contact the entities behind the flying saucer manifestations using short-wave radio and a ouija board. The latter procedure generated enormous amounts of material that could broadly be termed Theosophical UFOlogy. He was also a direct channel, speaking in weird voices and so on. A wild and wacky bunch of UFO entities came through such as Artok of Pluto, Wan-4 of the Safanian planets, Noro of the Saucer Fleet, Affa from Uranus and so on.

Williamson really hit his stride when he met up with Marion David Martin who had gone on to found another contactee cult called the Brotherhood of the Seven Rays. A series of works followed that looked at ancient history from two perspectives. Firstly, that of ETs being the source of all stories in various scriptures, particularly the Bible, of deities, angels, miracles, weird aerial phenomenon and suchlike. In this Williamson anticipated the work of Raymond Drake and in particular Erich von Daniken who would later create a spectacular career from such speculation. Secondly, an important theme running throughout the rewriting of history was that a central core of characters were continually reincarnating throughout the major dramas. The core of this material can be found in *Other Tongues - Other Flesh* (1957), *Secret Places of the Lion* (1958), and *Road in the Sky* (1959).

In *Road* Williamson can be spotted using some ideas and terminology taken from L. Ron Hubbard's Scientology which probably came via Dorothy Martin who had a long-standing interest in the subject. Between the doomsday cult and the Seven Rays group she had gone back to studying Dianetics. It may well be that some fascinating discoveries could be made through further investigation of these connections if the trail hasn't gone cold.

As is often the case in these unfolding cosmologies, it soon became apparent that there is war in heaven and not all of the ETs are playing on the same team. The good guys are from Sirius but some evil influences are coming from the vicinity of Orion. There is a secret society that has been in contact with the Sirius influence for a long time and they use an eye in the triangle symbol. Sirius was part of Pelley's cosmology but coupled with the name of Affa which crops up in Enochian it may well indicate that the eclectic Williamson had absorbed some Crowley material, whether from books or specific people who were members of Thelemic groups.

A strange atmosphere surrounds the activities of the decidedly odd group of people Williamson was involved with. Martin's case is well known. Another couple of channellers he briefly worked with named Wilbur Wilkinson and Karl Hunrath set out in a light plane in 1953 to check out a grounded saucer. The plane disappeared without trace. A friend of theirs named Hal Nelson was drowned. D. J. Detweiler, who had processed George Adamski's early photographs died not long after. Lyman Streeter who collaborated with Williamson in the radio experiments died of heart seizure.

Hints of controversial politics can also be discerned. There is a direct link with Pelley. *Other Tongues* contains a chapter dedicated to his ideas. Williamson can hardly have been unaware of the man's history. He seems to have fine-tuned some of Pelley's vagueness about the adversaries of the good-guy Sirians. The Orion baddies seem like a bunch of Nazi Jewish caricatures.

1958's *UFO's Confidential*, written in collaboration with John McCoy, was big on that perennial favourite "International Bankers" as the hidden hand behind global politics and surprisingly enough, to some extent, the saucer activity. They are at the heart of the recently formed United Nations Organisation. They have suppressed bits of the Bible. When conspiracists start using such terminology it usually soon becomes clear that they harbour suspicions that said bankers have a Judaic background in common.

Michael Barkun's *A Culture of Conspiracy* revealed that Williamson seemed to be making extensive use of a pamphlet published by a Cinema Educational Guild, an enterprise co-founded and largely bankrolled by Gerald L. K. Smith, considered to be the country's most notorious anti-Semite at the time.

This is all part of the weird psychology of the fifties that enabled the kind of ideas propounded by Pelley to continue to develop even after the war against the Nazis. America was in the grip of anti-communist hysteria. The alleged links made before the war between Jews and Communism were still circulating. It's worth remembering that although the Holocaust was known and discussed it remained strangely in the background during the fifties. Nazi scientists and intelligence operatives had been bought up wholesale at the end of the war by America and assimilated into the new CIA era on the basis of their usefulness in the fight against the reds. There was fear that the saucers might be part of some Russian secret strategy. The psychic airwaves were weirdly polluted and the legacy lives on in contemporary conspiracism.

As the fifties ended Williamson withdrew from public UFOlogy to immerse himself in South American mysteries, still very much from a channelled space brother angle. He eventually resurfaced in California as an ordained member of the Nestorian Church, dying in 1986.

THE FLYING SAUCER VISION

'*We scanned the skies with rainbow eyes and saw machines of every shape and size. We talked with tall Venusians passing through.*'

David Bowie. *Memory of a Free Festival.*

During the psychedelic sixties UFOlogy developed in a manner clearly reflective of the flavour of the time. LSD culture was hugely influenced by it, particularly in Britain, and vice-verca. It seemed to be an inevitable part of the trajectory of any dedicated hallucinogenic voyager that eventually they would encounter in some manner entities, external intelligences, guides etc who were often experienced as being extra-terrestrial. We have of course begun with Crowley. It does appear that hallucinogens were present at the time of whatever it was that lead to the production of the Lam drawing. Tom Wolfe's *Electric Kool-Aid Acid Test* describes such a moment amongst Ken Kesey's pioneering Merry Pranksters. Leary's case is so huge it has served as the portal for this wider investigation. John C. Lilly in *Centre of the Cyclone* provided a map of the territory. It's also clear that staring at the sky under the influence of various drugs makes it more likely that things seen may be mutated to fit the percipients mindset.

Over the August Bank Holiday weekend of 1965 thousands of visitors descended on the normally quiet small Wiltshire town of Warminster following widely publicised UFO phenomenon. The story of the enduring connection of the place with weird manifestations and the type of questers it attracted is a sociological study in itself that has been excellently covered by the *In Alien Heat* of Steve Dewey and John Ries. Sufficient here to note that this 1965 swarming was not a millennial host of hippy acid heads although many would soon follow. Just like the USA with Orson Welles, the wider population was primed with the possibility of response to symbolic stimuli of a certain kind, of things seen in the sky. By 1965 though, despite plenty of hostile depictions in movies, there was a profound attraction rather than fear and the urge to escape.

It must not be forgotten that the sixties were the decade of the amazing odyssey into space that culminated in the moon landing. Even if the current climate of conspiracism casts doubt on whether the great event actually happened back then the idealism and sense of adventure undoubtedly helped to broaden a huge number of people's mental frontiers at a rapid rate. As we have noted earlier, psychedelia was the extreme inner edge of what appeared in the external realms as the space race.

In 1967's *The Flying Saucer Vision* John Michell recognised the major difficulties of establishing the definitive cause of the phenomenon and advocated the usefulness of observing its effects. Interest in the mystery led to many people looking into other subjects on the edges of consensus reality and finding apparent connections. UFOlogy was a major impetus in the emergence of the so-called Earth Mysteries in the sixties of which Glastonbury was a focus. Landscape alignments named leys by their nineteen-twenties chronicler Alfred Watkins became of wider interest when theories circulated suggesting that the lights in the sky seemed to navigate along them. Dragon folklore seemed to have points of commonality. Were the flying fire-breathers really alien vehicles? As we shall see, faerie lore was re-examined. Light phenomenon did seem to be associated with sites of ancient sanctity and it seemed that this would have been a known factor in their placing and whatever activities occurred at them. The Bible and other religious texts were investigated with fresh eyes on the look-out for flying saucers and their crews. The motif of the winged disc found in a number of Middle Eastern cultures and on the Stele of Revealing became particularly popular as a possible symbol of the presence of the UFOnauts. Looking back from decades further on much of this seems naïve and the assorted subjects that the UFO mystery revitalised have mainly disowned the connections but the initial strange inspirational stimulus is undeniable and has led to speculation as to whether or not the phenomenon somehow deliberately serves such obscure purposes.

The psychedelic music scene was full of images of what could almost be termed flying saucer religion. London's hippest venue was the UFO Club where the likes of Pink Floyd made their name. The bands supremely atmospheric second album *Saucerful of Secrets* was full of references, such as this from *Let there be more Light*.

> 'Then at last the mighty ship
> Descending on a point of flame
> Made contact with the human race'

Alongside their fateful dalliance with the romance of Satan the rebel, the Rolling Stones' ranks contained some definite saucer enthusiasts. Keith Richards went out in the company of John Michell looking for them and the doomed Brian Jones perused the literature.

David Bowie, who would later achieve *Top of the Pops* immortality in 1972 with his rendition of the obviously ET themed *Starman*, featured on his 1969 *Space Oddity* album the evocative anthemic *Memory of a Free Festival* that concluded with an extended *Hey Jude* type chorus of

'The sun-machine is coming down and we're gonna have a party.'

The depiction of a loved-up tripped out crowd of hippies in a field experiencing a timeless afternoon permeated by flying saucer religion has long been a particular favourite of mine in providing a permanent snapshot of the feel of an era as effective as anything on *Sgt Pepper*. And, for me, the most enduring image of psychedelic sixties UFOlogy is the Luciferic blood ruby flying disc seen in the skies over Egyptian temples in Kenneth Anger's *Lucifer Rising*. The sun-machine was indeed coming down.

★ ★ ★

OUR LADY OF SPACE

In my opinion there are two indispensable works on UFOlogy that establish the necessary perspective. In *Passport to Magonia*, Jacques Vallée suggested that there seems to be one phenomenon which has been interacting with the human race from our earliest days. It takes on different forms in various cultures. He eventually came to believe there is a kind of control system for human consciousness that UFOs may form part of. They may be involved in the manipulation of belief and this makes them very difficult to study. Once again we have to look at the effects that can be attributed to their stimulus.

Firstly, faerie lore yields suggestive comparisons with abduction cases. The classic tales tell of dome-shaped mounds with open lighted entrances. Once lured within them, time/space becomes dangerously relative. After partying it up with the Little People, and maybe even having sex with one of them, it would become apparent on leaving that fifty years might have elapsed.

During the Christian Middle Ages, the most far-out possibilities of experience would be a visitation from Jesus and the BVM (Blessed Virgin Mary) or an encounter with an angel or demon. And such tales are by no means a thing of the distant past. Vallée studied modern accounts of apparitions of the BVM, most notably the 1917 Fatima event. I don't think anyone could really examine that episode with an open mind and fail to feel that something genuinely very strange had occurred. A group of Portuguese children claimed to have seen and talked to the BVM. She initially appeared in a globe of light, telling them she would return at monthly intervals, prophesying a spectacular culmination in October. They kept their appointments, accompanied by increasingly large groups of people. Only the children could see her. They were clearly in some kind of trance state. Some minor, but odd, external manifestations would weirdly validate their stories. Branches of a tree where the Mary figure was supposed to be hovering bent as if supporting weight, and so on. The climax saw a huge crowd, approaching a hundred thousand in size, gather for the last appointment. They witnessed a seemingly miraculous heavenly phenomenon. It was as if the sun fell from the sky and plummeted, revolving, with a spectrum of colours towards the earth. Whatever it was that was happening, it was witnessed miles away. Many converted to Catholicism on the spot. It seemed that the woman clothed with the sun from the *Book of Revelation* was tangibly present.

At the very least, a group of small children had been able to assemble a Biblical multitude with exact timing, to witness a spectacular and obviously rare atmospheric event that if it had happened half a century later may well have inspired UFOlogical speculation. That in itself is extremely odd. Looking at other famous BVM cases like Lourdes, it's interesting that the child visionaries at first don't necessarily identify their "contact" as Mary. The response of adults that it obviously must be, conditions what follows. What the being looks like often changes to more fully conform to the archetypal Catholic visuals. Once this is established, messages of the 'I am the Immaculate Conception' variety follow.

The earlier French case of La Salette in 1846 is another good example of fruitfully comparing the UFOlogical and Catholic realities. Two children saw a globe of light hovering above fields. It opened, disgorging a smaller but brighter light that came down and spoke to them. The Catholic children assumed it must be Our Lady. Prophecies were spoken concerning disease and pestilence which appeared to be validated within a decade. If this had happened in the America of the early nineteen-fifties it seems possible that the light might have taken on the form of the likes of the legendary Aura Rhanes, the female beach-babe flying saucer commander who wrecked the marriage of contactee Truman Bethuram. It has rightly been intuited that Crowley's devotion to Nuit is akin to Catholic adoration of the Virgin Mary. Nuit is Our Lady of Space and could be considered to be present in the UFOlogicaly aspected BVM manifestations.

The modern UFO era has mutated the forms and beliefs of an archetypal mythology to always be just ahead of the current science. In the fifties "aliens" talked of coming from Mars and Venus. Once it was established that those planets couldn't support life, the messages changed. The phenomenon seems to be interactive. We are intimately involved with it. Vallée came to feel that UFOs and their apparent occupants are not necessarily extraterrestrial.

ULTRATERRESTRIALS

Operation Trojan Horse by John Keel serves as a valuable companion piece to *Magonia*. Keel was wonderfully prepared to investigate the UFO enigma. From a young age he had fed his head on the full spectrum of the paranormal as well as stage magic. He became a journalist and radio presenter and was able to do a Halloween broadcast from the Great Pyramid. In his mid-twenties he had spent four years travelling on a quest for mysterious phenomenon. This had included him spending his twenty-fifth birthday with the legendary Yezidi, studying the arts of Indian fakirs and mastering their tricks, including being buried alive. He saw two possible Yeti on Himalayan slopes and communicated with a telepathic levitating Tibetan adept. These wonderful stories are featured in his autobiographical account of his early years, *Jadoo*. At Aswan in Egypt he later saw a flying metallic looking silver disc in daylight. From that point on he paid attention to the UFO sensation.

Keel likewise came to feel that one shapeshifting phenomenon has been interacting with the human race for aeons. It can be discovered in historical material from the same range of material Vallée covered. Keel also looked at ghosts, telepathy, automatic writing, trance mediumship, poltergeist manifestations, vampires, and psychic phenomenon in general along with anomalous airships and mystery planes from before 1947. All of this threw new light on the modern UFO events. Alien entities seem very similar to traditional angels and demons.

Very much at odds with most mid-sixties UFOlogy, Keel did not necessarily believe the source of it was off-planet. He coined the term Ultraterrestrial to designate the intelligences involved. As he later stated in *The Mothman Prophecies*, '*When you review the ancient references you are obliged to conclude that the presence of these objects and beings is a normal condition for this planet.*' Some other forms of consciousness are present here with us, albeit on an extended spectrum we normally do not suspect the existence of. The Ultraterrestrials '*operate outside the limits of our space-time continuum yet have the ability to cross over into our reality.*' They can manifest for brief periods in a bewildering variety of forms.

Keels "*Paraphysical hypothesis*" can be seen as an expansion of Meade Layne's ideas. He suggested that UFOs and their inhabitants originate in the astral realms familiar to occultists, mystics and spiritualists. Their bizarre home worlds that awestruck contactees sometimes journey to are not dissimilar to the spheres of the Qabalah or the Lokas and hidden kingdoms of eastern lore that blink in and out of consensus reality and can only be noticed by the prepared. Keel came to believe that human consciousness was an important factor in how the phenomenon manifested. The history and folklore of an area created a psychogeographical matrix that interacted with its inhabitants. Predisposition towards paranormal experiences was another aspect of the alchemical blend. The phenomenon was interactive.

ENLIGHTENMENT

We have already entered into the illumination mystery. It remains in the background throughout this work as a fundamental issue. Periodically it has been expanded to include a larger cast of characters who may perhaps all be participating in some greater drama.

Concerning the Ultraterrestrials, John Keel stated in *Trojan Horse* that this *'unknown extra-dimensional intelligence – controls important events by manipulating specific human beings through the phenomenon of mystical illumination'*. The most obvious spectacular modern accounts concern individuals who are caught in a beam of light from some aerial source. Making a similar point to Crowley on the St Paul illumination issue, he noted that *'persons caught in these beams undergo remarkable changes of personality. Their IQ skyrockets, they change their jobs, divorce their wives, – suddenly rise above their mediocre lives and become outstanding.'* The John Travolta movie *Phenomenon* gives a bitter-sweet depiction of the theme that has increasingly entered into popular culture through the vehicle of UFO mythology.

It's there in recent mystical history as well. There are numerous examples. A few will suffice. In 1925, an Indonesian who came to be known as Pak Subuh was out walking late one night when a brilliant light suddenly appeared above him and then seemed to fall down into his body. Believing himself to be experiencing a heart attack of some kind he was able to get home and lie down. Thinking he was about to die, he let go of all resistance.

Some strange force became active within him though. It delivered inner teachings and manifested an ongoing spiritual energy process that eventually was able to be transmitted to other people who in turn were able to open others. Such was the beginning of the movement known as Subud which continues to this day.

The mythology of Reiki speaks of its founder Mikao Usui engaging in a mystical mountain-top retreat that culminated in the descent of a beam of light which downloaded an entire system of healing and transformation into him like a lost Tibetan Mind Terma treasure. This was able to be transmitted by him and has since spread widely around the world.

The *Contact* mystery covers a wide spectrum from physical and psychical encounters to access to states of higher consciousness seeming to come from guardian angels or some Quantum super-self. Investigation of certain subjects seems to help stimulate its manifestation. UFOs and Crop Circles are modern examples. The Holy Grail and the Pyramids are old chestnuts. And there can be mysteries connected with locations such as Glastonbury, Rennes Le Chateau, and as we shall see, Montauk, that have the capacity to press initiatory on-buttons if approached in a particular way. Shamans and magicians, yogis and witches down through the ages have known something, sometimes plenty about the territory. Crowley's magickal system was specifically designed to bring it on and to provide the aspirant with the critical faculties necessary to navigate the process.

CHAPEL PERILOUS: ADVENTURES IN THE GOBLIN UNIVERSE

'If there is a universal mind, must it be sane?'

Charles Fort.

THE FUNDAMENTALS of the conundrums presented by material that connects UFOlogy with the wider study of occultism and the paranormal have perhaps best been characterised by Robert Anton Wilson in the 1977 *Cosmic Trigger: Final Secret of the Illuminati*.

'In researching occult conspiracies, one eventually faces a crossroad of mythic proportions (called Chapel Perilous in the trade).' 'Everything you fear is waiting with slavering jaws – but if you are armed with the wand of intuition, the cup of sympathy, the sword of reason and the pentacle of valor, you will find there (the legends say) the Medicine of Metals, the Elixir of Life, the Philosopher's Stone, True Wisdom and Perfect Happiness.' 'You come out the other side either a stone paranoid or an agnostic; there is no third way. I came out an agnostic.' There are 'those without the pentacle of valor who stand outside the door of Chapel Perilous, trembling and warning all who would enter that the chapel is really an Insect Horror Machine programmed by Death Demons and dripping fetidly with green goo.'

John Keel's awareness that many UFO cases contained elements of "high strangeness" where a whole spectrum of weirdness manifested led to his involvement and recording of the legendary events immortalised in his most famous work *The Mothman Prophecies* and his extensive logging of the Men in Black phenomenon. I am going to deal with these topics at some length because I believe they represent a clear topography of a zone we could call the threshold and the dwellers upon it. The Babalon Working and Crowley's *Vision and the Voice* Choronzon experience are journeys into the same zone. There appears to be an Abyss to cross and humanity as a whole may be plunged collectively in it. Such is the nature of the

Aeon of Horus. The esoteric millennium of 2012 has gathered about itself the allure of a threshold crossing, whether into disaster or ecstasy. We can readily see in such things as ecological issues and the Mega Ritual of 9/11 signs of external collective processes but what lies beneath the surface can be better mapped through examining the nature of the eruption of dark weirdness.

Studying the nature of the zone prepares researchers and aspirants with vital data because this material is archetypal and many people are likely to find themselves in the midst of their own version of it. The difficulties involved are considerable because it often deals with apparently real events in consensus reality. The main occupational hazard of the conspiracy researcher is the possibility of remaining lost in a hall of mirrors and reporting in ever greater detail on the shifting perspectives in the reflections forever more.

LOCH NESS LEVIATHAN AND THE BOLESKINE KIBLAH

Having already been drawn into a fantastic realism we now enter into a dream that is sometimes lucid and often incomprehensible to the conscious mind but carries with it an emotional tone that can't easily be shaken off and seduces with a feeling of meaning trying to reveal itself.

A fine example of the blending of categories in paranormal studies can be found at Loch Ness. The place has achieved world fame through the mystery of its most famous inhabitant, the monster. Bizarrely enough, links have been made with the second most famous inhabitant, Aleister Crowley.

The investigation of the monster usually assumes that the creature, if it has any reality, is considered to be solidly physical. A dinosaur survival is the most popular theory. There are other perspectives. Lake monster studies have similarities to UFO investigations in as much as there are similar divisions within the ranks of enthusiasts. There are dinosaur and nuts and bolts advocates who are clear that we are dealing with a purely physical phenomenon. Others note a level of weirdness that brings the mystery into the realms of the paranormal and human consciousness.

The Loch Ness monster is by no means a unique entity. A number of Scottish lakes, lochs and rivers have folklore traditions of beings known as Kelpies or water horses that have the ability to change shape and entice the unwary to their doom, usually carrying them off into the depths. They could appear as a beautiful woman or a wild hairy man.

It may be that lake monsters are part of the shapeshifting phenomenon noted by Vallée and Keel that includes faerie folk, angels, demons, and UFOs. They change appearance, seem to interact with their investigators, resist attempts at capturing through photography and other modern means of recording and seem to catalyse weird spiritual states and processes that are often uncomfortable.

What has occurred at Loch Ness represents a coming together of a number of disparate elements that give the location and its mythos added charisma and potency. A fault line known as Great Glen runs beneath the entire length of the loch and may be a factor in inducing altered states as a result of fluctuations in the earth's magnetic field. This kind of thing has been strongly linked to the UFO phenomenon with a clear indication that the human consciousness factor is a major part of the mix.

Researchers who actually visit Loch Ness and search local libraries for old records soon discover that the area seems to be what the UFOlogists call a Window area where a wide range of alleged paranormal phenomenon have been observed. In *The Circle Makers* and *Alien Energy* Andrew Collins mentions a visit he made in 1979 with Graham Phillips and Martin Keatman. They soon discovered accounts of UFO sightings, big cats, hairy monsters, and Little People. Perhaps most outlandish of all was a timeslip folk-tale concerning a couple who disappeared during the mid-eighteenth century at one end of the loch. A century later two disorientated people dressed in strangely old-fashioned clothes sought help from a priest in an almshouse during a freak storm. They remained for two days in a confused state, unable to account for themselves and on leaving were never seen again.

A fine example of the zone of interface can be found in the case of the legendary Anthony "Doc" Shiels, a man equally admired and reviled as shaman and mountebank. During the scorching summer of 1976 Morgawr, Cornwall's version of Nessie, manifested. Shiels party piece involved attempting to invoke the beastie to visible appearance, often with the aid of naked witches. This made for great publicity photos for the national press but also does rather seem to have been a factor in the generation of genuine weirdness. A lot of dark strange stuff was stirring in Cornwall that summer that bears comparison with the West Virginia Mothman scenario a decade earlier. It centred around the repeated appearance of a scary entity that came to be known as the Owlman. Jonathan Downes' masterpiece *The Owlman and Others* gives a detailed account. Sufficient to say that the sea monster cannot be separated from the Owlman, witchcraft, and a whole load of other weird shit and that the human factor exemplified by the magical trickster Shiels was of vital importance. The Doc inevitably took his talents to Loch Ness and produced a photo in 1977 that made front page news. Controversy over its authenticity lingers decades later.

In 1899 Alcister Crowley was fresh from his induction into the Hermetic Order of the Golden Dawn. He had progressed through a sequence of grades, engaging in an extensive magical curriculum to do so. In these early days he had tremendous respect for the head of the group. Samuel Liddell MacGregor Mathers had created an impressive romantic aura of power and authority about himself. This had partly been achieved through a number of translations he had published of powerful occult tomes. One that had not been particularly well known beforehand would achieve legendary status through Crowley's subsequent use. *The Sacred Magic of Abramelin the Mage* was allegedly written by a Jew named Abraham in 1458. It told of his journey to Egypt and meeting with the mage Abramelin who instructed him in a powerful magical mystical procedure designed to enable an aspirant to have the Knowledge and Conversation of their Holy Guardian Angel.

The text impressed Crowley because it combined a devotional mysticism with magical attainment and gave instructions which although daunting were practical and seemingly obtainable. The process outlined in Mathers version would take six months to complete. Beginning at Easter, a daily regime of prayer and purification would be undergone that would increase in intensity as the months went by. The most vital factor was to *'enflame thyself with prayer'* in order to experience communion with the angel.

It was recommended that a house be procured that would give the necessary seclusion and facilities for immersion in such an undertaking. Some of the details were very specific such as a main entrance facing north with a terrace of fine sand in front and windows facing in all directions. Crowley began to look for a home that would meet the Abramelin requirements. He found Boleskine House on the south-eastern shore of Loch Ness. It was soon given some modest structural adjustments to accommodate the magical instructions.

In the beginning of the Abramelin operation a sequence of angels were invoked. Once an initial HGA contact had been achieved the next somewhat controversial step required summoning a host of demons and getting them to swear allegiance, thus demonstrating the power of light over darkness and getting them to acknowledge one's angel and spiritual status. Needless to say, such an undertaking is fraught with peril. On successful conclusion a sequence of talismans consecrated to the assorted invoked forces would confer all manner of abilities and boons as well as the main bonus of HGA contact.

Crowley did not complete the Abramelin procedure at Boleskine. Problems in the Golden Dawn led to him breaking off during the sequence of demon invocations to travel to Paris to assist Mathers. This action has been considered to add even more danger to what was already a spiritually perilous endeavour. Standard magical practice demands the banishment of forces invoked at the conclusion of any rituals. Crowley himself was clear about this but there was no closing down before he left Boleskine. Many have speculated this was a fatal error for the young mystic who subsequently left himself open to obsession and possession. Crowley later returned to Abramelin, internalising the process and eventually claiming success.

It does seem that the initial Boleskine invocations stirred up enormous forces. Crowley's account of what transpired detailed a variety of physical manifestations over a period of months. Artificial light was needed during daytime in the sunniest room of the house at one point. Shadowy shapes manifested outside on the sandy terrace. He later wrote in his *Confessions* that

'I have little doubt that the Abramelin devils, whatever they are, used the place as convenient headquarters and put in some of their spare time in terrifying the natives. No one would pass the house after dark. Folk got into the habit of going round through Strath Errick, a detour of several miles.'

A number of tales recorded by Crowley tell of unfortunate circumstances that befell some of those who succumbed to such occult influence. Two friends helping Crowley at different times bolted in fear. A visiting clairvoyant departed to become a prostitute. The Boleskine gatekeeper, a confirmed teetotaller, got drunk enough to try and murder his family. A workman employed in redecorating the house tried to kill Crowley. Much later, in 1965, a later owner of the house committed suicide in Crowley's old bedroom.

Crowley would meet and impetuously marry Rose Kelly on August 12th 1903. They would spend a short time at Boleskine before embarking on the extended honeymoon that took in a night in the Great Pyramid in November and a fateful return to Cairo in March 1904. What Crowley stirred up at Boleskine should probably be thought of as an important ingredient in the mix. The shadow side is strongly present. Rose herself, vital muse for the reception of *The Book of the Law* was an early casualty.

Led Zeppelin lead guitarist Jimmy Page owned Boleskine for twenty years. There is a memorable fantasy sequence in the movie *The Song Remains the Same* that was filmed in the grounds there. Page is seen clambering up a tree-covered rocky cliff at night to meet a robed figure holding a lantern and staff like the tarot Hermit that had featured on the inside cover of the bands' fourth album. When finally looking at the figure face-to-face, Page sees it is himself, firstly as an old man, and then rapidly regressing to a foetus. A flash of lightning returns him back along the time-track to the wizened hermit who then brandishes his staff in an arc back and forth leaving a seventies special-effects rainbow trail behind it.

Despite this powerful linking of Page with Boleskine he barely spent six weeks there in all his time of ownership. He left a childhood friend named Malcolm Dent looking after the place. Dent knew very little about Crowley and was a fairly normal guy who brought up a family at Boleskine whilst restoring and maintaining the grounds. Despite a generally sceptical disposition he soon came to believe that the place was notably unusual and all manner of strange phenomenon occurred. On one occasion he was disturbed in his bedroom by a noise outside his door that initially sounded like a dog growling but soon developed into a full-blown door-shaking demonic roaring.

Crowley's period of press notoriety was strongly linked to his home of the time, the Abbey of Thelema at Cefalu Sicily, and it was there that the events for which he is most notorious occurred. For practitioners of his magick, Boleskine is considered to be more significant. In fact, as a result of Crowley's own instructions, Thelemic rituals should be oriented towards it as the radiating power-point for the Aeon of Horus. A passage in the third chapter of *The Book of the Law* instructs Crowley to *'Get the stele of revealing itself; set it in thy secret temple - and that temple is already aright disposed -*

& it shall be your Kiblah for ever.' The temple was his existing home at Boleskine. The passage has been taken to mean that Crowley should install an exact replica of the stele there. The term *Kiblah* is taken from Islam and refers to the direction that prayer should be addressed. The meteoric black stone of the Angel Gabriel at Mecca is famously faced by Muslims every day. The stele serves the same purpose. Magicians usually orient themselves to begin their procedures facing the east as the direction of sunrise. Boleskine is stated to be the *'magickal east'* for Thelemites. The practice is somewhat contentious in Thelemic circles. There is by no means any consensus agreement on its necessity and efficacy. Nonetheless, a tremendous amount of psychic attention has been focused on the place for around a century. Boleskine is not currently owned by Thelemites and no image of the stele is displayed there but some consider it to be an astral temple and Crowley pilgrims still like to visit the vicinity.

It may well be that in the bigger scheme of things, for which Crowley was acting as a not entirely conscious agent at that point, the Abramelin demons needed to be unleashed around a location that would come to be the focus for so much attention. A kind of folktale belief has gradually developed whereby Crowley's demon invocations in the immediate vicinity of the Loch were a factor in the modern appearances of the monster. The first group of demons Crowley would have had to invoke are known as the Four Superior Princes of Hell. Alongside Satan, Lucifer, and Belial is Leviathan, a sea monster of Old Testament vintage. It is generally taken to be some kind of coiled serpent with blazing eyes. The Babylonian goddess Tiamat came to be personified as a water serpent embodiment of primal chaos. In the most famous version of her mythos she was dismembered and her body used to make the world. Something of Tiamat may have contributed to the characteristics of medieval Leviathan.

Those who have investigated the manifestations of weird critters, *Alien Animals* as Janet and Colin Bord's excellent study has named them, often discover it is a study fraught with a certain peril. These creatures that seem to exist between two worlds often seem to emanate a baleful influence. John Keel and Jonathan Downes could both readily vouch for that. Lake monster studies are definitely included here. They do contain elements of high strangeness like UFOlogy that dinosaur hunters are in denial about. Regardless of any portrayal in cute American movies, the most famous inhabitant of the loch is a *monster*. It is also a being whose form varies considerably in different reports even if the approximation to a plesiosaur has become the most well known.

Monster hunters like to mention a passage in a biography of the sixth century St. Columba. The Irish monk was visiting Scotland when he met a group burying a man who had been attacked whilst swimming across the River Ness by some kind of water beast. Columba took massive action by despatching one of his companions to swim out into the river as bait. The creature duly appeared and Columba told it to clear off in the name of Jesus which it immediately did thus impressing the pagan Scots with the power of the new dispensation. This result seems to suggest the possibility that the beastie was considered to be in some sense demonic rather than a purely physical animal. The action takes place on the river rather than the loch. Such monster-bashing was standard fare for wandering saints of the time. The connections are tenuous but irresistible to modern mood-setters.

A modern exorcism of the loch was carried out on June 2nd 1973 by the Rev. Donald Omand accompanied by F. W. "Ted" Holiday, author of *The Dragon and the Disc* and *The Goblin Universe*. Holiday had begun as a seeker of a flesh and blood Nessie who he had initially speculated was a kind of giant slug. He came to realise that general paranormal and UFOlogical studies expanded his perspective on the mystery. Looking back into history he came to believe that the presence of dragons and discs in some kind of interplay was an important aspect of ancient culture representing the energies involved in the UFO phenomenon. He felt the loch did hold a bad vibe and that Crowley, who he characterised as a modern priest of an accursed ancient dragon cult, hadn't helped things much.

Omand was a famous demon-buster exorcist who travelled extensively in the name of his vocation. He and Holiday were part of a two-car-convey that made a complete sixty-mile circuit of the loch, stopping at four points to conduct the roving ceremony. The conclusion saw them out on a boat with Omand intoning over the waters.

'*I adjure thee, thou ancient serpent, by the judge of the quick and the dead, by Him who made thee and the world, that thou cloak thyself no more in manifestations of prehistoric demons, which henceforth shall bring no sorrow to the children of men.*'

A modest re-enactment of the scenario was staged soon after for BBC TV.

The immediate aftermath for Holiday was more than a bit strange. He had arranged to spend the night with friends, a Wing Commander Cary and his wife who lived in the vicinity of the loch. They had experienced a certain amount of weirdness themselves. Talk turned to Holiday's intention to investigate the nearby site of a UFO close encounter case he had initially heard about from John Keel. A Swedish student who had been wandering in woods near the loch claimed to have seen a landed craft in a clearing. Three weird dudes wearing grey suits and headgear like divers' helmets were visible by it. Barely had the Swede registered his feeling that they weren't human than a hatch opened in the craft into which they rapidly disappeared with the thing lifting off and flying away. It was a bizarre case and has aroused much suspicion. For Ted Holiday just thinking and talking about it seemed to set spooky events in motion.

Omand the exorcist had already cautioned against visiting the site of the close encounter. When discussing the topic with his hosts, Mrs Carey emphatically warned Holiday twice not to go, fearing the possibility of an abduction of some kind. This was enough to convince him to abandon the idea.

At the very instant the decision was made, Holiday heard a powerful rushing sound seeming to originate from outside the window. He saw a moving mass of dark smoke and heard heavy thuds shaking the door and wall. The episode lasted barely fifteen seconds and calm was soon restored. Mrs Carey had the same experience with the notable addition of seeing a beam of white light coming through the window to mark out a small circle on Holiday's forehead, an area he later realised had been marked with holy water during the exorcism. Wing Commander Carey, who was in the room at the same time saw and heard nothing whilst this peculiar scenario occurred.

When Holiday departed the next morning he was puzzled to see an odd-looking man wearing goggles and black leather seemingly waiting for him. Determined to immediately establish if it was an apparition he walked over to meet it. He kept his eyes fixed ahead but briefly glanced away for the briefest of moments during which the figure disappeared. A year later, Holiday had a heart attack at the same location. As he was carried on a stretcher he realised he was passing over the exact place where the enigmatic man in black had been standing. Five years later, in 1979, a further heart attack would kill him.

In the midst of what could easily be unravelled as a series of tenuous non-rational connections a mood of high strangeness has been encountered the nature of which serves as an orientation around which to expand the study. The magickal focal point of Crowley's New Aeon can be seen as a multi-dimensional Window area for a wide spectrum of paranormal weirdness, most notably the Loch Ness monster. In the period since 1904 it rather seems that similar areas have been energised and activated so that the critters have gained greater access to our world and our psyches.

CALL OF CTHULHU: WAIL OF SUMER?

'I cannot think of the deep sea without shuddering at the nameless things that may at this very moment be crawling and floundering on its slimy bed, worshipping their ancient stone idols and carving their own detestable likenesses on submarine obelisks of water-soaked granite. I dream of a day when they may rise above the billows to drag down in their reeking talons the remnants of puny, war-exhausted mankind - of a day when the land shall sink, and the dark ocean floor shall ascend amidst universal pandemonium.'

H. P. Lovecraft. *Dagon*.

'Nor is it to be thought that man is either the oldest or the last of earth's masters, or that the common bulk of life and substance walks alone. The Old Ones were, the Old Ones are, and the Old Ones shall be. Not in the spaces we know, but between them, They walk serene and primal, undimensioned and to us unseen. Yog Sothoth knows the Gate. Yog Sothoth is the Gate. Yog Sothoth is the key and guardian of the Gate. Past, present, and future, all are one in Yog-Sothoth. He knows where the Old Ones broke through of old, and where They shall break through again.'

H. P. Lovecraft. From the *Necronomicon* in *The Dunwich Horror*.

The idea of a monster being awoken from a primal sleep in the watery depths and returning to terrify the rational world was gestating in other places as well as Loch Ness during the early decades of the twentieth century.

The American Howard Phillips Lovecraft was a legendary figure in the development of horror/fantasy/sci/fi literature. Born in 1890, he suffered the appalling combination of the early death of his father from syphilis and the suffocating ministrations of an over-protective mother who likewise died insane, predisposing him to be a physically unhealthy man who lived almost entirely in his head. He was dead by 1937. An obviously eccentric figure who affected the persona of some kind of fastidious gentleman aesthete of a bygone age, he actually took the side of the British in any discussions on the War of American Independence. In this he was quaintly charming. In other aspects of his mindset he was more unpleasant to modern sensibilities, being a rabid xenophobe who penned some passages that would not have been out of place in Nazi propaganda.

Lovecraft was a fan of Edgar Alan Poe and wrote some acceptable but derivative early horror fiction and poetry. His physical weakness helped him from an early age to be receptive to an extraordinary dream-life from which he derived his most powerful inspirations. *'Space, strange cities, weird landscapes, unknown monsters, hideous ceremonies, Oriental and Egyptian gorgeousness, and indefinable mysteries of life, death, and torment, were daily – or rather nightly – commonplaces to me before I was six years old.'* Despite such a temperament he was clear in a letter to fellow writer Clark Ashton Smith that, *'I am, indeed an absolute materialist so far as actual belief goes; with not a shred of credence in any form of supernaturalism.'*

A whole range of recurring symptoms laid Lovecraft low. These included bad headaches, dizziness, and an intense detestation and agitation at any temperatures below seventy degrees. Anthony Roberts in *The Dark Gods* considered them to be signature signs of prolonged Ultraterrestrial contact.

Lovecraft is most famous for a series of tales now known as the Cthulhu mythos. Such is their peculiar potency that a number of other authors have taken up the themes and expanded them. Lovecraft introduced the motifs in the 1917 early tale *Dagon*, named after a Canaanite deity often depicted as human from the waist up but fish from below. A decade later the story was reworked and expanded into the *Call of Cthulhu*.

One of Lovecraft's many correspondents quoted him as saying that *'All my stories, unconnected as they may be, are based on the fundamental lore or legend that this world was inhabited at one time by another race who, in practicing black magic, lost their foothold and were expelled, yet live on outside ever ready to take possession of this earth again.'* In *Cthulhu*, in accordance with some vast heavenly cycle, the old gods are near again. Ancient cults they left in place aeons ago are re-energised in preparation for their return.

In one strand of the narrative a voodoo-style cult in fetid New Orleans swampland is busted. Lovecraft sets the scene where *'malevolent tom-tom'* can be heard in the *'black haunted woods'*. Approaching nearer there are the sounds of *'insane shouts and harrowing screams, soul-chilling chants, and dancing, devil flames'*.

A statuette of the deity that appears in the story depicts

> *'a monster of vaguely anthropoid outline, but with an octopus-like head whose face was a mass of feelers, a scaly, rubbery-looking body, prodigious claws on hind and fore feet, and long, narrow wings behind. This thing, which seemed instinct with a fearsome and unnatural malignancy, was of a somewhat bloated corpulence, and squatted evilly on a rectangular block or pedestal covered with undecipherable characters.'*

It may not seem on the surface that there any points of similarity between the aesthetically beautiful deities of Egypt and the slimy tentacled monstrosity Cthulhu. Nonetheless a zone of interface between Crowley and Lovecraft has come into being. It's a mighty strange space and there are many who argue that is not "authentic" in terms of being truly representative of what the two men were about.

In *The Call of Cthulhu* his demented devotees claimed that when the Old Gods regained control of the planet, *'Mankind would become free and wild beyond good and evil, with laws and morals thrown aside, and all men shouting and killing and revelling in joy – all the earth would flame with a holocaust of ecstasy and freedom'*. There are definite similarities to the characteristic of Crowley's Aeon of Horus here.

Lovecraft, like Crowley, is now strongly associated with a magical grimoire of terrifying potency. The *Necronomicon*, the Book of Dead Names, was a title he made up during a phase as a small boy when he had become enamoured of all things Arab after reading the *Thousand and One Nights*. The title was heard in a dream.

A *Necronomicon* mythology was created by Lovecraft in a document to help him maintain consistency in subsequent tales. It stated that the dread tome was written by a *'mad Arab'* named Abdul Alhazred during the 8th century AD. A poet from the Yemen, he had travelled widely, including the ruins of Babylon and Egyptian Memphis. During a decade alone in the Arabian desert he came upon the fabled lost city of Irem and discovered beneath a ruined town archives of a race that preceded humanity who worshipped terrifying gods. Alhazred himself became a devotee of Cthulhu and Yog Sothoth, eventually retiring to Damascus where he composed his accursed text.

As Lovecraft developed as a writer he moved into the new genre of science fiction. In doing this he evolved his conception of the creatures he portrayed from being medieval style demons to aliens with advanced technology. To modern sensibilities the two categories are not necessarily mutually inconsistent.

The publication of *The Magical Revival* in 1972 saw the first major attempt to link Crowley and Lovecraft. Kenneth Grant postulated that Lovecraft, regardless of his cynical persona, was an authentic channel for the magical energies of the new aeon. His peculiar temperament clothed his intuitions in fear, thereby distorting their truth.

A table of comparisons was included that began by placing the *Necronomicon* alongside *The Book of the Law,* showing the fundamental importance of two grimoires linking with extra-dimensional entities. Lovecraft's general term for his vastly archaic beings is the Great Old Ones. The Golden Dawn and Crowley had a ritual phrase, the *'Great Ones of the Night of Time'*. The various details are suggestive without being entirely convincing. This was only the surface of an ongoing assimilation of Lovecraft into Grant's version of Crowley's magick, his Typhonian OTO.

In his next work, *Aleister Crowley and the Hidden God,* Grant tried to clear up the fear factor in Lovecraft, seeing the forces involved

'not as an attack upon human consciousness by an extra-terrestrial and alien entity but as an expansion of consciousness from within, to embrace other stars and to absorb their energies into a system that is thereby enriched and rendered truly cosmic by the process.'

Below the Qabalistic Tree of Life lies another anti-matter version, a shadow realm where the spheres and paths are populated by assorted entities known as the Qlippoth. They were dealt with to some extent in the Golden Dawn. Crowley wrote of them.

Grant went further than anyone before him in mapping out the magic of what his fourth book *Nightside of Eden* called the Tunnels of Set. He located it behind rather than below the tree. Access to it was afforded through a zone called Daath, functioning for Grant as an eleventh sephiroth and situated right in the middle of the veil of the Abyss that featured so strongly in the lives of Crowley and Parsons and whose threshold guardian is Choronzon. Here were the zones to encounter Lovecraftian entities.

Grant equated Yog-Sothoth with Choronzon. Lovecraft's horror held him back from a successful navigation of the Abyss. In Grant's interpretation, even though Lovecraft's experiences were in dreams this doesn't in any way diminish their magical authenticity but enhances the sense of something primal stirring.

Daath means Knowledge in Hebrew. The Greek equivalent would be Gnosis so Kenneth Grant talks of a Necronomicon Gnosis that can be seen as a vital ingredient in the broader Extra-Terrestrial Gnosis.

In *Outside the Circles of Time*, Grant stated that 'The Necronomicon does not exist as a book in the mundane world, but it does exist in the dream state and is available to those who are able to penetrate the Veil and the Abyss and break open the seals of the qliphoth which guard it.' He also spoke of the Necronomicon mythos with the sense that the grimoire probably serves as a better designation than Cthulhu for the genre.

He speculated whether Lovecraft's visionary abilities were due to some past life when he far more consciously connected to the creatures of his dreams. They were not demons in the strict medieval sense but primal layers of the human psyche formed during our earliest years and therefore forgotten and profoundly "alien" in their feeling.

Grant's work has certainly opened the portals for the emergence of magical groups who work with Lovecraft's entities. Their attitudes vary in terms of what they believe they are doing and to what end.

Interest in Lovecraft and his fabled grimoire had already grown considerably in the sixties. The occult literature market had a potentially fertile gap for those willing to entertain the possibility that the *Necronomicon* could be for real. In 1977, with a dedication dated to mark the centenary of Crowley's birth two years earlier, such an item appeared in New York.

There is a one sentence quote from Crowley's unpublished writing included in *The Magical Revival* that has caused the most amount of occult tumult apart from the "bloody sacrifice" sequence:

'Our work is therefore historically authentic, the rediscovery of the Sumerian tradition.' No context is given. This sentence provided one of the foundations of what has come to be known as the Simon *Necronomicon*.

An excellent legend accompanied the publication of the work. Two monks engaged in an extensive pilfering of rare books from libraries gave a copy of a terrifying grimoire to an enigmatic translator of rare Arcanum, a consecrated bishop of some obscure Eastern Church known only as Simon. He worked on it and took the result to Herman Slater, owner of the *Magical Childe* bookshop in New York (then known as the *Warlock Shop*), purveyors of all manner of occult paraphernalia as well as books, and centre of a thriving social scene often fondly recalled as some kind of free-form sex and drugs apocalypse.

Slater was enthusiastic about the text and assembled a team to render it publishable. This included Peter Levenda who we have already met as the author of the much later Nazi occultism investigation *Unholy Alliance*. Levenda has often been suggested as the real identity of the mysterious Simon who has resisted any definite unmasking. James Wasserman of the OTO was apparently involved in the design and layout. The now notorious sigils were the work of a character calling himself Khem Set Rising.

In this version, the dread grimoire originated from the very dawn of civilisation in Sumeria and represents the mother lode of the tradition that Crowley was trying to rediscover. A preparatory tale of the *'Mad Arab'* seems to set a Lovecraftian scene. It also establishes the idea that the text is not necessarily a complete version of an incredibly ancient text but might have later layers of style and material.

Assorted Sumerian deities and demons are the sources of some of Lovecraft's creatures and his great grimoire. The mysterious Sumerians are depicted as working Necronomicon magic in their seven-levelled ziggurat temples. Kenneth Grant's comparative table of terms between Crowley and Lovecraft is obviously drawn upon and an additional column added to include the "Sumerian" elements.

Marduk, the chief god of Babylon, is in effect the warrior lord of the work. His battle with Tiamat, the ancient goddess who became degraded until portrayed as a chaos monster and became a probable Leviathan template, serves as the exemplar for a War in Heaven scenario. Tiamat, like Cthulhu, is a denizen of the deep waters.

This zone could be considered to represent an archaic strata of humanities' consciousness. In magical terms it can also signify the Abyss and the Daath portal into the Tunnels of Set. We have already noted one possible example of its eruption at Loch Ness. The Elder Gods and the Ancient Ones are in conflict and our planet is a potential battleground. 'The Ancient Ones, Lords of a time before memory, are being drawn by a smell of confusion and the hysteria and mutual hatred of the primitive life-forms on this planet: human beings.' The grimoire is presented as potential protection through its use of fifty different names of Marduk that serve different purposes.

There are also various invocations of entities who seem to be the very sort of creatures that Marduk and his associated deities were warring against. These demons are a right unfriendly bunch portrayed as exceedingly dangerous.

One of the most enduring aspects of the work concerns a sequence of gate openings that should be carried out in sequence over a period of a year or so. Each gate has associated planetary symbolism, colours, perfumes, and deities. The most famous myth that has endured from those far-off days is the story of the goddess Innana (who became the Ishtar of the Babylonians) and her descent into a seven-gated underworld. It seems likely it lies somewhere in the background of the *Necronomicon* framework whatever its provenance.

Stories suggestive of dangerous forces at work were thrown in to add to the atmosphere regarding the *'fearful hallucinations, physical incapacities, and emotional malaise that accompanied the work from the onset of the translation to the end of its final published form'*.

A fairly obvious attempt to emulate the mythology surrounding the successive publications of *The Book of the Law* and their apparent link to the outbreak of wars and the crumbling of dynasties accompanied the 1980 paperback edition. An introduction recalled the reign of terror of satanic-cult linked killer Son of Sam at the time of it original appearance. The Jonestown mass suicide and the ascendancy of the Ayatollah Khomeini in Iran with its hint of a stirring of Islamic problems were suggested as ripples spreading outwards from the opening of a potent portal.

So just how authentic is the Simon *Necronomicon*? For an extended consideration of the issues involved the best resource is *The Necronomicon Files* of Daniel Harms and John Wisdom Gonce III. A few important points will suffice here.

There was indeed a real case involving book-stealing monks but grimoires don't appear to have been on their wish-list. They focused on valuable atlases. The original manuscript the team worked on has never been displayed. This is partly explained by the suggestion that it is a thing of potentially dangerous power. Against this one might at least expect some photographs.

The Sumerians stand in relation to the later Babylonians in a broadly analogous manner to the Greeks with the Romans. There is a fundamental inspiration and connection but all kinds of differences. The basic source material for the Simon *Necronomicon* is Babylonian not Sumerian. It does rather seem that authentic texts that could be found in most good libraries have been rewritten with names of Lovecraftian deities or approximations thereof grafted on.

There is one example in *The Necronomicon Files* that adequately demonstrates the important issues surrounding the Sumeria/Lovecraft blend. Being as it tackles in detail something of central importance to the whole edifice's credibility it is worth quoting John Wisdom Gonce III at length.

> '*Simon's most infamous violation of Sumerian syntax is probably his claim that Lovecraft's Cthulhu is found among the ancient Mesopotamians in association with the town of Kutu (sometimes known as Cutha), which he refers to as "KUTU." Simon further states that "KUTU" is a Sumerian name for the underworld. Thus he claims that "KUTU-LU" or "Cuthalu" means "the man of the underworld" or "man of Cutha." First, the proper Sumerian idiom would be LU-KUTU. Second, while there was a real city of Kutu in Babylonia, where Nergal was worshiped at a temple called E-meslam (or Meslam House), its only association with the underworld was that its patron deities were Nergal and Ereshkigal, Lord and Lady of the underworld. And third, no God – even one with tentacles on his face – would ever be referred to by the humble title of "Lu" or "Man."*'

The fifty names of Marduk, derived from an authentic Babylonian text, and so important to the work and the subsequent *Necronomicon Spellbook*, are badly mashed so their order and meaning get confused. There is also the little matter that Marduk cannot be clearly traced back to a Sumerian original.

Even more problematical are the procedures for stirring up the assorted forces. Controversy attends the most basic details as no circles of protection are cast. This is at variance with Mesopotamian magical texts that repeatedly mention using flour for the purpose.

It is also strangely at odds with introductory notes indicating the necessity of a circle of protection. The work also says there is no protection against the forces invoked. That is at least a deliberately melodramatic statement if not a nasty little fear game. It's somewhat irresponsible.

A herb called Aglaophotis must be burnt to invoke a particular demon. An enormous amount of magical lore says however that the stuff is just the ticket for getting rid of demons. It's kind of like inviting some dodgy psycho round to your house and spitting in his face when he gets there. How will he respond? And this with no protective circle as preparation. In the planetary gate walking sequence the sun god Shamash has a fine sounding invocation that is actually a bit of authentic Sumerian/Akkadian. Unfortunately it is actually telling the Sumerian version of Shamash to clear off out of it.

The Gates may have inspirations deriving from the Qabalah, Enochian and Gnosticism but primarily from the Innana story that concerns a descent into an underworld. The Simon procedures have been criticised for perhaps leading into a qliphotic Tunnels of Set scenario without giving due warning. The magical correspondences seem to owe more to the Golden Dawn than Mesopotamia.

The whole work in general has a tone and structure similar to medieval grimoires. Harms and Gonce find all manner of source material. That in itself does not serve as proof of its fraudulence. Such texts often seem to contain older strata. We have encountered the barbarous names of evocation used in the Golden Dawn and Crowley systems. There is nonetheless a point when it becomes a cop-out to side-step issues concerning Sumerian authenticity by claiming that the material has been reused over the ages and the text is a late version. Harms and Gonce give numerous details that cast extreme doubt on any Babylonian never mind Sumerian provenance.

Although Crowley was known to put a few jokes and misdirections into his magickal texts this is something else altogether. The Abramelin grimoire is famously dangerous but the Simon *Necronomicon* is in a class of its own. There are a number of accounts, allegedly originating from people who were around the *Warlock Shop* social scene, that the whole thing was a deliberate spoof along the lines of "let's see how stupid people really are". Something was badly misjudged and got well out of hand, taking on a life of its own, perhaps (in a Lovecraftian touch) due to the predatory presence of assorted entities that smelled lunch and wanted to keep a good thing going.

A likely further stimulus for the format was the unlikely appearance of a Mesopotamian deity as Hollywood superstar. *The Exorcist* was released in 1973 to unparalleled controversy. It's assuredly one of the great horror movies and featured an unusual villain in a genre full of Christian devil clichés. Pazuzu was a storm lord of Assyrian Babylonian vintage who tends to be depicted as winged, with bird talons, a dog's face, scaly torso, and a snake-headed penis. He was actually thought of as a nice chap who protected pregnant women from a baby-stealing demoness named Lamashtu and also offered protection against disease-bearing winds. In order to fulfil such functions he needed to be a bit fierce and he certainly comes on that way in *The Exorcist*. It's may be not that much of a surprise that Pazuzu features in the Simon *Necronomicon*.

What about the Lovecraft/Crowley/Sumeria connection that is so fundamental to the presentation of the work? Lovecraft was intensely interested in Roman times. So great was this passion that he stated he had never really projected his imagination to any periods before it. He had very little knowledge or interest in Sumeria. The attempt to graft Cthulhu onto a Sumerian structure has been shown to be dubious.

Lovecraft was aware of Crowley, it was difficult not to be during the years of his press vilification, and referred to him in correspondence as '*rather over-advertised*'. He certainly didn't have a high opinion of him. He seemed to feel in general that his style was simply a hangover from the decadent diabolists of the Fin de Siecle. A 1936 unpublished letter to a friend named Richard E. Morse referred to the Beast as a *"mass of psychological putrescence"*.

If we take the Kenneth Grant approach it really doesn't matter if Crowley and Lovecraft were temperamentally worlds apart and might have hated each other on sight. They dreamed true as part of a picture far bigger than their external personas. By this criteria as well, Lovecraft could still have tuned in to the Mesopotamian current regardless of his conscious interests and level of knowledge.

It does rather seem that there is very little authentic Lovecraft in the Simon *Necronomicon*. Or Sumeria. What about Crowley? In *The Necronomicon Files*, Gonce wonders why '*If Crowley were so devoted to the Sumerian tradition, why didn't he call his coming age the "Aeon of Enki" and not the Aeon of Horus?*' '*Simon spares no stratagem to link two men who never met with a civilisation neither cared about.*' In Crowley's published work there are scarcely any references to Sumeria. One that Gonce mentions is evocative however when we add some additional data. The Cephaloedium Working, dating from the time of the Abbey of Thelema, refers to Aiwaz as *'the God first dawning upon Man in the land of Sumer'*. The variant spelling comes from Crowley's discovery that he could get the alternative version to add up to his favourite 93 by gematria.

Remember Crowley's description of the subtle form of Aiwass he perceived during the writing of *The Book of the Law?* He had *'the face of a savage king, and eyes veiled lest their gaze should destroy what they saw. The dress was not Arab; it suggested Assyria or Persia, but very vaguely.'* In the midst of a whole scenario in Cairo full of Egyptian god-forms there is no indication that the messenger of the process conforms to the same archetypes. If Crowley was just making it all up one would expect Aiwass to also be described as Egyptian in appearance. His name sounds out of place as well. This at least hints that there's more to the dynamic behind the Aeon of Horus than just Egypt.

During the thirties Crowley amazingly came to know a man whose surname was Aiwaz. This backed up his alternative spelling. What is also intriguing is the man's ethnic background. He was an Aisor. These people are the descendants of the ancient Assyrians.

There is no doubt that the genesis of Babalon can be traced, as we have already seen, back to Ishtar/Inanna. Her characteristics are far more clearly seen in the Mesopotamian goddess forms than Egyptian. Her very name is a variant on Babylon and her importance in Thelema is undeniable.

In *The Magical Revival*, Grant is quite clear that he believed the vital *Liber Samekh* ultimately derived from Sumerian sources through its barbarous names. This is more than a bit contentious but serves to broadly establish Grant's own context for the use of the mysterious Crowley quote. Whilst these snippets are a long way from an endorsement of the Crowley Sumeria slant in the Simon *Necronomicon* they do leave a few portals open.

Without wishing to extend this work into even greater length I would recommend that those interested in the attempt to find a vastly ancient disturbingly powerful magical tradition that links both Egypt and Sumeria and goes back beyond both of them would be well advised to look at Andrew Collins astonishing investigation of the legends of the Nephilim presented in his *From the Ashes of Angels*.

The Simon *Necronomicon* has become the grimoire of choice for all manner of satanic badasses and looks set to stay that way. There have been tragic cases where murders have occurred involving people who have become enamoured of its transgressive charisma.

The book has certainly found its way into popular culture in a manner surpassing any other grimoire. Some lines from it were chanted to stunning effect on the extended version of the epic Fields of the Nephilim occult-rock number *Psychonaut*. Gothic Chaos magicians have prayed for Leviathan. One of the most commercially successful and one of the coolest cult movies of the eighties, *Ghostbusters* and *The Evil Dead* respectively, both featured plot details inspired by it.

Is this just a complex sociological scenario or is the Simon *Necronomicon* packing some real voltage? Magicians might assert that if you call on various forces with sufficient intensity, especially ones lurking beneath the threshold of consciousness from the dawn of history, something will happen. If the procedure is framed with nuances full of emotional tone in the collective mind it will further colour and enhance the results. What does that mean? *The Necronomicon Files* rightly notes how well-established is the archetype of the dark grimoire that serves as a portal for dangerous entities that may consume the foolhardy magician. This theme is present in the *Arabian Nights* material that was a formative part of Loveraft's childhood. It's also there with the medieval grimoires and the likes of Abramelin. The aura of danger and potential doom may serve as an active psychological (if not magical) magnetic force that almost inevitably switches on even in the cases of those who are actually attracted to such legends.

There are those who believe that, regardless of any issues concerning its composition, the book has a unique identity and magical power. Interviewed for *The Necronomicon Files*, Peter Levenda suggested that '*The book protects itself, I think. It has a life of its own, now, and has not been out of print a day since that fateful December in 1977. What does it want? Where is it going from here? None of us – none of the original band – have the foggiest idea.*'

Tales of magical misfortune befalling *Necronomicon* users are legion. A magician named Martin Mensch went through the Gate procedure in double-quick time and shortly after completion was shot dead in an apparently random manner. Maybe these forces have some kind of independent existence and do broadly function in the ways described. The most potent magic is likely to be worked by those who are at least able to believe that it is true for the duration of their experiments.

Fake grimoires are nothing new. The Middle Ages and Renaissance periods were full of works falsely attributed to the likes of Moses and Solomon, consisting of various diverse elements stitched together. To the occultist the concept of fake is ultimately only applicable to something that doesn't work. If something is deliberately booby-trapped it may still stir things up. It is perhaps a post-modern irony that a fake grimoire should take up a genuine functional position across the Veil of the Abyss and the doorway into the Tunnels of Set. By genuine, in terms of the Abyss, I mean it has the capacity to ensnare the would-be-adept and permanently keep them off course in the manner of Choronzon. Those that may attain a true nightside gnosis through such means are rare indeed.

The aspirant would be well-advised to think carefully about attempting to navigate these realms using the Simon *Necronomicon* as a guide book. Kenneth Grant's oeuvre is problematical enough but arises out of a far greater bigger picture. Remember that Crowley only stirred up Abramelin demons after long preparation on the sunny side of the Tree of Life. The practice of invoking Goetic demons is supposed to occur on a balanced foundation. There are only a few modest suggestions along such lines in the Simon *Necronomicon*. The follow up *Spellbook* pretty much invites anyone to jump straight in and get whatever toys and jollies they want with the aid of Marduk *'without fear or risk'* as the back cover says. A necessary get-out clause does add that *'great care must always be taken when harnessing primal forces'*.

When it comes to Lovecraftian monsters, before Pazuzu hit the silver screen and the Simon *Necronomicon* was dreamed into being, a creature had already manifested in the realms of consensus reality to devastating effect that perhaps spoke more strongly of the reality those sources sought to portray and invoke than anything contained within them.

MOTHMAN

In West Virginia, centred on the town of Point Pleasant, during 1966 to '67 there were sightings of an entity that seemed to have strayed from a horror movie. The general consensus described it as semi-humanoid, grey, about seven feet tall, very broad, with large round glowing red eyes set in a not very pronounced head. Usually, shortly after being spotted, it would perform its party-piece of suddenly unfolding a ten foot wingspan and rising vertically to then head off without any movement of the wings, an aeronautically improbable manoeuvre. It was the eyes that lingered, along with a chilling feeling of something being far from right.

Incredibly, over a hundred people claimed to have seen the creature between November 1966 and December 1967. The local press, in the spirit of the era when *Batman* was a top TV show, soon named it Mothman. Large crowds went out at night looking for it. None could have guessed that their locale would soon feature in a disaster that would claim the lives of nearly fifty people and that a Hollywood film and the unveiling of a statue of the monstrous Mothman in Point Pleasant lay decades ahead.

The area was also hosting a classic UFO "flap" There were a large number of lights in the sky sightings and some bizarre closer encounters with absurdly improbable small flying objects in the vicinity of roads. Woodrow Derenberger achieved legendary contactee status through his repeated encounters with a human looking being who said its name was Indrid Cold.

Keel had noted a repeating pattern whereby contactees were fed prophetic information of various kinds that often proved to be correct thus leading them and their followers further into situations where they would always be let down. The promised climactic manifestation that would offer ultimate validation failed to appear. This was usually end of the world type stuff.

Sometimes contactees talking to space brothers and spiritualist mediums talking to their controls relayed identical prophetic messages independently of each other, convincing Keel they were tuned into one source. In June 1967 an entity calling itself Apol communicated that the Pope would be knifed to death in the Middle East by a man dressed in black there. Details repeated and expanded: it would happen at an airport, an earthquake would precede it and a general Armageddon crisis would be the consequence. Keel spoke to Apol through a hypnotised contactee who told him that Robert Kennedy was in danger. There were warnings of plane crashes that Keel says happened. Shortly afterwards the Vatican announced that the Pope would be visiting Turkey in July. A large earthquake in Turkey killed a thousand people. Obviously those who were aware of the prophecies became a bit freaked out. The Turkish visit came and went without incident. Three years later, in November 1970, the Pope was attacked at Manila airport in the Phillipines by a man dressed in black brandishing a knife. He was stopped before being able to use it. A channelled message that *'Robert Kennedy should "stay out of hotels"'* came to make horrible sense in 1968.

This material epitomises the problems of communicating with entities of whatever genus. The details get skewed, ie it was in the Far rather than Middle East, three years later than predicted, that a man in black with a knife did indeed confront the Pope at an airport but without fatal consequences. Nonetheless, as a whole, the prophetic package involving Pope, Kennedy, earthquake, and plane crashes really did seem to originate from a source beyond normal space-time. If you are receiving this kind of data and it is appearing to be validated it is understandable why anyone could get hooked into the process of looking for more and being willing to act on it.

The more Keel investigated the West Virginia web of weirdness a feedback mechanism seemed to be activated whereby his research appeared to be manipulated. There were mysterious phone calls, messages, and improbable synchronicities that seemed to be engineered to communicate to him that whatever intelligence was orchestrating the big picture it always knew exactly what he was doing and could easily engineer events for his benefit. Receiving information from contactees and psychics who didn't know each other but were bringing forth information that all gelled together was typical. A further good example came when he decided on a car journey that he would stop at a motel and simply pulled over at the first one that appeared. On arrival a letter was waiting for him that really just served to let him know that high strangeness was on his case. Keel found himself increasingly talking to the weird Apol over the phone via tranced-out contactees. He could ask any number of trivial questions to him and get an accurate answer. Where had he lost his watch? *'Look in the shoebox in the upper-right hand corner of the bedroom closet.'* This kind of paranoia inducing episode is handled very well in the *Mothman* movie.

Although Keel tended to deny it, I rather feel that he was a major factor in the mystery himself. His rich background of experience possibly helped the phenomenon to manifest more strongly. He came on the scene, prepared by his experiences in Egypt, Tibet, and the paranormal in general like some magician or shaman. It seems as if someone like him was required to participate in and record the events.

Further prophecies developed involving a major EM (Electro-Magnetic) effect. A date of December 15th 1967 was given via Apol.

A disaster on the Ohio River was looming involving heavy loss of life. The hints implied a factory explosion. Later details fine tuned it to be synchronised with the turning on of the Christmas tree lights on the White House lawn. At the very moment the switch was flipped a nationwide power failure would occur. The atmosphere in the Point Pleasant area intensified. Disturbing dreams were reported, including one of many people drowning in the river with Christmas packages floating amongst them. Keel's associates confided a feeling of foreboding and that sense of something being far from right that accompanied Mothman sightings. The frequency of sightings of Mothman and lights in the sky had noticeably decreased however.

In early December the entities seemed to change their mood and start terrifying their contactees. They circulated a story that Keel was dead. One experienced fires breaking out. Another woke in the night to find all of the gas jets on the kitchen cooker turned on. The White House Christmas tree lights went on with no problem but the TV broadcast was interrupted with a newsflash announcing the collapse of the Silver Bridge over the Ohio at Point Pleasant. Nearly fifty people died. Beyond the centre of the tragedy, a little way out in the surrounding hills a large number of red flying lights appeared for an hour or so.

Keel was of course devastated by the tragedy and became angry that the entities had not made their warnings clearer. He came to believe there was deliberate trickster malevolence in their activities. In *Trojan Horse,* written after the Mothman experiences, Keel registered his distrust saying that, '*the UFOnauts are the liars, not the contactees. And they are lying deliberately as part of the bewildering smokescreen which they have established to cover their real origin, purpose and motivation.*'

MEN IN BLACK

The worlds of the physical and psychical contactees were not entirely separate. There was a zone of overlap which shows elements from the world of occultism. Probably the most disturbing and instructive aspect of this involved the now legendary MIB (Men in Black).

Albert K. Bender was an American UFO enthusiast who set up one of the first investigation groups in 1952. His account of his experiences, *Flying Saucers and the Three Men* remains a classic controversial oddity of the genre. Bender came from a family whose history included ghostly experiences with which he had been regaled when young. This helped him develop a serious interest in the paranormal and Fortean anomalies in general. Bender entered UFOlogy as a minor local celebrity. He had painted characters from horror novels on the walls of his home. It also contained twenty chiming clocks, *'artificial human skulls, shrunken heads, bats, spiders, snakes, black panthers, and the like'*. Bender *'began reading books on Black Magic'*. There were unsuccessful séances. He experimented with a divination technique involving the Bible that a Native American woman had shown him when he was a child. Some thought him insane. He was featured in a newspaper story thus ensuring his home became known as a "Chamber of Horrors".

Bender's UFO group rapidly became very successful, establishing international branches. Barely a week after the issue of their first newsletter Bender had an experience that seemed like something in keeping with his Gothic background. Leaving a cinema he was suddenly overcome by an intense headache, feeling as if something had been put over him to shut everything else out. Looking up he saw a blue flash and felt as if his feet were being lifted off the ground and a telepathic message being communicated telling him to stop his UFO investigations. Returning home he noticed a blue light shining from behind his front door as he was about to enter. *'A large object of undefinable outline was aglow in the center of the room. It looked like a bright, shimmering mirage.'* On switching the light on it disappeared. A strong odour like burning sulphur filled the room. Bender discovered his UFO files were in disarray although nothing was missing. This was disturbingly strange.

One day in a semi-deserted cinema Bender had the feeling of being watched. He suddenly found that a sinister man with glowing eyes was sitting beside him. Thinking he was hallucinating, he briefly closed his eyes only to find that the man had suddenly shifted to be sitting on the other side of him. Leaving the cinema he encountered the man again in the street and realised that he did not consider him to be human.

Bender wondered if it might be possible to telepathically contact the intelligence behind the UFOs. He wrote a statement beginning *'Calling occupants of interplanetary craft'* and suggested to his study group that they try and beam it out in unison across various global time zones on what would be termed *World Contact Day* on 15th March 1953. There were expressions of reluctance and even hostility but the experiment went ahead. It would lead to events even more disturbing than the Carpenters seventies kitsch ET anthem it inspired.

Bender sent out the telepathic message from his Chambers of Horrors and immediately encountered the headache and sulphur smell again. He seemed to leave his body and float above it, hearing a voice conveying a dramatic message.

'We have been watching you and your activities. Please be advised to discontinue delving into the mysteries of the universe. We will make an appearance if you disobey.'

After the voice faded and Bender seemed to drop back into his body he became aware of a humanoid shadow in yellow mist. This concluded the episode but the sulphurous smell lingered for days.

A few months of comparative normality followed until in July, things really got going. Returning to his Chamber of Horrors after a short vacation, Bender was again confronted by the sulphur smell. Moving blue lights appeared in the room as headaches and dizziness overcame him and, suddenly icy cold, he fell onto his bed convinced that some malevolent force had him in its power.

Three shadowy figures appeared in the room, hovering about a foot above the floor. They *'looked like clergymen'*, wearing black clothes, including shirts, ties, shoes, and gloves. Their faces were not immediately discernable being partly hid by Homburg style hats but pearly white teeth stood out against their dark complexions. The eyes of all three then lit up *'like flashlight bulbs'*. *'They seemed to burn into my very soul as the pains above my eyes became almost unbearable.'* Another telepathic warning was conveyed. They had an agenda and were not to be disturbed. *'As you see us here, we are not in our natural form.'* Their craft were hidden on Earth. They had killed some humans and *'We also found it necessary to carry off Earth people to use their bodies to disguise our own.'*

The creatures left a small piece of metal behind which Bender could use to contact them by holding on to it, switching his radio on, and repeating the word *Kazik*. This is where his account displays an uncertain tone. His experiences to that point would be enough to terrify most people. Bender nonetheless tried to use the metal to contact the three beings again and appeared disappointed that some attempts were failures.

Subsequent visits change the mood of Bender's tale considerably.

It became not dissimilar to many tales from the fifties of experiences inside alien craft with the revealed history of ET races and their reasons for being on Earth. It's also clear that Bender was a sci-fi aficionado. He had been watching such a movie when the fire-eyed entity appeared in the cinema. The MIB repeatedly took Bender to their base in Antarctica. They appear in his room and instigate out of the body experiences which sometimes seemed to last a long time before his arrival in the frozen south leaving the obvious questions of what was the nature of the reality they occurred in. As a reader of horror literature as well, Bender may have been familiar with H. P. Lovecraft's *At the Mountains of Madness* with its depiction of a hidden alien city there. There's a lot of room for cynicism.

The locations he visits do seem a compendium of fifties sci-fi movie imaginings. They include a gigantic cavern with a ceiling made of ice, a large circular room with a transparent domed roof through which he could see a night sky and stars and a cigar shaped craft the size of an ocean liner. Bender watches TV screens showing movies of the alien's home world, sees laboratories and medical facilities of some kind. The visitors are processing sea water for some vital purpose they refuse to explain.

The creatures encountered were quite varied. A humanoid shape-shifter revealed its true form as a ten foot tall green thing with a glowing red face that had visited him in his home but was invisible at first. The head honcho of the whole operation was a being known as the Exalted One. He was a muscular, nine feet tall handsome humanoid, with silvery white hair and light brown skin, wearing a golden coloured uniform and sporting the standard glowing eyes. He communicated telepathically with quaint genteel civility, using terms such as *"cordial welcome," "deepest esteem,"* and *"honoured guest."* Bender had a few question and answer sessions with him. My favourite revelation is that beneath the surface of Earth are cavernous cities inhabited by creatures that can render themselves invisible when they visit the surface and cause all kinds of malarkey stealing stuff and scaring people. Devotees of weirdness will recognise echoes of the notorious Shaver mystery here. Again, it is quite possible that the relevant material could have been familiar to Bender.

A notable episode occurred when Bender met three women with translucent glowing skin *'dressed in tight white uniforms'* at the alien base. *'Their hair was a silver color, done up in a sort of bun with large silver halos about it.'* Bender considered them to be *'physically attractive'* despite the usual red glowing eyes and the headaches their appearance set off in him. The three foxy ladies all touched Bender and began stroking his body. He was carried away to a room where his clothes were removed and a vial of liquid poured over him. *'They massaged every part of my body, without exception.'* He was then given a going over by some kind of medical gizmo operated by a hooded figure who informed Bender that he would subsequently be safe from cancer.

In the middle of this curious chain of events Bender married a woman he had begun corresponding with from a British branch of his UFO group. She came to live with him in America and he visited the UK, extolling the virtues of the English countryside and *'a steaming cup of tea, scones with clotted cream and strawberries'*. As long as his mysterious piece of metal remained however, Bender knew that the aliens were still present and he had to continue his silence. One day it was gone.

Following the initial MIB appearances Bender dramatically announced that he was closing down the UFO group and withdrawing entirely from the subject. He hinted at dramatic events indicating he had become aware of the truth behind the flying saucers but was pledged to silence. Not surprisingly he was deluged by requests for information. Eventually he told a considerably edited version of his story to a friend from the UFO group named Gray Barker who wrote a successful book with the material. The 1956 *They Knew Too Much about Flying Saucers* introduced the MIB archetype into the UFOlogical field but without the distinctly demonic edge present in the full version.

What's immediately problematical is that Barker himself is a hugely controversial figure in UFOlogy, often considered to be an inveterate trickster and sometimes out and out liar. His presence haunts and distorts both MIB studies and the Mothman story as if understanding these enigmas wasn't difficult enough already.

In Barker's version of the story, Bender gains information from a government source regarding the true nature of UFOs. He posts a letter to an associate containing the details. Soon after, he is visited by three middle-aged men, all dressed in similar black clothing and wearing Homburg hats. They had the letter Bender had just posted. They were clearly intelligence operatives working for the government. It was explained to him that the truth he had discovered was powerful stuff that could not yet be made public and he should keep silent about it. There was something intimidating and sinister about the men who threatened a possible prison sentence if he did not comply.

Such was the level of interest in the story that Bender was not allowed to retire in peace. When the alien metal dematerialised the way was clear to tell the whole tale. *Flying Saucers and the Three Men* emerged in 1962. At the very least, some kind of psychological odyssey can be perceived in the narrative. From Bender's Chamber of Horrors bachelor pad to idyllic married life with tea and cakies encompassed quite a journey, moving as it did from the demonic MIB with their dire warnings on the threshold of unknown worlds to the healing hands of the women in white who perhaps evoke a triple goddess archetype. It could be said that he crossed some kind of Abyss.

Bender's story would be a remarkable document even if it stood alone. He repeatedly stated his concern for being considered insane. The peculiarity of mood evoked whereby the horrific, bizarre, and everyday elements sit beside each other in such a matter of fact manner invites strong response. It's not surprising that Bender has been considered as a nutjob/bullshit artist. Throw in doubts about Gray Barker who generally promoted MIB mythology for decades and it's clear why many people consider the whole field to be entirely fraudulent. Whatever the case, the story seemed to unleash the archetype of the MIB. Bender's encounters were only the beginning.

As the sixties moved on it gradually became apparent to some investigators that further MIB manifestations were occurring. What was fascinating about the cases was the similarity of bizarre details reported by witnesses scattered across the United States and eventually other countries including Britain as well at a time before they were widely known. There was always something distinctly strange about the intrusive visitors. The big black cadillacs they drove seemed brand new as did the old fashioned suits and shiny shoes of their occupants. The men seemed slightly oriental, often with olive skins and pointed features. They behaved as if unfamiliar with the commonalities of language and conversation in a way that would not be expected of government agents. These eccentricities were sometimes disturbingly bizarre. A very peculiar atmosphere accompanied them. Time seemed to warp out. They might give the impression of trying to emanate a baleful hypnotic influence.

John Keel came to pay particular attention to them, eventually having his own experiences of their style. In *Trojan Horse* he compared their general appearance to that of vampires. On occasions they displayed badges of some kind featuring an eye in a triangle.

WILHELM REICH'S CONTACT WITH SPACE

'It was as if someone had spread butter on all the fine points of the stars 'Cause when he looked up they started to slip.'

Patti Smith. *Birdland*.

As already noted, in the final phase of his mythic career Wilhelm Reich came into increasing conflict with the US Food and Drug Administration concerning his work with the primordial life energy Orgone and the devices he had created that in some way made use of it. The most famous of these was the Orgone Accumulator, closely followed by the Cloudbuster, both immortalised in song by Hawkwind and Kate Bush respectively. The FDA refused to accept the validity of any of Reich's experimental work and made him aware that the claims he was making for them and their transport across state boundaries contravened regulations. A Federal injunction was issued leading to the conclusion where his devices were destroyed and his books were publicly burnt. He died in prison.

This tragic trajectory was notable for a powerful accompanying mood set by Reich's simultaneous involvement in extreme high strangeness in the realms of UFOlogy. Once again there's something archetypal, dream-like, and disturbing about the case that serves as a pointer to the deeper forces at work and further belies the myth of the boring fifties. Reich's psychological theories and his orgone work make his place in the UFO mystery very interesting. Consensus opinion holds that he totally lost the plot during the flying saucer period but I'm far from sure about that.

Reich had established a research institute named Orgonon in north-east America at Rangeley Maine where he conducted experimental work, the most notable concerning what was termed Cosmic Orgone Engineering (CORE). He had wondered about the potential relationship between nuclear radiation and orgone. Perhaps radiation sickness could be alleviated. A controversial series of experiments known as Oranur (ORgonomic Anti-NUclear Radiation) brought the two forces together. After a small amount of radium was put in an accumulator box it apparently antagonised the orgone, generating Deadly Orgone (DOR). Some baleful force seemed to emanate from the laboratory and out into the local environment. Reich and his team went down with a variety of ailments. A tangibly oppressive feeling hung in the air. Unlike any of his other work, this experiment has been considered too dangerous to ever repeat which unfortunately makes evaluation of it rather difficult.

In 1953 the local blueberry crop was threatened by a drought. Some farmers offered to pay Reich if he could produce rain. At a time when weather forecasts predicted no rain for days, Reich began work. Ten hours later it began raining. Two inches fell in a few days and the crop was saved. Understandably it seemed a strong case of cause and effect and Reich became a local celebrity hero.

In January 1954 Reich noticed *'two bright yellow-orange lights moving in front of a mountain range toward a lake'*. This marked the start of an increasing interest in the UFO mystery. He had read one of the most successful books on the subject, Donald Keyhoe's *Flying Saucers from Outer Space*, a few years before. He had also seen the *War of the Worlds* movie. Both of these sources may have subtly predisposed him to form two opinions, firstly that nuts and bolts space ships were involved, crewed by creatures from other planets, and secondly that those beings may have hostile intentions. This material, coupled with the Cold War climate, led to a feeling of urgency and danger in what seemed to be occurring. When he discovered from friends that UFOs had been seen over Orgonon as far back as 1951, the time of the seminal Oranur experiment, this intensified the mood.

Reich reported his sighting to the local Air Force and duly received a questionnaire form in response. His secretary likewise saw unknown lights in the local sky. This initial consciousness of the intrusion of the UFO phenomenon into the Reichian world was all but simultaneous to the first injunction issued against the orgone devices and any literature deemed to be promoting them.

Communication with the Air Force continued to varying degrees. Reich sent them an essay on his theories about UFOs which he designated with his typical predilection for terminology coining, EA, meaning Energy Alpha. He was sure they made use of orgone.

In May 1954 an apparently accidental discovery was made. During a night-time sweep of the sky with a Cloudbuster it was observed by Reich and three colleagues that a point of light in the path of the flow faded out. There had been nothing to indicate it was not a star until that point. After pointing the device away, the light reappeared. Further similar effects soon followed. This understandably led to a strange mindset amongst Reich and his group. Firstly there was the uncanny feeling generated by not knowing how many of the lights in the night sky were perhaps craft from other worlds. Were they deliberately clustering around the orgone work to interfere and, in a massive escalation of standard Cold War paranoia, did this mean they stood on the front line of a possible inter-planetary conflict? The EAs were sucking up orgone and spewing out DOR. Perhaps it was a concerted strategy against humanity. At the same time Reich's legal position became increasingly precarious as the scale of the injunction against him increased in extent until eventually books that simply contained the word orgone were considered fair game for banning.

It was with this unusual background in the autumn of 1954 that Reich and his team were led to the climax of the weather modification Cloudbuster work during a spectacularly weird extended trip to Tucson Arizona. River beds had been dry for fifty years. It allegedly hadn't rained for five years. No prairie grass was visible anywhere. The desert seemed to manifest extreme forms of natural imbalance. Team Cloudbuster, including Reich himself and his young son Peter (who recorded the episode in his unique immortal childhood memoir *Book of Dreams*), soon succumbed to a general malaise which they felt went beyond what could be expected in a desert environment. DOR was deemed to be responsible and UFOs soon appeared. It was felt that they were actively resisting his rainmaking.

A bizarre pattern established itself. Initial Cloudbuster use was followed by a massive rise in humidity. Clouds began to appear shortly followed by UFOs. Some of the UFOs seemed to be cigar-shaped with windows. Humidity fell and the clouds dissipated as if in response to a negative ET influence. The Cloudbuster would be brought in again. Eventually the balance seemed to shift. Foliage began to appear. Prairie grass began growing in the vicinity of the Cloudbuster. Some radium needles that had been charged in an orgone accumulator were brought from Orgonon and put into a Cloudbuster. The device was now used against the UFOs.

It was on December 14th that the drama reached its climax when in Reich's words, '*a full-scale interplanetary battle came off*'. An enormous black cloud appeared over Tucson that took on a red and purple colouration and set off massive readings on Reich's Geiger counter. The team went down with a variety of unpleasant symptoms. Air Force planes buzzed the camp. Reich turned his radium charged Cloudbusters up towards the malevolent mass. Within twenty minutes the cloud had broken up and the background radiation reading returned to normal. Three weeks of lively UFO battles followed and finally the victory of rainfall. Grass grew to the extent that local ranchers drove herds of cows back into the area. In April 1955 Reich felt the job was done and returned to Orgonon.

What was really happening here? Was Reich deluded, his methodology faulty and his accounts untrustworthy? That tends to be the consensus view. Even some of his advocates prefer to ignore this final phase of his work, detailed in the book *Contact with Space*. He was not alone in Arizona or at Orgonon. There are many corroborative accounts. Was the power of his personality enough to create and sustain a weird little world where things were massively misinterpreted? The history of religion, psychology, and for that matter, politics, has seen many such episodes. Did he get himself enmeshed in some secret military scenario without realising and pay the ultimate price? For the record, I do believe in the essential veracity of the orgone work and that it vectored in some aspect of the UFO phenomenon and this led to something genuinely mysterious occurring in Arizona. In the absence of certainty however it is the mythic side of the drama that we are left to ponder and perhaps serves as its strongest factor.

Reich does rather seem to have encountered a version of the threshold of the Abyss experience. The FDA agents functioned as Men in Black. Their general look in the Kate Bush *Cloudbusting* video captures something of that nuance. Like an esoteric alchemist Reich entered into the realm of a profound arcanum concerning transmutational secrets. Some force of resistance kicked-in like an automatic programme and delivered all manner of difficulties. Yes, all of its elements were part of explicable historical factors but the manner of their assemblage seems to speak of something beyond the total understanding of any of the protagonists. Reich grasped something of it in his very last days when he stated that it was the Character Armour and Emotional Plague of the majority of people that prevented them from seeing the saucers. This has been interpreted as an example of his megalomania and paranoia and also sits uncomfortably with the nuts and bolts interpretation he seemed to favour but it does suggest a fascinating and perhaps fundamental mystery at the heart of UFOlogy that we are repeatedly encountering: the human equation.

ORGONE BIOFORMS

One of Reich's followers (albeit one not exactly endorsed as such) provides a great example of the role of the human percipient in the UFO mystery. He also formed definite opinions on the nature of the forces of resistance encountered in its study.

Trevor James Constable was present at the Giant Rock gatherings where George Van Tassell spoke in strange voices about esoteric matters. Whilst some of these performances could easily seem to border on the ridiculous, Constable was impressed by what he rated as oratory worthy of Orson Welles that Van Tassell in his usual life was incapable of. Fascinated by what was occurring he sought to encourage similar phenomenon in himself. Van Tassell instructed him personally. This resulted in a series of communications that contained some intriguing material. UFOs in part are manifestations of previously unknown life-forms that live in the atmosphere. In the time between dawn and sunrise they can potentially be photographed using infra-red film.

These mediumistic episodes disturbed Constable due to their increasing frequency and his lack of control. He found an occult teacher named Franklin Thomas who taught him how to maintain his equilibrium and ultimately dispense with the need for that particular type of input altogether. Constable was fortunate in coming to a sequence of remarkable teachers who progressively heightened his sensitivity to subtle energies. These included Radionics pioneer Ruth Drown, who was persecuted by the FDA in a manner very similar to Reich, Meade Layne, and Reich's widow, Eva. He was also considerably influenced by the teaching of Rudolf Steiner.

Constable's remarkable journey was described in 1976's *The Cosmic Pulse of Life*, a work indubitably worthy of cult classic status. Perhaps the most important issue he raises is the role of the state of consciousness of consensus humanity in the UFO experience. As Meade Layne had realised, the changing vibrational frequency effects whereby UFO phenomenon became periodically visible imply that they are present most of the time but outside the range of normal perception. Cleansing the doors of perception does seem of fundamental importance and this doesn't simply mean consuming hallucinogens.

In *The Cosmic Pulse of Life* Constable encouraged his readers by simple exercises to learn to see and sense the human aura and to apply similar adjustments to the normal methods of visual focusing to become aware of other forms of energy present in the everyday world. He endorsed Reich's conviction that the Emotional Plague and Character Armour that afflicts the mass of humanity prevent people from perceiving the UFO phenomenon. As we shall see, Constable came to believe that some of the forces involved seek to open our eyes whilst others prefer to keep them closed.

It has quite often been the case that UFO experiences have not arisen out of a vacuum for the percipient. Subjects may be found to have a history of at least moderate mystical and paranormal states. This may include the apparent sighting of ghosts, psychic abilities and so on. UFOs have also clearly catalysed the opening up of such faculties. Occultists have systematically trained themselves to become aware of other realms and work with a belief in the possible reality of discarnate intelligent forces. It seems fairly likely there will be some overlap.

The inspirations Constable received from his initial trance channelings proved to be fruitful. In 1957 he went out into the Mojave with a colleague to try and photograph the generally invisible life forms in the sky that he came to refer to as "critters". It was considered to be a vital part of the procedure for Constable to perform a kind of meditational invocation to attract them. The Star Exercise had been recommended to him by Franklin Thomas. It was because he had already successfully opened his doors of perception that he was able to effectively perform it. The procedure looks like something out of Qi-Gong or Tai Chi.

Facing east at dawn, Constable began with the assumption of an obvious star posture involving legs spread apart and arms held out parallel to the ground. He gently oscillated his body to try and atune with the Earth's magnetic fields. Having found to his satisfaction the resonance point in the east, he would then turn 180° around to the right to find it again. A further 90° turn to the right followed while facing north, then 180° to the south on the right. A 270° turn to the right to face the east and begin again completed the first sequence. Between sixty to one hundred repetitions would be performed around dawn. This produced what Constable called *'a regular pattern of bioenergetic pulsations in the ether.'* A beacon of this nature would be noticeable in supersensible realms.

Amazingly enough the duo photographed over a hundred biological looking images and more standard UFO-type "craft". The "bioforms" were pretty big, sometimes miles long. Constable believed them to have a kind of consciousness and intelligence. His record of this work and speculation on its meaning in the 1958 *They Live in the Sky* and *The Cosmic Pulse of Life* continues to inspire new generations. He believed the creatures arose out of the cosmic energy ocean of orgone described by Reich. Constable went on to major Cloudbuster work of his own and was clear that understanding of orgone was vital to the UFO mystery.

In 1962 in Ray Palmer's *Flying Saucers* magazine Kenneth Arnold, the man whose experience had started the whole UFO furore in 1947 and had investigated the mystery ever since, suggested that the saucers *'are not space ships from another planet at all, but are groups and masses of living organisms that are as much a part of our atmosphere and space as the life we find in the oceans. The only major difference in the space and atmospheric organisms is that they have the natural ability to change their densities at will.'* This obviously helped Constable to feel that he was on the right track.

Over the years it has been increasingly recognised that some of the lights in the sky reported as UFOs are manifestations of what have been termed Earth Lights. Studies have shown that stresses and strains in the earth's crust generate electromagnetic responses that can result in the discharge of various types of lights.

Perhaps the best example of the profound mysteries involved comes from a study conducted during the eighties at Hessdalen in Norway. The remote valley had become known for lights in the sky and a long term stake-out was arranged by various UFO groups. Many sightings and photographs resulted but the most notable thing was the way the lights gave the impression of somehow interacting with the observers. A modest example occurred when a slow moving light that was flashing with a regular rhythm changed its rate when a laser light was pointed at it. At the extreme end of the weirdometer a group of lights once gathered together to form a Christmas tree design and most absurdly of all, an unmistakeable depiction of the iconic billowing-skirt image of Marilyn Monroe. All of this can still be interpreted as linked with orgone.

To quote Andrew Collins in his development of Reich and Constable's work investigating the crop circle enigma, *The Circlemakers*, 'Each time we come into contact with one of these dense orgone masses through close encounters, we give it identity. Its base intelligence is continually re-programmed until it takes on some semblance of the very entities we believe it to be' – 'The orgone bioforms are the alien intelligences and the fairy folk of old, and both are generated, programmed and updated by us.'

So at least some of the UFO phenomenon may be a part of the still unknown life of the planet. This potentially links in with the Ultraterrestrial hypothesis of John Keel and the Magonia studies of Jacques Vallée. We may have found the stuff of which these dreams are made and something of how they come to manifest. This still leaves the mystery of the changing forms through the ages. It may not just be a case of evolving human consciousness. UFO entities may be the scientific era form of mythic beings from humanities past but the modern world also seems to be experiencing an upsurge of the reappearance of many mythologies in essentially their ancient form. Cycles of time may hold the key. We are back to Jung and Crowley. Certain god and goddess forms may be said to preside over different epochs. Human consciousness is central to the equation but the question still remains as to whether it is being acted on from outside and how far outside that might be? Orgone bioforms and Earth Lights may serve as a conduit for Ultra-terrestrials and Inter-dimensionals. Anything that malleable could filter forces through into the life of humanity from outside the planet, from space. Clearly we have arrived in a zone crucial to the understanding of all forms of magic and a further test of the psychology necessary to navigate such a realm.

Constable did draw a distinction between the orgone critter sky creatures and the etheric vehicles of the UFO beings. He took on Meade Layne's *Ether Ship* terminology. There is a diagram in *Cosmic Pulse* of one of the interdimensional craft and one of his published Mojave photos is claimed to show just such a thing briefly making itself visible. Whilst being willing to accept that some of the things seen in the sky may have a nuts and bolts explanation as machines from other worlds he felt that the majority were not. This further led to pondering on the nature of the entities involved.

AHRIMANIC DARK GODS

'There are essentially two factions at work in UFOs. There are the etherians, who enlighten and guide, and the Boys Downstairs who confuse and control mankind.'

Trevor James Constable. *The Cosmic Pulse of Life.*

Constable took on the War in Heaven mentality of Pelley, Williamson, and a number of others, and presented it in terminology derived from Steiner stating that Ahrimanic forces had become involved in the downfall of Reich following the Oranur experiment. Ahriman, the equivalent of the Christian devil in Zoroastrianism (possibly even a partial template for the later development of the church idea), was a figure of considerable importance to Steiner. He believed that Ahriman was set to physically incarnate around 1998 and that centuries of preparation had already occurred. This sits nicely alongside the Steiner-inspired spiel in *Mark of the Beast* about the spiritual forces at work behind the creation of the bomb. One type of the application of science can lead to an ever denser materialism for all the vast vistas it seems to open up. The result is an increasing limitation on human consciousness. Ahriman has been considered to be the personification of all that is potentially negative in the application of scientific method. A different perspective has the opposite effect. A new epoch is dawning and the consciousness of humanity is expanding to perceive other realms. The Etherians are becoming visible in response to this. Revolutionary science such as Reich's orgone work will help that process hence its targeting.

Constable, following Meade Layne, at least gives us a sense of good guys and bad guys. Others tended to focus more on just the "Boys Downstairs". After the Point Pleasant bridge disaster in the Mothman story John Keel's feelings about the Ultraterrestrials came to resemble the Medieval church talking about the devil and all his works. '*The demonologists have been studying the same thing as the UFOlogists.*' '*The manifestations are the same, only the frame of reference is different.*' The title of a later Vallée book *Messengers of Deception* recorded a similar process for the French author.

It's interesting to return to the case of Ashtar at this point. In the UFO era a being with this name has supposedly identified itself to a number of people as a benevolent big-chief helping humanity along with massed ranks of intergalactic entities of varying levels of density under his command. In the western magical tradition Ashtaroth is identified as a fallen angel trickster demon. He makes appearances in the Old Testament. The *Lemegeton*, generally known as the *Lesser Key of Solomon* or *Book of Evil Spirits* warns that he '*discourses willingly on the Fall but pretends that he himself was exempt from their lapse.*' The *Grimorium Verum* or *True Key of Solomon* is dated 1517, not long after Columbus. It makes the remarkable claim that Ashtaroth had migrated to America. Crowley was certainly more than familiar with this being as it is present in the Abramelin procedure, described as *'riding on an Infernal Beast like a dragon, and carrying in his right hand a viper'. 'He giveth true answers of things Past, Present, and to Come, and can discover all secrets.' 'He can make men wonderfully knowing in all liberal sciences'*

To complicate matters further it would appear that the Old Testament writers were distorting the name of Astarte in their depiction of Ashtaroth. She was a Phoenician goddess, famously painted by Dante Gabriel Rossetti, linked to Ishtar and part of the blend that makes up Babalon.

RAF Air Marshall Sir Victor Goddard, who had a distinguished military career during the Second World War, later became well-known for his interest in mystical topics in general and particularly UFOlogy. In a public lecture in 1969 quoted by Keel in *Trojan Horse* he recognised that the source of the phenomenon was not necessarily purely physical but came from paraphysical realms where,

> *'Seemingly some of its denizens are eager to exemplify principalities and powers. Others pronounce upon morality, spirituality, Deity etc.'* They *'propagate some special phantasm'* and seem to mess with people's heads *'simply to astonish and disturb the gullible for the devil of it'. 'We can only see the objects and the entities under certain circumstances, and perhaps only certain types of people can see them at all.'*

This mood gradually influenced the UFOlogical field to such an extent that a number of people left it altogether having become convinced after their own peculiar experiences that it was inherently evil. This in turn was happily accepted by certain evangelical types and a bizarre *UFOs: Angels of the Antichrist* genre emerged.

Perhaps the most readable product of such a mindset is the 1980 paranoid classic *The Dark Gods* by onetime Glastonbury residents, the great Avalonian Anthony Roberts, and Geoff Gilbertson. The UFOlogical research of Jacques Vallée and John Keel got a good going over. The authors essentially agree with Keel. Malevolent entities have been messing with our heads since the dawn of history. H. P. Lovecraft was their unwitting vehicle. Just about every single esoteric group in the western tradition reeks of diabolism and general contamination. Freemasonry is a hideous tentacled monstrosity aiming at Luciferic world domination. And so on.

Crowley is described as '*a creature of immense evil, indulging in virtually every perversion known to the mind of man.*' The whole Golden Dawn tradition was irredeemably tainted by its supposed roots in the notorious Illuminati, of whom much more later. Rather than the emergence of the genius of the angelic higher self, its techniques are really designed to make one a conduit for demonic forces.

Dion Fortune was a graduate of a reformulation of the Golden Dawn known as the Stella Matutina. To the authors of *The Dark Gods*, behind its '*top dressing of intellectual cosmetics that presented a pretty face to the world, there lay a raddled whore of Babylon: a whore eager to consume the clients who patronised her.*' Roberts and Gilbertson give a nod of approval to Fortune for her recognition of the significance of earth energies and her work on Glastonbury. She is ultimately characterised however, as an '*English Lilith,*' working for '*a return of paganism in the form of sex-magic through invocation of fierce elemental forces*' and showing '*a great interest in necrophilia, astral vampirism and sex interaction on the inner planes.*' Her role of Priestess of the Goddess was nothing more than '*the authoritarian, matriarchal essence of power through blood, ritual spells and endless sacrifice. That was her warped legacy through the Stella Matutina and all the other secret orders going back to at least the Bavarian Illuminati.*'

Even Rudolf Steiner was nowt more than a Luciferic Illuminati pawn. It is certainly true that he was once involved with the German occult scene, primarily the OTO. The real corpus of his work may well constitute the most remarkable manifestation of esoteric Christian mysticism of the twentieth century. Here was a man who wrote at length on the second coming of JC and the pivotal role of the Archangel Michael. Ahrimanic forces are endlessly castigated by Steiner. Somehow this just didn't land right with Roberts and Gilbertson. The work of Steiner's Anthroposophy in caring for the mentally handicapped and developing bio-dynamic farming shouldn't blind us to their essential dodginess.

The Dark Gods makes use of Trevor Ravenscroft's *The Spear of Destiny* to detail the occult background of Nazism. The fact that the same book is a hymn of praise to Steiner and names him as the greatest "white" adept in Europe, the only person who recognised and opposed the early Nazi's occultism, goes unmentioned by Roberts and Gilbertson. Likewise, if Dion Fortune was a channel for the same schools that lay behind the Nazis, how was it that she was able to focus the Magical Battle of Britain from Glastonbury?

As for the Great Beast, we have already seen where he stood in relation to Hitler and the Nazis. When it really mattered, Steiner, Fortune and Crowley clearly demonstrated what team they were playing for. Or at least thought they were.

SECRET CHIEFS

The various illumination cases examined so far have highlighted some diverse personalities to say the least. Although there are many points of similarity between the experiences the results have been spread across what one could term the religious and moral spectrum. Is it even a valid question to ask if the illumination produced can be said to be a true one or have people been misled by a false light? Are we dealing with something that is in essence amoral?

Even if Aiwass was a true Secret Chief was he telling the truth? Were Crowley and Parsons manipulated to further an agenda that was not an inevitable cosmic law of nature but a plan for mega demons to feast on the death of millions? They may not have realised. Indeed their conscious personalities might have believed they were working for an entirely different outcome.

Hermann Rauschning was a Nazi who had met Hitler and changed his mind about the whole scenario by the mid-thirties. He wrote *Hitler Speaks*, allegedly a record of numerous conversations about a huge range of subjects mixed with various anecdotes. One has been widely circulated in occult literature. A close associate of Hitler told Rauschning that the Fuhrer sometimes woke up screaming, sweating, and in convulsions, maniacally babbling weird sounding words and seeming to see some otherwise invisible being in a corner who had *'come for me'*. This has been construed as magnificent Ultraterrestrial demonic Secret Chief stuff and grist for the mill of the myth of Nazi occultism. Rauschning's work was treated as authentic for decades and used by reputable historians. More recent analysis has trashed it completely. A short story by Guy de Maupassant apparently provided the model for the night horrors episode. Shame really.

Perhaps the classic account of meetings with Secret Chiefs comes from Golden Dawn supremo Samuel Liddell Macgregor Mathers. He believed that *'they are human beings living on this Earth, but possessed of terrible and super- human powers.'* A terrific energy emanated from them that only an advanced adept could handle for more than a few minutes. It was strong enough to kill. Various intense physiological symptoms were reported during his different encounters such as problems with breathing, '*cold sweats and bleeding from the nose, mouth and ears.*'

Crowley himself was in no doubt of the reality and power of these forces, whatever they may actually be. In the late collection of letters *Magick Without Tears* he says of them, '*They can induce a girl to embroider a tapestry, or initiate a political movement to culminate in a world-war; all in pursuit of some plan wholly beyond the purview or the comprehension of the deepest and subtlest thinkers...But are They men, in the usual sense of the word? They may be incarnate or discarnate: it is a matter of Their convenience...*'. This may strike those of differing temperaments as an inspirational or terrifying idea.

So who or what are those apparently evil Illuminati that *The Dark Gods* claimed to lie behind so much western occultism. Are they the earthly vehicle of the centuries-wide plan of the Ultra-terrestrials who are the guiding forces and contacts of occultism and UFOlogy? Are we beginning to head into a paranoid cul-de-sac or will a change in the way we look at exactly the same thing transform it and ourselves? Time to examine in detail Robert Anton Wilson's definitive odyssey into such territory.

COSMIC TRIGGER

ILLUMINATI

COSMIC TRIGGER may be the most expansive and useful guide to the interface of occultism and UFOlogy. It catalogues the typical symptoms stirred by such studies through telling the interlinked tales of a number of major game-players. Crowley and Leary have a central role in the unfolding saga.

Robert Anton Wilson had co-authored with Robert Shea the cult classic *Illuminatus* trilogy. *Trigger* told the story of the astounding background of their researches into the mystery of the Order of the Illuminati, most certainly one of those topics capable of pressing an on-button.

Trigger begins with the basic historical facts concerning the notorious group. Founded by Adam Weishaupt on May 1st 1776 in Bavaria, they were a kind of secret society within the Masonic lodges of Germany. By 1785 they were suppressed by the Government for allegedly plotting to overthrow all European monarchies and the Catholic Church. Those few details are about as much as anyone will ever agree upon. Everything else on the topic rapidly degenerates into the most incredible speculations. Weishaupt himself has been variously considered to be an atheist rationalist, mystic occultist, fascist, anarchist, and democrat. His creation has been credited with arranging the French and Russian revolutions, controlling the international banking system and stage-managing most major wars since.

Ever since the early nineteenth century, the Illuminati have been periodically rediscovered along with a conspiracist view of history. This kind of thinking reached a peak during the era of Hitler and Stalin when the two most important figures on the world stage both based their policies on their beliefs in the machinations of enormously powerful secret societies and alliances. Occultist types have expanded the Illuminati mythos even further. It is often claimed that Weishaupt revived rather than invented them. Their lineage could be traced back, through the likes of the Knights Templar, to Egypt and Atlantis. They have even been linked to malevolent extra-terrestrials.

Wilson and Shea found the paranoid theories on the secretive Bavarian boys to be an interesting and amusing study. They conceived of using it as a backdrop for a satirical novel that lampooned such fantasies. This device would serve their greater purpose of holding the state up as the ultimate object of ridicule. It was the time of the ending of the sixties and the appalling ennui of the degeneration of the Nixon regime. A lot of paranoia was about. Some of it was justified. Wilson had worked for *Playboy* and read many of the letters they received requesting financial aid from a foundation that the magazine had created to help worthy causes. There were cases that could readily document real hassle they were getting from the authorities. Others were nutters with their heads full of complex plots against them. These crazy tales were perfect fodder for the creation of *Illuminatus*.

As the writing progressed, things began to get increasingly weird. Some kind of process was set in motion whereby Wilson was led to question to what extent there was a reality behind the mythos of the Illuminati. Information revealed itself in an impressively synchronistic manner, suggesting to him that he may have connected psychically to a magickal current that really did extend back down the ages to an astonishing source. Things he thought he'd made up proved to be the apparent calling cards of the mysterious ones. The way in which the whole thing unfolded was way beyond the sifting of data and ideas by an armchair academic to arrive at some theory. These ideas seemed to be alive. Connecting to them inevitably generated weirdness.

What Wilson underwent was a kind of initiation. It forced him to look at the very nature of reality and personal identity. It put him through intense personal dramas and ultimately, an appalling tragedy. And all of it was strangely synchronised with the bigger picture of the madness of the sixties.

SIRIUS MYSTERY

Wilson stated that his entry to Chapel Perilous began when he was reading Crowley's *The Book of Lies* in 1971. It is a work full of codes and riddles, Zen-type epigrams, poetry, jokes and magick. Crowley had stated that somewhere within it was concealed the inner secret of Freemasonry and Illuminism. Wilson experienced a flash of insight whereby he felt he'd cracked the code. It dealt with sex magick. This led him to suspect that the Illuminati had possibly been the lineage holders of methods of altering consciousness through sex and perhaps drugs as well. This stuff had to be kept secret as it carried a potential death sentence. Outsiders looking in experienced the immediate horrors of the threshold of Chapel Perilous, suffering as they were from Christian conditioning.

Already an experienced psychedelic voyager, Wilson decided to test his theory by combining acid with serious experimentation in Crowley's magickal techniques. As a result of this he found that synchronicities and strange experiences rapidly increased. It was through this doorway that information suggestive of an Illuminati signature fortuitously clustered around him. During the writing of *Illuminatus*, Wilson was inspired to make major use of the symbol of the eye in the triangle, treating it as a motif of the secret brotherhood. He knew that its portrayal on the dollar bill had been linked to Freemasonry. Gradually he came to know that it connects with the Egyptian Eye of Horus design and was used on ceremonial headgear by Crowley. The Beast referred to his work as '*scientific illuminism*', and occasionally to himself as '*Epopt of the Illuminati*'. Wilson began to notice that the number 23 seemed to appear in his synchronicities a disproportionate amount of times. William Burroughs had introduced him to the idea that some kind of strangeness surrounds the number. At first he wondered if it was a case of selective attention.

The process built up to a peak in 1973. On July 22nd Wilson performed a customised Crowleyan ceremony involving '*Tantric sex-trance*'. The next morning he '*awoke with an urgent message from Dreamland*'. It stated that '*Sirius is very important*'. Looking for relevant information in his occult books, he struck gold in Kenneth Grant's *The Magical Revival*. Wilson was impressed to read that

'*Phoenix was Crowley's secret name in the Ordo Templi Orientis... The Phoenix was also an ancient constellation in which Sothis, or Sirius, was the chief star.*' '*Crowley identified the heart of his magical current with one particular Star. In Occult Tradition, this is "the sun behind the sun," the Hidden God, the vast star Sirius.*'

Indeed, the Order that Crowley created himself, the AA, has been generally taken to mean "Argenteum Astrum" or Silver Star. The part of Wilson that was a careful researcher hesitated to weird-out too much as he had looked through some of Grant's book before and may have subconsciously absorbed some of the data.

Kenneth Grant stated in *The Magical Revival* that Crowley's personal papers show that he believed the 93 current to reflect an energy from Sirius and that the entities with which he had congress related to stars, planets, and the strange spaces between. If Grant's interpretation was valid, Thelemic Magick was clearly cosmic in its scope. Nuit was *Our Lady of Space*, after all.

Later on, at a public library, Wilson's doubts were dissolved. He read that July 23rd, that very day, was the date when the so-called "dog days" began. Sirius has come to be known as the dog star. This dates from Graeco-Roman times. It's located in the constellation of Canis Major, the Great Dog. It follows Orion the hunter as the dog at his heels. The ancient Egyptian calendar began when it was seen to rise above the horizon, behind the sun, at dawn, after a long period of absence from the sky. This return was noted across the classical world as the beginning of the season of scorching summer sun, the dog days. In Egypt, it was once broadly synchronised with the inundation of the Nile. The river dominated the agricultural cycle of Egyptian life so it was inevitable that the star heralding the season of its blessings would be regarded as important. To the Egyptians, Sirius was the star of the Goddess Isis. The river's fertile gifts could easily be associated with a divine mother. Nuit is not separate from Isis, rather a more expansive cosmic form of her. In *The Book of the Law* Nuit says, '*I am Infinite Space and the Infinite Stars thereof,*' showing how Isis is within her.

Wilson was obviously stunned by this. He couldn't resist speculating as to whether, via Crowley's work, he may have tuned in to a magickal frequency that really did link Earth to Sirius through hyperspace. Somehow he had been led to the most auspicious date in the calendar to make that connection. The eye in the triangle represented Sirius. Perhaps the 23 enigma had been leading him towards the July 23rd event. Things he had been pondering on for years seemed to have been inexorably leading him to that moment of revelation. Something that Wilson didn't mention is that the birthday of Rose Crowley, who had been so instrumental in the reception of *The Book of the Law*, was on July 23rd.

This was a typical synchronistic bringing together of material in a way sufficient to advance a process. It is worth noting that the Sirius date may have been true once but it's not anymore. The date has shifted. It is now in early August. What I have come to respect is that the July 22/23 time remains a most potent magical time to connect with certain energies.

From that moment on, Wilson was willing to entertain the possibility that he was in contact with some kind of intelligence connected with Sirius. This episode lasted for over a year. *Trigger* contains an extensive consideration of the "contact" phenomenon.

SUFISM

It wasn't just Crowley who seemed to have a Sirius connection. When discussing various mysteries of the European Middle Ages, Idries Shah had stated that the Illuminati had arisen from a Sufi impetus. He focused on a particular verse in the *Koran* considered central to the secret doctrines of this lineage. *'Allah is the Light of the heavens and earth. His light is resembled by a lamp within a niche. The lamp is within a crystal, like a shining star.'* Wilson felt that the star in question could well be Sirius. OTO documents, approved by Crowley, trace their origin to a famous martyred Sufi saint, Mansur el Hallaj. Wilson doesn't mention that Crowley was actually studying under a Sufi Sheikh at the very time that the events leading to the reception of *The Book of the Law* began. The teacher was of the school of the Sidi Isawiyya. Founded by Sidi Ibn Isa (1425-1526), they incorporated pre-Islamic shamanic magical rites into their practices, and were considered heretical in some Arab countries. Crowley made extensive use of one of the most notable Sufi techniques, the Zikhr. This is similar to Mantra Yoga, involving repetition of holy verses whilst cultivating exalted emotional states. It was this that had inspired the 1909 Algerian desert sequence of prostrations after Koran recitations.

Gurdjieff has been strongly linked to Sufism, and Wilson was led to connect him to the mystery as well. One of his most important followers, J. G. Bennett, had been willing to accept the allegedly autobiographical *Meetings with Remarkable Men* as primarily based on real events. The book can barely be validated in any of its details. Nonetheless those who were closest to Gurdjieff accepted its essential veracity. His father was a kind of bard who had memorised a vast storehouse of ancient tales, none of which he wrote down. One day the young Gurdjieff read details of the translation of some cuneiform tablets recently excavated in Babylon. They told the tale of the *Epic of Gilgamesh*. He was amazed to recognise the story as one that his father told. This meant that oral tradition was capable of preserving material in undistorted form for thousands of years. It raised the question of what other survivals may be retrievable. Gurdjieff and his friends engaged in a quest for ancient knowledge. In the ruins of a Greek Orthodox monk's cell, a manuscript was discovered. It told of a group known as the Sarmoun Brotherhood. This esoteric society had originated in Babylon and gradually migrated. Here was the evocative idea that some Christians had been guardians of hidden knowledge, passed secretly down through the ages, avoiding inquisitors and iconoclasts. There were hints that Sarmoun still existed. Gurdjieff made it his life's work to find them.

All manner of lyrical adventures followed. A map of "pre-sand Egypt" led him to the Sphinx. There was an expedition across the Gobi desert. Finally, after being led blindfolded on horseback and across a perilous ravine, Gurdjieff arrived at the Sarmoun Monastery. He was initiated into their mysteries. They had preserved a tradition of sacred dance. The movements had complex meanings. In learning to perform them the dancer would need to enter into a profound altered state. A whole cosmological system could be taught through them. Gurdjieff later achieved great success in Europe and the USA through public presentations of dances and music allegedly originating from esoteric sources.

It was always maintained that the Gurdjieff Work was essentially "Esoteric Christianity". He was born into a Greek Orthodox family and was buried to their funeral service. Evocative statements were made claiming that the liturgical details of early Christianity, which were better preserved in the Eastern churches, derived from the Egypt of the Pharaohs. There was also a science of number and proportion, known to architects and builders, which could create places that inevitably induced altered states in those who entered within them. The combination of the appropriate ceremonial and music in such temples and churches was a true science and had been largely lost.

The essential principles of Esoteric Christianity lie at the core of all religion. In Islam, similar wisdom has been transmitted through Sufi schools. Until recently most textbooks on the history of religion would state that the Sufis are simply the mystics of Islam.

Many of the groups themselves affirm that they are the carriers of wisdom from the very dawn of humanity. The Sarmoun Brotherhood may have seeded schools in central Asia with their knowledge. Possible candidates are a mysterious order called the Khwajagan or Masters of Wisdom. They may in turn have inspired one of the most important Sufi sects, the Naqshibindi. According to Idries Shah, some of the wisdom kept by the Sufis was transmitted to Christian Europe.

J. G. Bennett tried to discover the locations mentioned in *Meetings* with a view to finding the Sarmoun Brotherhood. Links with the Khwajagan and Naqshibindi Sufis seemed very likely. The idea of a Babylonian beginning was deemed acceptable. In his *Gurdjieff: Making a New World* Bennett mentions an occasion when Gurdjieff discussed why he rewrote some of his book *Beelzebub's Tales to his Grandson*. Passages were made deliberately obscure in order to "*bury the dog deeper*". Some thought that he meant to say "bone". He explained that the dog he was speaking of was Sirius, '*which stands for the spirit of wisdom in the Zoroastrian tradition*'. *Beelzebub's Tales* can be taken on one level as a kind of science fiction tale. It is set on board a space ship named Karnak. Wilson wondered whether this plot device was more than just a vehicle for allegorical teaching? There may be an implication that the source of Gurdjieff's teaching was extraterrestrial. Sirius was originally present in a way that revealed too much so it needed to be hidden.

There is confirmation of this in the revised updated version of Thomas and Olga DeHartmann's *Our Life with Mister Gurdjieff*, published after *Trigger*. The original had been the memoirs of Thomas. To this was added material from his wife. Olga had been Gurdjieff's secretary when he had begun *Beelzebub's Tales*. She had actually taken dictation of the initial draft. Included in the memoir was the original version of the very first page. The spaceship Karnak was specifically stated to be journeying from Sirius.

DOG DAYS

During the Kohoutek Watergate summer of '73, when Wilson was having his Sirius experiences, he kept getting images of Timothy Leary, who was back in prison, somehow flying over its walls and generally giving the impression that he was involved in weirdness. He later heard the whole story behind the *Starseed Transmissions*.

On July 23rd 1976 Wilson was inspired to perform, '*using all the paraphernalia of ceremonial magick,*' an invocation of Hadit, having linked this aspect of Crowley's cosmology with the eye of Horus, which is Sirius. There was a sense that the explosive energies at the very heart of matter and consciousness, characteristic of the Aeon of Horus, were an expression of a greater cosmic process linked with Sirius. Nothing as obvious as the events of 1973 immediately manifested as potential validation. Within a week however, Robert Temple's *The Sirius Mystery* appeared, to great publicity and amazement. It was difficult not to feel that the two events were connected, but no normal laws of causality could explain how.

Temple's contentious book rapidly attained cult classic status. It takes the reader on a memorable journey. The West African Dogon tribe know that Sirius has an invisible companion, although our modern astronomy didn't prove this until the twentieth century. They know its orbital period of 50 years and that it's one of the "heaviest" stars. They say that they know this because a visitor from Sirius told them, thousands of years ago. These beliefs are central to their whole culture and the rituals of its religious calendrical mythology. Temple believes that this information was carried, over a long period of time, across Africa from Egypt. He lingers there on the subject of Nuit/Isis, Anubis, and the Nile. He eventually postulates a starting point in Mesopotamia, involving an actual physical "contact".

There are also glimpses of a kind of esoteric cultural package, partially inspired by those events, surviving down through the ages. Fragments of it can be spotted within the western mystery tradition. Temple seemed generally unaware of the fact that the tradition remains alive and that Egyptian and Babylonian deities are invoked to this day. His historical search nicely complemented Wilson's. Robert Temple postulates "contact" at a similar time and place to where JG Bennett eventually came to believe that the lineage behind the Sarmoun Brotherhood originated, and Kenneth Grant traced the Thelemic current. It all leads back to the origins of our civilisation in Sumero-Babylonian times, with links also to Egypt.

Temple concluded by wondering if the human race has been left with a kind of initiative test. The beings from Sirius may have been monitoring our progress, waiting for us to finally realise the implications of the cultural package they have left us. They may be waiting to resume the contact. Perhaps *The Sirius Mystery* could represent a crucial moment? '*If what I propose in this book really is true, then am I pulling a cosmic trigger?*' Wilson was happy to affirm the possibilities and took the phrase for his own book's title.

The 1998 revised edition gave a few details of how the book came to be written. Temple was introduced to the basic mystery of the Dogon's Sirius knowledge by a university teacher and mentor, Arthur M. Young, who was a notable and influential figure in consciousness studies with a definite interest in all angles of the UFOlogical enigma. Young in turn had been given the basic data by Harry Smith, an artist, film maker, and hallucinogen enthusiast. Smith was a long-term member of both of Crowley's magickal orders, the OTO and AA. Having been introduced to Thelema in California back in the forties it is quite possible that he could have met Jack Parsons.

Given the associations of Sirius with the AA star and the High Priestess tarot trump, it seems a safe bet that Smith's magickal background was the stimulus for his interest in the Sirius enigma. He would surely have felt that he would be helping the New Aeon to manifest more fully by helping to reveal potential lineage mysteries. The interest shown by Freemasons in Temple's book is also probably due to the presence of Sirius in their own system.

MODELS AND METAPHORS

Eventually Wilson met Jacques Vallée and contemplated multiple model options to help understand his experiences. New Agers would be well advised to follow his example. Many are far too accepting and uncritical of the forms their strange experiences take. Firstly it could be argued that Wilson's Sirius experiences originated solely in his own brain. Evolutionary games like magick and psychedelia activate normally latent faculties that produce major weirdness. Different bits of our heads start engaging in dialogues and the result brings dreaming and waking together. We can affect the external world. Increased synchronicity can be a symptom of such stirrings. Shamans and yogis know the landscape. Our rational culture doesn't, hence confusion. The contact experience may be with parts of our own higher selves, dressed by our dream weavers in the cultural fabric of fears and expectations.

Robert Anton Wilson took stock of all of this. He came to feel that the sex and drug secrets of the magickal lineage he was investigating may well have stimulated contact experiences, linking with entities, and apparently external intelligences of some kind. In certain cases, that may have been the deliberate aim. The Cairo 1904 episode was a definitive example. There may really be external higher intelligences interacting with us. What are they though? Perhaps there are superhuman adepts who are playing head games with us? Maybe they are in physical bodies or maybe they once were but are now "ascended"? Some might be playing for one team, and others another. Good guys and bad guys. Theosophical Mahatmas and Gurdjieff's Inner Conscious Circle of Humanity against the Illuminati? Or were Blavatsky and Gurdjieff all part of the work of the dark forces against the Cosmic Christ? Were the Illuminati really evil or not? And where on Earth or beyond it were Aiwass and the Aeon of Horus? Extraterrestrials and/or Ultra-terrestrials could be involved. They could be in contact with and directing individuals and/or secret schools. There could be opposing camps amongst them as well. Somehow Wilson knew he had to balance all of these theories against each other and try not to get dogmatic about any of them. This was the inner sanctum of what he'd called Chapel Perilous and it does seem that it tends to produce either paranoids or agnostics. This was the initiatory test.

ORDEAL OF THE ABYSS

For all the feast of ideas therein, it was events that were heart-rendingly anchored to earth that served as a measure of the real intensity of Wilson's odyssey. After Temple's book had appeared, and all of the different strands of research been brought together, Wilson suffered an appalling tragedy. His fifteen-year-old daughter, Luna, was murdered. The family response to this was remarkable. Wilson had been studying cutting-edge theories on Immortalism. Some scientists affirmed that one day the secrets of aging and illness would be sufficiently understood to enable humans to effectively live forever. There was a feeling that if all of the resources put into warfare could be diverted into medical research, that outcome could be realisable within a few decades. Increased longevity and rising population would make space migration inevitable. Leary's *Starseed* had been infused by such ideas. A possibility arose of putting Luna into cryonic suspension. Unfortunately the body was already too decomposed. In the end her brain was preserved allowing future science an option of reconstruction currently unimaginable. She was the first murder victim in history to be cryonically frozen. The Wilson family's attitude was that at least science would potentially benefit from this. What was more important was that this noble act transformed the ghastly energy of the situation. The horrendous wheel of the nightmare of history, of sleepwalking humanity, was transcended.

In his emotional extremis, amazed by the love and support all round him, Wilson's multiple models were outshined by one all-encompassing one. He had wondered if what he was involved in was a kind of law of nature? The *'quantum net of synchronicity'* could be neutral and impersonal. What about the conscious circle, the awakened ones, the communion of saints? Finally Wilson *'entered a belief system in which the Network of Love was not one hypothesis among many but an omnipresent Reality'*.

Timothy Leary was there to demonstrate what entering into that reality actually means. At the time of Luna's murder, he was around to offer support. Wilson's wife Arlen thanked him for the example he had demonstrated in prison. *'You convinced us that it is possible to transcend suffering.'* Leary replied, *'That's the whole point of all my work on brain change!' 'Positive energy is as real as gravity. I've felt it.'* Later on that evening he was asked what he did when people kept giving him negative energy? With a grin, he responded by saying, *'Come back with all the positive energy you have.'* That was the climactic lesson that Wilson learnt in his incredible journey.

Repeated reading of Wilson's work, along with the study of Crowley and various adepts of eastern traditions, has convinced me that at certain stages in the process of initiation/individuation, an activation of levels of the psyche that resonate with the traditional demons and dark gods may well be inevitable. The Jungians would call it the Shadow. If a system of magic or mysticism stirs it all up, it by no means follows that it can therefore be considered to be inherently evil. That system or teacher could conceivably provide effective guidance through it. One simply has to form an appropriate relationship to such processes. The excruciating difficulty though, is the issue as to whether or not these "things" have an existence outside of the human psyche? In my opinion, Crowley and Steiner had confronted this process in their own ways and emerged largely triumphant. There are dodgy dudes about. Some schools undoubtedly have dubious motives. But which ones? This is part of the great intelligence test. Everyone accuses each other of being in the Black Lodge. However much I may be critical of the contents of *The Dark Gods*, I would endorse its final words: '*Be discerning.*'

THE MONTAUK LEGEND: CONSPIRICISM AS A MAGICAL PROCESS OF INITIATION

'As a general rule, if you think you have been involved in a space-time project, you probably have.'

Peter Moon. *Pyramids of Montauk.*

PARANOIAC PRELIMINARIES

'Total paranoia is total awareness.'

Attributed to Charles Manson.

HAVING TRAVELLED ALONG with Crowley, Leary, and Wilson, having confronted the Illuminati and the dark gods of the threshold, we are far better prepared to navigate through a time where conspiracism has developed to thoroughly permeate popular culture. It is omnivorous in its capacity to make use of absolutely anything at all. Some have become almost paralysed by paranoia. Following on from our Illuminati investigation it could be said that conspiracism presents another form of Chapel Perilous, of the Abyss of Choronzon. Whatever its vices and virtues, it also potentially presents a magical way of thinking that deconstructs consensus reality and serves our established theme of the undermining and breaking down of old forms. In this I can intuit the further playing out of the process of Crowley's Aeon. With this perspective established, conspiracism sits very interestingly alongside technological acceleration, quantum physics, LSD, the Nazis, UFOlogy, and the general magical mystical revival as part of a greater unity. With the Montauk legend we can see this blend blown up to epic proportions.

Jack Parsons was an important figure in the early days of what became the American space programme. Occultism played a major role in his life. An increasing density of material is surfacing suggesting a far bigger esoteric picture surrounding NASA.

There are hints in *Cosmic Trigger*. Robert Anton Wilson briefly summarised ideas of Illuminati Masonic capers circulated by W. N. Grimstad but primarily originating from the maverick American conspiracist James Shelby Downward. The first edition of the incendiary anthology *Apocalypse Culture* featured an article entitled *Alchemical Conspiracy and the Death of the West* by Michael Hoffman that is also inspired by Downward.

Downward claimed that from the thirties, the OTO revered Mount Palomar where Cal Tech would establish the world's greatest observatory in 1949. Parsons was certainly familiar with the mountain. Nobody living within sight of it could fail to be. On special occasions sex magick rituals involving intelligence operatives of various kinds and Downward's estranged wife would take place inside the observatory after the giant telescope had been focused on Sirius thereby bringing its influence down into the room.

These rites formed part of a giant master-plan that would take decades to fulfil. An alchemical work was being undertaken involving the creation and destruction of primordial matter, the "Killing of the King" (manifested as the Kennedy murder), and the bringing forth of what is hidden. Locations were chosen for specific reasons.

Mount Palomar is stated to be sited at 33 degrees latitude. California Institute of Technology incorporating Jet Propulsion Lab was founded at 33 degrees. The Trinity site in New Mexico where the first atom bomb was exploded is on the 33 degree latitude line. John F. Kennedy was assassinated on another 33 degree site. The moon rockets were launched from Cape Kennedy, another 33 degree site. The general 33 degree latitudinal locations are not exact but are near enough to be intriguing.

The 33 Degree Scottish Rite Masonic Temple in Washington contains some fascinating material researched by Richard Sauder and presented in his *Kundalini Tales*. In the temple museum a Masonic flag is prominently displayed that was actually planted on the lunar surface by the second man to set foot on it, Edwin "Buzz" Aldrin. This little event must have occurred with the knowledge and acceptance of Mission Control. There is also a letter from the astronaut expressing his pleasure on presenting the flag to the museum. A number of the early "Right Stuff" era astronauts were masons. Flags had been taken into space before. This leaves no doubt that something other than science and cold war rivalry was a factor in the space programme. It's a question of the level of importance involved. Once the space programme was up and running some esoterically inclined people with access to it may have made use of unusual opportunities. That's significantly different to suggesting the whole thing was created as a vehicle for occultist concerns from the outset.

The Masonic flag data is enough to make conspiracy freaks start frothing at the mouth. All kinds of effusions are now expanding exponentially and are often nothing like as interesting and entertaining as Downward. A general label for it could be the Illuminati conquest of space. As an example of the general standard of thought in this genre we have the fact that Crowley once referred to himself as Teitan, a 666 gematria variant on the Greek Titan, being considered enough to prove that the NASA Titan rocket was named in deference to the Beast by the Satanic group that's really in charge etc. The least that can be stated is that Jack Parsons now seems to have played out his astonishing career against the backdrop of a considerably expanded context.

In *Underground Bases and Tunnels* Richard Sauder also diligently researched the existence of a surprising number of underground military buildings of some kind in the USA. This complemented material in *Kundalini Tales* investigating the number of patents for devices that clearly had mind-control potential. Sauder has provided a foundation of extensive factual data for paranoid awareness to make use of.

During the fifties the CIA created an ongoing project known as MK ULTRA. This would involve amoral and reprehensible procedures with the generally common theme of mind control. The early testing of LSD on unaware subjects was the most well known work. All kinds of indignities and often dangerous procedures were inflicted in the name of science and national security. The presence of a large number of Nazi scientists and intelligence operatives who had escaped prosecution as part of Operation Paperclip, whereby the USA had scooped up any Nazis deemed useful for its own purposes, in the early days of the CIA and NASA may have been a factor here. The mood of MK ULTRA permeated other agencies.

Conspiracy mongers have speculated on *Manchurian Candidate* processes having been run on Lee Harvey Oswald and the extreme possibility of the Summer of Love as an MK ULTRA social experiment that was terminated by the unleashing of secret mind controlled operative Charles Manson. Regardless of the credibility of this material it has left its mark in the American psyche. Due to the horror and indignation felt at the very real abuses that have been discovered from the past it is widely believed that such secretive agencies are capable of virtually anything. The success of the *X Files* and the extent of 9/11 conspiracy theories show the scale of this.

Perhaps the most disturbing aspect of Downward's take on the sorcerous nature of the Kennedy killing is

'The ultimate purpose of that assassination was not political or economic , but sorcerous; for the control of the dreaming mind is the underlying motive'

The result, as Aeolus Kephas explains in *The Lucid View* is that

'paranoia, impotence, despair, - are consolidated in the dim, dark and mute acquiescence of the mass to the existence of malevolence and chaos, of conspiracy and deception and evil across the board. This is the "revelation of the method" employed by the Custodians to ensure that the bulk of "humanity" continue to sink ever further into the Consensus program.'

This little preamble sets the scene for a strand of material that stands out spectacularly from all of the rest. What can be termed the Montauk Legend might just be the most outrageous story ever told. The saga manages to contain so many modern classic conspiratorial elements as to feel like every episode of the *X Files* combined and then some. Its main chronicler Peter Moon likes to point out that the first published account of Montauk appeared before the show made its TV debut. Crowley and Jack Parsons' Babalon Working become a constant theme in the unfolding legend and they are not treated negatively. *Pyramids of Montauk* states clearly that *'Both of their writings reflect the fact they were warriors for consciousness.'* At various points in the proceedings Peter Moon comments on and interprets *The Book of the Law*, eventually coming to feel that he understood its *'Key'*. Regardless of the veracity or otherwise of its material, Montauk is a major modern myth and Thelema a significant core element within it.

★ ★ ★

SPACE-TIME PROJECT

In the pages of Preston Nicholls and Peter Moon's *The Montauk Project: Experiments in Time, Montauk Revisited: Adventures in Synchronicity, Pyramids of Montauk: Explorations in Consciousness, Encounters in the Pleiades: An Inside Look at UFOs*, and Moon's solo *The Black Sun: Montauk's Nazi-Tibetan Connection, Synchronicity and the Seventh Seal, The Montauk Book of the Dead*, and the novel, *Spandau Mystery*, can be found Crowley, the Babalon Working, Scientology, pyramids of Egypt and Mars, historical and legendary ancient civilisations, sacred geometry, a planetary grid of sacred sites, mind control, ETs, Illuminati, New World Order, Nazi occultism with its Antarctic, Tibetan, and UFO offshoots, time travel, Qabalah, John Dee and Edward Kelly, and above all, synchronicity.

The enormous range of material in these works has been strongly criticised for its large number of factual errors and the manner of its linking together. Tenuous is a word that comes to mind. The main Montauk protagonists, Preston Nicholls, Duncan Cameron, and Al Bielek have been repeatedly harangued as barking-mad bullshitters, and general disinformation artists. There's no doubt that their tales are about as outlandish as it's possible to get even in a field full of wackos. The basics of the overall story are near to impossible to prove in any consensus way.

Like *Morning of the Magicians* I have put aside my doubts concerning the factual errors and occult gossip in order to appreciate what I consider to be the merits of the story and the way in which it is presented which could be considered a form of fantastic realism that does potentially deliver a genuine gnosis. What I find of continuing interest is the odyssey of Peter Moon who co-wrote the early works with Nicholls and went on to the solo projects at the end of the sequence.

At the very beginning of the story in *The Montauk Project* it is stated that

> 'This book is an exercise in consciousness. It is an invitation to view time in a new manner and expand your awareness of the universe.' *Synchronicity and the Seventh Seal* makes it clear that 'It is absolutely crucial to realise that the Montauk Project itself, as originally recounted, is a blend of incredible legend and archetypal (cabalistic, if you will) mythology mixed with certain irrefutable facts.' *Montauk Revisited* begins with Moon priming his readers

with the most appropriate meta-perspective. *'Perhaps the most important point in dealing with the phenomena of Montauk is that we are dealing with "the stuff of which dreams are made". 'We are directly tapping into the creative zone of consciousness.'*

As he investigated Montauk he found that a powerful process of synchronicity was unleashed that he happily went along with as it led him into ever more extraordinary territory. He was always aware that much of the information he was led to and some of the unusual characters he encountered could be considered dubious but the bigger process was more important.

There is an original basic story that Peter Moon has been happy to call the Montauk legend. Once *The Montauk Project* was published in 1992 tangential ripples with a definite Thelemic flavour spread outwards in many directions. I shall begin by summarising the initial saga as it is given in the full knowledge that all kinds of details may well be significantly skewed at the very least.

The saga starts with an episode already established in American mythology. During the Second World War the US Government created a top-secret science research programme named the Rainbow Project. It came up with an experiment designed to make a ship invisible to radar detection. The vessel involved was the *USS Eldridge*. Results were spectacular. The *Eldridge* physically dematerialised from the Philadelphia Naval Yard, reappeared a hundred miles away, and was finally transported back. The crew on board suffered all kinds of horrors. Some died as a result of returning slightly at an angle to their original positions and therefore with body parts stuck through bulkheads and so on. Others went stark raving mad. Such is the core of the story known as the Philadelphia Experiment, subject of a number of books and an eighties movie.

In the Montauk legend the Rainbow Project continued after the war with research that included investigations into why interdimensional experience fried peoples' brains. The man credited as inventor of the modern computer, John von Neumann, had been a major player in the Philadelphia Experiment and now looked into how to connect machines with the human brain. Eventually crystal radio receivers were built that could pick up thoughts and store them on a computer as information bits. One development of this involved a psychic projecting thoughts that could be stored on a computer and then transmitted to influence other people. After a secret report to Congress the potential dangers were recognised and it was recommended that the project be shut down. Military interest recognised the potential of mind control. A covert Black Ops network secured massive funding from looted Nazi gold to transfer the project to a disused air force base at Camp Hero on Montauk Point, Long Island. It was deemed ideal due to its massive Sage radar antenna that produced a frequency range of 400-425 Megahertz, a range also used in the mind experiments. Various elderly Nazi scientists were involved and their ideas and techniques permeated the whole operation. By the early seventies what we can now call the Montauk Project was operational.

The first book on the subject, *The Montauk Project*, is primarily the story of Preston Nicholls and is relayed autobiographically with co-author Peter Moon never present in the first-person anywhere in the narrative. Nicholls depicts himself as an electronics buff with a particular predilection for all kinds of radio equipment. He had a degree in electrical engineering and worked for a defence contractor on Long Island. An interest in the paranormal led to him getting together with psychics for experimental sessions. In 1974 he began to notice that at a certain time each day their abilities seemed to mysteriously turn off. He suspected that an electrical signal of some kind might be responsible and used his gizmos to determine the truth of this, finding the source at Montauk Air Force base.

A decade went by before he was able to investigate further. A friend told him that the base was now abandoned and electrical equipment remained with the possibility of salvage. Nicholls collected a variety of old equipment, particularly relating to radio transmitters, and took the opportunity to visit. He met a homeless man there who claimed to have been messed up by a big experiment at the base that had gone badly wrong in 1983. The place was indeed in a state of disarray not indicative of an orderly departure and therefore unusual in a military context. He gave information about the machinery and spoke of a monster of some kind that had manifested and wrecked everything. He stated that he recognised Nicholls from those days as the man who had been his boss.

Gradually Nicholls met a whole bunch of people who all claimed to remember him being at Montauk. He began to realise his mind had been controlled so that he was living two compartmentalised lives simultaneously that had no memory cross-references. Psychics he worked with independently confirmed a gradually emerging story of a major mind control project. A vital moment in the investigation was the arrival of Duncan Cameron on the scene. He was extremely psychic and it soon became clear that he also had a whole database of suppressed memory around Montauk and would prove to be the key to unlocking the mystery.

Locals provided tales of high strangeness that further suggested powerful forces at work. There was snow in August. Hurricane strength winds suddenly arose with no warning. Animals exhibited bizarre flocking, entering the town and crashing through windows. There were weird repeating two-hour windows when a spate of crimes would be committed. Teenagers would also congregate together for similar periods and then disperse for no apparent reasons.

In the seventies the Montauk cabal started to turn their evil attention to children. The Nazi science legacy was continued when about fifty Aryan blonde-haired blue-eyed boys were kidnapped and subjected to psychosexual programming that often involved horrendous violence. Part of the purposes concerned genetics and the breeding of a New World Order master race. Duncan Cameron has memories of being a Montauk Boys programmer and that was not at all pleasant. There's film footage of him visiting the ruined base and entering a room where the nasties apparently occurred. Something is triggered off in him and he does seem to get genuinely upset.

After the initial publication and publicity of the idea of the Montauk Boys a number of young men started to surface claiming to be victims. Some had varying levels of memories. Others were more difficult to fathom. Preston Nicholls became involved in deprogramming some of them. The manner in which he accomplished this was a tad controversial. He masturbated them in an esoteric context utilising tantric massage, radionics and some kind of technique derived from Wilhelm Reich. The rationale was that it was necessary to get them back into a zone approximating the one whereby they had been initially programmed but without fear and violence. Quite obviously this scenario invites a variety of responses from laughter to disgust but it should be said in Nicholl's defence that none of the young men have ever complained about his approach. In fact, they thanked him for it. Something that was giving them considerable grief was dealt with. Such is the enigma of Preston Nicholls.

At the centre of the whole sci-fi mythos is the "Montauk chair". The device was initially created in the fifties through a design provided by ETs from the Sirius system. This is casually dropped into the story. We later learn in *Montauk Revisited* of US government interaction with numerous ETs going back at least as far as 1913. The chair was connected to computers and amplifiers so that a subject sitting in it could think of something and an image of it would appear on a monitor screen. Things really got going when the spectacularly powerful psychic Duncan Cameron became involved. A vital part of the agenda also included Cameron messing with people's minds by inserting thoughts into their heads thereby potentially controlling their behaviour against their will. This developed to include experimentation in control of groups of people, animals, and machinery. The climax of this exploration of Cameron's capabilities came when it was discovered that if, when connected fully to the amplifying power of the giant Montauk transmitter, he thought of a simple object like a can of beer it would actually materialise. You could crack open the can of Budweiser and it would taste the same as any other. It was noted that these manifestations did not necessarily occur instantly. The question of time delay expanded the research to include the mysteries of time itself.

Cameron became able to create time-portal vortex thingies whose co-ordinates could be stored on computer and then reactivated through the big transmitter enabling elite agents to go travelling in the manner of the sixties *Time Tunnel* TV series. Between 1981 and '83 time travel was fully operational. The standard history time-line was repeatedly messed with in a manner that no Star Trek crew member could ever have endorsed. Both twentieth century world wars were tinkered with. The special-ops team were sending film footage through from different time zones that was played on screens at base and stored on video. In a number of cases winos and derelicts were abducted off the streets and slung down time portals with recording equipment strapped to them for experimental purposes. According to Nicholls between three and ten thousand people were sent forward two to three hundred years into the future and abandoned there for reasons unknown! Okay, I allowed myself one exclamation mark there. I'm sure you understand. I could rightfully insert a hundred in this material but I have spared you.

Aryan Montauk boys were repeatedly sent forward in time on some mysterious special mission to 6037AD to a city in ruins with no sign of life and a gold statue of a horse on a pedestal at its centre (this is the image on the cover of *The Montauk Project*). The exact purpose was also unknown to Preston Nicholls.

Never small-scale in their thinking, the Montauk crew went into full *Stargate* mode, gaining access to an underground realm beneath the Martian Cydonia complex around the legendary face. Some kind of solar system defence array was in place and the dastardly Montauk operatives shut it down retroactively to 1943, helping to initiate the UFO era and much else besides.

Nicholls elaborated further a few books on in *Pyramids of Montauk*. The project ultimately reached 3.6 million years into the past as well as the 6037AD future. '*They fed these times back on themselves. What this mean is that we actually lived this time line twice.*' We may have even gone through more than twice. These time lines have created alternative realities. The first one was divinely created. The divergence represents original sin. '*Only by becoming conscious of the original time line can we blow off the false time.*'

A later arrival on the Montauk scene was Stewart Swerdlow (author of a few books of his own and initially portrayed as Stan Campbell in *Montauk Revisited*) who claims to have had a return of suppressed memories after hearing Preston Nichols lecture. Along with Duncan Cameron he recalls being a Montauk Boys programmer. Swerdlow was one of the time team sent on reality-bending missions, taking on some big tasks. He went back to meet Jesus to get a sample of blood from him and then shoot him. He was a bit non-plussed when JC told him he knew exactly who he was and what he was up to. He could have the blood but there was no way he could kill him. Swerdlow emptied a revolver into Christ to no effect. The blood was brought back to Montauk with the intention of mixing it with Duncan Cameron's in order to fake the Second Coming by getting his blood compared to the Turin Shroud. This was all a manoeuvre to help bring about the New World Order under the aegis of what would effectively be an Anti-Christ. Thankfully Christ's blood seems to have had the opposite effect on Cameron from that intended.

Getting back to the basic Nicholls/Moon narrative, huge events began in August 1983 when the big transmitter was turned on and left to run solidly for days. Suddenly, on the 12th, it fell into synchronisation with the Philadelphia Experiment and the *USS Eldridge* appeared at the end of the time vortex portal. It was exactly forty years on from the original event. Some arcane twenty-year planetary biorhythm sequence had made it possible to link in with 1943.

In this climax of the story, as 1943 and '83, came into synch we reach an outlandish time-paradox scenario with Duncan Cameron in the middle. Two brothers named Duncan and Edward Cameron were part of the crew on the *USS Eldridge* in 1943. They were operating special machinery on board that was part of the experiment. As things starting going a bit wonky they tried to shut the whole thing down and, on failing, jumped overboard, were propelled through the vortex and landed in 1983 at Montauk. They were rapidly briefed by the aging John von Neumann (forget conventional biographical accounts of his life and death, he was there), who had been waiting since 1943 for this exact moment, and recruited to the 1983 operation. They would have to go back to 1943 and successfully turn off the machinery there. With this accomplished Edward Cameron stayed in 1943 but Duncan returned.

Hang on a minute. Haven't we already got a Duncan Cameron in 1983, the Montauk chair psychic? Yes. When 1943 Duncan appeared, he was kept away from the 1983 model to avoid time paradox problems. Nonetheless 1943 Duncan started to rapidly age. His electromagnetic signature was somehow recorded and preserved. A time team operative went back to have a word with Duncan Cameron Sr. who apparently was an intelligence agent. He was briefed on the serious necessity of having another son. After a delay caused by the unfortunate birth of a daughter, Duncan 2 arrived in 1951. Using the planetary twenty-year biorhythm the Montauk scientists installed the electromagnetic signature into Duncan 2 in 1963. Whoever had been occupying that body since birth was forced out. Duncan Cameron has no memories of his life in his current body prior to 1963 but can recall Duncan 1 Philadelphia Experiment material.

Edward Cameron was brainwashed to forget the 1943 business and *'age regression techniques'* were used to put him into a new body in the Bielek family.

> *'The Bielek family was chosen as there was only one child in the family and that baby had died by the time of his first birthday. Edward was substituted and the parents brainwashed accordingly.'*

The technology for this was developed from work by Tesla who had been involved in the Philadelphia Experiment as well. Al Bielek, as well as co-authoring a book on the Philadelphia Experiment, has been sounding off at length on this kind of material as well.

Lecture material that is enough to run for days on end is available for those with the inclination and stamina to pursue it.

By the time of the events of August 1983 a number of the lower echelon Montauk operatives were getting worried about where things were heading. Trying to go back in time and kill Jesus, switching off the solar system defence array on Mars and stuff like that is a bit of a heavy scene, right? Preston Nicholls set up a plot to bust the project. Duncan Cameron, now transforming through the purifying force of Christ's blood, was crucially enlisted to secure success. He summoned up a monster from the Id which materialised as a kind of Bigfoot that ran amok smashing things up. A photo is featured in *The Montauk Project* taken a few years later in 1986 that when developed showed a dark form fitting the archetype that was not visible when the shot was taken. This effectively curtailed the work of the techno black magicians, at least for the time being. For a while the base was abandoned and the people involved had their memories wiped and were dispersed.

An important aspect of Preston Nicholl's background is absent from *The Montauk Project* but was revealed later in *Encounter in the Pleiades*. He was a contactee. As a young teenager in the early sixties, experimenting with radio equipment in a garden shed, he was perturbed when all of the equipment he had switched on started to hum. Power fluctuated and went off. He went outside, briefly registering a general neighbourhood electric failure, before looking up to see a bright white disc *'hovering above my front yard'*. It suddenly passed over Nicholl's head and shot upwards and away.

This was the sixties. Plenty of people were having such experiences. Nicholls went on to have many more, often in company. On entering college he put his electronics skill to the test by trying to film the phenomenon and get an electromagnetic understanding of it. Nicholls claims that things got very mysterious in his mid-teens. As a child he had never been in the best of health. Passing out twice with a heart murmur at the age of twelve is a good example. He was not very well physically co-ordinated. Medical tests revealed a form of cerebral palsy. At a certain point it went into complete remission. He emerged with a new level of health and also with his knowledge and abilities in electronics inexplicably increased to virtual genius levels.

During that time he had been having a series of intense dreams where he encountered seven-feet-tall, blonde-haired, blue eyed, Aryan master-race-type ETs from the Pleiades. This particular breed is not unknown in UFOlogy and are sometimes referred to as Nordics. He also heard a voice in his head that he was able to converse with. It would lead him to answers to questions he was investigating. Later hypnotic regression sessions revealed Nicholls had been transported to their home planet for medical treatment and education. Descriptions of their world and place in the general scheme of things in relation to other alien races were revealed in an archetypal contactee manner familiar since the fifties. Nicholls was not dogmatic about his experiences. *'Whether these encounters were in a dream state or in another constellation, I cannot really say. All I know is that after I had these experiences, I suddenly appeared to have a complete mastery of electronics.'*

The unfolding narrative portrays the usual War in Heaven scenario whereby there are benevolent forces monitoring the likes of Montauk and intervening in their own way. Nicholls was being primed for the project and no amount of messing with his head would be able to ultimately deflect him from the right course. He moved on to his compartmentalised dual life that included hands-on investigation of a captured alien craft that Tardis-like was hugely bigger on the inside than outside. Eventually the barriers between his different lives began to dissolve.

Publication of *The Montauk Project* definitely caused ripples. There was lots of interest and publicity. Whilst the time-travel sci-fi side of the saga could not be proven, all kinds of data came to light indicating the possible existence of a large underground complex that was having huge amounts of voltage pumped into it. Nicholls and Moon started to encounter the sort of hassle and blockages on all fronts that are archetypal challenges to all investigators of conspiratorial and Choronzonic material. This at least indicated that they had gotten close to something important.

BABALON RIPPLES

'Babalon opens the door to all possibilities in creation without discrimination. She welcomes all, and this means that everything that has been suppressed in the subconscious of mankind is going to come out of the woodwork. UFOs are a prime example of the unknown.'

Peter Moon. *Encounters in the Pleiades.*

* * *

'Two weeks after Jack died, the Capitol was stormed with UFOs. Government pursuit of Hubbard began in earnest shortly thereafter.'

Peter Moon. *Montauk Revisited.*

Peter Moon is unique in as much as he had significant contact with two of the participants in the Babalon Working. He spent eleven years in Scientology, which included time in their elite Sea Org navy where he was able to observe L. Ron Hubbard at close quarters. LRH features in all of the books from *Montauk Revisited* onwards and most extensively in *The Montauk Book of the Dead*, a fascinating and moving memoir that deals very clearly with why he presses so many buttons. It's a useful corrective for those previously fed exclusively on anti-Ron material.

In *Encounters in the Pleiades*, Moon discussed his first direct meeting with Hubbard and it was somewhat unusual. Assigned to the Sea Org vessel that was Ron's base, he was performing a menial deck-hand task scraping rust off a surface. He became aware of a presence behind him and knew it could only be LRH whose general vibe was entirely unique. The Commodore was well-known for *'skull-watching'*, an ability to look inside people's heads, and also for a remarkable ability to cause out-of-the-body experiences. After a short while, Moon felt himself to be in two places at once. Part of his awareness had been dulled but another was experiencing tremendous lightness and brightness. He remembered he had a body far away that was scraping rust off a deck. Hubbard could then be heard talking to Moon's superior on the deck above. Only when he departed did Moon fully rejoin his body.

Moon generally portrays Hubbard arriving on the Babalon scene primed with a number of early mystical experiences and with a background in naval intelligence, having already studied all kinds of top-secret psychiatric records from the war that included mind control, drugs, and areas in the realm of the paranormal. He was aware of the direction that American psychiatry was taking due to its unhealthy links with the increasing power of the Nazi infested intelligence agencies that would result in MK ULTRA. Following a further expansion of consciousness after the events of the Babalon Working during which he developed theories he had already formulated that would lead to Dianetics and Scientology, he broke ranks and took up a role in blatant opposition, developing some of the mind-tech for good rather than bad. This was the basis of Scientology's long established powerful anti-psychiatry stance.

Even a casual investigation into the American psychiatry scene of the fifties and its leading figures such as the notorious Ewen Cameron, a man who could have comfortably been a doctor in Auschwitz, would be enough to make one realise Hubbard's arguments were not without foundation. For his pains LRH was on the receiving end of a sustained campaign of hostility and disinformation that endured for decades. He had to resort to fighting fire with fire to survive.

It's rather interesting to note that government attacks on Hubbard have some definite similarities to the Wilhelm Reich case. Firstly LRH had made life force, named by him as *Theta*, of fundamental importance in the newly founded religion of Scientology. Helping to free it to its fullest functioning could be helped by a device known as an E Meter, broadly analogous to a lie-detector. There was even a kind of equivalent to DOR known as *Entheta*. The Feds didn't buy it and in a considerable show of force obviously intended to induce fear and compliance raided Scientology premises in Washington and took some of the devices away. Hubbard was also elaborating on a space opera cosmology that involved the human race in an intergalactic aeons-old drama. Life energy. A hugely expanded sense of human capabilities. Life on other planets. We can recognise these themes from Reich as ones that bring forth the emotional plague in response. For all his genius, Reich didn't know how to survive in such a game. Hubbard did and that is no mean feat, one that those who think of him as some crazed fantasist would do well to acknowledge.

Moon credits his time in Scientology, and particularly in the proximity of Hubbard, as crucial in enabling him to deal with '*the various psychological oddities that one encounters in researching the Montauk Project*'. LRH was running processes on dealing with mind control implants and suchlike decades before most people had even considered the idea of their existence. Moon summarises the issues: '*Implantation has everything to do with the nature of knowing exactly who you are and who might have caused you to think in ways that are not in your own interest.*'

Much later he had a number of meetings with Marjorie Cameron during the last years of her life. She strongly communicated to him that synchronicity is the key to magic. This became his fundamental research tool. He eventually wrote a whole book on the subject of synchronicity as not just an acausal connecting principle as Jung would have it but an intelligent initiatory principle. A good example of how this manifested for Moon occurred on January 24th 1986. He learned that L. Ron Hubbard had died a few days earlier and then, literally within a few minutes, heard that the space shuttle had exploded. In *Synchronicity and the Seventh Seal* he described it as *'like a one-two punch without any lag in between.'* It was as if the two events were connected. In terms of Moon's personal destiny and the dream logic of synchronicity they were but it took a few years for him to interpret the meaning of this waking dream. Jack Parsons was responsible for the development of the shuttle fuel, subsequently dying in an explosion. Now, as LRH left his body, there was a powerful echo of their connection and an affirmation that these were not ordinary men but major game-players in a bigger picture. This was an event fine-tuned for Moon himself. He could have found out about Hubbard at any time in the previous few days. It could have been maybe a few more hours before hearing about the shuttle.

There is not a single mention of Aleister Crowley in *The Montauk Project*. In their very first conversation however, Preston Nicholls told Peter Moon of supposed past life memories of an association with the Beast. He and Duncan Cameron had been brothers Preston and Marcus Wilson who were manufacturers of scientific instruments and friends of the Crowley family, having some kind of business association with his father. This work led to the formation of Thorn EMI. These details have yet to be verified and don't seem to gel with the known biography but they nonetheless pressed a potent on-button in a manner Moon began to recognise as typical of some of the odd material dispensed by Nicholls.

Looking for any possible verification, Moon read the immense autobiographical *Confessions* where Crowley mentioned that in 1918 *'I spent the summer in a tent beyond Montauk at the extremity of Long Island.'* This was the period between the Amalantrah Working and the public appearance of the Lam picture. There was also mention of a Duncan Cameron as well. Moon considered this to be a synchronistic affirmation that his line of research was worthwhile.

Indeed, names, family linkages, and the history of the meaning of words became a magical synchronistic research tool for Moon, a kind of surrealist, almost Chaos magic technique, that he used to guide him on. Its presence in the Montauk books is not dissimilar to Kenneth Grant's use of gematria. Both approaches are often difficult to read and would never convince those not temperamentally inclined to be supportive. Moon's results would certainly not persuade a conventional historian but they repeatedly proved their value to him by leading him to incredible information and bizarre meetings that always advanced his studies. One needs to actually read the Montauk books to fully appreciate this. A summary can't do the process justice.

Knowing that the legendary Aleister Crowley had been there in 1918 made Moon wonder if Montauk had some kind of significance prior to the arrival of the techno black magicians. This brought the Thelemic current and the revelation of remarkable layers of historical mysteries strongly into the mythos. That combination has powered the endless ripples that have reverberated out from the centre ever since.

A "Mr X" who supposedly had high level Montauk involvement told Moon that Crowley had been deliberately somehow manipulating time by magickal means during his American stay. This led Moon to connect this idea with the concept of the interdimensional portal that had opened during that time allowing Lam access. He came to wonder if this was a factor in the later success of the Philadelphia Experiment. Following this chain of associations the Babalon Working was powered by the same current and fully ushered in the UFO epoch.

Secret Agent 666 has another angle on Crowley's presence at Montauk. Richard B. Spence never suggests that his magickal mystical work was in any way a hoax. The retreat was essentially authentic but the location may have served multiple purposes. Crowley may have been keeping an eye on the American naval base there. The days of Britannia ruling the waves were numbered. The USA was rapidly moving into a position of dominance. The base housed wireless stations and other more obscure experimental items.

THE MEN-AN-TOL CROWLEY MYTH

A correspondence also occurred between Moon and self-proclaimed son of the Beast Amado Crowley. I am not going to enter into the general Amado controversy other than to refer the interested reader to Dave Evans *The History of British Magick After Crowley* which contains an excellently comprehensive demolition. One aspect only concerns us here. Following the first Montauk book, Amado wrote an account in his book *The Wrath of Aleister*

Crowley of an alleged ceremony he had been present at as a young boy presided over by his father with a group in attendance at the prehistoric Cornish site of Men-an-Tol. The story is further recounted in *Montauk Revisited*. The event occurred on August 12th 1943, the date of the Philadelphia Experiment. Amado noted a similarity to the place name sounds for starters. The site's centre is a large circular shaped stone with a further circular hole in the middle large enough for a modest-sized person to crawl through. This has generated a local tradition where this practice has healing qualities. Young Amado was placed on a large wooden board that was passed through the hole.

'It was like the ferrite rod that is put into an electric coil. Aleister performed a ritual which appeared to "cause" a line of "rough water" between this spot in southern England, and Long Island in the USA.'

Extant Crowley diary entries for the date and general time in question do not give the slightest indication of any such episode. Amado has cited the espionage angle to back up his general assertion that Crowley kept a lot back from his diaries. Dave Evans has made a number of good points concerning the dubious nature of this tale. Diary entries or not, it is known that in August 1943 Crowley was impoverished and in failing health. A journey to Cornwall, and in particular the remote Men-an-Tol would have been lengthy, tiring, and expensive. The final part, even if car transport had been available, would have involved a trek over terrain that an old ill man would have had definite difficulties with.

During this same period, American soldiers were arriving in Britain in huge numbers as part of the extensive build up to the invasion of Nazi Europe the following year. In the English countryside enormous military bases were being established. The area of Cornwall in question was full of soldiers in tent cities and security was very high. Travel was restricted. Non-local civilians would need good reasons to be moving through. As *Secret Agent 666* points out there were people in American intelligence circles who were extremely wary of Crowley.

Regarding the actual alignment of the site itself, which features two upright stones with the big donut, it does not remotely point in the direction of Montauk. Taking the curvature of the Earth into account it actually misses the USA altogether.

Crowley had a son by a woman who was living in Cornwall during the war. A letter dating from 1945 expressed concern as to their well-being as he hadn't heard from her since 1942. If he had travelled to Cornwall in 1943 his inevitable route would have put him in the proximity of their last known whereabouts. Surely he would have made efforts to contact them then?

I clearly understand that the Amado tale is highly likely to be a heap of hooey. It has already developed an internet life as established fact. I also note that it set Peter Moon off into the realms of his most mystically expansive work yet and by his own criteria of synchronicity as validation principle thereby carries a higher level of magical power behind it that ultimately affirms it as "true". He later met someone who claimed to know people who had been present.

There is another side to the controversy that is intriguing however. Men-an-Tol and Cornwall became a focus of attention in August 1999 at the time of the solar eclipse. It was noted that its path, which followed a curve rather than a straight line, moved across the Atlantic from North America to Cornwall and on to Egypt, rather nicely adhering nonetheless to Amado's *'line of "rough water"'.* The story circulated widely at that time. Understandably, Peter Moon took it as strong validation of a Montauk Men-an-Tol Cairo connection.

PYRAMIDS AND SACRED GRIDS

Robert Anton Wilson started with the Illuminati, Peter Moon with Montauk. The real action began in both cases when Crowley was encountered. He served as the trigger. It's with *Pyramids of Montauk: Explorations in Consciousness* that Peter Moon really got the full download and it continued into *Black Sun*. Initial investigation of Crowley and the Babalon Working had taken him *'to the very threshold of the mystery schools'*.

Moon had an ongoing concern to understand the history and meaning of the Montauk place name. Amado Crowley's letter noting a similarity between Montauk and Men-an-Tol nagged away in the back of his head. Like many American locations, the word has a history dating back before the arrival of white settlers. One afternoon in a library he found the 1911 *Historic Long Island* by Rufus Rockwell Wilson. Looking at the contents list of photo plates he was startled to notice *'The Pyramids – Montauk'*. There indeed was an odd pyramid-shaped mound about twenty feet tall with a man standing at its base. Two similar mounds were visible in the distance. There was no explanatory mention at all in the book itself. No sign of the mounds remain. The area became a military base around the time of the First World War so they may well have been levelled then.

Moon and Nicholls had already become interested in the issue of who owned the land on which the base was situated. This soon led them to the case of the Montauk Indians which opened up a whole new expansive level of the game. In 1910, in a court case where the Indians had tried to assert their land rights which had been enshrined through centuries in a variety of legislation, the tribe was declared legally dead despite the presence of Montauk Indians at the hearing. The reasoning was that they had become too Negroid due to intermarriage with blacks. This was a not untypical manoeuvre in the dealings between the US government and Native Americans but this case had its own unique aspects.

It's rather striking that an important family name in the Montauk tribe was Pharaoh. The language of the Montauk Indians was virtually extinct even as far back as the early days of the American republic. A member of the Pharaoh family was its last recorded speaker. Onetime president Thomas Jefferson made a personal journey to meet with the few remaining speakers to compile a dictionary. This suggests it was considered to be important. One of Moon's informants, a man who had a track record of seeming to know more than one could reasonably expect about the ever-growing Montauk mystery, stated that the language was known as Vril and came from Atlantis and was in turn linked with John Dee's Enochian. A wild suggestion indeed.

In *The Secret Doctrine* Blavatsky spoke of Vril, claiming it was known in Atlantis by the bizarre name of *Mash-mak*. In the immediate proximity of Montauk is a nature preserve on Mashomak Point. It's an old Native American name and typical of the kind of weird resonances that convinced Moon he was on the right path. It is of course possible that his informant knew of this Blavatsky idea and been inspired by it regarding the Montauk language.

The current air force base where the Montauk Project was carried out is situated on ground particularly sacred to the old tribe. Nearby was a place named Turtle Cove which some believed was the point from which the world had been created. It's not unusual in tribal landscapes to have a site designated as point of creation. Moon notes the prevalence of the turtle in a number of cosmologies and how in modern times the geometry of the turtle shell has been examined with the conclusion that maybe the apparent primitives were expressing something a lot more profound. The geometry of creation was implied, what gets called things like the morphogenetic grid-plan. The design of a turtle's shell is a good two-dimensional representation of the donut torus shape currently serving as a model for the shape of the universe. Was Montauk a global sacred site like Glastonbury, Shasta and Uluru? Were the New World Order Montauk Project mind control Nazis aware that they had picked a useful area to broadcast their bad vibes out on the planetary radio?

It started to look to Moon as if mystery schools have been keeping an eye on Montauk for some time due to its positioning on the global geometric energy grid of sacred sites. He started checking out the geology of Montauk and found it wasn't really a part of Long Island but had been pushed down by glaciers from the north. By the time we get to *Black Sun* it had been established that Montauk was originally part of Thule.

In *Pyramids* Moon takes his personal style of etymology to its limits in order to get a satisfactory understanding of the full meaning of the Montauk place-name. He travels though Latin, Tibetan, Native American, Gaelic, anything that sounds a bit similar in any field at all. With a certain good humour he gives over half a page to the final version. Amongst the most important details are

> 'Colloquial name for an interdimensional gateway that is a conduit to the circulatory system of the planet and the higher forces of creation.'
> 'Native American ground on eastern Long Island that was one time demarcated by pyramids and corresponds to an underlying energy body called the morphogenetic grid whereupon the Earth's consciousness and its entire physical construct have manifested.'

INSPIRED FORTH-SPEAKER OF MONTAUK

The pyramids in Egypt and the alleged pyramid on Mars are part of the bigger picture. The name Cairo is a rendering of the Arabic Al-Kahira, meaning Mars, usually thought of as god of war. This led

Moon to Egyptian war god Montu who had a temple at Karnak. The cover of *Pyramids of Montauk* has an image of a bull-headed Montu. He was certainly associated with bull cults but is usually depicted as falcon-headed and therefore very similar to Horus. Montu sounds enough like Montauk for Moon to have felt he was still being led on the right path. The Romans called him Mentu or Menthu and this was beginning to sound like Men-an-Tol.

A chain of associations were coming into view: Mars, Cairo, Horus, Ra-Hoor-Khuit, Montu, Mentu, Montauk. Moon was led to the events at the heart of the revelation of the Aeon of Horus.

Hieroglyphs on the funerary Stele of Revealing of Ankh-af-na-Khonsu (who Crowley came to consider a past life), praised him as *'inspired forth-speaker of Mentu'*. In terms of the unique magickal blend he was experiencing, Moon contemplated Crowley as Priest and *'inspired forth-speaker'* of Montauk.

The August 12th date so significant in 1943 and 1983 was also the day that Crowley married Rose in 1903. It was mentioned in *The Book of the Law* where there are instructions for it to be a feast day. Thelemic orders and individuals honour it as a major date in their magickal calendar. It fitted in with the twenty-year planetary biorhythm cycle mystery. It was exactly forty years before the Philadelphia Experiment as that in turn was forty years before Montauk 1983. Moon eventually wondered if the famous prophetic verses in *The Book of the Law* concerning the forties and eighties referred to those very events. The eighties being *'abased'* might hint at the catastrophic implosion of the Montauk Project.

Montauk Air Force base was named Camp Hero. Hero derives from Horus. Moon also wondered if this enigmatic passage in the third chapter might refer to the island of Montauk and what was to come?

'4. *Choose ye an island!*
5. *Fortify it!*
6. *Dung it about with enginery of war!*
7. *I will give you a war engine.*
8. *With it ye shall smite the peoples; and none shall stand before you.*'

Remember the unusual page in *The Book of the Law* with its grid squares and slanting line and the references to a code therein? Moon bravely gets stuck in and comes up with a solution. Please note: I said *a* solution, not necessarily *the* solution. I will give some of the details here but there are more in *Pyramids*.

The line lies at a 26 degree angle, apparently the same declination as some of the passages in the Great Pyramid, including one alleged to align with Sirius. In gematria IHVH Jehovah and HIVH Beast both add up to 26. One of the more enigmatic lines in *The Book of the Law* asks *'Is god to live in a dog?'* God and dog both add up to 26 in an English gematria.

Moon wrote down the letters touched by the line and found they could be jiggled around to read *'Easy if Bast'*. The Egyptian cat-headed goddess had suddenly made an appearance. Moon takes Bast as a variant on Beast. In this he was probably following a hint given by Kenneth Grant in the glossary of *The Magical Revival*. Due to an association with sexual heat and general lust and that she is sometimes portrayed with a lion head, Moon equates Bast with Babalon.

Ankh-af-na-Khonsu was not just a priest of Mentu. Khonsu was a moon god. There's a solar lunar balance being hinted at. Cats are archetypically lunar and associated with the female and witchcraft. This brings out another aspect of Babalon. She is initially full of leonine solar fire.

Bast gets linked to the sphinx. Sumerians are equated with Sirians. Wild sexual magick was the essential characteristic. We almost enter the realms of *Theozoology* on being told of Bast's role in *'the vast sexual experiments of Atlantis (and later Egypt) which gave rise to mermaids, minotaurs, centaurs, Pegasus, and the like.'*

The Sirians colonised Mars. Giza reflects both a Martian and Sirian influence. We have already seen what thinking about Sirius can do to your head. The Montauk mythology goes to far more extreme lengths than *Cosmic Trigger*. Al Bielek quite happily talks about hanging out with Sirians in the Montauk underground after they had kindly supplied the design for the legendary chair. They are humanoid looking, averaging about six feet tall, stocky, with cat-like slit eyes. They wear something over their heads including a possible communication device over their ears. They might be bald. *'At Montauk, they were generally affable and did their job.'* August 12th is right in the centre of the Dog Days so a Sirius influence is not a complete surprise.

When they settled in Sumeria the Sirians were cat and lion like. This is somewhat at odds with amphibious hints in *The Sirius Mystery* but has been stated elsewhere by the likes of Murry Hope. They turned up in the Cairo area and called it Babylon meaning

Baby Lyon! Looking to create a site to be a repository for their wisdom they began the construction of the whole Giza plateau Sphinx/Great Pyramid complex that included the legendary Hall of Records. The sphinx was originally a depiction of Bast. The New Aeon really began when Crowley spent the night in the Great Pyramid.

The base of the triangles in the sides of the Great Pyramid have angles of 51.51 degrees which *'correspond exactly to the geometric distortion of the Earth from a sphere to its current shape.'* The implication is that the pyramid builders knew the exact shape of the planet. Moon also mentions the original limestone casing of calcium carbonate stating that under a microscope it has two 51.51 degree angles at the base of each triangular molecule. There is also the little matter that the carbon-based universe hangs together on a 666 basis. A carbon atom has six electrons, six protons, and six neutrons.

Babalon has a magickal symbol associated with her. It is a seven pointed star and features in Crowley's own work. It can be seen on the Star card in the *Thoth* tarot deck. When drawn correctly there are 51.51 degree angles in the design. The Hindus and Tibetan Buddhists have a very exact art-form for this kind of thing. Geometrical designs called Yantras contain all sorts of information about the deities they represent. The Babalon star seems to be a successful western version.

Moon speculates that using this design in an altered state allowed Parsons, Hubbard, and Cameron to access something of the morphogenetic grid that the pyramid connects to. This goes some way to account for the enormous power involved that had such tumultuous effects on its participants.

In *Encounters in the Pleiades*, Moon mentions that Cameron read *Pyramids* and discussed it with him on what proved to be her last birthday, shortly before her death. She strongly affirmed the importance of geometry, mentioning that one of her lingering memories of her experiences during the Babalon Working was of visions of geometrical shapes. These actually persisted as an important factor in her consciousness for the rest of her life.

If all this train of thought seems too far-fetched it is nonetheless possible to appreciate something of Moon's state of mind during this process by the nature of information that came his way while he was involved in it. He discovered that an OTO lodge met at Montauk. Not only that, the order chief had edited Jack Parsons *Freedom is a Two-Edged Sword* whilst in their company.

Remember Moon got a whole book out of what started as a trip to the library stimulated by Amado Crowley's Montauk Men-an-Tol etymology which yielded an old photo of a pyramid shaped structure. By the end of *Pyramids of Montauk* we are not much the wiser about that photograph but we have been taken on quite a journey. Moon did meet some of the modern Montauk Indians and hear a few family tales that the structures were sacred to them and the focus of ceremonies of some kind. He became involved in publicising their land-rights cause and this was assuredly a good thing that was anchored to the real world, to the earth itself. The mystery expands again in Moons' *Montauk Book of the Living* but that is a story outside the scope of this narrative. A moving conclusion to *Pyramids* comes when a shaman of the tribe offers an amnesty to those who have committed crimes against humanity and the earth at Montauk. The only conditions for acceptance are a genuine confession and repentance to whatever higher power may be recognised. I can easily understand that *Pyramids of Montauk* is a book likely to strongly annoy many readers for a lot of reasons but I respect the intensity, expansiveness, and archetypal initiatory nature of the download it represents.

MONTAUK-THULE

As *Pyramids* proceeds there are increasing references to Nazi occultism. We are treated to a spectacular bit of occult gossip that gives an indication of where the journey will be heading in *Black Sun*. The 1943-83 time-rift was actually initiated in 1923 when Thule Nazi occultists collaborated with Crowley's AA on a time travel project. The intention was to go back and grab the Holy Grail for the purpose of helping to groom the Anti-Christ. Crowley was personally involved. The Spear of Destiny was somehow used as a power source. Such were the roots of another mystical sect, the Order of the Black Sun. Time rifts were created in a number of areas. Some kind of device including crystals was utilised for these undertakings. Someone stole them and things became increasingly complex. The basic details were channelled by an American woman.

Remember there are hints of Nazi mysteries from the very beginning of the Montauk story. The whole project was allegedly funded by Nazi gold looted from Europe. Nazi scientists became involved and the unpleasant use of the Montauk Boys stems from their obsessions. An increasing amount of rumours and real information led Moon to look at the presence of Germans on the Montauk end of Long Island. It seemed to date back prior to the First World War and Crowley's espionage activities but it really got going during the Nazi era.

An American organisation known as the German Bund set up a Camp Siegfried in a place called Yaphank in a rural part of Long Island. The density of Germans in the area was such that a place called German Gardens' main street was named Adolf Hitler Boulevard! The camp hosted large gatherings that were mini-Nuremberg Rallies. People in uniforms were goose-stepping around and generally sieg heiling. Swastika flags flew alongside the stars and stripes. The group's leader visited Hitler in Germany. Anti-Semitic speeches were made. There were even attempts to create boycotts of Jewish shops in a manner akin to the Fatherland. The Camp also had a kind of Hitler Youth contingent. It's important to note that many other locals were hostile to these developments. When war came a number of the Bund were arrested and interned. Nazis with connections there were involved in extensive espionage. Even after the war there remained areas where property was passed amongst those with German background. Camp Siegfried still exists under the same name today but the Nazis appear to have departed. This is a fairly amazing bit of forgotten American history and I can easily understand that Moon was stunned and excited to learn such details about his mythic landscape.

America also took on board a movement called Eugenics that advocated selective breeding to remove what were deemed to be the unhealthy and undesirable elements from society involving issues like race and mental illness. Under the authority of this "science" some disgraceful acts were carried out across the USA with full state authority including the enforced sterilisation of over 60,000 people. A 1924 Immigration Act limited the number of arrivals from Eastern Europe on the basis of their perceived racial inferiority. The Nazis took inspiration for their own policies from what was already happening in the USA and the apparent science that backed it up. Cold Spring Harbour Long Island was the most important Eugenics facility in the country. This is yet another piece of the shadow side of American history.

Maybe the proximity of such things lead over decades to all kinds of distorted folk memory gossip that generated tales like those surrounding the Montauk Boys. Moon got a number of first-person testimonies to what really did seem to be very odd data.

An elderly resident recalled Montauk wartime picnics watching large numbers of U Boats gathered just a little way out to sea. They were entirely distinct from American submarines and were easily in range of coast-guard guns but were left unmolested. The close proximity of a US Navy submarine pen at Montauk thickens the plot. Local legend recalled that in the closing days of the war a U- Boat crew landed at Montauk with a humungous sum of money and jewels. A deal was stuck with US military and some of the crew ended up settling in the area.

Moon examined the involvement of American business in Nazi affairs and how future legendary President JFK's father seemed to be rather sympathetic. In more recent times Prescott Bush has been likewise investigated. It's a tangled web rife with rumour but there's substance behind it. All kinds of duplicity was going down. The entry of America into the war was by no means as straightforward as most history books portray it.

A Montauk contact of Moon who had worked for the police mentioned the monitoring of Bon meetings. Moon thought he had misheard *Bund* in connection with the Camp Siegfried grouping but he was assured that it was most definitely *Bon*. Bearing in mind that Bon was the shamanistic pre-Buddhist religion of Tibet which still survives in many sometimes controversial forms and that Karl Haushofer (at least according to occult gossip) was an initiated Bon priest one can understand that Moon's mind was thoroughly blown by this outlandish configuration so typical of his investigations. It was difficult to get any hard data on the mysterious Bon group. They weren't a straightforward bunch of shamanic enthusiasts but discussed weird scientific ideas. Moon toyed with the idea that they were in some way between dimensions, acting as a conduit.

Such are the consensus co-ordinates behind *Black Sun*. The title denotes a motif central to what could be described as next generation Nazi occultism. There's no mention of it in Pauwels and Bergier or the first wave of works inspired by them. Nonetheless it is claimed that it was a fundamental concept of the Nazi mystical elite.

Two bizarre productions are largely responsible for the mutated Nazi occultism mythology that Moon encountered in the nineties. The first and most fundamental was a work by Wilhelm Landig, a member of the SS who claimed to have been close to Himmler. In post-war Vienna he was the focus of a small group who kept alive and regenerated Nazi mysticism, adding a whole new set of elements that would gradually spread out until by the time Peter Moon published *Black Sun* in 1997 they seemed such a well-established part of the total package that many simply accepted they had always been there.

A novel by Landig published in 1971 was the primary source of the subsequent dissemination of his ideas. *Gotzen gegen Thule* broadly translates as Godlets Against Thule. The secret order is portrayed as a global multi-racial grouping of advanced scientific capabilities. The novel is set at the very end of the war when two German airmen come to a Thule base in Arctic Canada where those who have stayed true to its original ideals have escaped the German defeat. Advanced experimental aircraft are in operation.

Despite a strong depiction of internationalism, featuring at one point a scene with a group appearing in their respective national costumes including a Tibetan Lama, black Ethiopian and Native American, Jewish representatives are notably absent. Landig stated that Thule idealism was perverted by Hitler and things took a wrong turn. Nonetheless, an eternal conflict with the Jews is described and justified in a similar manner to earlier Blavatsky variations. More insidious still is a brief interpolation claiming that the photographs of piles of concentration camp corpses had been faked using the bodies of German air raid casualties. The Jews remain an ancient and eternal enemy, the embodiments of the petty Godlets arraigned against Thule down through the ages.

Landig was primarily an advocate of a Thulean polar gnosis. He discussed what he claimed to be a concept that referred to the summit and source of that original physical and spiritual axis: the Black Sun. If nothing else, Landig was extraordinarily skilful in providing a mystical symbol that could be used in a world where open display of the Nazi swastika was not possible. It had the romance of arcane secrecy and the hint of a hidden brotherhood of the spirit. He believed the Black Sun was not just a potentially inspiring idea but a genuine source of energy that could regenerate the Aryan race. An associate of Landig named Rudolf Mund who was likewise a former SS member and part of the Vienna Circle linked the Black Sun with alchemy. It is an invisible anti-sun and designates the realm of spiritual force of which the material world is a shadow.

In a ground floor room of the North Tower of Wewelsburg where the SS elite gathered a design was carved on the floor. It takes the form of a twelve-spoke sun-wheel made from the notorious SS *sig* runes. It could be seen as three swastikas over a central point. Although there is some doubt it seems that the design dates from the Nazi reconstruction. From what is known of the conception of the grand plan for a projected complex of buildings that Himmler intended to build, the tower was an axis through a centre of the world.

It does not appear that Landig specifically linked the Black Sun with the Wewelsburg design but the connection is now firmly established. In this scheme of things, SS doesn't just stand for *Schutzstaffel* Guard Detachment but also *Schwarze Sonne* meaning Black Sun. Only the esoteric elite would have been aware of this. There are increasing numbers of people who are not just fascinated by Nazi mysticism but are active enthusiasts It's now possible to buy wrist-watches and coffee mugs displaying the Wewelsburg wheel.

A second design has also been displayed as an alleged Nazi Black Sun symbol. It is featured in Peter Moon's book and has started to appear with increased frequency, for example on the cover of Joseph Farrell's *Reich of the Black Sun*. This is two runes in the centre of a black sun-ray wheel. Unlike the Wewelsburg image it has no known authentic antecedents in the Nazi era.

One of the strangest and most haunting ideas in Landig's mythic mix concerns a variant on Roerichs's thought-form light disc as sign of Shambhala episode. For Landig, Thule is the equivalent of Shambhala as sacred centre and spiritual axis. *Manisolas* are living bio-machines who are born as circles of light that increase in density until becoming metallic. This eventually produces another light being, exploding in the process.

Depending on what stage of their life cycle and the time of day they are seen the Manisolas display different colours such as gold and silver and may have aureoles of flame or leave trails behind them. They are able to easily evade anything humans may send to pursue them.

These creatures have been observed since the earliest days of humanity and have been considered to be manifestations of the spiritual forces that inspire our greatest moments. Now their visibility is increasing with the dawn of a new era when the primal power of Thule will return.

Such ideas lead into the second strand of modern material that has fed the new Nazi occultism. This is most spectacularly found in the nineties video produced by Austrians Norbert Jürgen

Ratthofer and Ralf Ettl, *UFO Secrets of the Third Reich*. The duo were promoting the ideas of their neo-Templar group that in some respects could be seen as a successor to the dubious lineage of Lanz von Liebenfels and the SS.

Nazi UFO mythology has levels of material that become increasingly wild and unreliable. I am only going to very broadly summarise it. The most basic level suggests that the Nazis created a number of experimental circular flying vehicles powered by unconventional means. When the war ended and Operation Paperclip brought the whole Nazi rocket science package over to the USA these craft and blueprints for others were developed in secret and actually formed the reality behind the early UFO sightings. This topic has been much debated and is fervently believed and disbelieved. It is at least a fascinating and seemingly not too fantastic a hypothesis.

The Nazis did have a major interest in Antarctica. This has provided the foundation for stories of a huge complex built beneath the ice where flying discs were, and in some versions still are based. Variants have Hitler escaping there, gateways to a Hollow Earth where *Coming Race* super-beings live and suchlike. If nothing else, mystically speaking, these ideas complete the polar axis from the Thulean north with its black sun.

The wildest fringes of these beliefs, as presented in the *UFO Secrets* video, make out that the Nazis had ET contacts and developed craft capable of space travel and even interdimensional and time travel. The Vril Society drew together a number of secret groups including the Black Sun which was a kind of inner core of the Thule society. Whilst Thule increasingly focused on politics this new configuration looked into matters magical and mystical. They made use of mediumistic women who established contact with ETs from Aldebaran. This is round about the same period of time that Crowley drew Lam. The ETs were the original Aryans and had once landed on Earth and created the Sumerian culture. They now gave a high-tec download spec to the psychic women to build all kinds of devices that became the fabled Nazi flying disc programme. Karl Haushofer was present for these sessions. To Moon this linked in nicely with the channelled material about Crowley and Thule combining forces for the 1923 time travel working.

There's a big mix of modern Nazi occult themes heavily featured in *Black Sun* such as flying saucers, secret bases in Antarctica, Hitler's possible survival of the war, ancient Sumerian bloodline brotherhoods etc. A lot of material surfaced from German sources in the eighties and nineties, usually claiming a reliable background. Moon himself met up with people who told all kinds of tales, often of first-hand involvement. I'm inclined to treat their testimonies with caution. That they will throw some strangely pertinent real data into the brew doesn't reduce the need for discernment. Many of the ideas may well have originated with the Landig/*UFO Secrets* matrix.

Black Sun probably contains more data than any other Montauk book that is confidently stated to be historical fact or truth of some kind but is actually open to considerable doubt. Moon goes along with it because it came to him through a whole series of bizarre meetings and contacts so downright odd it's obvious something mighty strange was on his case. Whether there were attempts being made to manipulate him is not as important as what he actually made of it all.

Moon met a German who claimed connections with elderly Thule adepts who were depicted as life-respecting vegetarian mystics who claimed that the original intentions behind the group were good but things got seriously distorted along the way. Hitler deserted their ideals and started to cause concern. Haushofer knew Crowley and set up the Hess episode. He actually met Crowley in England, and so on. Moon had long discussions with a woman who claimed to have been specially mated with nefarious psychiatrist Ewen Cameron as part of a millennia old secret brotherhood bloodline cult dating back to Sumeria that linked the USA and the Nazis.

Robert Anton Wilson encountered all kinds of people with Illuminati tales to tell. He kept to a wise agnosticism and stayed sane. John Keel knew that he was thoroughly in the depths of the Mothman mystery when weird phone-calls, messages, and meetings conveyed to him the apparent presence of a higher guiding intelligence. He came to distrust it as potentially a liar and trouble-maker. When we are led towards the possibilities that the Nazis were potentially tuned-in to the mysteries of the universe, had advanced scientific projects, set up by ET contact and suchlike we need to be extremely cautious. I reiterate: at a point in the process archetypal stuff gets activated. As well as the synchronicity machine bringing pertinent data to hand, it may well also involve all kinds of people coming out of the woodwork who provide initiatory tests of discrimination.

There's an art and a science to effectively doing a bit of a Tai Chi dance with this stuff and not letting it stick to you. This is the trap that astonishing data of the Illuminati Montauk type lays for the aspirant. It's trying to drag you in and keep you there but the name of the game is to use it to understand something about how the world works and the process of initiation and move on beyond it.

THE BLACK SUN, SWASTIKA, AND SHIN

Peter Moon connected with the strange disturbing archetypal power of the new Nazi symbol, going on to express his own understanding.

> 'The Black Sun is an even more esoteric concept than that of Thule. Represented as the void of creation itself, it is the most senior archetype imaginable.'
> 'In Pythagorean teachings, the Earth itself geometrically unfolds from a void in the centre. This void has been recognised by many ancient groups, including the Sumerians, as the Black Sun. In this sense, Thule is synonymous with this Black Sun.'
> 'It creates the sun, wind, moon and stars.'

The swastika is clearly a symbol able to express such a cosmology. Thomas Wilson was a curator of the Smithsonian Institute who wrote a weighty tome on the swastika in the pre-Nazi days of 1898. Moon made use of his work noting his interpretation of the symbol in a Tibetan and Chinese context 'where it designated a whirling motion or a vortex of creation.' This is taken to equate with the Black Sun concept.

Crowley and Lam conclude the great journey. Thomas Wilson also discussed the word *lama* stating it was originally pronounced as *lam*, that the word means cross and is also equated with the swastika. Moon echoes the Typhonian OTO in referring to Lam as 'a guardian at the gateway to the hidden god which reaches us through the deepest aspects of our psyche'. Moon notes Kenneth Grant's use of gematria to connect Lam and Vril and links it all to his own favourite *Mon*. *Black Sun* includes a new artistic rendition of Lam with eyes far more noticeably open than the original, thus representing '*a new awakening of consciousness.*' Crowley called Lam "*the way*". Now the way has become the swastika in terms of '*the geometric unfoldment of existence and the source of all creation as coming from a black void or regenerative process as exemplified in the female.'* This is the *'Key'* mentioned in *The Book of the Law.* The final imagery shows us an eyes-opened Lam serving as guardian of the mysteries of the vortex of creation symbolised by the Black Sun. It's a gnosis that has been fought over and abused down through the ages and potentially offers a path back to the source.

In *Synchronicity and the Seventh Seal* another crucial complementary Key is examined. The famous Old Testament name of God passed down through the western mystery tradition has been written in English as the letters YHVH, the so-called Tetragrammaton. The letters have been taken to represent forces in nature depicted by the ancients as the four elements Earth, Air, Fire, and Water. Such are the teachings included in magical orders such as the Golden Dawn. The true pronunciation of the name has been a great mystery leaving the sense of something missing.

One clue seems to come with the Hebrew letter *Shin.* It has a double elemental attribution of Fire and Spirit with associations of the energy that enlivens matter. In *Genesis,* God breathed life into the basic material of creation that had been assembled. This breath of the Holy Spirit was called *Ruach Elohim.* Its gematria was 300. Shin has the same number. This supposedly shows that it represents some aspect of that force. Christian Qabalistic Occultists like the Renaissance Pico della Mirandola claimed that one could prove the divinity of Jesus through this. If you put Shin in the middle of the Tetragrammaton it spelled YHShVH, a Hebrew version of the name of Jesus. When tongues of fire came down into the disciples at Pentecost, it was the spirit/fire of Shin in operation. It can be compared with the Kundalini/Shaktipat spirit baptism of Hinduism. Shin turns the Tetragrammaton into a fivefold Pentagrammaton.

This missing ingredient is the key to synchronicity. Any system of magical mystical self-development should somehow activate it. Being as it is the life energy itself it is obviously already present in some way but inner work and coming into contact with people and situations where it is more fully functional create a turn-on effect. Peter Moon had the powerful combination of connecting to the voltage still rippling out from the Babalon Working for which he had been suitably prepared through his advanced Scientology training. At a certain point, the process takes on a life of its own outside of the conscious control of the limited third-dimensional everyday self but in synchronised accordance with the greater identity represented by such myths, models, and metaphors as the

Holy Guardian Angel or Operating Thetan.

In the Golden Dawn tarot attributions, Shin is attributed to the Judgement trump, usually portrayed as a Last Days *Revelation* scenario where an angel with a trumpet presides over the raising of the dead from their tombs. Believing that the old epoch was ending in fire and with essentially a new baptism of spirit, Crowley produced a new trump to replace Judgement. This was *Aeon* which features imagery taken from the Stele of Revealing such as Nuit and Ra Hoor Khuit and also the child of the new age, of the distinct divine individuality of all beings, Harpocrates. The Shin designation remained the same with a sense that it ties in with the energy depicted as Hadit.

There is indubitably a vast amount of material in the Montauk saga that is either plain wrong in the form of incorrect historical information or part of the great occult gossip section of the Akashic Records. Much of the personal testimony from a number of the unusual characters featured is so unusual or downright bizarre that many would consider it at best dubious. As someone who has read Israel Regardie's *The Eye in the Triangle* about a dozen times I find the suggestion that he may have actually murdered Aleister Crowley put forward in *Synchronicity and the Seventh Seal* entirely untenable. Nonetheless, Peter Moon's Montauk odyssey is a remarkable archetypal saga. From the initial starting point of the ultimate *X Files* sci-fi conspiracy it reveals deeper levels of unique data. Long Island really was full of Nazis. The case of the Montauk Indians and their land rights is a striking one. This kind of stuff simply isn't waiting to be uncovered anywhere. It's quite a combination.

A large amount of material in Moon's books has not been related here. There are further developments of the saga in his more recent works that cover some spectacular topics. The interested reader is assured that anyone enjoying the basic Montauk package would find them to be, at the very least, tremendous entertainment. As well as offering a unique memoir of life in the proximity of L. Ron Hubbard, *The Montauk Book of the Dead* is a striking treatment of the mystery of destiny, telling of the shattering moment when both of Moon's parents were killed in a car crash when he was only twenty-one years old. It expands still further the way in which he was primed for his mission.

I consider the Montauk legend and its potential trigger effect on consciousness to be a classic modern Aeon of Horus manifestation. It demonstrates the kind of things that can get activated when the necessary stimulus is applied. Moon's connections back to the Babalon Working show perhaps the most powerful sign yet of the tangential ripples still moving ever outwards from the Parsonage. Looming behind the turbulence is Crowley himself, enigmatically at Montauk during the period of his extensive past-life considerations that took his consciousness outside the circles of time and brought the image of Lam into the world. Crowley's ideas do rather seem to be able to press some spectacular on-buttons. When Shin, Kundalini, the Holy Spirit, gets increasingly switched on so the corresponding energies of oppression kick in.

With the ideas on Lam and the swastika in *Black Sun* and even more so with Shin in *Synchronicity*, Moon has provided some very useful material in getting to grips with the issues raised in *Extra-Terrestrial Gnosis* concerning the energies activated. If some mysterious force had to use the vehicle of occult gossip and assorted semi-crazies to get it to surface then so be it.

Whatever the exasperation of the dedicated researcher and their laudable desire to establish consensus facts, let's be clear here, in this work I am not just talking about history in itself but using history to put forth fantastic realism in the cause of magick and the New Aeon. Montauk and the Illuminati are great teaching tools to that end, calling us to develop a psychology able to accommodate and use such vehicles for the unveiling of our true shining genius rather than its distortion and destruction.

SECRET CIPHER: THE KEY OF IT ALL?

WE HAVE ALREADY NOTED Crowley's belief that numerical mysteries allegedly present in *The Book of the Law* are evidence of the presence of non-human intelligence in its creation. The link between numbers and letters that can be found in the Hebrew and Greek alphabets and is generally known as Gematria serves as the foundation of a kind of code whose signature can be found in the number ninety-three.

There is also a clear indication of a further level of hidden meaning with the mysterious grid page that we have briefly investigated in the Montauk section. The text itself tells Crowley to

'obtain the order & value of the English Alphabet; thou shalt find new symbols to attribute them unto.' 'Change not as much as the style of a letter; for behold! Thou o prophet, shalt not behold all these mysteries hidden therein. The child of thy bowels, he shall behold them', 'for in the chance shape of the letters and their position to one another: in these are mysteries that no Beast shall divine.'
'Then this line drawn is a key: then this circle squared in its failure is a key also.'

A body of work has now arisen based on the spectacular premise that the grid page code offers a key that demonstrates the unity of occultism and UFOlogy on a fundamental level. We now enter into what I would consider to be a triumph of fantastic realism where a number of the themes and motifs we have been examining can satisfyingly further cohere.

One of Crowley's most illustrious and enigmatic followers was Charles Stansfield Jones, often known by one of his magickal names, Frater Achad. In *The Magical Revival* Kenneth Grant covered a little of his career in a chapter called *Strayed Gods* that also dealt with Jack Parsons. Both men showed great promise and early achievement and then seemed to spectacularly fail. As the decades have passed many have looked at them again and found much of lasting value in their work.

Jones found a major numerical key to *The Book of the Law*. The circumstances leading up this event are of considerable magical interest. At the time of the Autumn Equinox in 1915, during his American stay, Aleister Crowley was engaged in sex magick workings with his Scarlet Woman of the time, Jeanne Foster, with the intention to produce a child who would be his magical heir. This was an issue that played upon him due to the prophecies in *The Book of the Law* indicating that he would not complete its interpretation and understanding himself but a *'child'* would do. No physical conception resulted.

On the Summer Solstice 1916 Achad took the Oath of a Master of the Temple. In magical terms this is a big deal, involving an undertaking to cross the Abyss and to interpret every single thing that happens to the aspirant as a particular manifestation of God's direct interaction. The difference between such a state of mind and what is generally considered to be insanity may not seem that much. In Achad's case it was rendered even more problematical by the fact that he had not worked through the relevant grades on the way up the Tree of Life that led to this. This is the same stage of the proceedings that propelled Jack Parsons on to the Black Pilgrimage from which he never returned.

This Oath was nine months after Crowley's workings to produce an heir. Achad had launched himself as a "Babe of the Abyss". This seemed to make him at least a magickal child. Crowley interpreted things that way and was thereby inclined to accept Achad's attainment as genuine.

This appeared to be entirely justified when shortly afterwards Achad discovered an important formula in *The Book of the Law* that had evaded Crowley. In the 60th verse of the first chapter, Nuit says, *'My number is 11, as all their numbers who are of us.'* Moving on eleven letters from A, starting the count with B will lead to L. AL together is an old Hebrew god name and adds by gematria to 31. The reverse LA will obviously also be 31. Achad then looked at the two tarot trumps numbered 20 and 11, *Judgement* or *Aeon* in the Thelemic update, and *Strength/Lust*. The Hebrew letters are Shin and Teth. Ignoring their specific numerical evaluation and instead simply adding together 20 and 11, Achad found a third 31 which makes 93. These letters were then arranged into the word *LAShTAL* that expressed a mystical magickal formula at the heart of Thelema.

At its most simple, AL as a Hebrew word for God is balanced by its reverse LA as 'Not-God.' The union of these opposites is equilibrated through the Shin force of spirit fire we have already encountered and Teth, the letter whose ideogram is a serpent and is attributed to the tarot trump *Lust* that depicts Babalon.

Crowley accepted this to the extent of changing the Latin title he used to generally designate *The Book of the Law, Liber Legis*, to *Liber Al vel Legis*, a format adopted by all Thelemites since. The work is now often referred to simply as *Liber AL*.

After this high point, things got a bit intense for Achad. He produced a revolutionary version of the Tree of Life that effectively turned it upside down. He fell out with Crowley and joined the Roman Catholic Church supposedly as an attempt to infiltrate it and ultimately affect a conversion to Thelema. Most notoriously of all, in Vancouver, Canada, Achad went out in public wearing nothing but a raincoat that he then discarded to wander the city naked as an affirmation of the extent to which he had cast off all restrictions. A predictable outcome saw him arrested and imprisoned. He continued to interpret the entire scenario right down to the conversational snippets of his fellow prisoners as God's inscrutable dealings with him. This obviously appears to be a descent into madness but Achad, like Parsons, has an increasing number of modern supporters who tend to feel he has unjustly experienced a bit of a legend of infamy himself.

Alongside the LAShtAL formula, Achad is now best known for proclaiming that the next epoch, the Aeon of the Egyptian goddess of justice, Maat, has dawned. It apparently began in 1948, a mere forty-four years after the Aeon of Horus was proclaimed. The difficulties in buying into this are immense. Kenneth Grant has come to believe in the possibility of concurrent aeons *Outside the Circles of Time*.

Achad is important here because his *Liber Al* code breaking provided the foundation for major discoveries later. In fact it seems downright odd that his initial insights were not used earlier to investigate the most vexed issue of secret coding there.

Having established the number eleven as the entry point one can take it another eleven letters on from L, starting with the next letter M, to get to W. This becomes our 1, 2, 3. An English occultist named Carol Smith completed the process in 1974. Looking at the *Liber AL* grid page we must forget all about the words on it and concentrate on the squares and the line. There are eight letters in alphabetical sequence horizontally along the top line of squares and ten numbers vertically down the side column. If the letter A is written in the top left-hand corner and then each subsequent letter of the alphabet entered vertically so that B takes up its place as number 2 and so on, the first column will go down as far as J, with K topping the next column. This process is followed through across the grid until the entire alphabet has been included three times with A, B ending the whole sequence in the bottom right hand corner. The primary diagonal line that can be drawn across the square goes firstly through the letters A, L, W, our 1, 2, 3, and then with H gives us our 4. This takes us to Z on the edge of the grid, our 8. The next letter along the top, K, starts a second diagonal line to bring us more numbers, and so on. Once the pattern is recognised it can be seen that it is working in sequence down along and across all diagonal lines that can be drawn across the grid.

A	K	U	E	O	Y	I	S
B	L	V	F	P	Z	J	T
C	M	W	G	Q	A	K	U
D	N	X	H	R	B	L	V
E	O	Y	I	S	C	M	W
F	P	Z	J	T	D	N	X
G	Q	A	K	U	E	O	Y
H	R	B	L	V	F	P	Z
I	S	C	M	W	G	Q	A
J	T	D	N	X	H	R	B

NEW AEON ENGLISH QABALAH

A=1	B=20	C=13	D=6	E=25	F=18	G=11
H=4	I=23	J=16	K=9	L=2	M=21	N=14
O=7	P=26	Q=19	R=12	S=5	T=24	U=17
V=10	W=3	X=22	Y=15	Z=8		

One of the most convincing early proofs of the veracity of the code came when examining perhaps the most perplexing of the obviously cryptic passages in *Liber AL*. The seventy-sixth verse of the second chapter states:

'4638ABK24ALGMOR3YX2489RPSTOVAL. What meaneth this o prophet?Thou knowest not; nor shalt thou know ever. There cometh one to follow thee: he shall expound it.'

If the letters are converted into their apparent numerical equivalents and the whole sequence added up it comes to 351. That's rather interesting being as if one also adds up the letters of the entire alphabet as per the newly revealed code they also come to 351.

With the onset of the computer era it was possible to quickly find numerical values for anything in *Liber AL*, whether words, phrases, or sentences, and run comparisons with other material.

So it appeared that what came to be called New Aeon English Qabalah (NAEQ) had come into being. The big question was did it satisfy its magickal requirements? What could actually be done with it?

Allen Greenfield is a veteran of the western mystery tradition, including Thelema, and also UFOlogy and general Forteana. This helped prepare him for some startling insights leading to his remarkable work, *The Secret Cipher of the UFOnauts*.

'When I started working with the 1974 cipher solution to The Book of the Law, however, as an idle experiment I began applying the cipher to the "funny" names from mediumship, contacteeism and trance channelling, and what I found constitutes the solution to the UFO mystery.'

The cipher solution fitted the type of cases we are already familiar with here such as the contacts of the fifties and the mothman case. These kind of things seemed to change after a final classic UFO flap in 1973. Greys and abductions became prevalent and the bizarre entities of the early days receded. Greenfield speculated that once a code of this kind is cracked the nature of the game will change in order for its players to stay one step ahead.

Secret Cipher tends to limit the comparative numerical equivalents to words and phrases that actually appear in *Liber Al*. This puts a limitation on how far one could look for validation without stretching credibility to the limit. In the following material then, words from various UFOlogical cases are assigned numerical values through NAEQ. The words given with equivalent values will be ones that can be found in *Liber AL*.

Lam = 24 = *God*. This is not taken to mean that Lam is exactly the same as the usual conception of God but that there is something about his name and function that casts a light upon his mystery. Perhaps we could suggest that Lam is effectively the god of Extra-Terrestrial Gnosis.

We have noted Meade Layne and his psychic Mark Probert with their group of discarnate teachers at the dawn of the modern UFO era. The Masters were known as the Inner Circle and were sixteen in number. In NAEQ the words *Inner* and *Circle* both add up to 88 which could be further reduced to 8+8 = 16. The two words together make 176. This is the same number as both *Instruction* and *Initiation*. These words indicate the nature and function of the Inner Circle group. One of the Circle was named Maharaja Natcha. Both words again have the same value, in this example, 57. Together they give us 114, equivalent to *The Name* and *Chosen One*. 57 also gives us *King*. This is appropriate to Maharaja. *The Name* is linked with the function. As Greenfield says, '*The connection is clearly there, but who made it, how, and why?* We can at least see something of how the cipher was intended to work. In this context we do have a definite mystical group and the possibility that Layne, a student of Achad's work, may have known and decided to make use of the cipher.

George Hunt Williamson has been established in our narrative as another pivotal figure in the interface between UFOlogy and occultism. Two of his close associates disappeared in mysterious circumstances after heading off in a plane in search of saucers, believing that a flight was on offer. Karl Hunrath and Wilbur Wilkinson had taken to referring to themselves as Firkon and Ramu, typical weird fifties contactee names. Wilkinson's home was found to contain a wall covered in symbols including the Royal Arch Masonic glyph for X written three times with an apparent translation beneath '*Births give cataclysms.*' In NAEQ, Firkon = 83 = *My Stars* = *Among Gods*. Ramu = 51 = *Sorrows* and *A Lie*. This is perplexing. Would anyone knowingly give themselves a magical name in a cipher that suggested that kind of grief? Highly unlikely. So what is going on? There's no quick and easy answer.

Remembering the importance of the number eleven in Thelema

and how it became the key to the code, it's notable how much it crops up with suspicious frequency right across the Secret Chief/Contact spectrum. Greenfield supplies an intriguing list that includes:

Aiwass = 38 = 3 + 8 = 11.
Ashtar = 47 = 4 + 7 = 11.
Aura Rhanes = 92 = 9 + 2 = 11.
Firkon = 83 = 8 + 3 = 11.
Morya (one of Blavatsky's Mahatmas) = 56 = 5 + 6 = 11.
Aia Aziz (magical name of head of Hermetic
  Brotherhood of Light) = 65 = 6 + 5 = 11.

The examples become still more perplexing when, having established a broad criteria of investigation, the bizarre adventures of Albert K. Bender are examined. For starters, his name as given for his book *Flying Saucers and the Three Men* (ie with just the first letter of his middle name), has a value of 195. This is the same value as *Alien Abductions*. When the controversial Gray Barker told a version of the story he shortened it to *Al K. Bender* which has a value we have just encountered of 114, in common with *The Name* and *Chosen One*. Again, there seems to be an implication that his name carried a key to his experiences. Barker referred to the MIB as the *lurking horror* which is rather interesting as the words carry the same numerical valuation, 142, as *Men in Black*. 142 also designates *Backward Darkness* and *All Lonely Places,* and *They Pass As Shadows,* very interesting phrases in the already established context.

Bender was given the weird magical sounding word *Kazik* to summon the MIB. It adds up to 50. *MIB* happens to score 64. Put them together for 114, the number of *Al K. Bender. Three Men* is 150. That plus the *Kazik* 50 gives 200, the number of *Black Pilgrimage,* a phrase we are familiar with through Jack Parsons.

This little mix presents all the issues involved. It seems to hang together very strangely in a kind of convincing way but also seems absurd. How is it supposed to work? Maybe Gray Barker knew the code and used it for his own purposes but it still had to fit the material very well to work. What about Bender himself and his *name*?

The Mothman case seems to yield an even higher rate of similar results. Remember that a major UFO flap was believed to be occurring around the area where the terrifying creature was being sighted. A classic bizarre contact case emerged from this when

Woodrow Derenberger encountered Indrid Cold and Carl Ardo and was told of the planet Lanulus. Cold had a wife named Kimi and was once accompanied by a man called Clinnel.

Indrid Cold −112. George Hunt Williamson was using the peculiar name *Mark III* during the fateful Firkon/Ramu period. It also adds up to 112. A phrase that recurs through assorted channelling lore *We are One* is similarly 112. Likewise *Word of the Law*, *Words and Signs*, and *Ra Hoor*.

Lanulus = 58, = *Hadit* and *Hawk's Head* and also *Seth*, a name associated with the first major New Age channelling and suggestive of the Egyptian god.

Carl Ardo = 54 = *Set* and *Snake*.
Kimi = 76 = *Night*, essentially Nuit.
Clinnel = 93 (an obvious Thelemic designation) = *Time*.

Again, what was happening here? Woodrow Derenberger has never seemed like a man who could hoax material in an obscure occult cipher. Perhaps he was massively duped by some mysterious tricksters in possession of the code. The role of Gray Barker, who wrote a novel *The Silver Bridge* on the West Virginia weirdness as well as his MIB book, is also problematical. None of it seems credible but following the code enhances the peculiar mood that the high strangeness has already established.

Greenfield is clear that many UFOnauts can be 'traced to their doorsteps'. An appendix to *Secret Cipher* features an interview with someone known as Terry R. Wriste. It contains some truly outlandish material that many would probably feel is a total wind-up. Amongst it is the tale of how Wriste used the cipher to actually physically locate Indrid Cold who was living in the Mothman locale decades after the initial furore. '*Mr Cold I presume?*' '*My friends call me Indrid*' Wriste describes him as a fugitive alien on the run from worlds conquered by the Greys who was invited to seek refuge by a representative of the same order of chiefs as Aiwass. He hadn't heard anything since. '*The whole Mothman thing was a distress beacon that failed.*' This doesn't seem entirely satisfactory.

Even less satisfactory to my mind is Greenfield's examination of the Babalon Working in his companion work *The Secret Rituals of the Men in Black*. Animated by an obvious dislike of L. Ron Hubbard, he theorizes that Jack Parsons' *Book of Babalon* is the result of some kind of post-hypnotic suggestion by LRH that was so complex and powerful that the text bears his signature in code throughout. That in itself would be a fairly unique feat. Greenfield believes that the cipher may have been circulating in sci-fi circles and Hubbard might have come across it then. The basic evidence is that Lafayatte Ron Hubbard by NAEQ = 248 and this is identical to Parsons' work ie *Liber 49 1.Yea it is = 248*. This doesn't work for me as for starters it is using a version of Hubbard's name that he didn't use himself. He was famously L. Ron. Secondly, the Parsons quote omits the end of the phrase. '*Yea it is I.*' Greenfield does have one definite and very mysterious hit though. The Xenu mythos has become famous amongst Scientology bashers for allegedly peddling an absurd sci-fi tale as true cosmology. In the material LRH used the name *Teegeeack* as a previous designation for our world. It seems bizarre and strangely jarring. NAEQ gives it a value of 158 which also happens to be the number for *Planet Earth*.

The issues here do call to mind the so-called Bible Code controversies. Briefly, a number of people using a basic principle of Equidistant Letter Sequence (ELS) have claimed to find in the Old Testament specific mentions of various historical characters and events. The thing has turned into a kind of Nostradamus almanac. One spectacular success seemed to be the discovery by such methods of a definite mention of the assassination of Israeli premier Yitzhak Rabin. Michael Drosnin has scored best-sellers giving the details and advocating their authenticity.

Endless debates have raged over the methodology used to find the prophetic material. I'm not going to cover the details which are all over the internet for those who want to know. One point concerns us here. Critic Brendan McKay has managed to use exactly the same criteria to find the Rabin murder and a bunch of other historical events such as the death of Martin Luther King in the text of Hermann Melville's great novel *Moby Dick*. This immediately detracts from the argument for Bible as unique divinely inspired work and the code in general. One also wonders at the bigger question. How is it that the universe somehow hangs together in terms of laws of mathematics and their potential relationship to languages that such results can be found at all ever in any text?

I don't know if the *Liber AL* ciphers' weird relationship to UFOlogy could be replicated in a novel by Jane Austen or something like that. To use one of Robert Anton Wilson's favourite words, *maybe*. Someone might have already figured that out. Arguments would follow.

For me, the most interesting application of the NAEQ that Greenfield makes, and a great triumph of fantastic realism that I affirm regardless of any arguments that can be made against the code, is in *The Secret Rituals of the Men in Black*. Its fundamental theme is the necessity of the contact experience in magick. All of the schools of the western mystery tradition can trace their material back to it. Another esoteric history lesson frames his presentation of a stunning magickal synthesis.

'Although the Cipher Solution is embedded in *The Book of the Law* it apparently does not originate there.' Greenfield came to believe it connects to a source that can be found a long way back through a chain of transmission not unlike the one Robert Anton Wilson traced in *Cosmic Trigger*.

Central to *Secret Rituals* is the significance of a being named Oannes, who strongly features in the Mesopotamian section of *The Sirius Mystery*. One of the most supremely enigmatic passages in the work of any ancient historian can be found in a fragment remaining of a three volume history of Babylon written by a priest of Bel named Berossus round about 300BC.

'In the first year after the flood appeared an animal endowed with human reason, named Oannes, who rose from out of the Erythian Sea, at the point where it borders Babylonia. He had the whole body of a fish, but above his fish's head he had another head which was that of a man, and human feet emerged from beneath his fish's tail. He had a human voice, and an image of him is preserved unto this day. He passed the day in the midst of men without taking food; he taught them the use of letters, sciences and arts of all kinds. He taught them to construct cities, to found temples, to compile laws, and explained to them the principles of geometrical knowledge. He made them distinguish the seeds of the earth, and showed them how to collect the fruits; in short he instructed them in everything which could tend to soften human manners and humanize their laws. From that time nothing material has been added by way of improvement to his instructions. And when the sun set, this being Oannes, retired again into the sea, for he was amphibious. After this there appeared other animals like Oannes.'

This is quite obviously a gold mine for ancient astronaut enthusiasts. Robert Temple linked this amphibious being with the entities revered by the West African Dogon. It seems that Oannes contributed to the form of the Philistine Dagon who helped H. P. Lovecraft create his Cthulhu mythos.

The Berossus passage has been taken to indicate the manner of the very beginning of western civilization and its mystery tradition. The lineage that led up to the modern revival of the Golden Dawn and Crowley has always preserved to some extent the memory of such beings and how to communicate with them. The name Oannes links with John and its variants. The whole Johannite tradition carried by the Templars and Masons is full of motifs that show this.

Greenfield presents another version of the War in Heaven theme that has recurred throughout this work, using terminology familiar to many mystical groups over the last century or so: The Great White Brotherhood and the Black Lodge, linked to Sirius and the Gnostic Demiurge respectively. In recent times, broadly coinciding with the birth of the New Aeon they have resurged together. It might surprise some to find Crowley speaking out against what he considered to be the bad guys. *'an organized conspiracy of the Black Lodges to prevent people from thinking'*. Greenfield repeats some *Morning of the Magicians* Nazi occult mythology. He believes that the secret cipher and others like it can help in assessing that perennial issue of who is playing for which team. *'Much of the "White Light Channeling" clearly bears the stamp of the Black Lodge and VALIS, an empty metaphysical blind of insipid psychic trivia.'*

In this scenario the Secret Chiefs have often been human beings involved in political games that made secrecy a matter of life and death. Blavatsky and her Theosophical Mahatmas were players in the political games of British India, definitely in favour of independence. Regardless of their spiritual attainments or the power of their physical presences (as best attested by Mathers' account) *'one should not conclude from this that they are immune to arrest, torture and execution.'* Cagliostro suffered such a fate at a time when his associates were involved in the American and French revolutions. We have already established that Crowley seemed to move in espionage circles throughout his adult life.

When it comes to the issue of how to be discerning in the Abyss of the goblin universe where dark gods and their human operatives may cross one's path, he states in *Secret Cipher* that *'The magick of the Black Lodge can be defined and thus identified in only one way and by one set standard: the subversion of the True Will. This is the essence of Black Magick and is its only true definition.'*

Affirming the virtues of the transformations wrought by effective magickal initiation he asserts that

> 'In elevated mystical states, the very secretions, psychic and otherwise, which humans emit and which desperate vampire-aliens consume like the soul-famished pathetic creatures they are, become poison to them in the Transformed Human. Cosmic Consciousness is literally poison to them.'

The MIB are used by Greenfield to refer to a whole class of generally Ultraterrestrial beings who appear in contact experiences related to the Oannes tradition as well as the Bender-model UFO fear-figures. Aiwass, who was tall and dark, can be considered of that ilk. Yes, the "black man" who supposedly appeared at medieval witch sabbats and was taken to be the Devil may not have always just been someone in a special costume.

The nature and effects of contact and illumination will be determined by the temperament and preparation of the recipient. Cosmic consciousness may be poison to the dark gods but also works like a magnet to attract those forces that are in harmony with it. With transformed vision the guardians of the threshold may be distinguished from the lurkers who seek to entrap. These characters can be understood by the already established criteria of using NAEQ to see whether they are a lurking fear or the glory of the stars and applying the general Black Lodge True Will subversion test. The final section of this work, *The Psychology of Thelema* is offered with the hope that it might aid in that discriminatory task.

Robert Anton Wilson provided a mixture of ideas that cohere together in a manner conducive to facilitating brain change with a particular flavor. Greenfield uses his own material to frame a magickal procedure in *Secret Rituals* that excellently complements *Cosmic Trigger*. Using all of the sources that Crowley drew upon, he created his own version of *Liber Samekh* incorporating the Sirius Mystery and the UFOnaut cipher to produce a workable "cosmic trigger" ritual intended to cultivate Extra-Terrestrial Gnosis and *'bring the glory of the stars into the hearts of men'*.

The invocation of the Bornless or Headless One is adjusted to "Beings Without Human Head", commemorated in the Oannes mythos, in other words fish-headed beings from Sirius.

'I call thee, the one without human head, that did appear upon Earth from the heavens, that did come by day and go by night, that came in the light and disappeared into the depths of darkness.

'You are an Adept of Kawi, the bornless, from the Knowledge Star whom no human hath seen before you arrived; you are the Fish Joshua, called John, called by the sacred word "Kazik"; you are Zarif, Abrasax; you have distinguished the worthy from the unworthy among us, male and female, you taught us to sow and harvest of old, you have taught us why we love one another or hate one another.'

The most radical innovation is to change the barbarous names to bring in some classic UFO and channelled entities and locations that have seemed notable through the use of the NAEQ to place alongside Thelemic material.

'You from Clarion, Baavi, Ashtar, Baavi, in Space. Manco! Omodra! Hanford! Fir Kon! Called Aiwaz of the six-fold star. Lazaris! Manco! Othra! Who spoke to Theon, Aiwaz of gold, O! Abuldiz! I say: SOLIM SOLARA! Orthon, appear unto me.'

'I am your Prophet in this time and space. Come in the Power of the Light of the Sacred Star, as now I behold it! Come in the Wisdom of the Stars; Come in the Benevolence of your Presence! The Light comes to me with healing in its wings. Unto you, Wise, Mighty, Incalculably long of Life, be praise and glory unto the end, who has permitted me, to partake of your Wisdom and Might, to penetrate thus far into the Sanctuary of your Mysteries.'

The star being is taken to appear and affirms:

'I am he, the Being without Human Head, having sight and feet, Strength, and the Fire of Immortality from the very Stars! I am he, the Truth. I am he who loathes that ignorance and disaster shall be wrought in your world. I come with roaring and flashing, showering down my light upon this Earth. I am he whose mouth seems to shoot forth flames.

'I am he the Giver and Shaper of the Light of Star Knowledge. I am that grace which descends from the Heavens unto your World. The Heart Girt with a Serpent is my Name.'

THE PSYCHOLOGY OF THELEMA

'Was it not the whole secret of personal life to find out what your innate nervous and mental fatality was, and then to drag it into your sorcerer's cell and work magic on it, and make of it your peculiar apparatus for testing your "truth" among all the "truths" of which the universe is crowded?'

John Cowper Powys. *Autobiography.*

'Let not the Magician forget for a single second what is his one sole business. His uninitiated "self" (as he absurdly thinks it) is a mob of wild women, hysterical from uncomprehended and unsated animal instinct; they will tear Pentheus, the merely human king who presumes to repress them, into mere shreds of flesh; his own mother, Nature, the first to claw at his windpipe! None but Bacchus, the Holy Guardian Angel, hath grace to be god to this riot of maniacs; he alone can transform the disorderly rabble into a pageant of harmonious movement, tune their hyaena howls to the symphony of a paen, and their reasonless rage to self-controlled rapture.'

Aleister Crowley. Magick. *Notes for an Astral Atlas.*

MAPS OF THE TERRITORY

'Important characteristics of maps should be noted. A map is not the territory it represents, but, if correct, it has a similar structure to the territory, which accounts for its usefulness.'

Alfred Korzybski. *Science and Sanity.*

'Offer thyself Virgin to the Knowledge and Conversation of thine Holy Guardian Angel. All Else is a snare. Be thou athlete with the eight limbs of Yoga for without these thou art not disciplined for any fight.'

Aleister Crowley. *The Book of Thoth.*

The most important word in *The Book of the Law* is the Greek *Thelema*, meaning both "*spell*" and "*will*". Crowley considered it to embody the single most significant formula for navigating the New Aeon. In studying the psychology of Crowley's Thelema we may be better able to understand what he was all about and what we ourselves can make of it.

It's useful to begin by looking at the overall rationale behind his various procedures. Crowley had a sort of recipe for preparation. He recommended that, before tackling the Great Work of Magick, aspirants should get their minds and bodies in order. Get fit, become competent in some athletic skill, some physical path. Study philosophy, comparative religion, and science. Understand the world around you in its own terms without necessarily losing yourself in it. If, neglecting this kind of balanced groundwork, you start trying to play games with reality you'll simply wreck yourself and have no fruitful understanding of the results.

All Crowley's masks and games were means not ends. His diaries over forty years show endless hours daily of mystical magical work. He was serious. His principle biographer, John Symonds, in my opinion, hasn't got a clue what he was all about and his mocking attitude and general condemnation has helped fuel the distortions of the legend of infamy. A far better doorway to Crowley is Israel Regardie's *The Eye in the Triangle*, which shows Crowley the mystic of immense self discipline, Crowley the poet and prophet, and outlines his real centre of gravity.

As well as his studies magickal and mystical, Crowley had great knowledge and insight on the latest developments in science, philosophy, mathematics, art, literature, and psychology. One of his most significant achievements was to synthesise his worldview in terms that seemed to fit the New Physics. '*The Method of Science. The Aim of Religion.*'

Even though we have entered the twenty-first century, our society hasn't really assimilated the epochal shifts in conceptions of reality from the period around 1904 detailed earlier. The old style Newtonian worldview where reality is "outside" waiting to be investigated, and science is a neutral objective process that can discover its true nature independent of the human equation had ended. Science can really only offer us statistical probabilities and possible models. Models that are always seen as metaphors and symbols that may be updated or replaced. This approach has generated the most spectacularly successful science in history.

Robert Anton Wilson mentions in *Cosmic Trigger* how the multi-model approach found its way into art and literature at the very start of the twentieth century. Picasso's paintings show the same scene from more than one angle, likewise the Futurists. James Joyce's novel *Ulysses* tells the story of one day from the standpoint of multiple narrators in a variety of different styles – comic, epic, poetic, tragic, encyclopaedic etc – because life isn't just either/or, it's *All*.

But we can't have a homosexual poet 22,000 feet up the Himalayas without oxygen, we can't have a god-intoxicated mystic out big game hunting. Some people rather than even attempt to face such problems will simply avoid them. To reiterate: '*Such a new world requires the development of a psychology of fluidity and multiple perspectives. At its very inception Crowley laid out detailed instructions for how to achieve such aims.*' Perhaps, if we tackle Crowley with the multi-model approach we may expand our horizons.

Following Crowley doesn't mean imitating him, his apparent vices and the nastier side of his character. He was brought up by fanatical Christians, mangled emotionally by fire and brimstone preaching on sin and guilt, bullied at school, crippled intellectually and sexually repressed. He had his own stuff to deal with. When you're working through such material all kinds of horrendous things may come to the surface. Getting it out of your system might involve some heavy-duty scenarios. It doesn't automatically follow that if you adopt Crowleyan techniques you'll end up killing a cat nine times over or encouraging your partner to have sex with a goat.

After leaving the Golden Dawn and receiving *The Book of the*

Law, Crowley founded his own magickal order, the Argentium Astrum. There he presented to aspirants his synthesis of all the techniques and knowledge he had worked with: magick, yoga, and the combination of the two, tantra. The backbone of the system was the Qabalah, a system of Jewish mysticism which serves as a filing cabinet into which many other systems can be absorbed without distortion. It was the centre of gravity of the Golden Dawn. A human figure, named Adam Kadmon can be drawn over the Tree of Life diagram. This cosmic being represents the true form of humanity, raised to its highest, fullest capacities. The middle pillar of the tree runs down the spinal column to the feet. The sephiroth spheres that are located along it have strong similarities to the yogic chakras. The other pillars give more obscure physical correspondences such as the shoulders. A series of experiences, work on oneself, is necessary to ascend the tree and activate its corresponding zones inside us.

Crowley's most notable initial aim was the Knowledge and Conversation of his Holy Guardian Angel. He chose this terminology because it was archaic and absurd enough to deter the cynical and hostile from even bothering to deride it. Nonetheless, it also conveyed something which most people can, simply by hearing the phrase, have some sense of its meaning and whether it may have significance for them.

We could say it's the true self, the higher will, personified. On some occasions though, Crowley said that it is most categorically something outside and beyond you. He gave both of these apparently contradictory explanations to two of his followers at almost the same time. How one might approach it will be a matter of temperament and preparation. It is both within you and without you. It's you and not you. It is an external entity but it is also that which, in essence, you have always been. A paradox, yes, but such paradoxes lie at the heart of mysticism and the practices necessary to achieve the aim also help resolve them. To attain this aim is to find ones True Will. This is the meaning of the formula "Do what thou wilt". It emphatically does not mean do what the hell you like. It means find out who you really are and be that, live it.

The experience of the Holy Guardian Angel can occur as part of the activation of the Qabalistic sphere of Tiphereth, located around the heart centre. To get there, you work through the elements and, in so doing, create a five-pointed star, a pentagram, inside yourself. This makes a temple of your inner realms. The upper point of the pentagram represents Spirit. The temple is empty until spirit infuses it. At that moment you are ready for your angel.

The work curriculum in Crowley's AA included magical practices very similar to those of the Golden Dawn. The Hebrew alphabet and tarot were thoroughly memorised. Pentagrams were drawn in the air and angels invoked. Some of the additional material might prove to be the most inspirational for the non-magickally minded. Much of it originally appeared in Crowley's *Equinox* publication. Some also resurfaced in the magnum opus, *Magick*. Israel Regardie later made a superb compilation of *Gems from the Equinox*. A variety of techniques and disciplines were recommended that did not involve actual ritual procedures. They all serve the purpose of the cultivation of the True Will.

So how do you find it? You may have to be brutal with yourself to discover how much of what you consider yours may be accidental conditioning, imposed externally. What if every piece of knowledge available on the cultivation of creativity had been engaged during your formative years? Imagine if, when you were a small child, you had lived in a household where many languages were spoken. What if your parents had engaged a whole group of master yogis, fitness trainers, and bodywork experts from toddler stage on your case? Chances are that the general level of fitness, of physical condition, the way that we are within our bodies and within ourselves would quite likely be extraordinarily different to what has come to be the case. Perhaps an expert tutor could have rendered you literate at a precocious age and introduced you to many subjects so as to superbly prepare you for later studies. Your parents might have set you up with piano or violin lessons that gave you competency by school age. The real geniuses in all these fields are assuredly born and not made but just think about it. In terms of the natural ability to learn that all healthy children have, anyone could potentially be a creative, multi-lingual, athletic, intellectual, musician. That we're not may be down to accident not intention.

In all of us reside groupings of personalities, sub-selves, some of which are latent only. We're all potentially very diverse. Crowley astonishes us because he seemed to bring out so many of his latent sub-selves and develop them to the full. Remember also, when thinking of your own sub-selves, that you wouldn't want to make the mistake of identifying yourself with any of them totally. They're not the whole you, the real you. So many people take one part of Crowley and define him by it. A more worrying thought perhaps, and the kind of meditation that Crowley also encouraged, concerns the persona you currently adopt, your apparent centre of gravity. Perhaps that may just be a random sub-self that stayed put? How much of your life may be dictated in such a way?

We can profitably look at one of Crowley's more enigmatic sides within such a context. He thoroughly enjoyed cultivating particular personalities and then composing elaborate works from their standpoint. These included the notorious pornographic *White Stains*, a thoroughly homosexual piece of Sufi mysticism, the *Bagh-i-Muattar*, and *Amphora*, a series of devotional verses to the Virgin Mary. In his *Confessions* Crowley wrote that

> 'I must not be thought exactly insincere, though I had certainly no shadow of belief in any of the Christian dogmas... I simply wanted to see the world through the eyes of a devout Catholic, very much as I had done with the decadent poet of *White Stains*, the Persian mystic of *Bagh-i-Muattar*, and so on. I was, in fact, adopting another alias – in the widest sense of the word. I did not see why I should be confined to one life. How can one hope to understand the world if one persists in regarding it from the conning tower of one's own personality? One can increase one's knowledge and nature by travelling and reading; but that does not tell one how things look to other people. It is all very well to visit St. Peter's and the Vatican, but what would be really interesting would be to know how they look to the Pope. The greatness of a poet consists, to a considerable extent, in his ability to see the world through another man's eyes; and my training in science is always suggesting to me that I should invent a technique for doing anything that I want to do. My technique for borrowing other people's spectacles was to put myself in their place altogether, either by actually adopting a suitable alias or by writing a book in their names.'

Similar ideas were taught by Gurdjieff to Ouspensky who recorded them in the classic works *In Search of the Miraculous* and *The Fourth Way*. It was stated that most of us can be said to be asleep in a trance of distraction. Each of us believes in a unique individuality but, on closer examination, most cannot demonstrate any real unity of functioning. We are full of small separate personalities. One part may proudly proclaim the intention to stop smoking, take up a regime of exercise, follow some idealised spiritual path etc. The "I" that likes to smoke or overeat or take drugs, be sexually deranged and so on, will later on assert its own claims and the lofty talk will be worthless. We have many I's. They can all be *'caliph for an hour'*. Work on oneself involves the conscious cultivation of a "magnetic centre". It is the responsibility of this aspect of oneself to seek out those influences conducive to the maintaining and expansion of its function.

What does that mean in the real world? The feeling of it can be better grasped by looking at it alongside another of Gurdjieff's teaching ideas. Ouspensky discusses the concept of "food". He takes it beyond the usual definitions. As well as what we eat in the normal sense, the case is made for regarding air as food. If anyone thinks it isn't, try living without it for a while. Most stimulating of all was the classification of "impressions" as food. What we input through our senses can nourish or poison us. To take an extreme example, a person feasting everyday on hardcore porn and horror, someone who regularly read the literature of hate, racism etc, would be thoroughly poisoning themselves. Contrariwise, a person who immersed themselves in great art, literature, music, and the religious classics of the world, with a view to changing themselves for the better, would be getting some kind of higher food vitamins and protein. Although just what constitutes appropriate input is hugely debatable and variable, the basic principle is a call to some sort of conscious awakening. Gurdjieff suggested that once this process was really in motion, somehow one magnetically attracted to oneself the necessary higher influences. The world is full of them, but to the average tranced-out sleepwalking person they are all but invisible.

In the early twenties Gurdjieff established a base in France in a large house with extensive grounds. Many people of a high level of culture and breeding joined him there. His teaching did not just consist of a series of lectures. He directly confronted the malfunctioning mechanical side of human life. To this end AR Orage, a leading figure on the London literary scene, was asked to go out into the garden and dig a ditch. Not exactly full of enthusiasm, he complied. Gurdjieff then told him to fill it back in again. Orage came to realise that such tasks are, in themselves, neutral. What matters is the quality of attention, the focus and emotional engagement we bring to them. They may frustrate and fatigue us but a kind of inner work could transform our relationship to them. The capacity for vast endeavours lies slumbering within us if we but knew how to awaken it. Gurdjieff gave out incredibly complex exercises to engage the full spectrum of functioning. Whilst performing ditch-digging type tasks someone might also be trying to memorise a list of Tibetan words and sensing different parts of their bodies in strange sequences. Orage and his colleagues began to experience threshold crossings where barriers of annoyance and lethargy gave way to heightened awareness and increased stamina. He ended up enjoying the digging. None of this would have been any surprise to Zen Buddhists. Their monastic traditions have a strong focus on the cultivation of a meditative attitude towards daily hard physical work.

The non-ritual disciplines that Crowley advocated for his AA all involved confrontation with our lack of unity and purpose. One of the more famous examples is outlined in *Liber III vel Jugorum*, a work of barely four pages concerning control of speech, action, and thought. A series of voluntary restraints of these functions are to be followed *'for a week or more'*. For example: *'avoid using the pronouns and adjectives of the first person; use a paraphrase'*. More simply put: do not use "I" in conversation. The idea is that speaking of oneself in the third person helps to confront the continual arising of the narrow separateness of conventional identity. Frustrate the relentless normal expression of the limited self and a strange trance begins to arise in which glimpses of something greater emerge. *'Avoid crossing the legs'* may seem a simple enough control of action but try maintaining it for a week. A more complex strategy involves creating two distinct personalities and switching between them when a ring is moved onto a different finger.

> *'On each occasion that thou art betrayed into doing that thou art sworn to avoid, cut thyself sharply upon the wrist or forearm with a razor; even as thou shouldst beat a disobedient dog.' 'Thus bind thyself, and thou shalt be forever free.'*

A photo was published of a suitably chastised pair of arms. Yes, this does seem to be a bit severe and not for everyone, but it shows that Crowley meant business and further debunks the myth of his lack of discipline. Other techniques taken straight from yoga helped undermine the arising of habitual tendencies in the body, mind, and emotions.

★ ★ ★

THE MAGICKAL DIARY

The normal state of the human mind often involves being forgetful and deceiving itself. Crowley placed great importance on the keeping of a detailed diary to record any kind of discipline or magical work undertaken. There's a remarkable tendency to be inaccurate in the recollection of fairly straightforward details. It is possible to under and overestimate ones' performance in any given situation. Real data is always the remedy.

When it comes to the general stirrings in the depths that inner work creates or the performance of specifically magickal ritual acts the recording and accurate dating of dreams, synchronicities and so on are vital. Apparently minor details can prove to be of significance years later.

Crowley himself produced what he considered to be a definitive template for such work with *John St John* which forms the core of the James Wasserman edited *Aleister Crowley and the Practice of the Magical Diary*. In the midst of everyday life in Paris, involving meals in restaurants, games of billiards, and romantic dalliances, Crowley undertook a magickal retreat during which he nonetheless continued his usual activities. There were invocations and meditations amidst failures of concentration and intensity. Yogic ecstasy overcame him. The document serves as an outstanding inspiration to integrate all of life into the process of initiation and that any avoidances produce unbalanced and therefore incomplete results. The whole process can be seen as further cultivation of Gurdjieff's Magnetic Centre. It affirms and builds unity of function.

Even if one has a busy life the keeping of a diary recording basic data is still easily possible. I have kept daily one-line entries, written on A4 paper, for over thirty years. I gradually increased the information that basic one line would carry to include things like books I was reading and films I'd seen. Later still, I began recording exercise sessions or drug and booze intake. This basic data has proved priceless to me again and again. I've also kept long-standing dream diaries and more detailed general diaries. Separate sheets for each year also kept lists of books read and movies seen in sequence. It's an easy way to keep track of one's functioning. I cannot recommend highly enough the necessity of keeping such records. The fun and games I have had with the data has rewarded the effort involved in keeping it a thousandfold.

THE LEARY EIGHT CIRCUIT MODEL

Timothy Leary developed an Eight Circuit model of consciousness that brought Crowley and Gurdjieff's work together. Beelzebub had significantly impacted on him as well as the Beast. In a prison letter to Robert Anton Wilson, Leary stated that, '*I love Him and I resonate to his wisdom more than anyone else's.*' His first presentation of the basic material dated from the darkest days of the ordeal of the Abyss. Kept in solitary confinement, Leary was allowed just a pencil stub to write with as anything longer was considered to be a potential weapon. His only supply of paper was in the form of the backs of legal briefs. Sitting on the floor of his cell by the dim light of a 20 watt bulb he scribbled a download of material that had been coalescing somewhere in the higher realms of his consciousness. Its initial form was a short pamphlet entitled *Neurologic*. It was later more fully developed in *Info-Psychology* and subsequently restated in a number of other works. Robert Anton Wilson gave a brief survey of it in *Cosmic Trigger* and then expounded on it to great effect in *Prometheus Rising* (from which the following quotes in this section derive) and the later *Quantum Psychology*.

There are plenty of other maps and models of the territory. At the risk of winding-up Scientology haters I shall mention that L. Ron Hubbard also presented an eight stage Dynamics of Existence in his early work that many have found extremely useful. Neuro Linguistic Programming has achieved considerable recognition in recent decades. I present Leary and Wilson's work here primarily because I consider it to be a masterful contribution to the psychology of Thelema. If you take its spirit on board you may find that you can playfully study and use all manner of ideas in a way that serves the True Will. I shall bring in some complementary diverse material alongside it to potentially demonstrate that.

CIRCUIT ONE: BIO-SURVIVAL

In animal studies the imprinting phenomenon is well known. When a bird hatches from an egg, the first thing it sees it treats as its mother even if it's a boot or a bicycle. That's an imprint. Leary believed that an imprinting sequence occurs in humans up to puberty and is reinforced by conditioning. This stuff is buried deep down inside us, virtually wired in. We progress through the first four neurological circuits as part of our natural biological development and imprint a certain pattern on each one of them, ideally in some kind of balance. Like Pavlov's dogs, when the appropriate bell rings we salivate. We're conditioned physically, emotionally, intellectually and sexually. The encouragement from Crowley, Leary and Wilson is to be aware of these circuits and play with them. That's where your latent sub-selves are hiding. They're all part of your totality. Don't disown them. Integrate them.

The first circuit corresponds to the magical element of Earth. It represents one's fundamental grounding strategy, the most basic of blueprints. A newly born child soon demonstrates a very simple script in all of its behaviour. It will advance towards any stimulus that appears to be nurturing or interesting and it will retreat from all things obviously dangerous and frightening. This serves a clear educational purpose. Good parenting will encourage a child to feel safe as it gradually begins to investigate the world around it. Difficulties may arise because there will be no rationality behind such decisions of advance or retreat. They come out of pure emotion.

These early life-scripts are written with internal physiology. The retreat stimuli produce distinct symptoms to make one back away. There's also a definite buzz about the confident advance forward that derives from infant responses. The first circuit is focused from a position of orality. Breast-feeding and the relation to the mother carry a whole state of consciousness through the deep body memory of that intimate connection. A feeling of comfort and security could end up being permanently linked with either withdrawal or advance. A child in an unhappy home full of conflict or even violence may adopt a posture of withdrawn retreat that might condition the rest of its life. As Wilson says in *Prometheus Rising,*

> '*A man or woman entering a new situation with the anxiety chemicals of a frightened infant coursing through the brain stem is not going to be able to observe, judge or decide anything very accurately*'.

This early circuit imprinting can determine whether a person goes forward in life with anxiety or self-confidence, a sense of rootedness or explorativeness, dependency or independence.

Work on the first circuit can be done through ensuring regular physical exercise. Crowley had his AA students practise Hatha yoga so they could sit in the lotus position with a saucer full of water balanced on their head and not a spill a drop of it for a period of up to an hour. The practice of the general postures stills agitation, promotes health and invokes the will, enabling one to not be as governed by advance/retreat. The long term practice of most athletic disciplines will tend to change body chemistry for the better. You can then start to play with your programming, maybe seek out new situations for the sake of it, or even weirder, avoid them when there's no need to and see if doing that dredges up childhood memories and some insights about yourself. It helps to break the mould, to regain a sense of freedom. More importantly, it helps to dissolve false identification with a limited accidental part of one's total identity.

Most magical orders, including the Golden Dawn, would have a list of deities associated with the element of Earth and procedures for invoking them in some way. Modern pagans might visit ancient sites of sanctity to connect with their sacred soil. All of that is fine. It's possible however, to do that kind of thing for years, decades even, and still be fundamentally the same person, still neurotic, toxic, overweight, underweight, rubbish at relationships, whatever. Israel Regardie eventually refused to take any magical students who hadn't undergone some form of psychotherapy. The additional techniques of Crowley and Robert Anton Wilson can really stir things up. Such movement in the depths, in combination with the usual magic, can press major initiatory "on" buttons and kick-start accelerated processes. In *Prometheus Rising,* Wilson is emphatic about the necessity of actually *doing* some of these psychological exercises. Each section of the book ends with a selection and the encouragement to develop more oneself. I am offering a few examples of my own in this section to give the general flavour.

CIRCUIT TWO: EMOTIONAL, TERRITORIAL

'For mind and body alike there is no purgative like Pranayama, no purgative like Pranayama.'

Aleister Crowley. *The Book of Lies.*

Freud believed in a sequence of developmental stages and the first circuit corresponds to his primary "oral". His second phase was named anal and this is where the second circuit activates. It corresponds to the magical element of Water. As a child begins to walk, it will also undergo toilet training. '*If the first (bio-survival) circuit is chiefly imprinted by the mother, the second (emotional-territorial) circuit is chiefly imprinted by the father – the nearest alpha male.*' Wilson shows how all kinds of complex associations between these earliest experiences of trying to control one's bodily functions and the "uptight" values of classic patriarchy may offer many possibilities for future dysfunction. During the toddling stage, complex negotiations of mammalian politics will determine the level of dominance or submission that a person may take forward in their life, where they stand in the pecking order, whether they're top or bottom dog. This can create a personality with self-confidence or self-doubt, a strong or weak ego, accustomed to giving or receiving orders.

Wilson postulates that:

> '*Ego is simply the mammalian recognition of one's status in the pack*', '*a single brain circuit which mistakes itself for the whole Self, the entire brain-mind apparatus*'. '*The standard "authority" reflex on the emotional-territorial circuit is to swell the muscles and howl. You will find this among birds as well as mammals, and in the Board meeting of your local bank. The standard "submission" reflex is to shrink the muscles, lower the head, and "crawl away." You will find this among dogs, primates, fowl and employees who wish to keep their jobs everywhere.*' '*Second circuit problems take the form of bullying or cowardice: "I will force them, or I will surrender and let them force me."*'

Crowley's AA used yoga breathing to work on this level as it is capable of transforming emotional upheaval whether it be active anger or sadly passive submission. He said that there is basically nothing to compare to these techniques in order to sort out your basic emotional complexes. Any form of powerful emotion, any agitation, any grief, any physiological disturbance involving the stomach and the general whole body can be potentially alleviated. If you practice these disciplines of pranayama then quite extraordinary transformations will come about in this. And if we want to perhaps doubt that Crowley was serious in his own application we know for a fact from his magical diaries from the period of time when he was in Ceylon in 1903, that there were periods when he would be doing yoga breathing exercises for eight hours, every single day. Can you imagine the amount of persistence that is necessary to go through this kind of process and the kind of physiological changes and altered states of consciousness that you would experience if you did?

Another way of experiencing the working of the circuit is Wilson's suggestion to, '*get roaring drunk and pound the table, telling everybody in a loud voice just what dumb ass-holes they all are*'. There are many ways to play games with it. If you're meek and mild, try acting loud and boisterous once in a while. State a strident opinion for the sake of it. If you're prone to being loud and proud, submit and admit you're wrong even if you're not.

CIRCUIT THREE: SEMANTIC SYMBOL DEXTERITY

If the second circuit represents the everyday ego, the third is the mind. It corresponds to the magical element of Air. The first thing that differentiates humans from other primates is our capacity to use symbols. '*The third, semantic circuit handles artefacts and makes a "map" (reality-tunnel) which can be passed on to others, even across generations.*' The first two circuits are rooted in biology and maintain a kind of equilibrium. The third inevitably creates a momentum of acceleration. Each generation doesn't have to reinvent the wheel. We can all benefit from the cumulative build up of knowledge. There's also however, a tension between new and old ideas. People who lived centuries ago can still dominate us through religious and political ideologies. New science and the ideas it generates can be socially disruptive. Peoples can be oppressed and nations go to war over ideas.

The third circuit begins to fully function about the age of twelve. It will deal with pictures, words, concepts and the use of tools, and music. It can set someone up for life as fluent or inarticulate, dextrous or clumsy. It's interesting to spot cases of arrested development on that level. The sort of people who are obsessive collectors, who have to get the whole set, who are maybe one pointed in their focus on a football team, a movie star, a pop group, religion or even a science (and it's not to say that good can't come from this), are eternal twelve year olds. We sense unbalance about them. A head trip. How many people do you see being dogmatic and absolutist about things? It doesn't matter how much education they've had, they're stuck on circuit three at about twelve years of age. And this reveals the worst abuse of this circuit in something that Gurdjieff called Formatory Thinking. Seeing everything in binary terms of left or right, wrong or right, black or white, has helped cause and perpetuate many a conflict over the ages. As Wilson sadly observed, *'the semantic circuit is notoriously vulnerable to manipulation by the older, more primitive circuits'*. Frighten the first circuit with hell and damnation or the second circuit with the threat of invasion or subversion by a hostile power and people will accept the Inquisition or the Nazis. The rational mind can always justify it, hence the cynical belief of some that Reason is a whore who will serve anyone.

There's a lot of work that can be done to free up the functioning of the intellect. Remember Crowley's advice to study widely in comparative religion, philosophy and science? Until recently many people followed the beliefs of their parents and cultural change was sometimes slow. It may be possible to annihilate intellectual imprints with the study of philosophy or paradoxical Buddhist meditations. You might not be able to spare the time for such reading but there is the option of not buying the same newspaper two days running. Try setting off papers that are politically opposite against each other. Try and suspend disbelief. Imagine what it's like to believe whatever opinions are stated. Read some Born Again Christian stuff or extreme political literature. Enter their reality-tunnel for half an hour. Be a true blue, be a Nazi, be a Trotskyist, believe Jesus loves you, for that time. How about checking out Scientology's enormous anti-Psychiatry material? If you cultivate this attitude you may begin to find you're not then able to be as absolute about the opinion you think you "really" hold. Repetition of mantras also serves as third circuit work, focusing and stilling the monkey mind.

CIRCUIT FOUR: SOCIO-SEXUAL

The "sexual moralistic" fourth circuit partakes of the qualities of the magical element of Fire. It can determine whether an individual becomes moral or immoral, a solid citizen or sexual outlaw. Puberty completes the biological developmental stages where the imprinting sequence is at work. Every society has had some form of taboos, some kind of beliefs around sex, acknowledging its power and importance. The most simple of them attempt to control breeding by determining which combinations of people can be allowed to mate. In the earliest of human cultures can also be seen a sense of the erotic as a possessing force that may afford a glimpse of the sacred. Early representations of deities glorify the mysteries of breeding, the Earth Mother, the phallic god etc. Out of all this has eventually emerged the "adult personality" of the parent. We have much in common with mammals in our early parenting behaviour but there's a lot of cultural variety as well. Clearly the parent role is necessary for the future of humanity. It is not necessary however, that every individual conform to it.

Some may discover that human sexuality seems unnecessarily prodigious if reproduction is its only purpose. A strong imprint on this circuit makes for physically attractive sexy horny types. Other knackered monkish sorts have taken a negative imprint and felt horribly bound to the wheel of birth and death, becoming celibate to deliberately step outside of the process. Deranged moral codes suggesting that natural functions are an evil force that we must be at war with may well be the greatest single cause of human misery in history. *'Fourth circuit problems take the form of guilt; "I cannot do what I am supposed to do".'* Wilhelm Reich believed that the muscular armouring that develops as part of the repression of the natural flow of life energy in the body can cause cancer in an individual and make entire societies vulnerable to manipulation and outbreaks of violence. His *Mass Psychology of Fascism* analysed the whole Nazi phenomenon from such a viewpoint.

None of this means that we shouldn't try to cultivate some kind of emotional-sexual morality. There is stuff that just doesn't work. Simply going to the opposite extreme from medieval Christianity is no guarantee of sanity and fulfilment. It's nice to believe that there may be an inherent wisdom of the body-mind. If the malfunctions of the earlier circuits are effectively adjusted, the force will freely flow. A vast literature now exists on the subject of sexuality and a right relationship to it. Nobody can fail to find some means or another of working out any fourth circuit dysfunctions if they're serious in that intention. Points will be disputed but many lives are changing for the better in a way that Crowley would surely have taken as a sign of the Aeon of Horus. Certain experiences of sexuality may open a door to the next level.

★ ★ ★

MAGNETIC CENTRE AND THE KUNDALINI ALCHEMY OF SHIN: STIRRINGS OF THE SECRET LOVER

> 'O Self Divine O Living Lord of Me!
> Self-shining flame, begotten of Beyond!
> Godhead immaculate! Swift tongue of fire,
> Kindled from thy immeasurable light
> The boundless, the immutable. Come forth,
> My God, my lover, spirit of my heart,
> Heart of my soul, white virgin of the Dawn,
> My Queen of all perfection, come thou forth
> From thine abode beyond the Silences
> To me the prisoner, me the mortal man,
> Shrined in this clay, come forth to me I say, to me,
> Initiate my quickened soul; draw near
> And let the glory of thy Godhead shine.'
>
> Aleister Crowley.

The fifth "holistic neurosomatic" circuit takes us into realms of human functioning which are latent in everyone but don't automatically manifest in the manner of the inevitable developmental stages of the earlier levels. It is possible to experience enhancements of sensory input that generate a high that may be experienced as permeating the whole body-mind. This kind of thing came to be called turning-on in the sixties. It doesn't necessarily involve the use of drugs. The kind of good sex with a sort of total-body orgasm, considered by Wilhelm Reich to be necessary for full health, will bring it on. Some yoga breathing may do the trick. The literature detailing peak experiences through sport show innumerable possibilities.

Some level of stability on the first circuits is usually the essential pre-requisite for this kind of function. It's unlikely that a medieval serf or African famine victim would be able to experience such benefits although India has produced some notable mystics from a background of poverty. At various stages in history, such as the Roman Empire, the Caliphate of Haroun el Rashid, Renaissance Italy, at certain epochs in the history of India, in the California of the sixties, some societies have reached the point where a leisured elite could cultivate these arts.

We have reached the unique stage whereby they are potentially available to millions. One sign of this is the pornogrification of the mass imagination with its attendant sexual obsessions. This has it's downside but it also means that reactionary newspapers may still print articles on Tantric yoga if celebrities like Sting are known to be practitioners and that can be useful. They at least alert the public that such things exist out there and if they're investigated for purely hedonistic purposes the possibility still remains that some may take it further. Massage, shiatsu, aromatherapy etc, allow people to open up to the inherent grooviness of a de-stressed body-mind.

Once a decent turn-on of this kind has been experienced, it becomes progressively more difficult to resume the seriously toxic lifestyle of normal culture: booze, cigarettes, caffeine, junk food. The "hit" they offer seems crap in comparison. Artful use of cannabis in the context of sex, music, and decent food has been known to assist the development of aesthetic sensibilities. As *The Book of the Law* advises, *'refine thy rapture!'* Ultimately, the assorted means of turning on the fifth circuit should become superfluous. A true yogic process would render the mutation permanent. There are such adepts alive right now and their numbers are growing.

Remember the elemental pentagram? The Golden Dawn tradition worked its way up through the Tree of Life, creating a stable foundation for the inner temple to receive the higher genius, the Holy Guardian Angel. The first four circuits correspond to the elements. The holistic neurosomatic circuit is the top tip of the pentagram. Wilson equates it with Gurdjieff's Magnetic Centre. It represents the awakening of spirit, Kundalini Shakti etc, the Shin of Pentagrammaton that Peter Moon placed so much importance on in *Synchronicity and the Seventh Seal*. The process takes one to the point of final preparation, of maximum receptivity for the invocation of the "angel".

The Holy Guardian Angel metaphor model is at the very least an immensely potent emotional archetype that when activated can facilitate gigantic shifts in consciousness. One of the most useful modern treatments of it can be found in Christopher Hyatt and Lon Milo DuQuettes' *Way of the Secret Lover: Tantra, Tarot and the Holy Guardian Angel*.

The authors affirm that we all have a Secret Lover, a profound inner aspect of our most fundamental identity, *'an ideal lover who has adored us since the beginning of our individual existence and who will never abandon us until the instant we merge our being in absolute Godhead.*' Our awareness of this may take the form of a response to certain types we might repeatedly fall in love with. Sexual ecstasy can be a doorway to communion with it, likewise the effects of the Arts. Our relationship with the Secret Lover, however unconscious it may be, nonetheless forms a kind of standard against which everything else may be compared. This can lead to melancholy, aching nostalgia, and general pangs for that which seems so near yet unattainable. *'The world still yearns for a love which few of us know. And this love is beyond anything any one individual can satisfy.'*

Surrendering to the Secret Lover can be considered to be a fundamental process at the real heart of all religions. Unfortunately, the assorted orthodoxies have always acted in ways that have prevented their adherents from experiencing the blessings of such a communion. Accounts that exist leave no doubt that the most obvious ways of expressing it always use the symbols of enraptured love and sexual ecstasy. This mode of being was never a favourite of the Inquisition. In the western mysteries the Secret Lover has been called the Higher Genius, Adonai, and the Daemon. The Golden Dawn/Crowley tradition used the term "Holy Guardian Angel." "Knowledge and Conversation of the Holy Guardian Angel" was the fundamental task of any would-be magus. Only thus equipped could the higher levels of initiation be navigated.

Hyatt and DuQuette summarise the issues involved in the statement that

> *'Magic and Mysticism - The Will To Self Mastery and The Will To Surrender are two sides of the same coin.'* '*Often this false distinction between magick and mysticism gives rise to strong prejudices against certain practices such as sex magick or the "Tantra of the Left Handed Path." The reason they have such bad reputations is that they teach surrender and self mastery. In other words they teach love and power and not simply love or power.*' *'The concept of surrender has become so distorted that many believe that "surrendering" is in opposition to power, sex and self mastery. This is one of the greatest lies. – self mastery is not possible without surrender.'*

The issue of Surrender has been known to cause many a twitch amongst westerners, especially narcissistic magicians. '*It is unfortunate but true that most of life's misery is caused by our inability to surrender to love. In a desperate attempt to fill this void people become addicted to alcohol, food, sex, endless affairs, fame, fortune and of course drugs.*' Surrender appears to be a negation of the will. The impression can be given that something of vital importance can be lost, integrity, or even the very soul itself. Hyatt and DuQuette assert that '*though the boundaries of the individual must necessarily fade away there is no way in the world that you can lose your Self. Your true Self is hard wired in and even if it were possible to lose one's self or be possessed it would have to be the result of one's true will.*'

When the great force of Shin becomes active the conscious ego can and should become swept up beyond itself. Accounts of experiences of mystical surrender tend to agree that they are centred in the heart region, whether it be the Qabalistic Tiphereth with its Holy Guardian Angel contact, or the yogic Anahata chakra. It marks a major stage in the activation of the True Will.

Quite clearly, given the points Hyatt and DuQuette raise, the level of preparation on the earlier circuits can be a strong influence on how things develop. When the force of Shin combined with the angel archetype is activated all kinds of nonsense from the early circuits may spontaneously dissolve if the psychological and physical preparation has been sufficient. This is why yoga prepares for the activation of Kundalini with the initial combined disciplines of posture, breathing, and various abstinences and so on.

There's a complementary phrase in *The Book of the Law* to '*Do what thou wilt*'. It's '*Love is the law, love under will*'. We may discover that all of the crap in our heads is weird defective imprinting. A load of mechanical hamster wheels stupidly turning. One realisation ought to run through all of our circuit games and our attempts to break our moulds: the idea of an open heart. It's our inherently natural condition. If we take negative imprints the heart contracts, in Vital Shock, and becomes poisoned, blocked, shut down, distorted. When we're not functioning at our best, that's what it means. What does it really all boil down to when we ask ourselves if we're happy and fulfilled? It's where our hearts are at. Can we give and receive love unconditionally? That's a good test definition of sanity. All else is determined by it.

Think of the crud in the first circuits. Fear and retreating in number 1. The need to dominate in 2. All the either/or, wrong/right, rubbish of the person in Circuit 3 head trip. Anyone with an open heart is far less likely to be perpetuating all that sort of thing. It often seems like nonsense to them. And, as a result, they're far less likely to have sexual problems. So, in breaking all of these moulds, playing with circuits, experimenting, looking for who you really are, how do you assess if you're on the right track? By feeling the trapped life energy flowing again. By a sense of relief and release, of freedom and joy, of regaining something you somehow recognise even if you don't know where from. *'Love is the law'.*

The word "Thelema" in Greek Qabalah adds to 93. So does "Agape", meaning "Love". This equivalence teaches that the two represent a vital unity. Say you break your moulds, then what? Balance and transcendence. Without that open heart it may be grey and uninspired and potentially dangerous. Some people are so alienated and unnatural they may say "how do we love?" One fundamental teaching of the Wisdom Tradition of humanity affirms that, in our fundamental nature, we are already one with that which is sought after. We are inherently free, intrinsically enlightened, essentially infinite love. If the blocks, distortions, barriers, conditioning and so on are dissolved that true nature will be automatically revealed as *the* most natural thing in the world. Why not adopt that belief system experimentally and see what happens?

As Hyatt and DuQuette say,

'This act of surrender can do nothing but add to one's autonomy and power, – Surrendering is a necessary experience for complete living and the will to surrender is the ultimate realisation of this fact. Giving love, being tender, showing compassion are as necessary as receiving them: none are a morality. They cannot be legislated. They cannot be enforced. They are a result, not a cause, of complete surrender.'

Pranayama practices can begin the purifying flow of the life force. There are some more explosive breathing practices that can be appropriate for this crucial fifth circuit Magnetic Centre Shin alchemy stage of the game. Wilhelm Reich was a pioneer. Christopher Hyatt incorporated dynamic breathwork into both his psychotherapeutic and magical work. Osho Rajneesh developed a Dynamic Meditation that created intense physiological results. Perhaps the most powerful of all such techniques is the deliberate hyperventilation induced through the Rebirthing of Leonard Orr. Rapid results are possible that unleash enormous emotion and physiological processes. Orr suggested that *'If the Biblical symbol for breath is fire, then hyperventilation may be the baptism of fire which Jesus talked about.'* This can also be considered to be putting on the wings and arousing the coiled splendour, '*the snake that giveth knowledge and delight and bright glory*', the Kundalini force. '*I am the secret serpent coiled about to spring. In my coiling there is joy, if I lift up my head, I and my Nuit are one*'.

PEAK EXPERIENCES AND NEW EXISTENTIALISM: A FIFTH CIRCUIT ASIDE

At this crucial fifth circuit stage it's worth a brief look at some very useful complementary ideas that help enhance appreciation of the processes involved. The American psychologist Abraham Maslow realised that the theories of Freud and Jung had been developed through studying people who considered themselves to be sick or to have problems of some kind. The same kind of attention had never been given by academics to those who felt healthy, sane, and fulfilled. Maslow decided that this potentially meant that the various psychoanalytical approaches might be unbalanced or incomplete and undertook research to rectify this.

He discovered that people from all ages, genders, and backgrounds reported what he came to call "peak experiences," a phrase that has passed into general cultural vocabulary. These broadly equate with the "turn-on" concept. In all kinds of different circumstances, a sudden feeling of extraordinary well-being and elevated sensibilities might descend on people. For example, a young drummer talked of occasions when, after extensive practising, he suddenly found himself in a superb focused state where it was if the drums played themselves. There are now so many reports of similar phenomena in sport that a whole literature and psychology has grown up around it. A mother preparing breakfast for her husband and children went into a state of profound joy and fulfilment when a ray of sunshine suddenly lit the scene. It seemed to simultaneously illuminate her higher emotions. She felt profound gratitude for what her everyday consciousness had started to take for granted. Once peak experiences were discussed, people began to remember many others. They also started to have new ones with increasing regularity. The psyche responds readily to all intimations of transcendent wholeness.

This sort of thing would be called gratuitous grace by Catholics. They are often simple transient versions of the states recorded by the more famous mystics. Maslow believed that the ground can be prepared for them but they can't really be induced to order. The preparation involves meeting the demands of what he called the Hierarchy of Needs. We have primal desires for food, shelter, and breeding. Freud developed a whole theory of human behaviour and the nature of society on the basis of these factors, feeling they were sufficient to explain everything. Maslow believed that if the basic needs are met, there is another dynamic that arises and also requires urgent fulfilment. He called it "Self-Actualisation". People need to have a sense of inner worth, of distinct individuality, of growth. Some kind of creativity seeks expression. Denial of these urges produces alienation, inertia, all manner of dysfunctional grief.

Colin Wilson knew all about this problem. His first book, cult classic *The Outsider*, was a study of the self-destructive path of many confused artistic types who had sought an outlet for their inner dynamism in a society that could not adequately accommodate them. The painter Van Gogh, the dancer Nijinsky, and philosopher Nietzsche, were all examples of intense talents that imploded. Their urge to super-consciousness came up against consensus pessimism, a major symptom of the sleepwalking trance of humanity that Gurdjieff had explained to Ouspensky. Wilson went on to write an Outsider series. One of them, *The Age of Defeat*, attracted the attention of Maslow in 1959 and the two began to correspond. Wilson had railed against the sense of doom and despondency that characterised European cultural thought. It led to people feeling passive, insignificant, and unable to lead a happy life or make a difference in the world. Colin Wilson considered this to be a fundamentally flawed and dangerous attitude. It could be summarised in the modern world as the "everything's bullshit, let's get the beers in" syndrome. Maslow told a story about how he had once asked one of his student classes which one of them would make significant contributions in their field in the future. None had raised their hands. "If not you, who will?" They got his point.

Eventually Colin Wilson wrote one of his most important works, *New Pathways in Psychology*, on '*Maslow and the Post-Freudian Revolution*.' Where Wilson diverged from Maslow was in his belief that we don't have to wait for the peak experiences, the turn-ons, for neurosomatic rapture. We have many ways to cultivate them as part of intentional self-actualisation, a kind of new existentialism that is assuredly a revelation of the True Will. To summarise, where Maslow and Wilson help us at this point in the journey through Leary's eight circuits and up the Tree of Life, is to underline the importance of firm foundations: the study of the psychology of health and sanity should form a vital part of any magical mystical curriculum.

With that in mind, do not despise the American cultural institution of Self-Help books. Long before Maslow, in 1908, Napoleon Hill was challenged by the fabulously wealthy philanthropist steel magnate Andrew Carnegie to dedicate twenty years studying what the most successful people across the whole spectrum of life in America had in common. The result was the *Law of Success,* a gigantic compendium of functional intelligence with practical guidance in its achievement. Hill's most famous and contentious work was *Think and Grow Rich.* This leads us back into Leary and Wilson and the zones where thought, empowered by dynamic equilibrium of developmental balance in the earlier circuits, and energised by the resulting turn-ons, can be said to *space-out.*

TO INFINITY AND BEYOND:
A META-PROGRAMMING, NEUROGENETIC, NON-LOCAL, MAGICAL REVIVAL

'Thou, who art I, beyond all I am,
Who hast no nature and no name,
Who art, when all but thou are gone,
Thou, centre and secret of the Sun,
Thou, hidden spring of all things known
And unknown, Thou aloof, alone,
Thou, the true fire within the reed
Brooding and breeding, source and seed
Of life, love, liberty and light,
Thou beyond speech and beyond sight,
Thee I invoke, my faint fresh fire
Kindling as mine intents aspire.
Thee I invoke, abiding one,
Thee, centre and secret of the sun,
And that most holy mystery
Of which the vehicle am I!'

Aleister Crowley. *The Ship/Gnostic Mass.*

We have been programmed, but in saying that, it's vital to see that a part of ourselves has co-operated in the process: the mechanism that wired this stuff in, having received it from outside. We have our own programmer. It usually functions in an automatic, passive, unconscious manner. Perhaps the most controversial of all the theories that Leary derived from his work with LSD suggested that in certain circumstances imprints can be dissolved and replaced by new ones. Some government brainwashing specialists exploited a negative side of this insight. When games are played with the different aspects of ones potential, the programmer will be confronted. What follows is an even greater insight: you are not the programmer. You can program the programmer. Leary always emphasised freedom of choice to select ones own inner reality.

The sixth "meta-programming" circuit (named in part as a tribute to the work of another great consciousness pioneer John C. Lilly) reveals itself whenever there is an awareness of the functioning of the earlier circuits as if from some kind of viewpoint outside them. When we decide to play games with our circuits we have started to free ourselves from their enslavement. Each of the first four circuits is like one of Gurdjieff's multiple "I"s. The fifth circuit begins to transmute their energies towards a functional unity. Modern techniques like Neuro-Linguistic Programming and the work of Anthony Robbins are making use of meta-programming. It's the active function of the sixth circuit to be able to step outside and then step back in and change something.

My favourite Crowley meta-programming strategy can be found in *Liber Astarte*, part of the magnum opus, *Magick*. Find a deity, a god/goddess or even a living guru, and cultivate a love bond. Fill your life up in every possible way with this figure. Do regular rituals to invoke it. Be totally one pointed. Devote yourself to it. Make shrines in your home. Put up pictures. Recite aloud or internally the associated prayers and mantras. Catholics are like this with Jesus and Mary. *Something* will happen, one way or another. The end result may be a stunning vision or experience. To most people that's *the* result. If a Catholic sees JC or the BVM then that's their whole life sorted. Not so Crowley and Robert Anton Wilson. The minute you get a result, stop. Choose another deity. Start again until a result comes and then again.

After a while you find out things about how the mind works with archetypes and natural forces. That's not to say that's there's no external reality involved, but it teaches one to be philosophical.

As Crowley said *'these things may or may not exist. It is immaterial whether they exist or not. By doing certain things, certain results follow. Students are most earnestly warned against attributing objective reality or philosophical validity to any of them.'*

We've seen how Crowley was, in his experimental attitude to himself, a kind of 21st century man ahead of his time. Here's another seeming paradox as Crowley believed that he was actually reviving the most ancient and primordial cultus. This idea has been considerably expounded in the works of Kenneth Grant such as *The Magical Revival* and *Aleister Crowley and The Hidden God* to which much of what follows is indebted. His interpretations are by no means universally accepted by Thelemites but I have found them to be profoundly useful. *The Book of the Law* states that although the law is for all, the fundamental principles, the ordeals, the magic, are not.

Grant takes us into what I would call interstellar darkness. It's best to make sure we're relatively sane before taking that leap because, so the magicians tell us, having sorted out your contact with your Holy Guardian Angel in Tiphereth, the next biggie involves crossing the Abyss and we have seen the kind of things that might be waiting there. At this point the requirement necessitates the abandonment of all of your previous achievements, including initial communion with your Angel. Wave bye-bye and leap in surrender. The nature of the void then experienced will be determined by what you already have or haven't sorted out. Meta-programming skills are a necessity.

Perhaps the most well known of all stories from Egyptian mythology concerns the goddess Isis and her husband Osiris, who was dismembered by his evil brother Set. Their son Horus sought revenge and eventually defeated Set, leaving him to become the original bad guy and all purpose stooge in Egyptian religion. He contributed to the formation of the later figure of Satan. What we have to bear in mind is that Egyptian religion extended over thousands of years and that each dynasty, even each city, favoured a particular mythos where one or another deity was predominant and another relegated to also-ran. The later form of some of these myth-cycles reflect centuries of politics, rivalries between priesthoods, and warfare. Much spiritual/magical truth may be embodied in their respective traditions but distortions do arise.

Kenneth Grant presents Set as one of the earliest Gods of Egypt, dating from a time when stellar cults were predominant. In one tradition he was associated with the seven stars of Ursa Major and, in particular, with Sirius, known as the sun behind the sun.

Crowley's Thelemic Magick does not perpetuate the usual antagonism between Horus and Set. In *The Book of the Law* Horus has a twin form. One represents manifestation and the other, silent potentiality. The silent form is an aspect of Set. Horus and Set are brothers here, in a sort of yin-yang interplay. This alchemy is explained by Grant as representative of crucial processes in the magical path across the Abyss.

Set is the absorption of the projected energy of Horus. The silence of the death of desire. This process, over which the Set energy presides, has a further two differentiated aspects, Hoor-Paar-Kraat and Harpocrates, usually conceived of as being an infant form of Horus. He is generally depicted as a naked youth, with a finger raised to his mouth in a gesture of silence. We have already noted an image of Harpocrates, dating from the early centuries AD, showing him sitting cross-legged on a lotus flower with a finger touching his lips. This seems to invite eastern comparisons.

An analogous conception in one figure is the Hindu God Shiva who some have linked to both Set and Satan. He embodies both destruction and creation simultaneously. The Indians are quite happy to accept these apparently paradoxical qualities in one figure.

Horus, as spirit, is the solar body of light, the sun. Daytime. Manifestation. Set is the double, the astral shade, the soul, stellar light in darkness, the sun behind the sun of Sirius. Night. Set represents a means of return to Nuit. I call him the Void Self. The Void Self is your real higher-circuit self, of which your manifesting Will as Horus is only a limited form. The greater Will is that which your manifestation arises out of. There's a point where the greater Will begins to seem like an Abyss. When the energy of Horus turns inward, instead of outward, the normal Ego can die and the Eye of Set, in India the Eye of Shiva, can open. This "destruction" can better be described as "absorption". To be reabsorbed into primal selfhood the ego must die so Set, as leader of that process, from life to death, Hadit to Nuit, can be seen as terrifying. The form of Set is another kind of dweller on the threshold to place alongside Lam, Choronzon and assorted entities.

Beyond that threshold is the chalice of Babalon, the glittering body of Nuit. This leads to another important consideration. What's the role of women here? Horus and Set are obviously male but Nuit is the whole universe and thereby contains them. Crowley is known to have partnered many women who were fairly unstable and later came to grief with alcohol and drugs so he's often been portrayed as an abuser of women. There's yet another of the Crowley paradoxes here. He was also a worshipper of them who knew quite early on in the twentieth century, that the whole system of magic that he was restoring was nothing without the shakti energy to empower it. Endless poems show his passionate and sincere capacity for love. Just because that love wasn't limited to one person for fifty years doesn't make it any the less real.

Think of Set-Horus as one figure like Shiva. Recall the union of Nuit and Hadit, which results in Set-Horus. In recent years Eastern artwork featuring a male sitting in a lotus posture with a female sitting upon him in sexual union has become increasingly well known. Shiva and Shakti as the Indians call it. The Shakti is the force of Nuit. Modern Witches affirm that every woman is a Priestess, "Thou Art Goddess". The great Thelemic polarity is Babalon and the Beast conjoined. This was Jack Parson's passionate ideal of the path from Tiphereth across the Abyss.

The *Book of the Law* can be considered to be a Tantric scripture. Many Eastern ideas help to clarify it. According to Kenneth Grant there are complex mysteries of a biochemical nature hidden within it concerning various chemicals produced within women's bodies. These menstrual mysteries were presented to a wider audience in the epochal *Wise Wound* of Penelope Shuttle and Peter Redgrove and Redgrove's *The Black Goddess and the Sixth Sense*. In these mighty works the real power of the Scarlet Woman reveals itself amidst the hideous story of her suppression. Sex magick can be a potent factor in the path through the higher circuits but again is susceptible to distortion by any factors unresolved from earlier stages of development.

From the fifth circuit upwards, especially if the processes outlined by Hyatt and DuQuette are successfully activated, the conventional sense of identity begins to be undermined. Boundaries blur. Feelings of separateness dissolve. Strangely enough this at first can lead to greater control of the apparently separate egoic bodymind through meta-programming techniques. Then comes the enigma of just what may be directing the technique. Our individual lives may be partial dramas of the global being. At first the mystery of some kind of higher self is revealed and comfort can be derived from trying to abide within it. Then it becomes clear that it too connects to something vaster and impersonal. The Hindu *Upanishads* talk of how once one goes to a certain depth within the individual self there comes a point where it simply dissolves into the universal consciousness. In this tradition, using the terminology of the great adept-realiser Adi Da Samraj, enlightenment might be defined as when one is no longer lived by the individual self but by the self that is alive as all beings.

This is where those meta-programming skills can be useful. To relax back from the constant arising of the standard human tendencies and watch them from a position of benevolent detachment represents a most fulfilling passive function. This is a meditation coming from a space that's been called the Witness. The Witness consciousness stands half way between two worlds. It is as if it can see in front of it the world of form in which the drama of our personal lives with their imprinting and conditioning is played out. Behind it lies the infinitely vaster formlessness that we are constantly arising out of. The meta-programming circuit offers a potential connection to the global brain and beyond.

Wilson and Leary suggest it may be possible to experience genetic memory, to access material from within DNA. This occurs with the "neurogenetic" circuit. Leary has it as number six. Wilson changes it round the other side of the meta-programming level. This at least shows the theories are not intended to be regarded as carved in stone. Those investigating them can at least ponder how the two levels may sit together and the necessity of developing meta-programming awareness when collective atavistic material begins to rise up from the depths.

A foetus goes through developmental stages that run through evolutionary history in rapid acceleration. At one stage it's virtually a fish. We do, in effect, have the memory of other lives within us. Timothy Leary wrote of an acid trip where he seemed to recall the whole process of evolution back to the pre-Cambrian slime, as if activating this cellular memory.

Apparent past life experiences, and the visions of mythic figures and deities spoken of by Jung, the peculiar entities of world mythology and UFOlogy, may all be manifestations of this collective neurogenetic circuit. The energy that infuses the Horus-Set alchemy may be partly derived from it. If the planet is a living being with some kind of consciousness could it be said to dream in some respect? Are the ghosties and lake monsters, black dogs, faeries, shining ones, UFOnauts and Fatima visions part of the dreaming mind of Gaia? There may be traumatic and dangerous dreams therein that require therapy of some kind. Many of the inhabitants and guardians of the Abyss may derive something of their form and tendencies from this collective historical layer even if they in some sense vector in from beyond it.

Hardcore acid mystics and New Agers may suggest that one of the reasons that individuals are able to access such strange states is to assist the greater global consciousness, the great DNA Being to become more conscious of itself.

The non-local quantum circuit constitutes the final part of Leary and Wilson's map of consciousness. Many people have reported experiences where they have believed themselves to have somehow left their physical bodies. There are the increasingly well-known near-death episodes. What's interesting about such endeavours and the experiences they produce is the way in which they may be shaped by beliefs about the nature of consciousness.

Psychics and Occultists speak of an "astral body" that somehow co-exists with the physical body but can go walkabout during sleep and be trained to function through the conscious mind. In the Golden Dawn tradition there is a practice known as "rising on the planes" which involves taking this "body of light" on journeys up the Qabalistic tree. The magician has to become sufficiently in control of their imagination to be able to travel clothed in magical apparel, armed with appropriate tools, and interact with various weird entities that are the guardians of the different zones. They may want to see particular gestures and signs of initiation in the aura before allowing entry to their spaces. It may all be occurring in a world that works a lot more strangely than most would imagine but there's still a touch of the 3D mind in the schemata of its functioning. In all this there remains assumptions of distance of some kind, a here and there, separation, outside and inside, and so on.

Crowley had a sense of limitation in this. When he gave instructions on the practice it was stated that the Golden Dawn method was a preliminary one. Having assumed the body of light, the magician should be able to, in a way, bring their intended location to them without moving. Even then, there's still the feeling of something that was somewhere else moving through distance to a point of arrival. The successful practice will involve a sense of simultaneity. There will be no movement, no distance. Crowley paid a lot of attention to developments in physics. He was trying to update the magical worldview to accommodate the new science. The variant on the usual rising on the planes procedure may be an example of a sound intuition on his part.

He died before the concept of non-locality was developed. I think he would have appreciated it. Bell's Theorem suggests that, in Robert Anton Wilson's words, *'every particle in the universe is in "instantaneous" (faster-than-light) communication with every other particle. The Whole System, even the parts that are separated by cosmic distances, functions as a Whole System.'* A problem here is that Einstein's Relativity work states that there can be no faster-than-light communication. The maths behind both approaches seem sound, so somehow they must both be "true". Perhaps the "stuff" communicated is not energy in the Einsteinian sense. Perhaps *'what does move faster than light, and holds the Whole System together, is "consciousness".'* Not just the global brain but the cosmic brain. *'The synchronicities of circuits 5 to 7 are just the dawning notes of the symphony of all inter-related harmonies revealed to those who have experienced Circuit 8 in action.'*

In a cosmology reminiscent of some Gnostic systems, L. Ron Hubbard stated that we are Thetans, immortal beings who have taken physical form in different galaxies over a period of trillions of year. We are potentially masters of Matter Energy Space Time who created the game of the universe and physical form for our amusement and challenge but have forgotten or been tricked into believing otherwise as a result of a major Space Opera. In this system, we don't ultimately blend into everything else but have an identity that is untouched by all the laws of the physical universe. This Thetan is a good model of the non-local self. The higher level teachings of Scientology deal with Exteriorisation and the ability to function comprehensively beyond the body. The modern vogue for Remote Viewing can be interestingly traced back to some Scientology adepts.

The body of Nuit is the whole universe. She could be said to embody mystical concepts like the voids of various traditions that are often symbolised as female in nature. Their "emptiness" is nurturing, in a womb like way, and, paradoxically, full and overflowing. Such concepts can be seen in the archetype of the Grail chalice, the Emptiness of Tibetan Buddhism, the Sunyata of Zen, and the Chinese Tao. Here we can contemplate Blavatsky's Voice of the Silence as the source of Extra-Terrestrial gnosis. These terms could be considered to designate an omnipresent non-local matrix.

All of these teachings encourage the cessation of striving and the inescapability and ultimate blissfulness of surrender to that which we are constantly arising from and sustained by. We're not separate from Nuit. '*I am above you and in you*'. The Thelemic work is to '*bring the glory of the stars into the hearts of men*", for we are already stars in the body of Nuit if we did but know it. On the basis of the ancient magical principle of "as above, so below", we are universes in miniature, we're full of our own constellations. Our bodies can dissolve into infinite space within. We must consciously reconnect to our source, which is not somewhere other than where we already are. This game of life, this dance, this illusion of separation, is summed up by Nuit, '*I am divided for loves' sake, for the chance of union*'.

There may well be, on one very fundamental level, potentially no distance, no separation, between any human brain and any place in the universe. Everything in spacetime could be considered to be here and now. An astral or higher mental, or whatever else one's "other bodies" may get called, may be frequencies of perception that are not as individual as some may imagine. We're left with a mind-fucking paradox for the Zen masters to laugh about. We're clearly separate individuals in this 3D world but we're made up of stuff that isn't in any way limited by such co-ordinates. We're made up of stuff that isn't even stuff. We can't even say it's in any one place at any one time. Whatever the hell it might be could potentially be in instantaneous communication with the entire universe. It may even be going continually back and forth between this and other universes in eleven different dimensions. Any model of reality that far-out gives tremendous opportunities for fun and games.

A void conceived of as female is the place where all may be resolved, truth revealed, and the aspirant reunited with their Holy Guardian Angel. The differing experiences of that Angel, below and above the Abyss, are determined by the governing principles in those varying realms presided over by the twin forms of Horus as manifester and absorber. It's not as if manifestation now ceases and life becomes static and withdrawn. There has now been an alchemical transmutation of the relationship between the realm of potential and the form of its manifestation.

A more energised return into the worldly realms is entirely necessary for the formula of this age is, after all, "*Do* what thou wilt". This becomes like breathing in and out. In every moment what one does as an act of Will is arising out of a formless mystery which is its source and sustainer but now that process is conscious and ones centre of gravity has become permanently mutated to abide in it.

APPENDIX A:

NOTES TOWARDS A MODERN HISTORY OF THE STELE OF REVEALING

THE FUNERARY STELE of the Egyptian priest Ankh af na Khonsu is of central importance in the transmission of Aleister Crowley's *Book of the Law*. Having come into its physical proximity for the first time during the writing of this book, I found myself recalling what I know of its modern history and appreciating how many uncertainties surround it.

The first mystery concerns the fact that Crowley, a noted traveller, doesn't seem to have ever returned to the scene of the fundamental revelation of his life. There is actually a passage in *The Book of the Law* that seems to indicate he was required to '*abstruct*' it, which is suggestive of actually physically obtaining it, in other words stealing the stele. Thelemic folklore suggests he may have swapped the original for a copy back in 1904 but this has to be considered extremely doubtful. The stealing and black market dealing of Egyptian antiquities was certainly rife at that time. The greatest of all archaeologists, Howard Carter and his patron Lord Caernarvon, appear to have extracted a huge number of items from the tomb of Tutankhamun for their personal purposes. This occurred before the official opening of the tomb however. The Stele was already in a museum. I simply don't believe Crowley could possibly have stolen it and then smuggled it out of the country. There is a brief mention of the abstruction instruction again during the twenties but it seems a passing thought even though the Beast did find himself comparatively nearby in North Africa during that decade.

I am not aware of any accounts of Thelemites travelling to Egypt and checking out the stele during Crowley's lifetime. In fact the stele seems to disappear off the radar. Its original home in the Boulak Museum closed and it was transferred to its current location.

My knowledge of the modern history of the stele begins in 1979.

The extraordinary American visionary Robert Coon, a direct descendent of Mormon founder Joseph Smith, was engaged in a massive sequence of astrologically determined global magickal events that he had received the inspiration for beginning in the sixties. An extensive account of his total work is featured in my *Avalonian Aeon*. Sufficient to say here that Crowley, Egypt, and Glastonbury played a major role in his bigger picture.

Working with a profound belief in the possibility of physical immortality and that a planetary throat chakra is focused in Cairo, Robert Coon's mission was to ensure that, '*the archetypal thought of Physical Immortality, the Key Word of the Aquarian Aeon, was energized within the collective consciousness of humanity.*' Timing was of vital importance in this grand plan and two major magickal acts would be involved.

Coon believed that it was vital for him to be in Cairo at the time of the 1979 Autumn Equinox. This was partly inspired by studying strange prophecies derived from the dimensions of the Great Pyramid, in particular by Adam Rutherford, who although meticulous in his adherence to genuine measurements could readily be described as a Bible nut and fellow traveller of the likes of Jehovah's Witness founder Charles Taze Russell who had earlier used the pyramid to support an extreme evangelical prophesying. Basically, the epoch of the Second Coming of Christ would begin in 1979 ushering in a millennium lasting until 2979. This material has very specific locations within the pyramid linked to it. The entrance to the Queen' Chamber marked the 1979 moment.

Coon believed that a new era was set to unfold and it would involve a shift in consciousness which Coon linked with his major concern, Immortalism. He informed Rutherford's group that he intended to actually be inside the pyramid in the Queens Chamber at the exact moment of the prophecies' fulfilment. They had a bit of a fire and brimstone attitude to what was upcoming. The response was one of fear with a definite warning to stay away. There's a strange flavor here. Crowley himself, as is well-known, was born into the intense fundamentalist Plymouth Brethren sect. His father was a lay preacher within the group. From there he learnt the Bible in depth and had his lifelong nickname of the Beast bestowed upon him by his fanatical mother. The oppressive life-negating misery of his Christian childhood was a huge factor in his subsequent development. There is something about the Old Testament and, to a certain extent, *Revelation,* that permeates *The Book of the Law.*

Regardless of the belief that its ultimate source was a non-human intelligence and that it announces an end to the Christian era one can at least say that it somehow required a scribe thoroughly imbued with a mentality steeped in the Bible.

In 1979 a man descended from the founder of Mormonism and who himself had experienced visitations from non-human entities and advocated the possibility of physical immortality tuned into a prophecy from the realm of pyramidology, a genre full of Christian millennialism of various kinds that had been endorsed by the founder of the Jehovah's Witnesses whose famous slogan was "Millions Now Living May Never Die". Coon's presentation of the topic of Immortalism is infinitely more sophisticated and interesting than the JWs (he finds many Immortalist motifs in *The Book of the Law*) but the thematic continuity is there. It's an amusing oddity to remember that the first date put forward by the JWs for the end of the world was 2nd October 1914, the very day that Thelemic superstar Jack Parsons was born.

Following on from the prophetic moment in the pyramid Robert Coon would then immediately set out to rediscover and *'realign'* the Stele of Revealing and recite an appropriate invocation in its vicinity. On 24th September 1979 this was accomplished with Coon invoking assorted deities and angels in front of the Stele. The culmination was a spontaneous outpouring which included the words:

> *'May the total frequencies,*
> *May the full force,*
> *May the unique True Will*
> *Of the Stele of Revealing*
> *Be directed upon this first day of the Millennium*
> *Unto the Total Purification*
> *Of every Heart – individual and planetary –*
> *And unto the Complete Manifestation*
> *Of the Revelation of Everlasting Life!'*

The 1979 events were considered to be a vital part of a process leading supposedly to the activation of a Global Omega Point from Glastonbury Tor at the moment of Easter Sunday sunrise in April 1984 and to further ramifications in 1987. Back in the sixties Coon had highlighted dates in the Meso-American calendar system that would later be widely publicised by Jose Arguelles and achieve lasting fame as the Harmonic Convergence. Coon, who had very much his own take on the proceedings, was closely involved in the Glastonbury side of the event.

For a number of years Coon kept fairly quiet about the full details of his 1979 adventure with the Stele. There were broad mentions in some of his books such as *Voyage to Avalon*. In 1997 he decided it was time to tell the whole story for the first time publicly in Glastonbury in an event timed to coincide with the perihelion of Comet Hale-Bopp. Comets had been important in Coon's long-term work and he noted that Crowley's death in 1947 had been within 24 hours of the perihelion of another great comet.

Avalon and the AA was presented by Robert Coon on 1st April 1997. The comet attained perihelion at 4.13am BST that day. A small booklet entitled *The Cairo Working* was printed in a very limited edition of eleven copies to accompany it.

The single most important element of the evening was the magickal affirmation of the new museum exhibit number of the Stele. Its original 666 designation was a major part of the story of how Crowley was drawn towards the reception of *The Book of the Law*. 9422 doesn't seem anywhere near as promising. Coon believed that in fact Gematria higher intelligence was definitely on the case. '*Immediately after the consecration of the Stele*' he was inspired to write down a sequence of twelve numbers incorporating two of Crowley's favourites 666 and 777. Thus:

777666666777

This was followed by a sequence of multiplication and addition symbols.

.+.+.+.

This led to

$7.7 + 7.666 + 666.7 + 7.7 = 9422$

I can understand why this would blow Robert Coon's mind in 1979 and leave him feeling like he was definitely on a winner. I am not making any big claims about it but it is rather interesting and deserves to be better known. There was more 9422 numerical material presented in *The Cairo Working* but that is Coon's story to tell. The pamphlet does periodically surface online and is worth keeping an eye out for.

Crowley commissioned a copy of both sides of the Stele of Revealing. Images of this reproduction are what feature in any books displaying it right up into the nineties. A centenary OTO edition of *The Book of the Law* published in 2004 actually contained a photographic reproduction, permission having been granted by Cairo Museum. Following Robert Coon's perihelion presentation in April 1997 I gave the information concerning its whereabouts to Andrew Collins who I knew was shortly to be travelling to Egypt himself. He had already asked me to give a presentation on Crowley's role in Psychic Questing for a conference in the autumn. This was the 93rd year of the Thelemic era and therefore a good time to affirm such things. I recognised an interesting opportunity and asked him to try and photograph it with a view to publicly showing it later on in the year. Since those days it has become impossible to take photos in the Cairo Museum on pain of expulsion and possible arrest. I did indeed feature a slide of the Stele in my Questing Conference presentation. I think this might have been only the second time an actual photograph rather than copy painting of the Stele had ever been publicly displayed. I could be wrong. I welcome any further information on this subject. It was certainly done as a very deliberate year 93 magickal act further sending out the Glastonbury ripples from Robert Coon's perihelion event.

Andrew Collins passed on the information about the Stele's location to researcher Simon Cox. This in turn led to a photo appearing in the 1999 *Stargate Conspiracy* of Lynn Picknett and Clive Prince. I believe that this may be the first time a photo of the Stele appeared in a book. Again, I may be wrong and welcome further information on the subject.

It does seem strange to me that there are so many gaps in the details surrounding this supremely evocative artefact and I rather feel it would be useful for a fuller modern history to be compiled so it's in that spirit that I have put together this piece as I believe it presents some interesting Thelemic information that deserves to be more fully in the public domain.

APPENDIX B:

L. RON HUBBARD AND THE BABALON WORKING

SCIENTOLOGY ACCOUNTS of L. Ron Hubbard's life leave blank the incredible period from 1945-6 when he was involved with Jack Parsons and the legendary magical Babalon Working. An extensive account of this episode has already been given but LRH's role is so contentious and mysterious it is worth considering separately. I believe I have brought together data that has not been thus arranged before and that it does at least a little to unravel some of the calumny surrounding LRH in this context and suggest that he might be a bit more interesting than his denigrators would contend.

With each passing decade Jack Parsons becomes increasingly well known. He may now be a candidate for the title of coolest man of the twentieth century, being referred to by Richard Metzger as the *'James Dean of the occult'*. Whatever one might feel about the nature of the spiritual forces he invoked, a quick perusal of his writings soon reveals a powerful and passionate advocate for freedom. He was obviously a quite incredible man.

The general feeling of Hubbard's role has scarcely developed at all. Occultist lovers of Parsons see Ron as a scoundrel who laid Jack low by cheating him out of a large sum of money and running off with his former partner. We will see how when confronted with the story of the Babalon Working the Church of Scientology portrayed LRH as a man on a covert Intelligence mission to infiltrate and undermine the Parsons scene.

With Peter Moon's Montauk books the possibility of a wider perspective began to present itself. As we have seen, Moon was able to offer unique insights through having known both L. Ron Hubbard and Marjorie Cameron. She recalled how the two men had been like brothers and she herself was not hostile to Ron. She even added a detail missing from other accounts that Hubbard had actually contacted Parsons again, years after their tumultuous parting, when *Dianetics* had just appeared. He invited Jack to invest in it! This might be seen as colossal nerve on his part but it hints at a bigger picture of their interaction.

Is it possible to create a narrative that in some way allows the different versions to all be essentially true? Beyond Moon's beginnings I'm not aware that anyone has ever really tried to do so. This is a tentative speculative attempt that may well be an imaginative fiction. I'm not asking anyone to necessarily endorse it. I would hope it might be found interesting and show that when approached in the right spirit this compelling topic still has some open doors.

On October 5th 1969 the London *Times* published a lengthy article going into considerable detail on L. Ron Hubbard's involvement in the Babalon Working. This information had never been disseminated before and was known only to a few occultists. Given that Scientology was a topic of some controversy at the time it was quite a story. Before long the Church responded with a threat of litigation unless the story was withdrawn. The paper eventually agreed to print a statement from Scientology in December which was written by Hubbard himself. All subsequent enquiries to the church concerning the Parsons period in LRH's life are simply referred back to the original statement.

> *'Hubbard broke up black magic in America: Dr Jack Parsons of Pasadena, California, was America's Number One solid fuel rocket expert. He was involved with the infamous English black magician Aleister Crowley who called himself "The Beast 666." Crowley ran an organization called the Order of Templars Orientalis over the world which had savage and bestial rites. Dr Parsons was head of the American branch located at 100 Orange Grove Avenue, Pasadena, California. This was a huge old house which had paying guests who were the USA nuclear physicists working at Cal Tech. Certain agencies objected to nuclear physicists being housed under the same roof.*
>
> *L. Ron Hubbard was still an officer of the US Navy because he was well known as a writer and philosopher and had friends among the physicists, he was sent in to handle the situation. He went to live at the house and investigated the black magic rites and the general situation and found them very bad.*
>
> *Parsons wrote to Crowley in England about Hubbard. Crowley "the Beast 666" evidently detected an enemy and warned Parsons. This was proven by the correspondence unearthed by the Sunday*

Times. Hubbard's mission was successful far beyond anyone's expectations. The house was torn down. Hubbard rescued a girl they were using. The black magic group was dispersed and destroyed and never recovered. The physicists included many of the sixty-four top US scientists who were later declared insecure and dismissed from government service with so much publicity.'

To begin with, it is important to set the statement in the wider context of the time period it appeared in. Hubbard and his church were already receiving a lot of flack and had black propaganda being flung at them. A year before, in 1968, LRH had commissioned an investigation to try and figure out where it was coming from and decided that a global cabal of big-pharma psychiatrists were heavily involved.

Less than one week after the *Times* article, on Crowley's birthday October 12th for those appreciative of such detail, Charles Manson was arrested. It wasn't long before he became the biggest story in America and all aspects of his past were being investigated. Perhaps the biggest issue was how he was able to "program" his followers? Where might he have learnt mind control techniques? It soon surfaced that he had received fairly extensive Dianetic auditing in prison and used a lot of Scientology terminology. It appeared that he did check out the organisation on his release. One of his followers took a somewhat mysterious journey to England and some unexplained deaths and unsolved murders cluster around it.

Scientology distanced itself from the Manson connection. They weren't exactly the only ones. Charlie had spent a lot of time at the prestigious Esalen Institute, a place where some of the biggest names in the Human Potential movement put on events. Manson was there very shortly before the Tate murders but people weren't exactly queuing up to talk about it. The Hollywood set that Charlie and his girls provided a rent-a-drug-orgy service to went a bit quiet too. Of course they did. I consider it to be perfectly straightforward that Scientology would want to play down any Manson connection. His major warp-outs derived from other sources, primarily his own head.

Nonetheless there is material circulating on the internet that states that Charles Manson was a Scientologist in a manner virtually suggesting he was a fully paid up member and that somehow LRH was responsible for his crimes or variants thereof. This is entirely untrue and unreasonable. In fact those that know the

Manson story in greater detail will be aware that in the last crazy days of Helter Skelter one man named Paul Crockett persistently stood his ground against Charlie and even helped some of his followers break free from him by effectively de-programming them. He was able to do this because of a strong background in Scientology.

The OTO weren't looking too good then either. Jean Brayton's Solar Lodge achieved notoriety through the decidedly unpleasant episode, mentioned earlier in the *Strange Days* section, of the child chained in a box in the desert. The subsequent trial was widely reported at the end of October 1969. The actions of one lodge were not representative of the organization worldwide but try telling that to the media. The *Times* article showing some kind of Hubbard involvement with an OTO linked scenario appeared just a few weeks before the Boy in the Box trial was reported. It is again understandable that a damage-limitation exercise would be deemed necessary. The *'savage and bestial rites'* may be reflective of that peculiar situation.

The kind of cultic milieu that Manson arose from and was later so well portrayed by Ed Sanders in *The Family* seemed to be very interdependent. One part of the equation was the Process Church which had undoubtedly been founded by two former Scientologists even though the end result was a long way away from its source.

As for Crowley, after his *Sgt Pepper* appearance, 1969 was the year that he really began to re-emerge with the reissue of the *Confessions*. We have seen that the legend of infamy hasn't gone away and isn't likely to. In many minds Crowley equals black magic equals evil. Is it that much of a surprise that at the end of '69, an OTO Crowley Manson association was the kind of thing Scientology could do without? The Crowley connection is there though. It does rather seem that the interest continued after Hubbard's break with Jack Parsons and this will be investigated shortly.

Beyond that, what about the basic story that LRH was sent in as part of an Intelligence operation to infiltrate the Parsonage? It makes sense that considering the circles Parsons moved in he would be thought of as a potential huge security risk. Hubbard, who, regardless of controversies around his biography, definitely did have a military background, would have been absolutely the perfect person to send in on such a mission. It's also fairly obvious that the chances of finding corroborating information in any government documents are virtually zero. If such a mission ever existed no paper trail would ever lead to it.

One of the biggest realms of contention in Hubbard's biography concerns his military career during the Second World War. Dedicated Ron haters have spent considerable time going through an enormous number of Scientology publications comparing details given of that period of time. There are undoubtedly inconsistencies. Ron spoke of medals and wounds and some interesting exploits. Russell Miller in *Bare Faced Messiah* attacked these stories armed with other documents that paint a picture of Ron as incompetent or problematical and leave the impression he was an out and out liar.

In today's conspiratorial climate it's rather interesting to find someone who has published extensively on CIA black-ops, the Kennedy assassination, and a whole other bunch of controversial topics coming out with a startling extended defence of Ron and his military career. The man in question was no stranger to controversy himself and has been harangued as an unreliable fantasist but the fact that his take on LRH even exists is notable.

Fletcher Prouty may be best known for being an advisor on Oliver Stone's *JFK* movie. The character designated only as X played by Donald Sutherland was based on him. The man does seem to have had a most intriguing military career. After joining up in 1941, within a month of LRH, he had a distinguished war in the air force and worked in the mid-fifties from US Air Force HQ for a decade creating a system of "Military Support of the Clandestine Operations of the CIA". He moved in the highest circles and retired with quite a collection of medals. His knowledge and experience led to his authoring of a number of contentious works, primarily *The Secret Team: The CIA and Its Allies in Control of the United States and the World*, and *JFK: The CIA, Vietnam and the Plot to Assassinate John F. Kennedy*. Prouty spoke of a global elite behind international events and believed that the CIA manipulated the notorious Jonestown cult mass suicide/murder.

Considering LRH and Scientology are so often on the receiving end of paranoid conspiracism it's rather intriguing that Prouty spoke out at length in their defense. Although never a member, he was hired out by the Church to investigate and hit back at what they considered to be black propaganda against themselves and in particular their founder.

When *Bare Faced Messiah* was published Prouty wrote a long letter to the publisher protesting in the strongest terms about the general tone of the work and what he took to be its selective abuse through omission and distortion of source material. This letter is readily available on a number of internet sites. Inevitably it has in turn likewise been denigrated but its contents are rather intriguing and provide the source for some of Peter Moon's material on Ron in the Montauk books.

Prouty seizes on Russell Miller's playing down of what he considers to be crucial data, mentioning only in passing that in 1941 Hubbard was posted for training as an Intelligence Officer. This is the information that changes ones awareness of all the rest. He further runs through Miller's data highlighting areas that show to someone with Prouty's background that,

> *'Almost all of Hubbard's military record is replete with markings that signify deep intelligence service at the highest levels. Many of his records, copies of official records, revealed that even the originals had been fabricated in the manner peculiar to the intelligence community in a process that we call "Sheep Dip". I myself have supervised a lot of that function in the offices I managed during 1955-1964.*
>
> *"Sheep Dip" is a process that provides, customarily, three files. One is the true civilian record of the agent. One is his agency or military true record. The third is his "cover" personality and all that it takes to support it.*
>
> *Thus when one researches these files, in a routine manner, he may get copies from any one of three... or of various kindred files that are maintained for special reasons. Some of Hubbard's records are kept in from 8 to 18 files as is clearly noted in codes on the records.'*

Prouty also noted that a Washington Congressman named Magnuson had written to President Roosevelt urging him to personally ensure Hubbard's request for active duty was processed quickly, a procedure that was *'most unusual'*.

> *'Miller failed to note that Hubbard's first Active Duty Orders were signed by none other than Chester Nimitz, later the famous five-star Admiral and hero of Pacific campaigns. A small code number on those same orders identifies Hubbard as being placed on duty with Naval Intelligence'.*

Miller mentioned in passing that Hubbard went *'on a four-month course in 'Military Government' at the Naval Training School, Princeton,'* and was later *'transferred to the Naval Civil Affairs Staging Area in Monterey, California for further training'*. Prouty asserts that these were important high grade establishments.

'Unlike MI-5's Peter Wright, Ron Hubbard was of the old school. He never revealed important intelligence sources and methods.' The inconsistent tales of where he was and when and what he was doing were partly to fulfil old obligations. He nonetheless felt it acceptable to let it be known he had a somewhat colourful war.

Prouty also stated that Ron was very familiar with the dark mind control direction that the newly formed Nazi infiltrated CIA was taking that would lead to MKULTRA. A lot of the source material they would abuse is there in the background of his own research prior to *Dianetics*. In this version of events he chose to break ranks and use the ideas for good. Of course there are plenty of people who would never endorse this idea but it needs to be stated for the sake of balance and the possibility that it might actually be true.

The official Church statement on breaking up black magic in America might just be Ron being ironic about some of the original intentions of his mission as he was given it. In 1969 it was obviously not true in any literal sense.

LRH has been portrayed as virtually a dribbling deranged nutcase. I've already noted that he started taking flack from the Feds round about the same time as Wilhelm Reich and for broadly similar reasons. The difference is that he handled it and not only survived but thrived. Indeed, over a period of decades when various governments and intelligence agencies were on his case, he managed to create his own departments within Scientology to deal with such hassle. This side of the church has always been controversial and likely to attract bad publicity but it has held its own, fought fire with fire, and generally played the spooks at their own game. The name of the game was set out by LRH in minute detail. Quite clearly it was a subject he knew about. He was in fact bloody good at it. No other self-help guru, mystic or occultist in history comes anywhere near it. Pathological dysfunctionals won't last very long in such scenarios. Hubbard was together enough to play it whilst formulating all of the Operating Thetan material for which Scientology is now so well-known and misunderstood for: Xenu etc.

Some might look askance at a spiritual movement that involved such activities. The same people might be captivated by the legend of the Knights Templar, a fabulously wealthy organisation that protected and served its esoteric interests through money, espionage, and warfare. The devil-worship accusations thrown against them tend to be seen as vulgar and stupid. Those guys are generally considered to be pretty cool. Reich died in prison. Gnostics and heretics down through the ages have been massacred for want of the knowledge of how to survive and protect themselves. It is perhaps useful to look at Scientology activity in that light.

I don't think it is at all unlikely that Hubbard could have been working on some kind of covert mission when he got to know Jack Parsons. That brings us to the next problem. It is clear that LRH was a full-on participant in the proceedings. In fact his visionary material considerably shaped the details of the magick rites. There must have been something occurring in the scenario that served his own mystical process. Most accounts are hampered by a predisposition on the part of the writer to view Ron with hostility. This is often coupled with a tabloid mentality towards Crowley. Such a combination is unlikely to produce any new insights even when the source material has been used.

A good example is *Bare-Faced Messiah*. The author detests his subject and goes out of his way to portray Ron as liar, madman, etc. There's a whole chapter dealing with the Babalon Working. Firstly, Crowley is referred to as a *'sorcerer and Satanist'*. Jack Parsons was *'worshipping the Devil'*. His home had become the *'headquarters of a black magic group which practised deviant sexual rites'*. It's clear that Russell Miller hadn't got much of a handle on the western mystery tradition. To describe the OTO Gnostic Mass regularly performed at the Parsonage as a deviant sexual rite is to allow one's critical faculties to descend to the level of a fundamentalist Christian. There are written accounts from other residents who likewise had no real understanding of Thelema and Parsons' passionate libertarian mysticism and simply thought in terms of "people in robes chanting equals black magic". Miller is happy to set his scene with such material. Add to that a number of skewed facts concerning Parsons its clear that the mystery of Hubbard's involvement will not be solved through Miller.

A pivotal event in Hubbard's life that may shed some light on his participation in the Babalon Working was recalled on various occasions by his onetime literary agent and major sci-fi aficionado,

Forrest Ackerman. Interviewed by Russell Miller he spoke of an occasion in 1947 when Ron told him how he had died on an operating theatre during the war and

> 'rose in spirit form, and looked back on the body that he had formerly inhabited. Over yonder he saw a fantastic great gate, elaborately carved like something you'd see in Bagdhad or ancient China. As he wafted towards it, the gate opened and just beyond he could see a kind of intellectual smorgasbord on which was outlined everything that had ever puzzled the mind of man. All the questions that had concerned philosophers through the ages - When did the world begin? Was there a God? Whither goest we? - were there answered. All this information came flooding into him and while he was absorbing it, there was a kind of flustering in the air and he felt something like a long umbilical cord pulling him back. He was saying "No, no, not yet!", but he was pulled back anyway. After the gates had closed he realised he had re-entered his body.'

After establishing with a worried nurse that he had effectively died Ron jumped up from the operating theatre and dashed home to get ' *two reams of paper and a gallon of scalding black coffee*' and within two days produced a manuscript he was calling *Excalibur* or the *Dark Sword*. This legendary work is the cornerstone of the official Hubbard biographies. It is said to contain the very foundations of everything that came afterwards. It is a legend because it was never published. Ron liked to tell how those he showed it to were immediately overwhelmed, with suicides and madness resulting.

Ackerman has a date and context for this episode that is at variance with the usual timeline. A modest preface from *Excalibur* has been published and bears a date of New Years Day 1938. The near-death experience happened under the influence of gas anaesthetic at Dr Elbert E. Cone's dental office in Bremerton, Washington. There is no mention of the gate and the great download of knowledge but in this version Ron returned agitated with the feeling of still being in contact with something that if he could remember would give him the secret of life. This state endured for days until one morning he awoke with enough recall to start on the great manuscript. We shall return to the gate and Babalon after noting another tale from Ron's early days.

The young Hubbard was a daredevil glider pilot. Nobody doubts this. He told a rather interesting story in the thirties to fellow writer

Arthur J. Burks. On occasions when he ran into trouble a red-haired smiling woman would appear on a wing and all would be well. Burks speculated on her as a possible guardian angel. Hubbard would name this being the Empress by the time he met Jack Parsons who mentioned in a letter to Crowley that he believed Ron to possibly be in contact with a higher intelligence of some kind that may have been his guardian angel. There is an incredibly evocative fragment concerning the early days of Dianetics when he was asked by an associate how he had managed to write the work so quickly and he hinted that it was in certain respects a kind of automatic writing dictated by the Empress.

In *The Montauk Book of the Dead* Peter Moon discusses the LRH 1938 "Gate" experience and notes how Babalon is taken to mean gate and therefore the two things hang together. I believe the links can be established in some detail through the Qabalistic framework of Crowley and Parsons' magick.

The Qabalistic Tree of Life is depicted with three vertical columns linked by twenty two paths. The middle pillar is taller, connecting upwards to the point of white light (known as Kether) whence the formless breaks through into the realms where it will become form. The tops of the left and right hand pillars are joined by a path that passes between them beneath the level of Kether. This path lies just above the veil of the Abyss which we have given so much attention to.

The Abyss contains the controversial zone named Daath where Crowley encountered Choronzon. It is known as Knowledge. Spheres called Understanding and Wisdom top the left and right hand pillars.

The assorted paths have attributions with the tarot trumps and Hebrew letters which are ideograms, meaning they are taken to broadly resemble artefacts in the world such as a hook, house, or camel. The letter associated with the path just above the Abyss that runs between the two pillars is *Daleth*. It means *door*. In the Golden Dawn/Crowley tradition, its tarot card is the Empress with a planetary association of Venus.

Whether or not he knew this before entering the Parsonage, LRH would more than likely have become aware of this magical data during the initial brainstorming before the Babalon Working. It doesn't seem unlikely that he might have recalled his experience with the great gate and his ongoing connection with the Empress and found a lot of things starting to make sense. Babalon, residing across the Abyss, primarily in the sphere of Binah partook of many of the qualities of Hubbard's red-haired Empress.

It would be easy enough to interpret the near-death experience in magical Qabalistic terms. LRH was briefly catapulted across the Abyss to the Daleth doorway where Knowledge, Understanding, and Wisdom were downloaded. The Daath side of it is covered by the fact that he had to virtually die to get there and faced the struggle of bringing back what he had found. Being a writer already who was famous for his prodigious fast output was a major bonus here. The experience fits the framework very well and the level of energy, power, and influence he went on to wield were entirely uncommon.

So Hubbard may have gone in to undermine the situation but would soon have experienced a conflict of interest. The forces invoked were extremely powerful. We have noted the resonance with the saga of Dee and Kelly. Ron took action that did indeed detonate the scene when he went off with a large sum of Parsons' money and his former partner, the girl 'rescued' in the 1969 statement.

There are indications that Hubbard's interest in a Crowley-flavoured magick continued. This means that the official Scientology line only covers some of the story. It does not address whether LRH actually found any interesting lines of enquiry when he came into contact with Crowley's work and is therefore incomplete but also worded in such a way that it cannot be said to be untrue.

A controversial court case in 1984, the details of which do not concern us here, made visible some documentation relating to the period after the Babalon Working. The details were covered in the anti-scientology work *A Piece of Blue Sky* by Jon Atack. Similar problems are faced to dealing with Russell Miller's Babalon chapter.

The waters have also been considerably muddied by the fact that L. Ron Hubbard Jr., generally known by his childhood nickname "Nibs", spectacularly fell out with his father and has sounded forth for decades, most notably with a *Penthouse* interview in June 1983, with the most outlandish accounts imaginable of his experience of dad as a drug crazed, woman beating, baby aborting, megalomaniac, sexual tyrannosaurus, black magician. Those temperamentally predisposed to be Ron haters have completely accepted this material and rehash it uncritically. *Blue Sky* is no exception.

In *Penthouse* Nibs told how when Crowley died dad

'decided that he should wear the cloak of the Beast and become the most powerful being in the universe.' 'I believed in Satanism. There was no other religion in the house! Scientology and black magic.

What a lot of people don't realize is that Scientology is black magic that is just spread out over a long time period. To perform black magic generally takes a few hours or, at most, a few weeks. But in Scientology it's stretched out over a lifetime, and so you don't see it. Black magic is the inner core of Scientology – and it is probably the only part of Scientology that really works. Also, you've got to realize that my father did not worship Satan. He thought he was Satan. He was one with Satan. He had a direct pipeline of communication and power with him. My father wouldn't have worshiped anything. I mean, when you think you're the most powerful being in the universe, you have no respect for anything, let alone worship.'

'Hitler was involved in the same black magic and the same occult practices that my father was. The identical ones. Which, as I have said, stem clear back to before Egyptian times. It's a very secret thing. Very powerful and very workable and very dangerous. Brain-washing is nothing compared to it. The proper term would be "soul cracking." It's like cracking open the soul, which then opens various doors to the power that exists, the satanic and demonic powers.'

In a 1984 taped interview Nibs went on to say that *'the same individual that transmitted the various Magick tech to Adolf Hitler as a young man also transmitted them to Dad. And like Dad, Hitler, when he came to power, promptly had his teachers and the occult field in general wiped out'*. This is classic material that will run forever in cyberspace getting more and more distorted as dark forces paranoid types with progressively less knowledge make use of it.

The Empress called in the Archangel Michael in guardian capacity at one point in the Babalon Working. Bearing in mind his role in the *Revelation* War in Heaven as God's bouncer when it comes to rebel angels it seems a tad odd that the supposed Satan worshipping badass portrayed by Ron Jr. would want his help.

An extensive Hubbard magical diary full of "affirmations" came to light and had brief quotations aired in the court case referred to in *Blue Sky* where it is stated that *'Hubbard hypnotized himself to believe that all of humanity and all discarnate beings were bound to him in slavery.'* This detail has been pumped-up to giant proportions in the Ron as black magician mythology.

The fabled document is not available for inspection but I am inclined to feel it may be part of an experiment by Ron to follow or create his own version of Crowley's Holy Guardian Angel ritual

Liber Samekh, presented in *Magick* as the distillation of his experience with the Abramelin procedure. The ritual is intended to be performed daily by anyone engaging in a serious HGA intensive. The four elements and Spirit are invoked with visualisations that we have already noted with Jung. At the end of each section this "affirmation" is recited:

> *'Hear me, and make all Spirits subject unto Me; so that every Spirit of the Firmament and of the Ether: upon the Earth and under the Earth, on dry land and in the water; of Whirling Air, and of rushing Fire, and every Spell and Scourge of God may be obedient unto Me.'*

It may appear a tad full-on to a tabloid mentality but it's really about profound balance as much as power and the one can't happen without the other. It's not proof of a Ming the Merciless mentality.

Another document that got a brief court airing was described by LRH himself as "The Blood Ritual". Those with their minds conditioned by Dennis Wheatley novels, horror movies, and Fundamentalist Christian fulminations will start twitching at the mere sight of the words. Only a few details were revealed. Ron and his "rescued" woman mingled some of their blood together to become one in the context of an invocation to Hathor, an Egyptian goddess of love quite similar to Isis. Nibs mentioned that dad also knew his Empress as Hathor. Maybe we can actually go along with him there. *Blue Sky* manages to find a way to make this seem like more malevolent sorcery.

Hathor was an Egyptian goddess of Love and Beauty whose myth cycle links her with lion-headed Sekhmet who on one occasion, which started as a mission of justice, went on a destructive blood-drinking rampage that threatened to destroy the human race. We have here a definite sense of Babalon and that ancient unity of the divine feminine that was fragmented by Christianity whereby seemingly contradictory aspects can exist together.

Jon Atack focuses on Sekhmet as *"destroyer of man"* and produces an interpretation of the Blood Ritual that is surely transparent in its desperate desire to paint as black a picture as possible. *'To Crowley, Babalon was a manifestation of the Hindu goddess Shakti, who in one of her aspects is also called the 'destroyer of man'. It seems that to Hubbard, Babalon, Hathor, and the Empress were synonymous, and he* was trying to conjure his 'Guardian Angel' in the form of a servile homunculus so he could control the "destroyer of man".' "Guardian Angel" and "servile homunculus" don't really blend together that easily. They are somewhat disparate concepts. Homunculus relates back to the moonchild idea in the Babalon Working whereby a conception is manipulated to embody a non-human force. And there's no indication that Hathor was intended to bring forth Sekhmet. If that was what he wanted then Hubbard would have mentioned her by name. A group of other deities including Nuit, Re, and Osiris got a mention as well but no Sekhmet. Perhaps the best clue comes from the inclusion of Mammon in the forces invoked. This is a Biblical concept for extravagant wealth, sometimes considered to be a demon by those who needed to control people through selective poverty consciousness. In modern terms it sounds like Ron was using the Secret to put in a cosmic order for mega-bucks. He's not alone in such activities. If you want to bring abundance and money into your life you don't stir up the destroyer of man!

In his epic 1952 *Philadelphia Doctorate Course* lectures, one of the most important foundations of Scientology, Ron did have a few things to say about Crowley.

'*The magic cults of the 8th, 9th, 10th, 11th, 12th centuries in the Middle East were fascinating. The only work that has anything to do with them is a trifle wild in spots, but it's fascinating work... written by Aleister Crowley, the late Aleister Crowley, my very good friend... It's very interesting reading to get hold of a copy of a book, quite rare, but it can be obtained, The Master Therion... by Aleister Crowley.*" And also, "*One fellow, Aleister Crowley, picked up a level of religious worship which is very interesting - oh boy! The Press played hockey with his head for his whole life-time. The Great Beast - 666. He just had another level of religious worship. Yes, sir, you're free to worship everything under the Constitution so long as it's Christian.*'

The *"good friend"* designation is certainly interesting as the two never met. The book referred to as The *Master Therion* is *Magick*, where *Liber Samekh* can be found.

Whilst it was only moderately controversial and potentially problematical to mention Crowley in 1952, by 1969 things had got a lot worse and this was before Nibs got involved. The *Philadelphia Doctorate* Crowley quotes, taken from original recordings, can be found all over the internet in video exposes by Christians, cult bashers and suchlike in the usual manner. In the Nibs mythology dad was going home every night during the lecture series and reading *Magick* to get ideas for the next day.

There are always going to be people who warp-out on Crowley and Hubbard. Put the two together and there is very little chance of any rational discussion. We can begin to see why the 1969 statement was made and why it has remained as essentially the only Scientology statement on the subject. It really wouldn't matter what else they might ever say, occult gossip will have its way.

Just supposing Hubbard had come out and admitted to a big interest in Crowley and significant experimentation with his work on the basis of the Beast's remarkable knowledge and experience of the world's magical and mystical traditions and how nobody interested in such topics could afford to ignore him, that checking him out constituted an essential part of a general education in the mysteries of consciousness. Would the results have been any more inspiring? Of course not. The same level of negativity would still circulate.

A lot of comparisons between Scientology material and bits of Crowley and the Golden Dawn have been made with the implication being that this reveals the secret core of the Church. I'm not going to examine that here. It's possible to find all kinds of other big influences as well such as Freud and Korzybski. Hubbard was always looking for what worked and he wouldn't necessarily keep it in its original context.

A student of comparative religion could probably place Scientology in with the Gnostic revival. There are many common themes. We are immortal beings trapped in a prison world by a lapse in our awareness often caused by external agencies whose purpose is served by keeping us that way. It is possible to awaken, become free, and regain the full power of our divine potential. In this Ron possibly absorbed some Thelemic Gnostic nuances via Parsons but was maybe also affected by what Jung experienced with Abraxas and what Philip K. Dick experienced as the Nag Hammadi plasmate generally in the airwaves. Nonetheless, coming to birth in the UFO Cold War fifties, his creation was unique.

THE STELE OF REVEALING.
Photo by Andrew Collins.

APPENDIX B: L. RON HUBBARD & THE BABALON WORKING

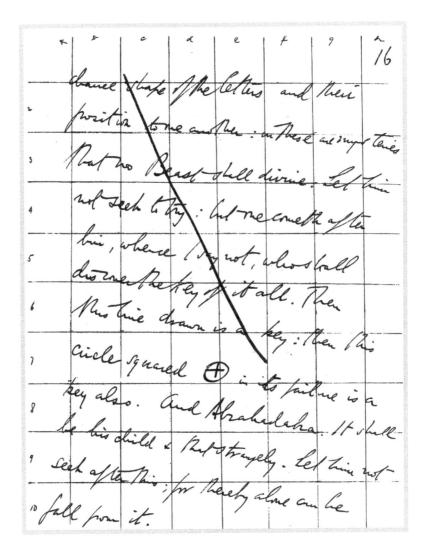

THE ENIGMATIC GRID PAGE IN
THE THIRD CHAPTER OF THE BOOK OF THE LAW.

'Then this line drawn is a key.'

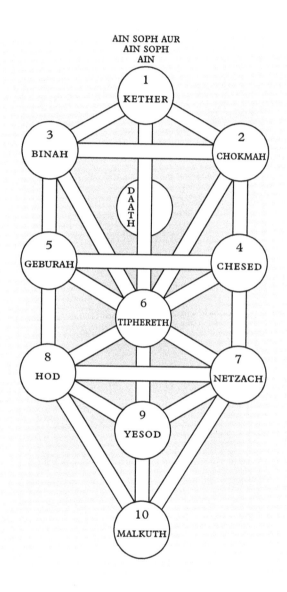

THE QABALISTIC TREE OF LIFE.

BIBLIOGRAPHY

a, *Necronomicon*, Avon, New York, 1980.
Adams, Henry, *The Education of Henry Adams*, Massachusetts Historical Society, 1918.
Anger, Kenneth, *Hollywood Babylon*, Dell Publishing, New York, 1975.
Atack, Jon, *A Piece of Blue Sky*, Carol Publishing Group, New York, 1990.
Barritt, Brian, *The Road of Excess*, PSI Publishing, UK, 1998.
Bender, Albert K, *Flying Saucers and the Three Men*, Paperback Library, USA, 1968.
Bennett, J. G., *Gurdjieff: Making a New World*, Harper & Row, UK, 1973.
Booth, Martin, *A Magick Life*, Hodder & Stoughton, London, 2000.
Bugliosi, Vincent, & Gentry, Curt, *Helter Skelter*, The Bodley Head, UK, 1975.
Carter, John, *Sex and Rockets*, Feral House, Los Angeles, 1999.
Chapman, Janine, *Quest For Dion Fortune*, Weiser, Maine, USA, 1993.
Churton, Tobias, *Aleister Crowley: the Biography*, Watkins Publishing, London, 2011.
Collins, Andrew, *The Circle Makers*, ABC Books, Essex, 1992.
Collins, Andrew, *Alien Energy*, ABC Books, 1994.
Collins, Andrew, *From the Ashes of Angels*, Michael Joseph, London, 1996.
Collins, Andrew, *Gods of Eden*, Headline, London, 1998.
Collins, Andrew, *The Cygnus Mystery*, Watkins Publishing, London, 2006.
Constable, Trevor James, *The Cosmic Pulse of Life*, Neville Spearman, UK, 1977.
Coon, Robert, *Voyage to Avalon*, Griffon Gold Publications, Somerset, 1986.
Coon, Robert, *The Cairo Working*, Glastonbury, 1997.
Crowley, Aleister, *The Book of the Law*, Red Wheel/Weiser centennial edition, USA 2004.
Crowley, Aleister, *Aha!*, New Falcon, USA, 1983.
Crowley, Aleister, & Neuberg, Victor, & Desti, Mary, *The Vision and the Voice*, Red Wheel/Weiser, USA, 1998.
Crowley, Aleister, *The Book of Lies*, Red Wheel/Weiser, USA, 1981.
Crowley, Aleister, *Magick: Liber ABA Book Four*, Red Wheel/Weiser, USA, 1998.

Crowley, Aleister, *The Book of Thoth*, Red Wheel/Weiser, USA, 1981.

Deacon, Richard, *A History of British Secret Service*, Granada, London, 1969.

Dewey, Steve, & Ries, John, *In Alien Heat*, Anomalist Books, UK, 2005.

Dick, Philip K., *VALIS*, Victor Gollancz, London, 1981.

Downes, Jonathan, *The Owlman and Others*, CFZ Press, North Devon, 2006 ed.

Drury, Neville, *Don Juan, Mescalito, and Modern Magic*, Routledge & Kegan Paul, London, 1978.

DuQuette, Lon Milo, *The Magick of Thelema*, Red Wheel/Weiser, New York, 2003.

Eliade, Mircea, *Occultism, Witchcraft, and Cultural Fashions*, University of Chicago Press, 1976.

Evans, Dave, *The History of British Magick After Crowley*, Hidden Publishing, UK, 2007.

Evans, Dave, *Aleister Crowley and the 20th Century Synthesis of Magick*, Hidden Publishing, UK, 2007.

Festiger, Leon, & Riecken, Henry W, & Schachter, Stanley, *When Prophecy Fails*, University of Minnesota Press, 1956.

Forte, Robert (Ed), *Timothy Leary: Outside Looking In*, Park St. Press, USA, 1999.

Godwin, Jocelyn, *Arktos*, Thames and Hudson, London, 1993.

Gorightly, Adam, *The Shadow Over Santa Susana*, Creation Books, USA, 2009.

Grant, Kenneth, *The Magical Revival*, Frederick Muller Ltd, London, 1972.

Grant, Kenneth, *Aleister Crowley and the Hidden God*, Frederick Muller, London, 1973.

Grant, Kenneth, *Nightside of Eden*, Frederick Muller, London, 1977.

Grant, Kenneth, *Outer Gateways*, Skoob Books Publishing, London, 1994.

Grant, Kenneth, *The Ninth Arch*, Starfire Publishing Ltd, London, 2002.

Graves, Robert, *The White Goddess*, Faber & Faber, London, 1948.

Greenfield, Allen, *Secret Cipher of the UFOnauts*, IllumiNet Press, Georgia, 1994.

Greenfield, Allen, *Secret Rituals of the Men in Black*, Lulu.com, 2005.

Guenon, Rene, *The Lord of the World*, Coombe Springs Press, North Yorkshire, 1983.

Harms, Daniel, & Gonce III, John Wisdom, *The Necronomicon Files*, Weiser Books, New York, 2003.

Hay, George, Ed., *The Necronomicon*, Skoob, London, 1992.

Higgs, John, *I Have America Surrounded*, Friday Books, London, 2006

Hoeller, Stephan A., *The Gnostic Jung and the Seven Sermons to the Dead*, Quest, Illinois, 1982.

Holiday, F. W., *The Dragon and the Disc*, Sidgwick and Jackson Ltd, UK, 1973.

Holiday, F. W., *The Goblin Universe*, Llewellyn Publications, USA, 1987.

Hyatt, Christopher, & DuQuette, Lon Milo, *The Way of the Secret Lover*, New Falcon, USA, 1991.

Jung, C. G., *Flying Saucers*, Princeton University Press, USA, 1978.

Keel, John, *Jadoo*, Julian Messner, New York, 1957.

Keel, John, *Operation Trojan Horse*, G. P. Putnam's, New York, 1970.

Keel, John, *The Mothman Prophecies*, Dutton, New York, 1975.

Kephas, Aeolus, *The Lucid View*, Adventures Unlimited Press, Illinois, 2004.

Lachman, Gary, *Turn off your Mind*, Sidgwick & Jackson, London, 2001.

Landis, Bill, *Anger*, Harper Collins Publishers Inc, New York, 1995.

Leary, Timothy, *The Politics of Ecstasy*, G. P. Putnam, USA, 1968.

Leary, Timothy, *Info-Psychology*, New Falcon, USA, 1988.

Leary, Timothy, *Neuropolitique*, New Falcon, USA, 1991.

Leary, Timothy, *Flashbacks*, J. P. Tarcher, USA, 1983.

Levenda, Peter, *Unholy Alliance*, Continuum, New York, 2002.

LePage, Victoria, *Shambhala*, Quest Books, US, 1996.

Lovecraft, H. P., *H. P. Lovecraft Omnibus 2: Dagon and other Macabre Tales*, Grafton Books, London, 1985.

Lovecraft, H. P., *H. P. Lovecraft Omnibus 3: The Haunter of the Dark*, Grafton Books, London, 1985.

Masters, Anthony, *The Man Who Was M*, Grafton Books, London, 1986.

Metzger, Richard (Ed.), *Book of Lies*, Disinformation Company Ltd, USA, 2003.

Michell, John, *The Flying Saucer Vision*, Sidgwick and Jackson Ltd, UK, 1967.

Miller, Russell, *Bare-Faced Messiah*, Michael Joseph Ltd, UK, 1987.

Moon, Peter, *Black Sun: Montauk's Nazi-Tibetan Connection*, Sky Books, New York, 1997.

Moon, Peter, *Synchronicity and the Seventh Seal*, Sky Books, New York, 2004.

Moon, Peter, *The Montauk Book of the Dead*, Sky Books, New York, 2005.

Moon, Peter, *Spandau Mystery*, Sky Books, New York, 2007.

Murray, Margaret A., *The God of the Witches*, Sampson Low, Marston & Co. Ltd, 1931.

Nicholls, Preston B., & Moon, Peter, *The Montauk Project*, Sky Books, New York, 1992.

Nicholls, Preston B., & Moon, Peter, *Montauk Revisited: Adventures in Synchronicity*, Sky Books, New York, 1994.

Nicholls, Preston B., & Moon, Peter, *Pyramids of Montauk: Explorations in Consciousness*, Sky Books, New York, 1995.

Nicholls, Preston B., & Moon, Peter, *Encounter in the Pleiades: An Inside look at UFOs*, Sky Books, New York, 1996.

Noll, Richard, *The Aryan Christ*, Macmillan, London, 1997.

Orpheus, Rodney, *Abrahadabra*, Looking Glass Press, Stockholm, 1994.

Orr, Leonard & Ray, Sondra, *Rebirthing in the New Age*, Celestial Arts, California, 1983.

Ouspensky, P. D., *In Search of the Miraculous*, Harcourt Inc, USA, 1949.

Parfrey, Adam (Ed), *Apocalypse Culture*, Amok Press, New York, 1987.

Parsons, John Whiteside, *Freedom is a Two-Edged Sword*, OTO/Falcon Press, USA, 1989.

Pauwels, Louis, & Bergier, Jacques, *The Morning of the Magicians*, Editions Gallimard, France, 1960.

Pendle, George, *Strange Angel*, Weidenfeld & Nicholson, London, 2005.

Picknett Lynn & Prince, Clive, *The Stargate Conspiracy*, Little, Brown & Co., UK, 1999.

Randles, Jenny, *MIB*, Judy Piatkus, London, 1997.

Ravenscroft, Trevor, *The Spear of Destiny*, Corgi, London, 1974.

Ravenscroft, Trevor & Wallace-Murphy, Tim, *The Mark of the Beast*, Sphere Books Ltd, London, 1990.

Regardie, Israel, *The Eye in the Triangle*, (Edition with introduction by Robert Anton Wilson and Preface by Christopher S. Hyatt, Ph.D.) Falcon Press, Phoenix, Arizona, USA, 1982.

Roberts, Anthony, & Gilbertson, Geoff, *The Dark Gods*, Rider/Hutchinson, & Co, UK, 1980.

Rudgley, Richard, *Pagan Resurrection*, Arrow Books, London, 2006.

Sanders, Ed, *The Family*, Panther Books, UK, 1972.

Sanders, Maxine, *Firechild*, Mandrake, Oxford, 2008.

Sauder, Richard, *Underground Bases and Tunnels*, Adventures Unlimited Press, Illinois, 1996.
Sauder, Richard, *Kundalini Tales*, Adventures Unlimited Press, Illinois, 1998.
Settegast, Mary, *Mona Lisa's Moustache*, Phanes Press, USA, 2001.
Spence, Richard B., *Secret Agent 666*, Feral House, USA, 2008.
Starr, Martin P., *The Unknown God*, Teitan Press, USA, 2003.
Steiner, Rudolf, *The Esoteric Aspect of the Social Question*, Rudolf Steiner Press, London, 2001.
Suster, Gerald, *Hitler and the Age of Horus*, Sphere Books, London, 1981.
Temple, Robert, *The Sirius Mystery*, Century, UK, 1998.
Thompson, Damian, *The End of Time*, Minerva, London, 1997.
Ulansey, David, *The Origins of the Mithraic Mysteries*, Oxford University Press, New York, 1989.
Vallée, Jacques, *Passport to Magonia*, Neville Spearman Ltd, UK, 1970.
Wasserman, James (Ed), *Aleister Crowley and the Practice of the Magical Diary*, New Falcon, USA, 1993.
Williamson, Jack, *Darker Than You Think*, Street & Smith Publications Inc, USA, 1948.
Wilson, Colin, *The Outsider*, Victor Gollancz, London, 1956.
Wilson, Colin, *Introduction to the New Existentialism*, Hutchinson & Co, London, 1966.
Wilson, Colin, *The Occult*, Hodder & Stoughton Ltd, Great Britain, 1971.
Wilson, Colin, *New Pathways in Psychology*, Victor Gollancz, London, 1972.
Wilson, Colin, *Alien Dawn*, Virgin Publishing, London, 1998.
Wilson, Robert Anton, *Cosmic Trigger: Final Secret of the Illuminati*, And/Or Press, USA, 1977.
Wilson, Robert Anton, *Prometheus Rising*, New Falcon, USA, 1983.
Wilson, Robert Anton, *The New Inquisition*, New Falcon, USA, 1986.
Wilson, Robert Anton, *Cosmic Trigger II*, New Falcon, USA, 1988.
Wilson, Robert Anton, *Quantum Psychology*, New Falcon, USA, 1990.

INTRODUCTORY INDEX

Abraxas 36, 38-43, 50, 113-114, 167, 375

Anger, Kenneth 10, 120, 153, 168, 173, 176, 188, 214, 335

Babalon Working 44, 101, 106, 107, 109, 111-113, 116, 118-120, 136, 148, 178, 180, 188, 191, 193-194, 205, 220, 278-279, 288, 291, 293, 298, 307, 309, 317, 361-362, 368, 370-372, 374

Beatles, The 12, 51, 164, 166, 168, 170, 172

Cameron, Marjorie 109, 111, 116, 120, 174, 194, 289, 361

Dick, Philip K. 112-113, 375

Fuller, JFC 79-80

Gardner, Gerald 138-150

Grant, Kenneth 42-43, 116, 190-195, 232-234, 238-239, 241, 265-266, 270, 290, 297, 306, 310, 312, 348-350

Graves, Robert 125, 133-136

Gurdjieff, George Ivanovitch 15, 17, 44-46, 48, 55, 59, 62, 76-78, 149, 196, 267-269, 272, 328-329, 331-332, 337, 340, 345, 347

Hess, Rudolf 17, 41, 53, 67, 73, 92-96, 98-100, 256, 305

Himmler, Heinrich 13, 67-70, 73, 90, 92-93, 301

Hitler, Adolf 12-13, 16, 36, 51, 53-58, 61, 63, 66-68, 72, 74, 76, 78-80, 87, 92-95, 98, 102, 104, 140, 154, 166, 170-171, 203-204, 261, 263, 300, 302, 304-305, 372

Hubbard, L. Ron 105, 107, 157, 205, 208, 210, 288, 290, 308, 317-318, 332, 353, 361-362, 371

Huxley, Aldous 154-156, 158-159, 160, 162, 166, 168, 186

Jung, C. G. 16, 36, 38-44, 48, 51, 53, 55-56, 72, 75, 112-114, 120. 159, 163, 189-190, 194, 257, 290, 344, 351, 373, 375

Keel, John 216-218, 220, 222, 226, 228, 242-244, 250, 257-260, 305

Lam 192-195, 205, 212, 290, 291, 304, 306-307, 309, 315, 349

LaVey, Anton Szandor 168-169, 171-172, 175

Layne, Meade 199-201, 204, 210, 217, 254, 257-258, 315

Leary, Timothy 16, 151, 157-163, 165, 167, 2669, 177-180, 183-188, 212, 263, 270, 273, 275, 332-333, 345-347, 351-352

List, Guido von 61, 68, 133

Lovecraft, H. P. 165, 229-234, 236, 238, 247, 260, 320

Manson, Charles 16, 167, 170-172, 174-175, 187-188, 275, 278, 363-364

Parsons, Jack 16, 103-107, 109-114, 116-119, 122-124, 146-148, 161, 163, 170-171, 194, 205, 208, 233, 261, 271, 275-278, 290, 298, 311-312, 316, 318, 358, 361-362, 364, 368, 370-371, 375

Pelley, William Dudley 201-205, 210-211, 258

Reich, Wilhelm 160-162, 250-256, 258, 282, 289, 303-304, 338-339, 343, 367-368

Sanders, Alex 148-150, 170

Sirius 203, 211, 265-267, 269-271, 275-276, 283, 297, 319-321, 349

Steiner, Rudolf 52-53, 57-58, 67, 73-75, 93, 201, 254, 258, 260-261, 274

Stele of Revealing 31-34, 176, 213-214, 296, 308, 358, 360

Vallée, Jacques 215-217, 222, 257-258, 260, 271

Van Tassell, George 206-208, 254

Williamson, George Hunt 147, 209, 210-212, 258, 315, 317

Wilson, Robert Anton 19, 104, 160, 178, 186, 220, 262-267, 269-276, 293, 305, 319, 321, 325, 332-337, 340, 347, 351-353